Palgrave Studies in Global Entrepreneurship

Series Editor

Vanessa Ratten, La Trobe University, Bundoora, Melbourne, Australia

This Palgrave Macmillan book series on global entrepreneurship provides an urgently needed platform to focus on issues related to entrepreneurship from a global perspective. It showcases the global nature of entrepreneurship and provides a home for high quality and novel research. These include a broad range of topics related to entrepreneurship that incorporate a global mindset. By focusing on the global aspect of entrepreneurship it combines an international element to how micro, small, medium and large enterprises need to consider international ramifications into their business decisions. In doing so, the series covers new areas including digital technology, crisis management, sport business and sustainability. Each book in the series will encompass a different ground breaking area related to global entrepreneurship. While the series focus is on global entrepreneurship, it is interdisciplinary in nature as it will link global aspects of entrepreneurship to new subject areas. These will contribute to a more global discussion on how entrepreneurship is fundamentally entrepreneurial in nature. The series responds to the need to incorporate global thinking amongst students, practitioners, policy makers and researchers.

Deepak Kumar · Ramswarup Bhaskar ·
Chandra Sekhar
Editors

Evolving Trends in Technology Entrepreneurship

palgrave
macmillan

Editors
Deepak Kumar
Department of Computer Science and Information Technology
La Trobe University
Bundoora, VIC, Australia

Ramswarup Bhaskar
Business Policy, Strategy and Entrepreneurship
Indian Institute of Management Jammu
Jammu, India

Chandra Sekhar
Department of Business Administration
National Institute of Technology Kurukshetra
Kurukshetra, Haryana, India

Palgrave Studies in Global Entrepreneurship
ISBN 978-981-95-7440-7 ISBN 978-981-95-7441-4 (eBook)
https://doi.org/10.1007/978-981-95-7441-4

This Palgrave Macmillan imprint is published by the registered company Springer Nature Singapore Pte Ltd.
The registered company address is: 152 Beach Road, #21-01/04 Gateway East, Singapore 189721, Singapore

Preface and Acknowledgements

The landscape of entrepreneurship has been profoundly reshaped by rapid technological innovation. From artificial intelligence and blockchain to sustainable innovation models, the entrepreneurial ecosystem has entered a phase where digital transformation is not merely an enabler but the foundation of new business paradigms. *Evolving Trends in Technology Entrepreneurship*, as part of the Palgrave Macmillan book series on *Global Entrepreneurship* series, aims to capture this transition by providing scholarly and practice-oriented insights into how technology is redefining entrepreneurial thought and action across industries and geographies.

This edited volume brings together a diverse collection of chapters addressing critical dimensions of technology entrepreneurship. It opens with reflections on the ethical foundations of digital and AI-driven Business models, highlighting the need to embed responsibility in innovation. It then explores the practical adoption of new technologies in startups, including perspectives from emerging economies such as Kosovo. Several contributions examine how blockchain, artificial intelligence, and responsible innovation intersect with financing, sports, entertainment, and education, thereby presenting a comprehensive view of opportunities and challenges faced by entrepreneurs today. Collectively, these contributions emphasize that technology entrepreneurship is not a uniform journey but one shaped by context, industry, and societal demands.

The volume is designed to serve multiple audiences including researchers, educators, practitioners, and policymakers. For scholars, it provides conceptual and empirical insights into the dynamics of technological disruption. For entrepreneurs and managers, it offers frameworks and real-world cases that can inform strategic decision-making. For educators and students, it provides pedagogical perspectives on nurturing sustainable and responsible technology-driven entrepreneurship.

This book underscores that technology entrepreneurship is more than the creation of ventures; it is about shaping the future of economies and societies through innovation that is inclusive, ethical, and sustainable. We hope that the perspectives shared in these chapters will spark dialogue, inspire new research, and guide entrepreneurs in leveraging technology as a force for long-term value creation.

The completion of this edited volume has been made possible through the collective efforts of many individuals and institutions. We would like to extend my deepest gratitude to all the contributing authors, whose chapters reflect rigorous scholarship, thoughtful analysis, and a shared commitment to advancing knowledge in technology entrepreneurship. Your expertise and dedication have shaped the intellectual richness of this book.

We are sincerely thankful to our reviewers, Dr. Chinmaya Kumar Sahu (CMS Business School, Jain University), Prof. Manoj Patwardhan (ABV IIITM Gwalior), Dr. Arghya Ray (International Management Institute Kolkata), Dr. Umamaheswararao Jada (NIT Durgapur), Dr. Sourav Mondal (IIM Jammu), and Dr. Ashutosh Pandey (FORE School of Management), for their constructive feedback and critical insights that enhanced the quality and clarity of the chapters. Their commitment to academic rigor has been invaluable in shaping this work.

We extend our sincere appreciation to Prof. Vanessa Ratten, Series editor of Palgrave Macmillan book series on global entrepreneurship, for the opportunity, guidance and support throughout the development of this volume. Her vision for fostering global dialogue on entrepreneurship has provided an inspiring platform for this work. The authors extend their sincere gratitude to Palgrave Macmillan for the opportunity, and for their unwavering trust and support throughout the entire journey of this book.

Finally, we wish to acknowledge the encouragement and support of colleagues, friends, and family, who provided both intellectual and emotional sustenance during this journey. Without their patience and motivation, this project would not have reached fruition.

It is our hope that this book will serve as both a resource and a catalyst for future scholarship and practice in technology entrepreneurship.

Bundoora, Australia	Deepak Kumar
Jammu, India	Ramswarup Bhaskar
Kurukshetra, India	Chandra Sekhar

Contents

1 **Conceptual and Theoretical Foundations of Technology Entrepreneurship** 1
Deepak Kumar, Ramswarup Bhaskar, and Chandra Sekhar

2 **Ethics in Emerging Digital and Artificial Intelligence Business Models** 29
Christina Öberg

3 **Using New Technologies in Startup Environments: Perspectives from Kosovo Startups Via UTAUT-3** 51
Flokart Aliu and Asdren Toska

4 **Fostering Sustainable Growth: Integrating Responsible Innovation in Technology Startups** 79
Apurva Verma and Anoop Singh

5 **Leveraging Blockchain Technology to Enhance Speed of Adjustment in Technology Startups: A Financial and Strategic Perspective** 97
Neha Sharma, Mayank Arora, and Darren Henry

6 **AI-Based Start-Ups and Applications in the Sports Industry** 121
Halil Erdem Akoğlu, Övünç Erdeveciler, and Kadir Yıldız

7 **Transforming Entertainment and Recreation: The Impact of Changing Technology on Work and Workers** 143
Tolga Beşikçi and Ezgi Abay Beşikçi

8 **Navigating Tech Startup Financing: A Critical Review of Models, Challenges, and Future Trends** 173
Ananthi Rajayya, Smarty P. Mukundan, and Fezeena Khadir

9 **"Tech for Good" as a Catalyst for Social Entrepreneurship: Revealing Research Topics with Unsupervised Topic Modeling with Latent Dirichlet Allocation (LDA)** 193
Richa Goyal and Swati Garg

10 **Education for Sustainable Technology Entrepreneurship** 209
Usha Shree Rathod and M. Rajyalaxmi

11 **Opportunities, Challenges, and Strategies and Educational Approaches for Advancing Sustainable Technology Entrepreneurship Education** 247
Anojan Vickneswaran

12 **The Intersection of Sports and Technology Entrepreneurship** 271
Esra Emir and Kadir Yıldız

13 **Building a Framework of Startup Growth in Evolving Economies: Empirical Scale Development and Validation** 297
Pinky Bahuguna

14 **The Future of Technology Entrepreneurship in Fitness Business** 319
Yeşer Eroğlu-Eskicioğlu and Kadir Yıldız

15 **The Evolving Dynamics of Technology Entrepreneurship: A Descriptive Approach** 339
Rajendra Sharma, Preeti Singh, and Kishan Jee

Index 383

Editors and Contributors

About the Editors

Dr. Deepak Kumar is an Associate Lecturer in the Department of Computer Science and Information Technology at La Trobe University, where he teaches courses on entrepreneurship and blockchain technology at both the undergraduate and postgraduate levels. He holds an integrated degree in Information Technology (B.Tech) and Finance (MBA) from the Atal Bihari Vajpayee Indian Institute of Information Technology and Management, Gwalior. Deepak completed his PhD at the Indian Institute of Technology Kanpur and La Trobe University, focusing on 'Blockchain-based Decentralized Financing for Small and Medium Enterprises.'

Dr. Ramswarup Bhaskar is an Assistant Professor in the area of Business Policy, Strategy & Entrepreneurship at IIM Jammu. He has received his master's and doctorate degrees in Entrepreneurship from IIT Kanpur, India. With over nine years of experience in entrepreneurship research, education, and mentoring, he has contributed to various projects, publications, and policy interventions related to technology management, and commercialization. Dr. Bhaskar's research interests include startup financing, knowledge partnerships, and technology commercialization. He is passionate about fostering entrepreneurial ecosystems that address societal challenges and create economic opportunities.

Dr. Chandra Sekhar is Working as an Assistant Professor in the Department of Business Administration at the National Institute of Technology, Kurukshetra, India. With over six years of experience in teaching and research, he has received numerous grants from the Government of India. His research areas include Entrepreneurship development, career management in family business firms, career management of sports personnel, Strategic HRM, AI in HRM, Playful Work Design, Agile Work Practices, Strength Based Leadership, Dark Triad Person, HR Flexibility, Employee Well-being, and Employee Time Theft. He is a life member of many professional bodies, including the Indian Society for Training and Development (ISTD) in New Delhi. Dr. Sekhar also served as coordinator and convener for several one-week workshops organised by the Department of Business Administration at NIT Kurukshetra.

Contributors

Halil Erdem Akoğlu Department of Sports Management, Faculty of Sports Sciences, Niğde Ömer Halisdemir University, Niğde, Türkiye

Flokart Aliu Department of Management, Faculty of Economics, University of Prishtina "Hasan Prishtina", Prishtina, Kosova

Mayank Arora Department of Electrical Engineering IIT Kanpur, Uttar Pradesh, Kanpur, India;
Department of Computer Science, La Trobe University, Melbourne, VIC, Australia

Pinky Bahuguna University School of Business, Chandigarh University, Mohali, Punjab, India

Tolga Beşikçi Department of Recreation, Faculty of Sport Sciences, Manisa Celal Bayar University, Manisa, Türkiye

Ezgi Abay Beşikçi Department of Recreation, Faculty of Sport Sciences, Manisa Celal Bayar University, Manisa, Türkiye

Ramswarup Bhaskar Indian Institute of Management Jammu, Jammu, India

Esra Emir Department of Coaching Education, Faculty of Sport Sciences, İstanbul Aydın University, İstanbul, Türkiye

Övünç Erdeveciler Department of Sports Management, Faculty of Sports Sciences, Ankara University, Ankara, Türkiye

Yeşer Eroğlu-Eskicioğlu Department of Physical Education and Sport, Faculty of Sport Sciences, Duzce University, Duzce, Türkiye

Swati Garg Department of Business Administration, National Institute of Technology, Kurukshetra, Haryana, India

Richa Goyal Department of Business Administration, National Institute of Technology, Kurukshetra, Haryana, India

Darren Henry Department of Accounting and Management, La Trobe University, Melbourne, VIC, Australia

Kishan Jee Dr. Shantilal K. Somaiya School of Commerce and Business Studies, Somaiya Vidyavihar University, Mumbai, India

Fezeena Khadir School of Management Studies, Cochin University of Science and Technology, Kochi, Kerala, India

Deepak Kumar Department of Computer Science and Information Technology, La Trobe University, Melbourne, VIC, Australia

Smarty P. Mukundan School of Management Studies, Cochin University of Science and Technology, Kochi, Kerala, India

Christina Öberg School of Business and Economics, Linnaeus University, Kalmar, Sweden

Ananthi Rajayya Amrita School of Business, Amrita Vishwa Vidyapeetham, Kochi, Kerala, India

M. Rajyalaxmi School of Business, SR University, Warangal, Telangana, India

Usha Shree Rathod School of Business, SR University, Warangal, Telangana, India

Chandra Sekhar National Institute of Technology, Kurukshetra, India

Neha Sharma Department of Management Studies, IIT Kanpur, Uttar Pradesh, Kanpur, India;
Department of Accounting and Management, Business School, La Trobe University, Melbourne, VIC, Australia

Rajendra Sharma Rajarshi School of Management and Technology, Varanasi, India

Anoop Singh Department of Management Sciences, Indian Institute of Technology, Kanpur, Uttar Pradesh, India

Preeti Singh Rajarshi School of Management and Technology, Varanasi, India

Asdren Toska Business Administration—Faculty of Business and Economics, South East European University, Tetovo, North Macedonia

Apurva Verma Department of Management Sciences, Indian Institute of Technology, Kanpur, Uttar Pradesh, India

Anojan Vickneswaran School of Business and Creative Industries, University of the Sunshine Coast, Sippy Downs, QLD, Australia; Department of Accounting, Faculty of Management Studies and Commerce, University of Jaffna, Jaffna, Northern Province, Sri Lanka

Kadir Yıldız Department of Sports Management, Faculty of Sports Sciences, Manisa Celal Bayar University, Manisa, Türkiye

List of Figures

Fig. 1.1	Integrative conceptual framework of technology entrepreneurship. (*Source* Created by Authors)	12
Fig. 3.1	Characteristics of respondents. (*Source* Authors)	62
Fig. 5.1	Overview of the Synergies and Interconnections Between Blockchain Technology, Entrepreneurial Finance, and Capital Structure. (*Source* Author)	106
Fig. 6.1	Artificial intelligence applications in the sports industry and examples of start-ups	127
Fig. 8.1	PRISMA flow diagram illustrating article selection. (*Database searched*: Scopus)	177
Fig. 8.2	Framework for determining the choice of financing models for startups across technology sectors, compiled by the authors	180
Fig. 8.3	Framework for challenges in securing funding across different stages of development, compiled by the authors	185
Fig. 9.1	Steps for LDA topic modeling	197
Fig. 9.2	Word Cloud	199
Fig. 9.3	Selection of the number of topics for LDA modeling	200
Fig. 9.4	The topic-by-word distributions for each of the five topics	201
Fig. 9.5	Topic visualization with LDAvis	201
Fig. 10.1	Intersection of education, technology, and sustainability	214
Fig. 10.2	Role of education in shaping conscious entrepreneurs (*Source* author)	231
Fig. 11.1	United Nations Sustainable Development Goals	249

Fig. 11.2 Challenges, opportunities, strategies, and approaches for sustainable technology entrepreneurship education 261
Fig. 13.1 Measurement model of start-up growth factors 311
Fig. 15.1 Conceptual framework of digital entrepreneurship. (*Source* Paul et al., 2023) 355
Fig. 15.2 Digital entrepreneurship orientation cycle. (*Source* Paul et al., 2023) 356

List of Tables

Table 2.1	Search terms and results	35
Table 2.2	Articles on ethics, business models, and digitalization or AI, from oldest to newest	36
Table 2.3	Business model types and ethical issues	42
Table 6.1	Cluster-based classification of AI start-ups in the sports industry	126
Table 6.2	Examples of AI-enabled wearable technology and performance monitoring start-ups	128
Table 6.3	Examples of AI-enabled athlete rehabilitation start-ups	129
Table 6.4	Example start-ups supported by artificial intelligence in training applications	132
Table 6.5	Example start-ups developing match prediction systems with artificial neural networks	133
Table 6.6	Example start-ups supported by artificial intelligence in athlete transfers and talent scouting	135
Table 7.1	Timeline of key technological developments in entertainment and recreation	149
Table 7.2	Comparison of emerging technologies in entertainment and recreation	155
Table 7.3	Technological shifts in job roles within the entertainment industry	161
Table 10.1	Key strategies to integrate technology	228
Table 10.2	Key policy interventions	234
Table 10.3	Primary implications across domains	236
Table 13.1	Demographics of respondents	303

Table 13.2	The result of KMO and Bartlett's test	304
Table 13.3	Communalities	305
Table 13.4	Total variance explained	306
Table 13.5	Rotated component matrix	307
Table 13.6	Factor loadings of items in the measurement model	308
Table 13.7	Reliability statistics	309
Table 13.8	Indicators of convergent and discriminant validity	309
Table 13.9	Model fit indices	312
Table 15.1	Review of literature	342
Table 15.2	SWOT analysis of digital entrepreneurs	366

CHAPTER 1

Conceptual and Theoretical Foundations of Technology Entrepreneurship

Deepak Kumar, Ramswarup Bhaskar, and Chandra Sekhar

1.1 Introduction

Digitalization and artificial intelligence (AI) have fueled the development of new Business models. Business models refer to the ways in which businesses are organized, capturing both the provision and customer sides of operations. Meanwhile, digitalization expands across various IT solutions not only as technology but also as a means of organizing business and

---

D. Kumar (✉)
Department of Computer Science and Information Technology, La Trobe University, Melbourne, VIC, Australia
e-mail: D.Kumar@latrobe.edu.au

R. Bhaskar
Indian Institute of Management Jammu, Jammu, India
e-mail: rbhaskar@iimj.ac.in

C. Sekhar
National Institute of Technology, Kurukshetra, India
e-mail: chandrasekhar@nitkkr.ac.in

D. Kumar et al. (eds.), *Evolving Trends in Technology Entrepreneurship*, Palgrave Studies in Global Entrepreneurship,
https://doi.org/10.1007/978-981-95-7441-4_1

providing content to Business models. AI, with its separation between its role as a decision tool and its generative capacity for constructing Business models and producing creative solutions, further adds to this development by creating ever-new ways of organizing in the market space, producing new offerings, and fueling data as a valuable resource.

The notion of data as free and access provided on a non-monetary basis is increasingly scrutinized in the context of integrity, exploration, and regulations designed to restrict the use of personal data. With many digital Business models focusing on personal data and transparency rather than trust among parties, traditional ethical frameworks are challenged by these developments. Furthermore, AI introduces challenges related to the ownership of ideas and determining when it is possible to claim intellectual property rights relative language models and AI-generated ideas. Ethics, defined as the moral norms that guide how individuals should behave, is concerned with the impact of human actions on others. Over time, these norms may evolve in tandem with changes in regulations and the legal system, or work opposite to such developments.

Based on the emergence of digital and AI-fueled business modes, the purpose of the chapter is *to discuss how new Business models, as entrepreneurial expressions emerging from digitalization and AI, may challenge current ethical behaviors and regulations*. The chapter is based on an integrative, prospector literature review that encompasses ethics, digitalization, AI, and Business models.

The chapter identifies various ethical issues and explores how these issues are related to different business model types and the development over time. More precisely, it demonstrates how past research deals with AI decision-making as potentially non-ethical, changes in marketing and data use, and privacy concerns (Ashok et al., 2022).

The chapter contributes to existing research by highlighting contemporary ethical issues related to Business models and the way in which these issues emerge in the context of digitalization and AI. A key contribution of the chapter is its development of business model configurations, the associated ethical issues, the identification of responsible parties, and recommendations for addressing these issues. The analysis links various ethical issues to business model types, while showing how the development is dynamic, not only following technological transformations but also in terms of business modeling, who is regarded as responsible and what ethical issues emerge. By extending the review to incorporate missing perspectives and themes, the chapter identifies central ethical concerns associated with digitalization and AI development. Given the time-critical nature of AI, future avenues of development along with the potential shifting role of regulations relative to ethics are also discussed.

The rest of the chapter is organized as follows. First, Business models, AI, and digitalization are further discussed to set the stage for the chapter's topic. Next, ethics is examined in greater depth. The method section describes how the literature review was conducted, justifies methodological choices, and explains the data analysis process. The findings section presents the evolution over time, outlines business model types, and identifies central ethical issues. Subsequently, the findings are discussed, and paradoxes are derived from this analysis as the ethical issues contain co-existing contradictions. The chapter concludes with a final remark.

1.2 Background and Rationale

The twenty-first century has witnessed an unprecedented convergence of technological disruption and entrepreneurial dynamism. Advances in artificial intelligence (AI), blockchain, the Internet of Things (IoT), and digital platforms have redefined not only how firms operate but also what entrepreneurship itself entails. Technology entrepreneurship has emerged as a distinctive domain of inquiry that examines how digital and technological capabilities create, transform, and diffuse new forms of value (Nambisan et al., 2019). At its core, this field involves the systematic exploitation of technology-based opportunities through innovative Business models that address complex economic, social, and environmental challenges (Autio et al., 2018).

The digital transformation of global markets has blurred the traditional boundaries between production and consumption, as well as between firms and users, and public and private value creation (George & Zahra, 2022). Technological entrepreneurship now extends beyond venture creation to encompass the institutional, ethical, and educational structures that enable innovation. This shift aligns with contemporary calls for a more inclusive and sustainable innovation paradigm, one that recognizes technology's dual role as both an enabler of progress and a source of profound societal disruption (von Krogh et al., 2022). Consequently, scholars have increasingly emphasized the need for integrative frameworks that connect digitalization, responsible innovation, entrepreneurial ecosystems, and sustainable development (Kraus et al., 2023).

This edited volume responds to that call. It situates technology entrepreneurship as a multidisciplinary and context-sensitive phenomenon shaped by interactions among entrepreneurs, technologies, institutions, and values. The contributing chapters collectively examine how emerging technologies, from AI and blockchain to data analytics and green innovation, reconfigure entrepreneurial behavior and opportunity structures across industries. By spanning diverse settings, including startups, sports, education, and entertainment, the book demonstrates that technology entrepreneurship cannot be understood through a single theoretical lens. Instead, it must be interpreted as a dynamic system of evolving relationships among technological change, strategic intent, and social purpose (Audretsch et al., 2022).

The need for such a holistic perspective is underscored by several trends. First, the acceleration of digital transformation has intensified competition while lowering entry barriers for new ventures. Digital infrastructures enable entrepreneurs to scale rapidly, but they also expose them to ethical risks related to privacy, bias, and data governance (Ashok et al., 2022). Second, the sustainability imperative, amplified by the United Nations' Sustainable Development Goals, demands that innovation contributes not only to economic performance but also to environmental stewardship and social inclusion (Murray & Fisher, 2021). Third, the rise of decentralized and platform-based ecosystems challenges conventional notions of firm boundaries and ownership, compelling entrepreneurs to navigate new logics of collaboration and competition (Acosta et al., 2023). Finally, technological ethics has become central to entrepreneurial legitimacy: responsible innovation and governance mechanisms now shape public trust in technological ventures (Stilgoe, 2019).

This book, *Evolving Trends in Technology Entrepreneurship*, seeks to articulate an integrative conceptual framework for these developments. Its objective is threefold. *First*, it provides a theoretical synthesis that links foundational entrepreneurship theories, such as the Schumpeterian view of innovation, the Resource-Based View (RBV), and Dynamic Capabilities, with contemporary perspectives on digital transformation and sustainability. *Second*, it highlights how emerging technologies alter entrepreneurial processes, financing models, and value creation logics. *Third*, it establishes an agenda for responsible, inclusive, and human-centered technology entrepreneurship capable of addressing global challenges.

The volume is therefore both descriptive and normative. It describes how technology shapes entrepreneurial ecosystems and, simultaneously, advocates for frameworks that ensure these technologies serve collective welfare. In doing so, it emphasizes that the future of entrepreneurship research lies in integrating ethics, sustainability, and digitalization (George et al., 2022; Ratten, 2023). Each subsequent chapter contributes a complementary perspective, ranging from ethical AI and blockchain-enabled financing to sustainable education models and sectoral applications, all tied together by a shared focus on innovation, responsibility, and transformation.

The rationale for this volume stems from an awareness that technology entrepreneurship is no longer an optional subset of entrepreneurship studies but the central paradigm through which new ventures, industries, and societies evolve. Understanding the theoretical foundations, ethical boundaries, and practical implications of technological change is essential for scholars, policymakers, and practitioners seeking to harness it for equitable and sustainable growth.

1.3 Conceptualizing Technology Entrepreneurship

Technology entrepreneurship has evolved into a central construct linking technological innovation, venture creation, and socioeconomic transformation. While traditional entrepreneurship research emphasized opportunity recognition and firm formation (Shane & Venkataraman, 2000), technology entrepreneurship foregrounds how technological change shapes those opportunities and the ways they are exploited. It encompasses the identification, development, and commercialization of innovations based on scientific or engineering knowledge (Autio et al., 2018; Bailetti, 2012). Yet, its contemporary form extends beyond the confines of high-tech ventures to include digitally enabled startups, platform-based ecosystems, and social enterprises that integrate technology to address complex global challenges (Kraus et al., 2022).

At its core, technology entrepreneurship reflects a co-evolutionary relationship between innovation and value creation. Schumpeter's (1934) notion of the entrepreneur as an agent of "creative destruction" remains foundational; however, modern interpretations recognize that digital technologies diffuse innovation across boundaries, allowing non-traditional actors, such as users, developers, and communities, to become co-creators of value (Nambisan, 2017). The rise of open innovation and digital platforms has disrupted the linear view of innovation, replacing it with distributed, networked models where technological resources and knowledge flow across organizations (Chesbrough & Bogers, 2014). Consequently, technology entrepreneurship is increasingly understood as a socio-technical process that blends managerial agency with technological affordances (Autio et al., 2021).

1.3.1 From High-Tech Ventures to Digital and Sustainable Entrepreneurship

Early conceptualizations of technology entrepreneurship focused on high-technology industries such as semiconductors, biotechnology, and aerospace (Zahra & Nambisan, 2012). These ventures were characterized by significant R&D intensity, intellectual property creation, and high capital requirements. However, the diffusion of digital technologies has democratized entrepreneurial entry. Cloud computing, AI, and blockchain have reduced the cost of experimentation and resource acquisition, enabling "lean" technology startups that operate through agile and scalable Business models (Blank, 2013; Nambisan et al., 2019). This shift from high-tech exclusivity to digital inclusivity has redefined both who the entrepreneur is and what constitutes a technological venture.

Moreover, the intersection of technology entrepreneurship with sustainability has given rise to **green and responsible innovation.** Emerging concepts, such as "sustainable digital entrepreneurship" (George et al., 2021) and the "tech for good" movement (George et al., 2022), highlight how technology-driven ventures can simultaneously pursue economic viability and societal impact. Scholars argue that addressing grand challenges such as climate change, inequality, and digital ethics requires a reorientation of entrepreneurial intent from purely profit-seeking to purpose-driven innovation (Muñoz & Cohen, 2018; Ratten, 2023). As reflected in this volume, several chapters situate technology entrepreneurship within broader paradigms of ethical responsibility, inclusivity, and long-term value creation.

1.3.2 Digital Transformation and Entrepreneurial Processes

The digital transformation of business has fundamentally altered entrepreneurial processes. Digitalization enhances the entrepreneur's ability to sense, seize, and reconfigure opportunities through data-driven insights and algorithmic decision-making (Teece et al., 2016). Digital platforms enable entrepreneurs to leverage network effects and user participation, transforming how value is created and captured (Autio et al., 2021). Furthermore, artificial intelligence facilitates predictive analytics, automation, and personalization, while blockchain technologies ensure transparency and decentralization in transactions and governance (Catalini & Gans, 2016).

These affordances have produced a new generation of technology entrepreneurs (digital natives), who operate in globally connected ecosystems. Such entrepreneurs often pursue scalable solutions addressing both commercial and social challenges, combining technological literacy with ethical and environmental awareness (Kraus et al., 2023). Digital transformation, therefore, is not merely a technological shift but a cultural and strategic reconfiguration of entrepreneurship itself, requiring novel capabilities and governance models.

1.3.3 Entrepreneurial Ecosystems and Institutional Dynamics

Technology entrepreneurship does not occur in isolation but within interconnected ecosystems that include universities, incubators, investors, policymakers, and digital infrastructures (Stam, 2015; Autio & Levie, 2017). These ecosystems provide legitimacy, resources, and institutional support for technological ventures. The literature emphasizes that successful technology entrepreneurship depends on the quality of the surrounding institutional environment including intellectual property regimes, venture capital networks, and policy frameworks that encourage innovation (Wurth et al., 2022).

In emerging economies, ecosystem dynamics have a particularly significant influence. Weak institutions and funding constraints often necessitate creative adaptation, leading to distinctive models of frugal or inclusive innovation (Bhatti et al., 2021). Several chapters in this book explore these themes by examining technology entrepreneurship in diverse contexts, such as Kosovo and India, as well as sustainable education ecosystems. By synthesizing these studies, the volume illustrates how institutional diversity shapes entrepreneurial pathways and highlights the need for context-sensitive theoretical approaches.

1.3.4 Defining Boundaries and Future Directions

Given its breadth, technology entrepreneurship is inherently multidisciplinary, drawing from innovation management, information systems, strategy, and sociology. While definitions vary, three features consistently distinguish it:

1. **Technological basis**—ventures exploit or develop technological innovation as their core driver of value.
2. **Entrepreneurial agency**—actors intentionally mobilize resources and networks to transform technological ideas into market or societal impact.
3. **Contextual embeddedness**—technological entrepreneurship is situated within specific ecosystems, institutional environments, and cultural contexts that shape outcomes (Autio et al., 2021; Zahra et al., 2022).

Contemporary scholarship increasingly views technology entrepreneurship as a mechanism for *systemic transformation*, not merely firm creation but the reconfiguration of markets, industries, and social systems. The integration of ethical reasoning, responsible innovation, and sustainable development represents the next frontier in theorizing this domain (Ratten, 2023; Stilgoe, 2019). Accordingly, this book adopts a transdisciplinary lens that captures the dynamic interplay among technological capabilities, entrepreneurial intent, and societal imperatives.

1.4 Theoretical Frameworks Underpinning the Volume

Technology entrepreneurship has matured into a multidisciplinary research field supported by several interrelated theoretical foundations. While the phenomenon manifests through technological, managerial, and institutional processes, its intellectual roots extend across strategic management, innovation studies, and entrepreneurship theory. This section consolidates five dominant frameworks that inform the conceptual core of this volume: The Resource-Based View (RBV), Dynamic Capabilities Theory, Institutional Theory, Entrepreneurial Ecosystem Theory, and the Responsible Innovation (RI) Framework. Together, these perspectives explain how technology-driven ventures create, sustain, and govern value in a rapidly transforming digital economy.

1.4.1 The Resource-Based View: Capabilities as Drivers of Technological Value Creation

The Resource-Based View conceptualizes firms as bundles of heterogeneous, imperfectly mobile resources that form the basis for sustained competitive advantage (Barney, 1991; Wernerfelt, 1984). Within the context of technology entrepreneurship, RBV provides a micro-foundational explanation for why some ventures leverage technological knowledge more effectively than others. The key lies in *valuable, rare, inimitable, and non-substitutable (VRIN)* resources such as proprietary algorithms, data assets, or intellectual property that underpin innovation (Teece, 2014).

However, RBV's relevance in digital contexts depends on recognizing that technological resources are often open, replicable, and rapidly evolving. Thus, competitive advantage increasingly derives from *combinatorial capabilities* such as the ability to integrate, configure, and recombine digital tools and data (Nambisan et al., 2020). Digital startups frequently rely on externally sourced technologies, yet differentiate through design, user experience, or ecosystem positioning (Autio et al., 2021). Chapters in this volume, such as those addressing blockchain-based financing or AI-driven Business models, demonstrate how entrepreneurial ventures transform technological potential into strategic value through the orchestration of resources rather than their possession.

1.4.2 Dynamic Capabilities and Entrepreneurial Agility

While RBV emphasizes what resource firms own, Dynamic Capabilities Theory explains how these resources are renewed and reconfigured over time. Defined as the firm's ability to *sense opportunities and threats, seize opportunities, and transform its resource base* (Teece et al., 1997, 2016), dynamic capabilities are particularly salient in technology entrepreneurship, where volatility and uncertainty are inherent.

Digital technologies expand the entrepreneur's capacity to sense through real-time data analytics, to seize through agile experimentation, and to transform through continuous learning loops. For instance, startups employing blockchain smart contracts can iteratively adapt governance mechanisms, while AI-enabled ventures continuously refine algorithms to align with shifting market conditions. These dynamic processes reflect the *entrepreneurial agility* necessary for surviving technological turbulence (Helfat & Peteraf, 2015). The chapters in this volume highlight such adaptability, as seen in Kosovo startups adopting UTAUT-3 frameworks and educational ecosystems embedding sustainability in digital curricula, demonstrating how entrepreneurs translate dynamic capabilities into scalable innovation.

1.4.3 Institutional Theory: Legitimacy, Policy, and Ethical Alignment

Technological innovation unfolds within institutional environments composed of regulative, normative, and cognitive structures (Scott, 2014). Institutional Theory explains how these structures shape the legitimacy of entrepreneurial action. For technology ventures, legitimacy is often contested because their innovations disrupt established norms, laws, and ethical expectations (Zietsma et al., 2017). Institutional theorists argue that entrepreneurs must engage in *institutional work*, which involves activities that create, maintain, or transform institutional logics, in order to gain acceptance and support (Lawrence & Suddaby, 2006).

In the context of emerging technologies such as AI and blockchain, legitimacy is increasingly contingent upon ethical conduct, transparency, and societal trust. Institutional environments now embed expectations of *responsible innovation* and *digital governance* within entrepreneurship policy (Stilgoe, 2019). Accordingly, technology entrepreneurs must navigate complex policy landscapes and moral frameworks while fostering innovation. Several chapters, particularly those on ethics, responsible innovation, and sustainable education, illustrate how ventures build institutional legitimacy by adhering to global standards, such as the GDPR, OECD AI Principles, and ESG metrics.

1.4.4 Entrepreneurial Ecosystems: Networks and Interdependencies

Building upon RBV and Institutional Theory, Entrepreneurial Ecosystem Theory provides a meso-level lens to understand the interactive relationships among entrepreneurs, investors, universities, and policymakers (Stam, 2015; Autio & Levie, 2017). These ecosystems act as enablers of technological entrepreneurship by supplying resources, legitimacy, and connectivity. Unlike clusters or networks, ecosystems emphasize *co-evolution* and *mutual dependency* among diverse actors (Spigel & Harrison, 2018).

Technological change accelerates this interdependence. For example, blockchain-based decentralized finance (DeFi) ecosystems rely on coders, validators, regulators, and users who co-produce value without hierarchical control. Similarly, educational ecosystems that integrate sustainable technology entrepreneurship thrive on collaboration among academia, industry, and policy institutions. The cross-chapter linkages within this book reflect these dynamics, demonstrating how digital infrastructures, regulatory frameworks, and collaborative norms jointly nurture innovative outcomes. The entrepreneurial ecosystem thus provides the connective tissue linking micro-level entrepreneurial agency to macro-level institutional transformation (Wurth et al., 2022).

1.4.5 Responsible Innovation: Ethics, Sustainability, and Societal Alignment

The Responsible Innovation (RI) framework introduces a normative dimension to technology entrepreneurship, emphasizing anticipation, inclusivity, reflexivity, and responsiveness in innovation processes (Stilgoe et al., 2013). RI asserts that innovation should not only be technologically feasible and economically viable but also ethically acceptable and socially desirable. This framework aligns closely with the sustainability-oriented chapters of this book, which advocate integrating environmental, social, and governance (ESG) principles into entrepreneurial practice.

Incorporating responsible innovation reshapes the identity of the entrepreneur from an opportunistic disruptor to a *steward of societal progress*. Ethical AI design, privacy-by-design architectures, and sustainable blockchain applications exemplify this paradigm. Moreover, responsible innovation complements Institutional Theory by embedding moral legitimacy within entrepreneurial ecosystems and reinforces Dynamic Capabilities Theory by extending the concept of "sensing and seizing" to anticipate and reflect (Owen et al., 2012). Throughout the book's chapters, this normative commitment is evident in frameworks that promote sustainable education, ethical governance, and technology for the greater good.

1.4.6 Toward an Integrative Conceptual Framework

Synthesizing these five theories enables us to conceptualize technology entrepreneurship as a multifaceted, dynamic, and ethically embedded process. The proposed integrative framework (Fig. 1.1) links individual entrepreneurial agency, firm-level capabilities, ecosystem-level interactions, and societal-level governance structures.

- At the *micro-level*, the Resource-Based View and Dynamic Capabilities explain how entrepreneurs leverage technological and cognitive assets to innovate.
- At the *meso-level*, Entrepreneurial Ecosystem Theory captures interdependencies and resource flows within networks of innovation actors.
- At the *macro-level*, Institutional and Responsible Innovation theories provide the normative and regulative scaffolding that legitimizes and directs technological progress.

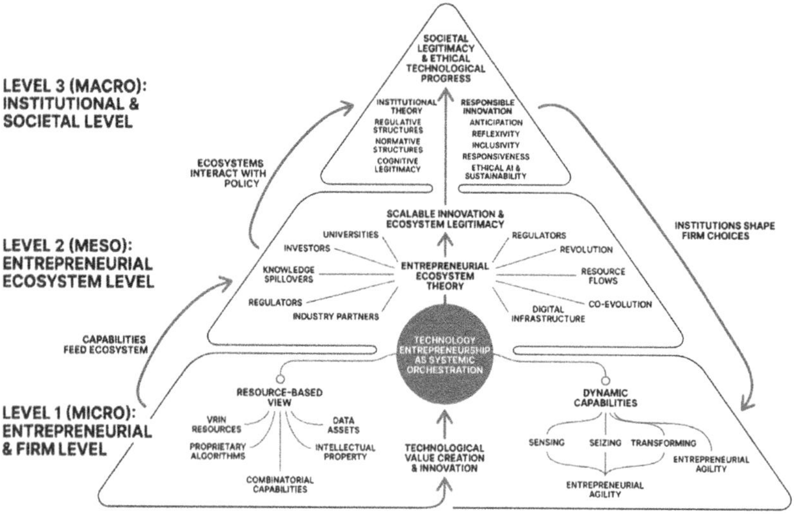

Fig. 1.1 Integrative conceptual framework of technology entrepreneurship. (*Source* Created by Authors)

This integration underscores that technological entrepreneurship is not merely about opportunity exploitation but about *systemic orchestration* aligning technological potential with ethical responsibility and institutional viability. As later chapters in this volume demonstrate, the future of technology entrepreneurship depends on striking a balance between agility and accountability, innovation and inclusion, and competition and collaboration.

1.5 Mapping and Synthesizing the Chapters

The chapters within *Evolving Trends in Technology Entrepreneurship* collectively illustrate how digital transformation, ethical innovation, and sustainability converge to reshape the theory and practice of entrepreneurship. Together, they portray technology entrepreneurship not as a monolithic construct but as a continuum spanning ethics and governance, adoption and diffusion, financing and growth, and education and societal impact. This section maps these contributions across four thematic clusters, highlighting continuities, discontinuities, and the connective frameworks that bind the volume into a coherent whole.

1.5.1 Cluster I: Ethics, Governance, and Responsible Innovation (Chapters 1–3)

The opening chapters establish the ethical and conceptual foundations of technology entrepreneurship. **Chapter 1**, *Ethics in Emerging Digital and Artificial Intelligence Business models*, interrogates the moral dilemmas and governance challenges arising from AI- and data-driven Business models. It draws attention to ethical paradoxes such as privacy versus innovation and automation versus accountability and positions ethics as an evolving institutional force. The chapter's typology of Business models (digitally intermediated, user-data, and AI-generated) aligns with the *Responsible Innovation* and *Institutional Theory* perspectives discussed in Sect. 1.3, emphasizing that entrepreneurial legitimacy increasingly depends on both moral and economic performance.

Chapter 2, *Using New Technologies in Startup Environments: Perspectives from Kosovo Startups* via *UTAUT-3*, extends this discourse to adoption behavior and contextual adaptation. By integrating technology acceptance theories with local entrepreneurial ecosystems, it demonstrates how social influence, perceived value, and performance expectancy shape technology adoption among startups. This chapter operationalizes the *Dynamic Capabilities* framework at the micro-level, illustrating how entrepreneurs sense and seize digital opportunities under institutional and cultural constraints.

Chapter 3, *Fostering Sustainable Growth: Integrating Responsible Innovation in Technology Startups*, synthesizes the ethical and managerial strands by embedding sustainability and responsibility within startup strategy. Drawing on systems thinking, circular economy principles, and stakeholder engagement, it translates *Responsible Innovation* theory into actionable entrepreneurial practice. Collectively, these three chapters provide the normative, cognitive, and practical scaffolding for understanding technology entrepreneurship as a socially embedded and ethically governed phenomenon.

*1.5.2 Cluster II: Blockchain, Artificial Intelligence, and Sectoral Transformation (*Chapters 4–6*)*

The second cluster of chapters explores how specific technologies, particularly blockchain and AI, are transforming industries and organizational models. **Chapter 4**, *Leveraging Blockchain Technology to Enhance Speed of Adjustment in Technology Startups*, reframes financial management through decentralized and transparent architectures. Anchored in the *Resource-Based View* and *Dynamic Capabilities* theories, it demonstrates how blockchain can accelerate capital structure adjustments, reduce transaction frictions, and expand financing access for startups. By bridging technological innovation with financial agility, it connects entrepreneurial finance literature with emerging fintech ecosystems.

Chapter 5, "*AI-Based Start-Ups and Applications in the Sports Industry,*" *and Chapter 6,* "*Transforming Entertainment and Recreation: The Impact of Changing Technology on Work and Workers,*" *together exemplify the* sectoral diffusion of technology entrepreneurship. Chapter 5 maps AI-driven ventures in sports, classifying startups according to innovation clusters, including performance tracking, fan engagement, and predictive analytics. It highlights how platform-based ecosystems and data-driven value creation redefine the concept of competitive advantage. Chapter 6 extends this logic to the creative industries, where AI, virtual reality, and streaming technologies are reshaping labor relations, skill requirements, and creative autonomy. Both chapters reveal how technology entrepreneurship induces not just business innovation but also profound shifts in work, culture, and identity, reinforcing the *Institutional Theory* perspective that entrepreneurship transforms societal structures alongside markets.

*1.5.3 Cluster III: Financing, Growth, and Measurement (*Chapters 7–12*)*

Chapters 7 through 12 examine financial models, empirical analyses, and metrics for evaluating technology entrepreneurship. **Chapter** 7, *Navigating Tech Startup Financing: A Critical Review of Models, Challenges, and Future Trends*, synthesizes venture financing theories, from bootstrapping and crowdfunding to decentralized finance (DeFi). It illustrates how financial innovation complements technological entrepreneurship, emphasizing the interplay between *ecosystem enablers* (venture capital, accelerators) and *institutional legitimacy*.

Chapter 8, *"Tech for Good" as a Catalyst for Social Entrepreneurship*, adopts a computational perspective, using topic modeling to identify emerging research themes in socio-technological entrepreneurship. Its findings underscore how digital innovation facilitates social impact ventures, connecting to *Responsible Innovation* by positioning technology as a moral force for good.

Chapter 9, "*Education for Sustainable Technology Entrepreneurship,*" *and Chapter 10, "Opportunities, Challenges, and Strategies for Advancing Sustainable Technology Entrepreneurship Education,"* extend the discussion into pedagogical and policy domains. They conceptualize higher education as an entrepreneurial ecosystem that cultivates ethical awareness, sustainability-oriented mindsets, and interdisciplinary collaboration. These chapters operationalize *Institutional* and *Ecosystem* theories through education, illustrating how curricula and learning environments shape technological capabilities and moral agency.

Chapter 11, *The Intersection of Sports and Technology Entrepreneurship*, revisits the sports industry to analyze value creation through AI, IoT, and data analytics, further consolidating sectoral insights. **Chapter 12**, *Building a Framework of Startup Growth in Evolving Economies*, contributes empirical rigor through a validated scale that measures determinants of startup success, including innovation capabilities, financial support, and market dynamics. This chapter operationalizes the book's theoretical integration—linking *Dynamic Capabilities*, *RBV*, and *Ecosystem* perspectives to measurable constructs of growth and resilience.

1.5.4 *Cluster IV: Emerging Trends and Future Directions* (Chapters 13–14)

The final cluster envisions the future landscape of technology entrepreneurship. **Chapter 13**, "*The Future of Technology Entrepreneurship in the Fitness Business," explores how digital health, IoT, and AI are reshaping* wellness ecosystems. It situates fitness entrepreneurship within broader trends of platformization and data-centric personalization, embodying the *Dynamic Capabilities* of continuous innovation and adaptation.

Chapter 14, "*The Evolving Dynamics of Technology Entrepreneurship: A Descriptive Approach," synthesizes* global and national case studies to trace the digital transformation journey of traditional enterprises. Through a *SWOT* analysis and comparative insights, it highlights drivers such as globalization, government support, and ethical challenges, concluding with strategies for sustaining innovation. Conceptually, this chapter serves as a mirror to the entire volume illustrating how ethical, institutional, and technological dimensions converge in shaping the next wave of digital entrepreneurship.

1.5.5 *Cross-Cutting Continuities and Discontinuities*

Across these clusters, several continuities emerge. First, ethics and responsibility persist as unifying threads, whether through AI governance, blockchain transparency, or sustainable education; each chapter recognizes moral legitimacy as intrinsic to entrepreneurial success. Second, digital transformation serves as both a context and a catalyst, redefining entrepreneurial processes and organizational boundaries. Third, ecosystem interdependence recurs throughout the volume, reaffirming that technological entrepreneurship is a relational, not solitary, endeavor.

Discontinuities, however, enrich the discourse. The chapters differ in disciplinary grounding, ranging from information systems and finance to education and sociology, and employ diverse methodologies from conceptual frameworks to empirical validation and topic modeling. This diversity reflects the field's pluralism and underscores the need for integrative theories that can bridge quantitative precision with ethical reflection.

1.5.6 Conceptual Integration Across the Volume

Synthesizing these themes, the book's conceptual trajectory mirrors the theoretical model proposed in Sect. 1.3:

- **Micro-level**: Entrepreneurial cognition, dynamic capabilities, and ethical agency (Chapters 1–3).
- **Meso-level**: Industry and ecosystem transformations through technology adoption and financing (Chapters 4–8).
- **Macro-level**: Institutionalization of sustainability and education-driven capacity building (Chapters 9–12).
- **Futures level**: Strategic adaptation and socio-technical foresight (Chapters 13–14).

Through this multi-level integration, the volume collectively advances an agenda for technology entrepreneurship that is ***innovative yet ethical, digital yet human-centered, and global yet contextually grounded***. The next section distills these patterns into emergent findings and implications for future research and practice.

1.6 Key Findings and Emerging Directions

The chapters in *Evolving Trends in Technology Entrepreneurship* collectively reveal an evolving paradigm, one that positions technology entrepreneurship as both a driver and consequence of socio-technical transformation. By integrating theories of resources, capabilities, institutions, ecosystems, and responsible innovation, this book constructs a multidimensional view of entrepreneurship in the digital age. This section synthesizes key patterns, theoretical insights, and emergent research directions arising from the contributions.

1.6.1 Convergence of Digital Transformation and Ethical Governance

A defining theme across the volume is the convergence between technological advancement and ethical governance. As digital infrastructures proliferate, entrepreneurs face new responsibilities in data stewardship, algorithmic transparency, and social accountability (Floridi & Cowls, 2022). The chapters on ethics, responsible innovation, and education underscore that sustainable competitiveness increasingly depends on *moral legitimacy* as much as on technological capability.

AI- and blockchain-based ventures exemplify this tension: while they promise efficiency and decentralization, they also challenge norms of privacy, consent, and fairness (von Krogh et al., 2022). The emerging consensus is that responsible innovation must be integrated into the entrepreneurial process from inception, not retrofitted after commercialization (Stilgoe et al., 2013). This integration transforms the entrepreneur's role from a disruptor of incumbents to a *custodian of responsible transformation* (George & Zahra, 2022). Thus, the volume collectively asserts that ethical reflexivity is now a *dynamic capability*: entrepreneurs must continuously sense and respond to evolving societal expectations in tandem with technological change.

1.6.2 Democratization of Technology and the Rise of Inclusive Ecosystems

A second insight is the democratization of entrepreneurship through accessible technologies and inclusive ecosystems. Digital platforms, low-code development tools, and decentralized finance mechanisms have lowered entry barriers for innovators worldwide (Kraus et al., 2024). Several chapters particularly those focusing on developing economies and educational contexts illustrate how digital tools enable new entrepreneurial identities among youth, women, and marginalized communities.

This trend resonates with recent research on *inclusive digital ecosystems*, which emphasizes that innovation capacity is distributed rather than concentrated (Autio et al., 2018; Nambisan et al., 2019). However, democratization also amplifies risks of uneven capability building and digital divides (Giones & Brem, 2023). Therefore, future scholarship and policy must strike a balance between openness and equity, ensuring that ecosystem participation leads to sustainable outcomes rather than transient access.

1.6.3 Integration of Sustainability and Entrepreneurial Purpose

The third pattern emerging from the volume is the fusion of sustainability with entrepreneurial intent. Chapters addressing green entrepreneurship, responsible innovation, and sustainability-oriented education emphasize that technological progress must align with the UN Sustainable Development Goals (SDGs). The notion of *entrepreneurial purpose*, the moral and social rationale underpinning business creation, is increasingly central to how startups define value (Muñoz & Cohen, 2018).

This evolution marks a shift from the profit-maximizing logic of traditional entrepreneurship toward a *quadruple bottom line*: economic, environmental, social, and ethical performance (George et al., 2021). By embedding purpose within pedagogy, policy, and practice, technology entrepreneurship becomes a vehicle for systemic sustainability transitions. Future research could deepen this integration by exploring circular Business models, impact measurement tools, and cross-sector partnerships.

1.6.4 Reconfiguration of Entrepreneurial Capabilities in the Digital Era

The digital transformation of industries has redefined what constitutes entrepreneurial capability. Traditional strategic assets, such as physical infrastructure and proprietary knowledge, are increasingly being replaced by data-driven, algorithmic, and network-based competencies (Teece, 2021). Entrepreneurs now operate within ecosystems where agility, learning, and connectivity outweigh static resource ownership.

Across the chapters, four recurring dynamic capabilities are evident:

1. **Sensing**—identifying emerging technological opportunities through analytics and foresight.
2. **Seizing**—mobilizing resources and partnerships to exploit these opportunities.
3. **Transforming**—reconfiguring organizational processes for scalability and sustainability.
4. **Reflecting**—aligning technological decisions with ethical and societal considerations.

These capabilities form the backbone of the *Technology Entrepreneurship Capability Framework, which is* implicit throughout the book. Importantly, reflection, often neglected in earlier models, emerges as a crucial dimension linking entrepreneurial agility with moral responsibility (Ratten, 2023).

1.6.5 Hybridization of Sectors and Business Models

Another insight is the growing hybridization of sectors through technology convergence. AI-driven applications in sports, entertainment, and fitness industries (Chapters 5, 6, and 13) demonstrate how digital tools dissolve sectoral boundaries. This hybridization produces *platform economies* where value creation occurs through interaction, not ownership (Acosta et al., 2023).

The trend aligns with the literature on *boundary-spanning entrepreneurship*, which views innovation as a cross-sectoral phenomenon integrating social, cultural, and technological capital (Bouncken et al., 2022). Future inquiry could explore governance mechanisms for hybrid ecosystems, balancing competition and collaboration among startups, corporates, and regulators.

1.6.6 Emerging Research Directions

The book collectively identifies several promising trajectories for technology entrepreneurship research:

1. **Ethical AI and Governance**—Advancing frameworks that operationalize responsible innovation XE "Responsible Innovation (RI)" principles in algorithmic entrepreneurship (Floridi & Cowls, 2022; Stilgoe, 2019).
2. **Blockchain and Financial Inclusion**—Investigating decentralized finance and tokenization as enablers of inclusive entrepreneurial ecosystems (Catalini & Gans, 2016).
3. **Digital Education for Entrepreneurship**—Exploring pedagogical models that embed sustainability, ethics, and digital literacy in entrepreneurship curricula (George et al., 2021).
4. **Sustainability Transitions and Ecosystem Resilience**—Understanding how entrepreneurial ecosystems evolve toward regenerative and circular innovation pathways (Wurth et al., 2022).
5. **Cross-Disciplinary Integration**—Bridging strategy, information systems, and ethics to build unified theories of digital entrepreneurial value creation.

Together, these directions chart a holistic research agenda that connects micro-level entrepreneurial behavior with macro-level institutional and ecological transformations.

1.6.7 *Practical Implications*

For practitioners and policymakers, the book offers actionable lessons. Entrepreneurs must cultivate *ethical agility*, the ability to innovate responsibly under uncertainty. Educators and universities should design curricula that integrate ethical reflection with technological literacy, while policymakers must align innovation policies with sustainability frameworks. Financial institutions and investors, meanwhile, should recalibrate evaluation criteria to reward long-term impact over short-term gains. Such systemic alignment can transform technology entrepreneurship from a disruptive force into a *stabilizing catalyst* for sustainable progress.

1.6.8 *Intellectual Contribution of the Volume*

By weaving together ethical, technological, and institutional perspectives, *Evolving Trends in Technology Entrepreneurship* makes three central contributions:

1. It conceptualizes **technology entrepreneurship as a moral and systemic practice**, extending beyond firm creation to societal transformation.
2. It offers an **integrative theoretical synthesis** that connects dynamic capabilities, ecosystems, and responsible innovation into a unified framework.
3. It establishes an **interdisciplinary research agenda**, advancing the field toward a human-centered, sustainable, and digitally enabled future.

1.7 Conclusion and Future Research Agenda

The preceding sections demonstrate that technology entrepreneurship has entered a decisive new phase, one where innovation is inseparable from ethics, sustainability, and systemic transformation. This volume positions itself at the intersection of these paradigms, synthesizing theoretical, empirical, and sectoral insights into a coherent narrative of how digital technologies reshape entrepreneurial ecosystems and societal value creation.

1.7.1 *Toward an Integrated Theory of Technology Entrepreneurship*

The conceptual synthesis across this book advances the argument that technology entrepreneurship must be understood as a multi-level system of interaction among individual capabilities, organizational resources, institutional contexts, and societal imperatives. The integrative framework proposed in this chapter combines the *Resource-Based View*, *Dynamic Capabilities*, *Institutional Theory*, *Entrepreneurial Ecosystems*, and *Responsible Innovation* into a unifying lens. This framework moves beyond the atomistic view of entrepreneurship as firm-level behavior to a systemic perspective where value creation is relational, reflexive, and ethically grounded.

Future theoretical developments must extend this integration through longitudinal, cross-disciplinary inquiry. Bridging strategic management with ethics and sustainability scholarship can yield a comprehensive "theory of responsible digital entrepreneurship" capable of guiding both practice and policy.

1.7.2 *Reimagining the Entrepreneur in the Digital Age*

The entrepreneurial identity is being redefined. No longer confined to risk-taking or innovation, the modern technology entrepreneur embodies *ethical stewardship* and *systems thinking*. As technologies such as AI, blockchain, and quantum computing evolve, the entrepreneur's role increasingly involves mediating between technological potential and societal consequences (Ratten, 2023).

The volume emphasizes that future entrepreneurs must cultivate both digital fluency and ethical reflexivity, striking a balance between technical mastery and moral judgment. This dual competency forms the foundation of a new archetype: the *responsible technopreneur*. Future research should explore how education, mentorship, and institutional frameworks can foster this identity through experiential learning, ethical reflection, and interdisciplinary training.

1.7.3 From Ecosystems to Ecologies: Expanding the Unit of Analysis

A key insight emerging from the book is that entrepreneurial ecosystems, though valuable as analytical constructs, often underestimate ecological interdependence. The metaphor of the *entrepreneurial ecology* better captures the complex interconnections among human, technological, and environmental systems. In this ecology, technologies are not neutral tools but active agents that influence norms, behaviors, and sustainability outcomes (George et al., 2021).

Future research should adopt *ecological and systems-based methodologies* to understand how technological entrepreneurship contributes to planetary well-being. This entails studying not only venture success but also the cumulative environmental and societal footprint of technological innovation.

1.7.4 Emerging Research Frontiers

The intellectual frontier of technology entrepreneurship lies in addressing its paradoxes such as innovation versus inclusion, disruption versus stability, and autonomy versus accountability. Drawing from the chapters and theoretical synthesis, several future research priorities emerge:

1. **AI and Algorithmic Accountability**—Investigate governance mechanisms that embed ethical oversight in AI-driven entrepreneurial ventures (Floridi & Cowls, 2022).
2. **Blockchain for Institutional Trust**—Explore decentralized mechanisms that enhance transparency and inclusion in finance, supply chains, and education (Catalini & Gans, 2016).
3. **Entrepreneurial Education for Sustainability**—Examine pedagogical frameworks that integrate responsible innovation and ethics into curricula and entrepreneurial incubation (Muñoz & Cohen, 2018).
4. **Socio-Technical Resilience**—Analyze how ecosystems adapt to shocks such as pandemics, geopolitical conflicts, or climate crises through digital transformation (Wurth et al., 2022).
5. **Hybrid Innovation Systems**—Study cross-sector collaborations among startups, corporations, and governments in addressing global challenges (von Krogh et al., 2022).

These themes collectively point to a research agenda that positions technology entrepreneurship as a lever for inclusive, transparent, and sustainable development.

1.7.5 Policy and Practice: The Path Ahead

For policymakers, the findings emphasize designing innovation ecosystems that are open yet regulated, dynamic yet equitable. Governments must incentivize responsible experimentation while establishing ethical and environmental guardrails. Educational institutions should reframe entrepreneurship not merely as venture creation but as *value co-creation* within planetary limits.

For practitioners, the path forward involves embedding ethics and sustainability into Business models from the outset. This requires developing governance frameworks, impact metrics, and transparent reporting mechanisms that align entrepreneurial ambition with societal trust. Investors and accelerators, too, must evolve, prioritizing ventures that balance innovation with responsibility.

1.7.6 Closing Reflection

The central message of *Evolving Trends in Technology Entrepreneurship* is that the future of entrepreneurship is *technological, ethical, and human-centered.* As digital technologies permeate every aspect of life, entrepreneurship becomes the primary mechanism for negotiating the balance between innovation and integrity. The challenge is not merely to create new technologies, but to ensure that those technologies contribute to a more just, sustainable, and inclusive world.

The volume, therefore, stands as both an academic contribution and a call to action: to scholars, to extend theoretical integration across disciplines; to educators, to nurture ethical agency among future entrepreneurs; and to policymakers, to design ecosystems where innovation serves collective prosperity. By aligning digital transformation with ethical responsibility, technology entrepreneurship can truly fulfill its transformative promise, not only as an engine of economic growth but as a force for human and planetary flourishing.

References

Acosta, P., Cavallaro, E., & Foss, N. J. (2023). Digital platforms and the boundaries of the firm: An ecosystem perspective on value creation and appropriation. *Technological Forecasting & Social Change, 187*, Article 122194. https://doi.org/10.1016/j.techfore.2022.122194

Ashok, M., Madan, R., Joha, A., & Sivarajah, U. (2022). Ethical framework for artificial intelligence and digital technologies. *International Journal of Information Management, 62*, Article 102433. https://doi.org/10.1016/j.ijinfomgt.2021.102433

Audretsch, D. B., Belitski, M., & Caiazza, R. (2022). Technology transfer, entrepreneurship, and sustainable regional development. *Small Business Economics, 58*(3), 1273–1291. https://doi.org/10.1007/s11187-021-00464-0

Autio, E., & Levie, J., et al. (2017). Management of entrepreneurial ecosystems. In R. Blackburn (Ed.), *The SAGE Handbook of Small Business and Entrepreneurship* (pp. 355–377). SAGE.

Autio, E., Nambisan, S., Thomas, L. D. W., & Wright, M. (2018). Digital affordances, spatial affordances, and the genesis of entrepreneurial ecosystems. *Strategic Entrepreneurship Journal, 12*(1), 72–95. https://doi.org/10.1002/sej.1266

Autio, E., Nambisan, S., & Zahra, S. A. (2021). Digital entrepreneurship and transformation: Theoretical foundations and research directions. *Entrepreneurship Theory and Practice, 45*(5), 1028–1053. https://doi.org/10.1177/10422587211001795

Bailetti, T. (2012). Technology entrepreneurship: Overview, definition, and distinctive aspects. *Technology Innovation Management Review, 2*(2), 5–12. https://doi.org/10.22215/timreview/520

Barney, J. (1991). Firm resources and sustained competitive advantage. *Journal of Management, 17*(1), 99–120. https://doi.org/10.1177/014920639101700108

Bhatti, Y. A., Basu, R., Barron, D., & Ventresca, M. J. (2021). Frugal innovation and institutional work: Making the hidden visible. *Organization Studies, 42*(5), 765–789. https://doi.org/10.1177/0170840620929977

Blank, S. (2013). Why the lean start-up changes everything. *Harvard Business Review, 91*(5), 63–72.

Bouncken, R. B., Kraus, S., & Roig-Tierno, N. (2022). Entrepreneurial ecosystems, hybrid innovation, and new Business models. *Journal of Business Research, 144*, 1081–1091. https://doi.org/10.1016/j.jbusres.2022.02.007

Catalini, C., & Gans, J. S. (2016). Some simple economics of the blockchain. *MIT Sloan Research Paper No. 5191-16*. https://doi.org/10.2139/ssrn.2874598

Chesbrough, H., & Bogers, M. (2014). Explicating open innovation: Clarifying an emerging paradigm for understanding innovation. In H. Chesbrough, W. Vanhaverbeke, & J. West (Eds.), *New Frontiers in Open Innovation* (pp. 3–28). Oxford University Press.

Floridi, L., & Cowls, J. (2022). A unified framework of five principles for AI in society. *Harvard Data Science Review*. https://doi.org/10.1162/99608f92.9a15dc4f

George, G., Merrill, R. K., & Schillebeeckx, S. J. D. (2021). Digital sustainability and entrepreneurship: How digital innovations are helping tackle climate change and sustainable development. *Entrepreneurship Theory and Practice, 45*(5), 999–1027. https://doi.org/10.1177/1042258721998948

George, G., Ratten, V., & Zahra, S. A. (2022). Tech for good: Harnessing technological innovation for social impact. *Technological Forecasting & Social Change, 180*, Article 121703. https://doi.org/10.1016/j.techfore.2022.121703

George, G., & Zahra, S. A. (2022). Institutional voids, technological innovation, and entrepreneurship in emerging markets. *Journal of Business Venturing Insights, 17*, Article e00317. https://doi.org/10.1016/j.jbvi.2021.e00317

Giones, F., & Brem, A. (2023). Digital entrepreneurship: Trends, challenges, and opportunities. *Technological Forecasting & Social Change, 191*, Article 122407. https://doi.org/10.1016/j.techfore.2023.122407

Helfat, C. E., & Peteraf, M. A. (2015). Managerial cognitive capabilities and the microfoundations of dynamic capabilities. *Strategic Management Journal, 36*(6), 831–850. https://doi.org/10.1002/smj.2247

Kraus, S., Bican, P. M., Giones, F., & Reyes, G. (2022). Digital transformation and entrepreneurship: A research agenda for future inquiry. *Technological Forecasting & Social Change, 186*, Article 122111. https://doi.org/10.1016/j.techfore.2022.122111

Kraus, S., Parastuty, Z., Kallmuenzer, A., & Tiberius, V. (2023). Technology entrepreneurship in the era of artificial intelligence: Challenges and opportunities. *Journal of Business Research, 171*, Article 114288. https://doi.org/10.1016/j.jbusres.2023.114288

Lawrence, T. B., & Suddaby, R. (2006). Institutions and institutional work. In S. Clegg, C. Hardy, T. Lawrence, & W. Nord (Eds.), *The SAGE Handbook of Organization Studies* (2nd ed., pp. 215–254). SAGE.

Muñoz, P., & Cohen, B. (2018). Sustainable entrepreneurship research: Taking stock and looking ahead. *Business Strategy and the Environment, 27*(3), 300–322. https://doi.org/10.1002/bse.2000

Murray, A., & Fisher, E. (2021). Sustainability, innovation, and entrepreneurship: Rethinking purpose in digital economies. *Business Strategy and the Environment, 30*(6), 2773–2786. https://doi.org/10.1002/bse.2776

Nambisan, S. (2017). Digital entrepreneurship: Toward a digital technology perspective of entrepreneurship. *Entrepreneurship Theory and Practice, 41*(6), 1029–1055. https://doi.org/10.1111/etap.12254

Nambisan, S., Wright, M., & Feldman, M. (2019). The digital transformation of innovation and entrepreneurship: Progress, challenges and key themes. *Research Policy, 48*(8), Article 103773. https://doi.org/10.1016/j.respol.2019.03.018

Nambisan, S., Zahra, S. A., & Luo, Y. (2020). Global platforms and ecosystems: Implications for international business theories. *Journal of International Business Studies, 50*(9), 1464–1486. https://doi.org/10.1057/s41267-020-00290-6

Owen, R., Macnaghten, P., & Stilgoe, J. (2012). Responsible research and innovation: From science in society to science for society, with society. *Science and Public Policy, 39*(6), 751–760. https://doi.org/10.1093/scipol/scs093

Ratten, V. (2023). Responsible innovation and technology entrepreneurship: Integrating ethics into entrepreneurial ecosystems. *Technological Forecasting & Social Change, 190*, Article 122343. https://doi.org/10.1016/j.techfore.2023.122343

Schumpeter, J. A. (1934). *The theory of economic development*. Harvard University Press.

Scott, W. R. (2014). *Institutions and organizations: Ideas, interests, and identities* (4th ed.). SAGE.

Shane, S., & Venkataraman, S. (2000). The promise of entrepreneurship as a field of research. *Academy of Management Review, 25*(1), 217–226. https://doi.org/10.5465/amr.2000.2791611

Spigel, B., & Harrison, R. (2018). Toward a process theory of entrepreneurial ecosystems. *Strategic Entrepreneurship Journal, 12*(1), 151–168. https://doi.org/10.1002/sej.1268

Stam, E. (2015). Entrepreneurial ecosystems and regional policy: A sympathetic critique. *European Planning Studies, 23*(9), 1759–1769. https://doi.org/10.1080/09654313.2015.1061484

Stilgoe, J. (2019). *Who's driving innovation?* Palgrave Macmillan. https://doi.org/10.1007/978-3-030-14002-3

Stilgoe, J., Owen, R., & Macnaghten, P. (2013). Developing a framework for responsible innovation. *Research Policy, 42*(9), 1568–1580. https://doi.org/10.1016/j.respol.2013.05.008

Teece, D. J. (2014). A dynamic capabilities-based entrepreneurial theory of the multinational enterprise. *Journal of International Business Studies, 45*(1), 8–37. https://doi.org/10.1057/jibs.2013.54

Teece, D. J. (2021). Dynamic capabilities and entrepreneurial management in large organizations: Toward a theory of the (entrepreneurial) firm. *European Economic Review, 140*, Article 103974. https://doi.org/10.1016/j.euroecorev.2021.103974

Teece, D. J., Peteraf, M. A., & Leih, S. (2016). Dynamic capabilities and organizational agility: Risk, uncertainty, and strategy in the innovation economy. *California Management Review, 58*(4), 13–35. https://doi.org/10.1525/cmr.2016.58.4.13

Teece, D. J., Pisano, G., & Shuen, A. (1997). Dynamic capabilities and strategic management. *Strategic Management Journal, 18*(7), 509–533. https://doi.org/10.1002/(SICI)1097-0266(199708)18:7%3c509::AID-SMJ882%3e3.0.CO;2-Z

von Krogh, G., Haefliger, S., Spaeth, S., & Wallin, M. W. (2022). Digital transformation and innovation ecosystems: Research opportunities. *Journal of Product Innovation Management, 39*(2), 131–151. https://doi.org/10.1111/jpim.12646

Wernerfelt, B. (1984). A resource-based view of the firm. *Strategic Management Journal, 5*(2), 171–180. https://doi.org/10.1002/smj.4250050207

Wurth, B., Stam, E., & Spigel, B. (2022). Toward an entrepreneurial ecosystem research program. *Entrepreneurship Theory and Practice, 46*(3), 729–778. https://doi.org/10.1177/1042258721998948

Zahra, S. A., & Nambisan, S. (2012). Entrepreneurship and strategic thinking in business ecosystems. *Business Horizons, 55*(3), 219–229. https://doi.org/10.1016/j.bushor.2011.12.004

Zahra, S. A., Wright, M., & Abdelgawad, S. G. (2022). Contextualizing technology entrepreneurship: An integrative agenda for future research. *Journal of Business Venturing, 37*(2), Article 106106. https://doi.org/10.1016/j.jbusvent.2021.106106

Zietsma, C., Groenewegen, P., Logue, D., & Hinings, C. R. (2017). Field or fields? Building the scaffolding for cumulation of research on institutional fields. *Academy of Management Annals, 11*(1), 391–450. https://doi.org/10.5465/annals.2014.0052

CHAPTER 2

Ethics in Emerging Digital and Artificial Intelligence Business Models

Christina Öberg

2.1 Introduction

Digitalization and artificial intelligence (AI) have fueled the development of new business models (Zhang, Yang, & Zhu, 2023; Öberg, 2023a). Business models refer to the ways in which businesses are organized, capturing both the provision and customer sides of operations (Osterwalder et al., 2005; Zott & Amit, 2010). Meanwhile, digitalization expands across various IT solutions not only as technology but also as a means of organizing business and providing content to business models (Verhoef et al., 2021). AI, with its separation between its role as a decision tool and its generative capacity for constructing business models and

C. Öberg (✉)
School of Business and Economics, Linnaeus University, 391 82 Kalmar, Sweden
e-mail: Christina.oberg@lnu.se

D. Kumar et al. (eds.), *Evolving Trends in Technology Entrepreneurship*, Palgrave Studies in Global Entrepreneurship,
https://doi.org/10.1007/978-981-95-7441-4_2

producing creative solutions (Öberg, 2024b), further adds to this development by creating ever-new ways of organizing in the market space, producing new offerings, and fueling data as a valuable resource.

The notion of data as free and access provided on a non-monetary basis is increasingly scrutinized in the context of integrity, exploration, and regulations designed to restrict the use of personal data. With many digital business models focusing on personal data and transparency rather than trust among parties, traditional ethical frameworks are challenged by these developments. Furthermore, AI introduces challenges related to the ownership of ideas and determining when it is possible to claim intellectual property rights relative language models and AI-generated ideas. Ethics, defined as the moral norms that guide how individuals should behave, is concerned with the impact of human actions on others. Over time, these norms may evolve in tandem with changes in regulations and the legal system, or work opposite to such developments.

Based on the emergence of digital and AI-fueled business modes, the purpose of the chapter is *to discuss how new business models, as entrepreneurial expressions emerging from digitalization and AI, may challenge current ethical behaviors and regulations*. The chapter is based on an integrative, prospector literature review that encompasses ethics, digitalization, AI, and business models.

The chapter identifies various ethical issues and explores how these issues are related to different business model types and the development over time. More precisely, it demonstrates how past research deals with AI decision-making as potentially non-ethical (Diab & El Hajj, 2024), changes in marketing and data use (Davenport et al., 2020), and privacy concerns (Ashok et al., 2022).

The chapter contributes to existing research by highlighting contemporary ethical issues related to business models and the way in which these issues emerge in the context of digitalization and AI. A key contribution of the chapter is its development of business model configurations, the associated ethical issues, the identification of responsible parties, and recommendations for addressing these issues. The analysis links various ethical issues to business model types, while showing how the development is dynamic, not only following technological transformations but also in terms of business modeling, who is regarded as responsible and what ethical issues emerge. By extending the review to incorporate missing perspectives and themes, the chapter identifies central ethical concerns associated with digitalization and AI development. Given the time-critical nature of AI, future avenues of development along with the potential shifting role of regulations relative to ethics are also discussed.

The rest of the chapter is organized as follows. First, business models, AI, and digitalization are further discussed to set the stage for the chapter's topic. Next, ethics is examined in greater depth. The method section describes how the literature review was conducted, justifies methodological choices, and explains the data analysis process. The findings section presents the evolution over time, outlines business model types, and identifies central ethical issues. Subsequently, the findings are discussed, and paradoxes are derived from this analysis as the ethical issues contain co-existing contradictions (cf. Cunha & Putnam, 2019; Poole & Van de Ven, 1989; Smith & Lewis, 2011). The chapter concludes with a final remark.

2.2 Theoretical Background

2.2.1 Business Models, AI, and Digitalization

Business models thus refer to how operations are organized to create value for stakeholders (Osterwalder et al., 2005; Schneider & Spieth, 2013; Zott & Amit, 2010). With its emergence in the business and management literature, emphasis was placed on the firm as a vehicle for value creation, while also stressing that parties external to the firm would be active in such processes. The traditional business model would be designed to create value for customers, packaged as value propositions (Osterwalder et al., 2005). The shaping of new ways of exchange has, though, put emphasis on the need to create value also for upstream stakeholders—providers supplying for reasons beyond monetary return, and for society in the light of sustainable solutions (Öberg, 2023c, 2024a, 2024c). Not only does this development expand the organizing of business upstream and into various forms of collaborative or open ways of operating, it also demonstrates that values are not purely monetary, but can be based on notions of doing good, visibility, and future opportunities (von Krogh et al., 2012). What could be described as a paradigm shift is fueled by the technological development acting as an enabler for such ways of operating as the sharing economy, data-driven business models, and indeed AI-generated entrepreneurship (Öberg, Grinevich, Tamvada, & Audretsch, 2024).

When business models are conceptualized in research, they are often divided into value creation, value offerings, and value capturing, portraying a resource-driven linear process from supply to customer offerings (Osterwalder & Pigneur, 2010). Alternatively, they are described as activity systems, which importantly depict not only what activities are pursued, but how they are linked and who performs them (Zott & Amit, 2010). In comparison to past research on offerings, the business model, regardless of conceptualization, thereby not only concerns the customer side of operations but entails a focus on such offerings throughout the firm. The linkages among various parts of the firm are in the definition of Osterwalder and Pigneur (2010) only understood as how the value creation ties the firm together across departments, while Zott and Amit (2010) describe these more explicitly as structures. The inclusion of external parties is primarily addressed in terms of key partners (Osterwalder & Pigneur, 2010) or through describing the business model as an open system. Meanwhile, research on open business models may still describe these in a company-centric manner, thereby illustrating how the firm benefits from contributions to ideas and innovations by others (Chesbrough, 2006; Vanhaverbeke & Chesbrough, 2014).

As we move into the digital and AI landscape, the very value proposition, linkages among activities, and the stakeholders included reach a new potential state. Notably, digitalization has led to algorithmic intermediation between users and providers, as expressed in the sharing economy (Geissinger et al., 2021). Data becomes the resource sold, and customers may "pay" with their data on platforms. We can also envision how AI becomes the entrepreneur, seizing business opportunities and turning them into value propositions and business models. Along such current and visionary developments, business models may start challenging moral norms related to, for instance, intellectual property and integrity. They may also contravene current legal regulations or require new ones. This chapter discusses how new business models, as entrepreneurial expressions emerging from digitalization and AI, may challenge current ethical behaviors and regulations.

2.2.2 Ethics

Ethics thus refer to moral norms about how individuals ought to behave (Gerwith, 1978). It can be seen as framed within the legal system, while at the same time providing insights into what is legal and not. Within such frames, ethics could also be described as desirable behaviors, thereby aspiring to not only do right but also do good. As times evolve, past notions of what is ethical and not change, influenced by progressive developments and the questioning of past behaviors. The social or institutional disruption related to digitalization in business is one such example, which has introduced sustainability while fostering a more liberal interpretation of ownership and use (Öberg, 2023b). This aspect is not least visible when we discuss digitalization and AI in relation to business models. However, and in parallel, the regulatory framework for data usage tends to restrict such liberal interpretations and uses. For instance, the GDPR requires consensus for use of personal data with clearly defined purposes. This, in turn, has implications for business modeling, the development of new business models, or the reconfiguration of existing ones (Andreini et al., 2021) in areas using data as a resource.

When scholars such as Diab and El Hajj (2024) discuss ethics in the context of AI, they do so on the organizational level, addressing ethics as a component of corporate culture. Meanwhile, we can also—and most often do—envision ethics as societal norms, standards that, although not always followed, generally define what is considered good or bad, core or at the fringes of acceptable behavior. Indeed, Sudhir and Murthy (2001) describe ethics along dimensions of business and ethics, business and society, and business and individuals. While doing so, the business remains the analytical unit, raising questions about whether firms require distinct ethical norms from those of the society at large, and whether individuals or firms are responsible for upholding these norms. Meanwhile, ever since the boundaries between individuals, firms and society have become less distinct, operations may be handled by individual peers, and open systems create resource uses across corporate borders with stakeholders other than pure business actors.

Sudhir and Murthy (2001) describe ethics as dynamic, and Marshall (1999) points out how technology creates new ethical dilemmas. While much has happened since Marshall (1999) raised this concern, we can thereby envision ethics evolving to highlight new dilemmas and a reshaping of moral norms.

Diab and El Hajj (2024) elaborate on ethics in the implementation of AI, focusing on how corruption, for instance, negatively impacts such implementations. Meanwhile, Ashok et al. (2022) refer to technoethics, computer ethics, information ethics, roboethics, machine ethics, computational ethics, information and communication technology ethics, and machine learning ethics to reflect ethics in the context of AI, addressing the development, use, and interaction between humans and machine.

Combined this suggests how AI has led to new ethical dimensions; however, Ashok et al. (2022) do not discuss these in the light of business models, nor do they include machine-to-machine interactions, generative AI, or societal moral norms related to AI.

2.3 Method

This chapter is based on a prospector literature review. As a specific type of literature review, it aims to combine literature across domains, while reaching for new conceptualizations and narratives. In the emergence of AI and in the realm of changing ethics, legal questioning, and renewal, the prospector review enables an extension beyond existing research. It traverses the organization and categorization of current literatures, questions and problematizes them, and exposes contradictions within them. Moreover, it builds non-preexisting bridges across related literature.

Past research has treated business ethics as a specific type of ethics, expressing it as culture, which suppresses other notions of ethics that can become relevant as business models include parties beyond the firm and affect individuals as well as society. Therefore, ethics is for this chapter addressed more broadly, ensuring that it reflects both internal and external considerations and ethics as moral norms to ensure that it not only expresses the firm as operandi. Meanwhile, business models have been defined in various ways throughout the literature (e.g., Casadesus-Masanell & Ricart, 2010; Desyllas et al., 2022; Zott & Amit, 2013). Here, they are used to capture the entire firm and its engagement with external parties, not just the value-offering side of operations. Digitalization and AI lastly evolve as technology develops. What was once described as AI in the 1970s is quite different from today, and generative AI has dramatically challenged past notions of AI.

To allow a dynamic perspective across concepts while still incorporating variants of business models and dimensions of ethics, the search terms used were defined as "business model", "artificial intelligence", "digital", "digitalization", and "ethics". Using these and not other search terms posed the risk of omitting certain publications, yet it helped maintain the core of this chapter. Meanwhile, non-relevant uses of the concepts were addressed during the analysis.

The chapter used *Web of Science* as its database focusing on high-quality journals. While there are other alternatives, such as *Google Scholar* and *Scopus*, these either include many non-peer-reviewed publications or overlap extensively with *Web of Science*.

Different search combinations were used to capture overlapping and distinct discussions, all of which included "ethics" as a component: for example, "business model" and "ethics" as well as "digital" and "ethics". From all searches, *MDPI*-journals were excluded to filter out questionable publications and to reflect the author's stance on these sources as publishing research without rigorous review processes and thereby quality assurance of articles.

The first search, including all concepts—"ethics" and (digital OR digitalization OR artificial intelligence") and "business model"—resulted in 35 articles. Table 2.1 then depicts search results across different combinations of concepts.

With business models as a central focus for the chapter, and indeed the digital and AI dimensions, the initial search served as the point of departure for the analysis. The analysis of this search also showed relevance for capturing ethics related to digital and AI business models. Only three articles (Bartels et al., 2022; Beleigoli et al., 2022; Zhao, Fieldson, & Duran, 2025) were omitted as irrelevant following the analysis because they solely discussed ethics in relation to data collection. Meanwhile, wherever gaps were identified, broader searches were used to fill these gaps and provide complementary insights. Table 2.2 summarizes the key 32 articles (the initial 35 less the 3 irrelevant articles).

Table 2.1 Search terms and results

Search term	*Results (number of articles)*
"ethics" and (digital OR digitalization OR artificial intelligence") and "business model"	35 articles
"ethics" and "digital" and "business model"	27 articles
"ethics" and "digitalization" and "business model"	4 articles
"ethics" and "artificial intelligence" and "business model"	12 articles
"ethics" and "business model"	210 articles
"ethics" and (digital OR digitalization OR artificial intelligence")	10,823 articles
"ethics" and "digital"	6,656 articles
"ethics" and "digitalization"	349 articles
"ethics" and "artificial intelligence"	5,099 articles

Table 2.2 Articles on ethics, business models, and digitalization or AI, from oldest to newest

Authors	*Year of publication*	*Area of publication*	*Topic of study*	*Ethics*
Busch (2011)	2011	Informatics	Ensuring citizens' access to IT	Fairness of knowledge distribution; responsible business models to ensure such access
Weijters et al. (2014)	2014	Business ethics	Consumers' preferences in downloading music	Illegal versus legal as dichotomies for for-free and paid downloading
Vezyridis and Timmons (2015)	2015	Informatics	Health care data business models introduced and questioned as empowering consumers	Health care data handling as business models
Stojanovski and Marusic (2017)	2017	Medical journal, publication on publishing	Predatory journals	Transparency of editorial policy and charge for open access for payment business models
Park and Skoric (2017)	2017	Business ethics	Google glass customized advertising posing challenges to legal system for data	Policies related to personal advertising
Díaz (2019)	2019	Informatics	Storage of data from apps, etc., as ground for possible (future) business models	Digital inscriptions of our everyday life
Goldkind and McNutt (2019)	2019	Ethics	Sharing, gig, and collaborative consumption business models exploiting individuals. Do governments provide social security? Need for new policies and regulations	Sharing economy ethical dilemmas, benefitting few while exploiting many

Authors	*Year of publication*	*Area of publication*	*Topic of study*	*Ethics*
Jung and Pfister (2020)	2020	Innovation	Written medical consent using blockchain technology	Ethical development of AI applications in health care
Kreitem and Ragnedda (2020)	2020	Informatics	User-generated content related to blockchain technology, reducing digital divides	Fair revenue models
White and Boatwright (2020)	2020	Public relations	Facebook and related business models causing ethical dilemmas	Algorithms and AI raising new ethical and social responsibility issues
García-Avilés (2021)	2021	Media	Review of journalism	Ethics of journalism. New business models implicit
Geiger and Gross (2021)	2021	Management	Firms creating data business models from consumers' health care data	Digital capitalism when exploiting health care data in new business models
Carvajal and Barinagarrementeria (2021)	2021	Media	Using commercials in editorial work	Ethics of hiding paid-for advertisement in journalism
Luitse and Denkena (2021)	2021	Informatics	Large language models leading to new business models	Monopoly and dependency
Saurabh et al. (2022)	2022	Informatics	AI fueling new business models	Ethical digital transformation

(continued)

Table 2.2 (continued)

Authors	*Year of publication*	*Area of publication*	*Topic of study*	*Ethics*
Barbazzeni, Haider, and Friebe (2022)	2022	Health	Digital transformation transforming ethics, business models in health	General transformation of ethics following from digital development
Berbenni-Rehm (2023)	2023	Informatics	AI to develop structured knowledge. AI by design needs to walk hand in hand with ethics by design. Opportunities and challenges	Ethics by design
Sweeney, Barton, and Nebeker (2023)	2023	Informatics	Mobile app advertising, sensitive data collected without consumers' knowledge (focus on elderly)	Privacy policy
Holmqvist and Kowalkowski (2023)	2023	Marketing	Traceability in supply chains of luxury goods. Digitalization/AI only assumed as solution	Ethics through traceability
Roffarello and De Russis (2023)	2023	Informatics	Data wellbeing through regulating self-data use	Ethics in data wellbeing
Read and Smith (2023)	2023	Media	Data-driven business models in sports: e.g., platform broadcasting partnerships, e-ticketing in smart stadiums, and cryptocurrency-based fan tokens	Vulnerability of consumers
Smith et al. (2024)	2024	Health	Mental health and digitalization of it	Biomedical ethics
Bickley et al. (2025)	2025	Entrepreneurship/ Economics	AI and big data positively while weakly affecting sustainable entrepreneurship	Sustainability
Rana et al. (2024)	2024	Marketing	Ethics among others impact digital transformation adoption	Ethics as values in business

Authors	*Year of publication*	*Area of publication*	*Topic of study*	*Ethics*
Jones (2025)	2025	Media	Risk with AI related to firms capitalizing on surveillance, invade privacy through data use, disrupt moral autonomy and harm democracy and how this can be overcome	Media ethics
Palau-Sam and Iranzo-Cabrera (2024)	2024	Media	Mixing commercial content into editorial	Media ethics (ethics of transparency)
Ji, Zhou, Zhang, Cheng, and Luo (2024)	2024	Informatics	AI-driven data analytics shaping business models	Privacy and security safeguarded by automation and control
Aburass and Abu Rumman (2024)	2024	Informatics	Copyright when AI produces text, monetized business models to use machine generated text	Copyright
Espíndola (2024)	2024	Politics	Mass atrocity raising normative and conceptual challenges in big tech firms such as Meta. Enabling human right violations, toxic speeches, and manipulation	Human rights
Norton (2025)	2025	Management	Ethical dilemmas and pressure to adopt to AI in business	Ethical issues of AI in business models
Sonni (2025)	2025	Journalism	Review of digitalization in journalism	Ethics of automated journalism
Ernst and Matter (2025)	2025	Innovation	Ethics is responsible innovation: Why not adopt?	Ethics in responsible innovation

The articles were analyzed in terms of areas of publication and years of publishing to capture the spread and development over time. The time stamp was important for understanding the evolutionary character of digitalization and AI, and it proved to be equally significant for tracking the ethical issues at hand, indicating how moral norms developed in tandem with technology or even acted as an opposing force to that development. For a content analysis (Holsti, 1969; Krippendorff, 2004), key ethical questions raised were captured as initial codes. Each article—not least review or conceptual articles—may entail multiple ethical dilemmas, resulting in an uneven number of ethical issues across publications.

The various ethical issues and their relation to business models, digitalization, and AI were coded across repeated rounds of comparison and code reductions. More precisely, the content analysis followed the steps of first-order constructs, second-order themes, and aggregate dimensions as outlined by Gioia et al. (2013) to ensure a structured progression from empirical coding to theorized constructs.

By working across the dimensions of ethics, business models, and technology (digitalization and AI), the analysis captured the relationships among these aggregated themes (cf. Gioia et al., 2013), while considering their development over time. This process revealed some paradoxical findings, including tensional co-existences of developments with contradictory characteristics (Poole & Van de Ven, 1989; Smith & Lewis, 2011; Öberg et al., 2020). More specifically, the evolution of ethics and technology appeared to follow a reverse order over time, while the literature suggested both democratized and exploitative relations with similar business models.

As digitalization and AI, business models and ethics continue to evolve, the chapter eventually searched for areas not well covered in past research. To do so, it revisited how business models have been described in previous studies—particularly in terms of e-activity systems and value creation characteristics—and examined the ethical issues arising from these processes, including their content, structure, and governance (cf. Zott & Amit, 2010). This approach helped ensure the chapter's relevance for the future.

2.4 Findings

The literature review indicates how the discussion on ethics related to digital and AI business models has risen over time. First, which may relate to the overall emergence of digital business models and indeed the business model concept, the oldest publication was released only in 2014. Second, AI is included for the first time in 2019, thereby indicating that the technology addresses changes over time. Third, the number of publications was somewhat sporadic until 2019.

Meanwhile, it is not only the technology that has developed and transformed; the topics at hand—business models and ethics—have also evolved. In terms of business models, three main types emerge over the years: 1) digitally intermediated business models, such as the sharing economy and the hype surrounding distributed ledgers; 2) business models that utilize user data as a resource, particularly in relation to health data and buying patterns; and 3) AI-generated content business models. Although all three types remain present, their evolution in research shows that digitally intermediated business models appear in the oldest publications, whereas AI-generated content business models are featured in the most recent ones.

For each such type, different ethical issues are raised. *Digitally intermediated business models* are linked to illegal uses, where user eligibility is closely tied to payment requirements. For example, research on digital platforms for music sharing (Weijters et al., 2014) and on predatory publishing houses (Stojanovski & Marusic, 2017) illustrates this connection. Additionally, both the unlawful use and the exploitation of providers by platform firms are discussed (Goldkind & McNutt, 2019), and more recently, the manipulation of public opinion has also been examined in relation to these business models (Espíndola, 2024).

Research on *user-data business models* extensively discusses health data (Barbazzeni et al., 2022; Vezyridis & Timmons, 2015) and the collection of customized data based on purchasing patterns and behaviors (Park & Skoric, 2017; Read & Smith, 2023). Here, a distinction is made between using data for the benefit of the user and selling it to others (Geiger & Gross, 2021). The latter is seen as exploitative, while the former is considered partly beneficial, albeit still involving the use of user data in ways that users may not have consented to (Sweeney et al., 2023). Jones (2025) describes how AI poses risks of enabling firms to exploit surveillance opportunities, compromise privacy through data misuse, undermine moral autonomy, and threaten democratic processes.

Business models based on AI-generated content (e.g., Norton, 2025) include how firms sell AI-produced services (Ji et al., 2024; Sonni, 2025) and generate content sourced from others without acknowledging or compensating for the data (Aburass & Abu Rumman, 2024). Copyright issues thus become central ethical dilemmas here. Table 2.3 summarizes the three types of business models, their main ethical issues and proposed solutions.

As can be read from Table 2.3, the focal actors vary among the three types: For digitally intermediated business models, the party potentially acting unethically or even illegally is often the user/consumer, while the platform may potentially be at fault related to leveraging service or input providers (White & Boatwright, 2020). Meanwhile, the user-data-driven business models place the business model owner at the center, highlighting how such firms might use data without proper consent—either toward the customer or to create business models directed at others, essentially selling the data onward. The business models based on AI-generated content, similar to user-data business models, tend to hold the producer accountable to some extent. However, the discussion is complicated by questions of editorship over data not originally generated by the party, and whether these business model "owners" have the right to the models and data. As can also be seen from Table 2.3 the literature currently offers few solutions for such business models.

Importantly, across all three types, both positive and negative issues are discussed, including ethical considerations. For instance, digitally intermediated business models are thought to enhance accessibility for those at the bottom of the pyramid and contribute to the democratization of IT knowledge, sometimes relying on the business models to achieve this (Busch, 2011; Kreitem & Ragnedda, 2020). Kreitem and Ragnedda (2020) point to the potential of blockchains to close digital divides in society, and Holmqvist and Kowalkowski (2023) discuss supply-chain traceability. Díaz (2019) examines the potential for new business models

Table 2.3 Business model types and ethical issues

Business model type	*Ethical issue*	*Solution*
Digitally intermediated business models	Using what is not yours as a consumer; exploiting providers; manipulation	Paying for using
User data business models	Using data to convince consumers; selling critical data	New policies
AI-generated content business models	Selling AI-generated content. Copyright; Ethics of responsibility (editorship, etc.)	–

based on user data, and research indicates that the collection of user data may lead to improved health care precision (Roffarello & De Russis, 2023). Berbenni-Rehm (2023) describes how AI facilitates the structuring of knowledge, and Bickley et al. (2025) discuss the role of AI in creating sustainable business models.

Ethics in digital and AI-driven business models thus demonstrate that ethical considerations extend beyond business ethics (cf. Diab & El Hajj, 2024; Sudhir & Murthy, 2001) to encompass various parties, societal norms, and individuals as potentially harmed by unethical behavior. These perspectives expand upon past notions of business ethics in relation to digitalization and AI as expressed in previous research (e.g., Diab & El Hajj, 2024).

2.5 Analytical Discussion

As we move across the digital and AI development in society and business, the emergence of new business models is pronounced. In this context, technological advancements foster innovative ways of conducting business, with content, structure, and governance (cf. Zott & Amit, 2010) being redistributed and critically questioned across parties, and what is offered as value and at whose expense. The evolution—or dynamics—of technological and business model development raises new ethical issues. Notably, these issues either call for new policies or require changes in individuals' behaviors. Meanwhile, and over time, the definitions of ethically right and wrong shift—a phenomenon previously described as a social disruption (Öberg, 2023b)—influencing both the assignment of responsibility and the conception of ethical behavior.

From digitally intermediated business models to the user-data business models, a shift emerges from using what is not yours to selling what is not yours, where the user as a private person is no longer the main target of discussion, but rather portrayed as the victim of digitalized business models. Meanwhile, in both the user-data and AI-generated content business models, ethical responsibility is predominantly centered on the producer (i.e., the business model owner, whether a platform or a producer of materials), although in AI-generated content models, the delineation becomes blurred regarding editorial control over data not originally generated by them.

Currently, issues of manipulation, exploitation of user data, and risks associated with content ownership remain central ethical dilemmas.

Ownership, however, has shifted from the mere act of using what is not yours to creation of new content without proper acknowledgment of sources in AI. Thus, while partly echoing past concerns of ownership right, AI introduces new and less traceable challenges regarding copyright and content ownership.

The development pertains to three co-existing contradictions, or paradoxes:

P1: Morals include paying for content, yet receiving payment can indicate exploitation.

This first paradox is predominantly related to digitally intermediated business models. Here, users are perceived as stealing when they use content provided, and if they supply content, they do so without the proper right. This is exemplified by music sharing (Kask & Öberg, 2019; Weijters et al., 2014) and other forms of content sharing, where the notion of paying to gain usage rights is emphasized, while compensated provision is seen as exploitative. The payment is particularly challenged as sustainability becomes debated and as it indicates how someone earns money on someone else's data.

P2: As perceptions of ownership become more relaxed, regulatory measures become stricter.

Along the development from digitally intermediated to user-data business models, ownership has become more flexible. Today, many content-sharing operations are no longer viewed as illegal, whether or not they involve payment (Öberg, 2023b), reflecting a disruption of traditional social or informal institutions. Instead, the benefits of non-ownership are highlighted in the sustainability debate. However, as these perceptions relax over time, regulations regarding ownership—and particularly the control over personal data as expressed in GDPR—have become more stringent. This includes how user data is dependent on consent, thereby transferring ownership of user data back to the user.

P3: Although digital business modelsare described as democratizing society, they can lead to increased exploitation of individuals.

Among the positive ethical outcomes of digital and AI business models are the democratization of access, the closing digital divides, and the provision of services to those at the bottom of the pyramid (Broccardo et al., 2023; Busch, 2011). Conversely, it is argued that these business models may exploit these individuals and even harm democratic processes (Jones, 2025). This applies across the three business model types outlined in Table 2.3, while being stressed related to digitally intermediated models in the debate. These business models are described as creating access for those that cannot afford past services, while the provision side is heavily linked to exploiting the same individuals. As user data becomes a resource, as in the user-data business models, we can only envision how these individuals' data become a commodity for sale and even to experiment with.

Drawing on the development trends observed across the three business model types and the evolving nature of ethics, we can anticipate that technological advancement will continue to raise new ethical concerns. In particular, regarding generative AI and its foray into creativity, AI-generated business models—where AI acts not merely as a facilitator of content but as the entrepreneur—could emerge (Öberg et al., 2024). This scenario would prompt ethical considerations about responsibility, potentially shifting the focus from the user in digitally intermediated models, to the business model owner in user-data and AI-generated content models, and ultimately to the machine or the prompting party in AI-generated entrepreneurship. Issues will again center on the challenge of machines replicating human functions and whether business models as such can be effectively protected.

2.6 Concluding Remark

This chapter discusses how new business models, as entrepreneurial expressions emerging from digitalization and AI, may challenge current ethical behaviors and regulations. The chapter outlined three business model types: (1) digitally intermediated business models, (2) user-data business models, and (3) AI generated content business models. These models reveal distinct ethical issues associated with exploiting what is not yours, while also suggesting solutions based on payment or regulation. Together, they highlight the increasing focus on the individual when discussing ethics in the business sphere.

References

Aburass, S., & Abu Rumman, M. (2024). Authenticity in authorship: the writer's integrity framework for verifying human-generated text. *Ethics and Information Technology, 26*(3).

Andreini, D., Bettinelli, C., Foss, N. J., & Mismetti, M. (2021). Business model innovation: A review of the process-based literature. *Journal of Management and Governance, 26*(4), 1089–1121.

Ashok, M., Madan, R., Joha, A., & Sivarajah, U. (2022). Ethical framework for artificial intelligence and digital technologies. *International Journal of Information Management, 62*, Article 102433.

Barbazzeni, B., Haider, S., & Friebe, M. (2022). Engaging through awareness: Purpose-driven framework development to evaluate and develop future business strategies with exponential technologies toward healthcare democratization. *Frontiers in Public Health, 10*.

Bartels, S., Johnsson, S., Boersma, K., Flink, I., McCracken, L., Petersson, S., Christie, H., Feldman, I., Simons, L., Onghena, P., Vlaeyen, J., & Wicksell, R. (2022). Development, evaluation and implementation of a digital behavioural health treatment for chronic pain: study protocol of the multiphase DAHLIA project. *BMJ Open, 12*(4).

Beleigoli, A., Nicholls, S., Brown, A., Chew, D., Beltrame, J., Maeder, A., Maher, C., Versace, V., Hendriks, J., Tideman, P., Kaambwa, B., Zeitz, C., Prichard, I., Tavella, R., Tirimacco, R., Keech, W., Astley, C., Govin, K., Nesbitt, K., Du, H., Champion, S., de Plaza, M., Lynch, I., Poulsen, V., Ludlow, M., Wanguhu, K., Meyer, H., Krollig, A., Gebremichael, L., Green, C., & Clark, R. (2022). Implementation and prospective evaluation of the Country Heart Attack Prevention model of care to improve attendance and completion of cardiac rehabilitation for patients with cardiovascular diseases living in rural Australia: a study protocol. *BMJ Open, 12*(2).

Berbenni-Rehm, C. (2023). Evidence-based AI, ethics and the circular economy of knowledge. *AI & Society, 38*(2), 889–895.

Bickley, S., Macintyre, A., & Torgler, B. (2025). Artificial intelligence and big data in sustainable entrepreneurship. *Journal of Economic Surveys, 39*(1), 103–145.

Broccardo, L., Zicari, A., Jabeen, F., & Bhatti, Z. (2023). How digitalization supports a sustainable business model: A literature review. *Technological Forecasting & Social Change, 187*, Article 122146.

Busch, T. (2011). Capabilities in, capabilities out: Overcoming digital divides by promoting corporate citizenship and fair ICT. *Ethics and Information Technology, 13*(4), 339–353.

Carvajal, M., & Barinagarrementeria, I. (2021). The creation of branded content teams in Spanish news organizations and their implications for structures, professional roles and ethics. *Digital Journalism, 9*(7), 887–907.

Casadesus-Masanell, R., & Ricart, J. E. (2010). From strategy to business models and onto tactics. *Long Range Planning, 43*(2–3), 195–215.

Chesbrough, H. W. (2006). *Open Business models: How to thrive in the new innovation landscape*. Harvard Business School Press.

Cunha, M., & Putnam, L. (2019). Paradox theory and the paradox of success. *Strategic Organization, 17*(1), 95–106.

Davenport, T., Guha, A., Grewal, D., & Bressgott, T. (2020). How artificial intelligence will change the future of marketing. *Journal of the Academy of Marketing Science, 48*(1), 24–42.

Desyllas, P., Salter, A., & Alexy, O. (2022). The breadth of business model reconfiguration and firm performance. *Strategic Organization, 20*(2), 231–269.

Diab, B., & El Hajj, M. (2024). Ethics in the age of artificial intelligence: unveiling challenges and opportunities in business culture. *Cogent Business & Management, 11*(1).

Díaz, A. (2019). The digital ordinary: Digitalization of everyday life as a form of labour. *Cuadernos De Relaciones Laborales, 37*(2), 313–330.

Ernst, L., & Matter, P. (2025). The ethical innovator: Bridging the gap for integrating ethics into digital innovation practice. *Journal of Responsible Innovation, 12*(1), 49–65.

Espíndola, J. (2024). Attributing responsibility to big tech for mass atrocity: Social media and transitional justice. *Perspectives on Politics.*

García-Avilés, J. (2021). Review article: Journalism innovation research, a diverse and flourishing field (2000–2020). *Professional De La Informacion, 30*(1).

Geiger, S., & Gross, N. (2021). A tidal wave of inevitable data? Assetization in the consumer genomics testing industry. *Business & Society, 60*(3), 614–649.

Geissinger, A., Laurell, C., & Öberg, C. (2021). Copycats among underdogs—Echoing the sharing economy business model. *Industrial Marketing Management, 96*, 287–299.

Gerwith, A. (1978). *Reason and morality.* University of Chicago Press.

Gioia, D. A., Corley, K. G., & Hamilton, A. L. (2013). Seeking qualitative rigor in inductive research: Notes on the Gioia methodology. *Organizational Research Methods, 16*(1), 15–31.

Goldkind, L., & McNutt, J. (2019). Vampires in the technological nist: The sharing economy, employment and the quest for economic justice and fairness in a digital future. *Ethics and Social Welfare, 13*(1), 51–63.

Holmqvist, J., & Kowalkowski, C. (2023). Traceability in luxury: Harnessing B2B relationships to enhance ethical practices in the luxury industry. *Industrial Marketing Management, 111*, 257–267.

Holsti, O. R. (1969). *Content analysis for the social sciences and humanities.* Addison-Wesley.

Ji, F., Zhou, Y., Zhang, H., Cheng, G., & Luo, Q. (2024). Navigating the digital odyssey: AI-driven business models in industry 4.0. *Journal of the Knowledge Economy.*

Jones, J. (2025). Don't fear artificial intelligence, question the business model: How surveillance capitalists use media to invade privacy, disrupt moral autonomy, and harm democracy. *Journal of Communication Inquiry, 49*(1), 6–26.

Jung, H., & Pfister, F. (2020). Blockchain-enabled clinical study consent management. *Technology Innovation Management Review, 10*(2), 14–24.

Kask, J., & Öberg, C. (2019). Why "majors" surge in the post-disruptive recording industry. *European Journal of Marketing, 53*(3), 442–462.

Kreitem, H., & Ragnedda, M. (2020). Distributed pool mining and digital inequalities, From cryptocurrency to scientific research. *Journal of Information Communication & Ethics in Society, 18*(3), 339–355.

Krippendorff, K. (2004). *Content analysis: An Introduction to its methodology.* Sage.

Luitse, D., & Denkena, W. (2021). The great transformer: Examining the role of large language models in the political economy of AI. *Big Data & Society, 8*(2).

Marshall, K. P. (1999). Has technology introduced new ethical problems? *Journal of Business Ethics, 19*(1), 81–90.

Norton, L. (2025). Artificial intelligence and organizational strategy: Ethical and governance implications. *Consulting Psychology Journal—Practice and Research.*

Öberg, C. (2023a). Disruption and the ecosystem: The changing roles of ecosystem stakeholders in the course of disruption. *Technological Forecasting and Social Change, 194,* Article 122679.

Öberg, C. (2023b). *Piracy Entrepreneur.* Paper presented at the SCANCOR Weatherhead Alumni Conference 2023, Harvard University.

Öberg, C. (2023c). Towards a typology of sharing economy business model transformation. *Technovation, 123,* Article 102722.

Öberg, C. (2024a). Sharing economy models and sustainability: Towards a typology. *Journal of Cleaner Production, 447,* Article 141636.

Öberg, C. (2024b). *Socially disrupted—The ARA-model in the light of machine-to-machine interaction.* Paper presented at the IMP Seminar, Urbino.

Öberg, C. (2024c). A typology on business model integration. *Thunderbird International Business Review, 66 (6).* 583-594.

Öberg, C., Dahlin, P., & Pesämaa, O. (2020). Tension in networks. *Industrial Marketing Management, 91,* 311–322.

Öberg, C., Grinevich, V., Tamvada, P., & Audretsch, D. (2024). *The roles of artificial intelligence in entrepreneurship.* Paper presented at the NFF Nordic Academy of Management, Reykjavik.

Osterwalder, A., & Pigneur, Y. (2010). *Business model generation: A handbook for visionaries, game changers, and challengers*: Wiley.

Osterwalder, A., Pigneur, Y., & Tucci, C. (2005). Clarifying business models: Origins, present and future of the concept. *Communications of the Association for Information Systems, 15,* 751–775.

Palau-Sam, D., & Iranzo-Cabrera, M. (2024). Quality index of informative branded content in Spain: Criteria and assessment. *Revista De Communicacion-Peru, 23*(1), 395–412.

Park, Y., & Skoric, M. (2017). Personalized ad in your Google glass? Wearable technology, hands-off data collection, and new policy imperative. *Journal of Business Ethics, 142*(1), 71–82.

Poole, M. S., & Van de Ven, A. H. (1989). Using paradox to build management and organization theories. *Academy of Management Review, 14*(4), 562–578.

Rana, S., Singh, J., Mishra, V., Khan, S., Quttainah, M., & Prashar, S. (2024). How digital transformation impact firm performance? The unmet needs of Indian exporting firms. *Journal of Strategic Marketing, 32*(8), 1317–1335.

Read, D., & Smith, A. (2023). Data as capital and ethical implications in digital sport business models. *Convergence: The International Journal of Research into New Media Technologies, 29*(5), 1389–1408.

Roffarello, A., & De Russis, L. (2023). Achieving digital wellbeing through digital self-control tools: A systematic review and neta-analysis. *ACM Transactions on Computer-Human Interaction, 30*(4).

Saurabh, K., Arora, R., Rani, N., Mishra, D., & Ramkumar, M. (2022). AI led ethical digital transformation: Framework, research and managerial implications. *Journal of Information Communication & Ethics in Society, 20*(2), 229–256.

Schneider, S., & Spieth, P. (2013). Business model innovation: Towards an integrated future research agenda. *International Journal of Innovation Management, 17*, 134–156.

Smith, K., Hardy, A., Vinnikova, A., Blease, C., Milligan, L., Hidalgo-Mazzei, D., Lambe, S., Marzano, L., Uhlhaas, P., Ostinelli, E., Anmella, G., Zangani, C., Aronica, R., Dwyer, B., Torous, J., & Cipriani, A. (2024). Digital mental health for schizophrenia and other severe mental illnesses: An international consensus on current challenges and potential solutions. *JMIR Mental Health*, 110–123.

Smith, W., & Lewis, M. (2011). Toward a theory of paradox: A dynamic equilibrium model of organizing. *Academy of Management Review, 36*, 381–403.

Sonni, A. (2025). Digital transformation in journalism: mini review on the impact of AI on journalistic practices. *Frontiers in Communication, 10*.

Stojanovski, J., & Marusic, A. (2017). Does small equal predatory? Analysis of publication charges and transparency of editorial policies in Croatian open access journals. *Biochemia Medica, 27*(2), 292–299.

Sudhir, V., & Murthy. (2001). Ethical challenge to businesses: The deeper meaning. *Journal of Business Ethics, 30*(2), 197–210.

Sweeney, M., Barton, W., & Nebeker, C. (2023). Evaluating mobile apps Targeting older adults: Descriptive study. *JMIR Formative Research, 7*.

Vanhaverbeke, W., & Chesbrough, H. (2014). A classification of open innovation and open business models. In H. W. Chesbrough, W. Vanhaverbeke & J. West (Eds.), *New frontiers in open innovation*. Oxford: Oxford University Press.

Verhoef, P., Broekhuizen, T., Bart, Y., Bhattacharya, A., Dong, J., Fabian, N., & Haenlein, M. (2021). Digital transformation: A multidisciplinary reflection and research agenda. *Journal of Business Research, 122*, 889–901.

Vezyridis, P., & Timmons, S. (2015). On the adoption of personal health records: Some problematic issues for patient empowerment. *Ethics and Information Technology, 17*(2), 113–124.

von Krogh, G., Haefliger, S., Spaeth, S., & Wallin, M. W. (2012). Carrots and rainbows: Motivation and social practice in open source software development. *MIS Quarterly, 36*(2), 649–667.

Weijters, B., Goedertier, F., & Verstreken, S. (2014). Online music consumption in today's technological context: Putting the influence of ethics in perspective. *Journal of Business Ethics, 124*(4), 537–550.

White, C., & Boatwright, B. (2020). Social media ethics in the data economy: Issues of social responsibility for using Facebook for public relations. *Public Relations Review, 46*(5).

Zhang, F., Yang, B., & Zhu, L. (2023). Digital technology usage, strategic flexibility, and business model innovation in traditional manufacturing firms: The moderating role of the institutional environment. *Technological Forecasting & Social Change, 194*.

Zhao, J., Fieldson, R., & Duran, O. (2025). Build it and they will come?—A case study of a 'softer landings' approach in creating a low-carbon community. *Sustainable Futures, 9*.

Zott, C., & Amit, R. (2010). Business model design: An activity system perspective. *Long Range Planning, 43*(2–3), 216–226.

Zott, C., & Amit, R. (2013). The business model: A theoretically anchored robust construct for strategic analysis. *Strategic Organization, 11*(4), 403–411.

CHAPTER 3

Using New Technologies in Startup Environments: Perspectives from Kosovo Startups Via UTAUT-3

Flokart Aliu and Asdren Toska

3.1 Introduction

For organizations worldwide, the swift advancement of technology, particularly artificial intelligence (AI), has brought along both new opportunities and difficulties. In the global startup landscape, the integration of these technologies has proven to be a driving force for innovation, efficiency, and competitiveness (Obschonka & Audretsch, 2020). However,

F. Aliu
Department of Management, Faculty of Economics, University of Prishtina "Hasan Prishtina", Prishtina, Kosova
e-mail: flokart.aliu@uni-pr.edu

A. Toska (✉)
Business Administration—Faculty of Business and Economics, South East European University, Tetovo, North Macedonia
e-mail: t.asdren@gmail.com

D. Kumar et al. (eds.), *Evolving Trends in Technology Entrepreneurship*, Palgrave Studies in Global Entrepreneurship,
https://doi.org/10.1007/978-981-95-7441-4_3

due to a variety of circumstances, including cultural dynamics, regulatory frameworks, and economic development, the degree and kind of technology adoption differ greatly throughout locations.

As a transformational force, artificial intelligence has started to significantly affect a number of industries by boosting competitiveness, efficiency, and creativity. AI holds significant potential for family businesses, particularly in optimizing operations, enhancing decision-making, and strengthening customer engagement (Kumar & Ratten, 2024). For example, the integration of AI platforms into business, and other Business models, is an indication of how it drives significant value creation and competitive advantage, as organizations use AI to innovate their processes and offerings (Reim et al., 2020); (Ruiz-Real, Uribe-Toril, Torres, & Pablo, 2020). According to the authors (Ratten et al., 2024), predictive analytics, personalization, and AI analytics aid international business expansion. However, the adoption of these technologies has not emerged in unison across all business environments across the globe. Several factors appear to play a critical role in influencing the extent and nature of technology adoption. Businesses operating in regions characterized by strong regulatory environments and advanced economic structures tend to adopt AI technologies more quickly and effectively than those in less developed areas (Lawalata & Yuliana, 2024); (Mazher & Tramankuti, 2024). Additionally, cultural background might affect how businesses view and use AI, which can affect their readiness to adopt such revolutionary technologies (Fang, 2023).

A fascinating case for researching technology adoption within its entrepreneurial environment is Kosovo, a newly established and extremely dynamic state in the Western Balkans. Despite being an emerging economy, Kosovo has seen an increase in the number of startups that use technology. Technological innovation thrives there because of its young adult population, developing digital infrastructure, and burgeoning entrepreneurial spirit. However, Kosovo faces distinct challenges, including limited access to finance, underdeveloped support systems, and a lack of research focused on its entrepreneurial ecosystem.

It seems that startups that effectively use AI technologies are often at the forefront of creating disruptive Business models that challenge traditional market structures (Horák & Turková, 2023). Such a trend highlights the importance of understanding regional differences in technology adoption, as startups in economically advanced regions may have better access to resources and support systems that facilitate AI integration (Singh & Chouhan, 2021).

The structure of this chapter begins with the literature review, methodology, discussion, analysis of results, and finally, the conclusion. The results of this chapter aim to contribute to the corpus of research on technology adoption by using the UTAUT-3 paradigm in a developing country setting. This study has both theoretical and practical consequences for regulators, investors, and entrepreneurs who want to help enterprises in Kosovo become more technologically proficient. The chapter acts as a guide for encouraging technology-driven entrepreneurship and developing a more sustainable startup environment in the Western Balkans by highlighting important motivators and obstacles.

3.2 Literature Review

3.2.1 *Adoption of Technologies in Startups*

A wide range of theoretical frameworks have been applied in the extensive research on new technology adoption by startups. The Unified Theory of Acceptance and Use of Technology (UTAUT) and its variations, including UTAUT-3, are among the most dependable models for analyzing the variables influencing the acceptance of new technology. Because UTAUT-3 incorporates dimensions like price value, social impact, performance expectation, and effort expectancy, it is especially well-suited to analyzing the complex nature of technology adoption in dynamic settings like startups. The UTAUT framework offers a thorough basis for comprehending how people accept and utilize new technologies by combining findings from several models of technology acceptance. By adding other components like price value and habit, extensions like UTAUT-2 and UTAUT-3 improve this methodology and provide deeper insights into situations like startups (Venkatesh et al., 2012); (Wong et al., 2015); (Shaw & Sergueeva, 2019); (Ananda et al., 2020); (Souiden et al., 2021); (Aliu, 2024).

3.2.2 *Critical Perspectives on UTAUT-3 and Contextual Adaptation*

Although the UTAUT-3 model provides a comprehensive framework for understanding technology acceptance, its direct application to resource-poor and institutionally fragile settings, such as Kosovo, requires careful consideration. Existing literature typically evaluates UTAUT-3 in relatively advanced or technologically mature settings, where infrastructural, institutional, and socio-economic conditions differ significantly from those in developing economies. Scholars such as Ahmad (2014) and Rabaa'i (2017) point out that technology acceptance models often produce different results depending on cultural, institutional, and economic contexts, emphasizing the importance of contextual adaptation rather than assuming universal validity. Critics further warn that frameworks such as UTAUT-3, rooted in broad behavioral constructs, may oversimplify adoption phenomena while overlooking broader socio-political factors, power dynamics, or systemic challenges that strongly influence technology use in fragile settings.

In Kosovo, factors such as institutional gaps, widespread informal business networks, and complex socio-political dynamics significantly shape entrepreneurial activity (Avdullahi & Hoti, 2020; Toska et al., 2022). These contextual elements can transform both the perceived benefits and barriers associated with the adoption of emerging technologies, including AI. For example, inadequate legal frameworks, limited access to capital, and reliance on informal networks can fundamentally change how theoretical constructs such as Performance Expectation and Social Impact manifest in this context. Consequently, this study refrains from treating UTAUT-3 as a rigid and universally applicable model; instead, it investigates how UTAUT-3 constructs interact within Kosovo's distinctive entrepreneurial ecosystem, recognizing the necessity to adapt the model to local realities. Moreover, socio-technical perspectives on AI adoption highlight that technology adoption cannot be viewed solely as a technical or economic decision; it is deeply embedded within social, organizational, and institutional processes (Fang, 2023; Horák & Turková, 2023). Such perspectives are particularly relevant when examining startups in fragile economies, where trust, social networks, and informal mechanisms often serve as alternatives to underdeveloped formal infrastructure. Integrating these critical perspectives into the UTAUT-3 framework increases its explanatory power, providing a more nuanced understanding of AI adoption within the startup landscape in Kosovo.

3.2.3 The Context of SMEs in Kosovo

The core of Kosovo's economy is made up of small and medium-sized businesses (SMEs), which contribute significantly to both employment and economic activity. These companies have particular difficulties implementing new technology since they frequently have little resources and immature organizational structures. SMEs in Kosovo exhibit a strong entrepreneurial spirit in spite of these limits, and many of them use digital tools to get around resource constraints and reach new markets. Contextualizing the use of AI and other cutting-edge technologies within Kosovo's startup ecosystem requires an understanding of the unique dynamics of SMEs in the country.

SMEs are crucial contributors to Kosovo's economy, representing a major source of job creation and economic output (Loku & Loku, 2020); (Krasniqi et al., 2022); (Aliu & Kutllovci, 2025). Many firms, however, find it challenging to adopt cutting-edge technologies due to their severe budgetary restraints. A shortage of trained personnel, restricted access to technology, and a lack of finance are some of the major barriers preventing their development and innovation (Draga, 2021). Many SMEs in Kosovo actively employ digital tools to increase their efficiency and penetrate new markets in spite of these challenges. For instance, it has been discovered that digital marketing and information technology are crucial elements in increasing the profitability and competitiveness of SMEs (Emini & Merovci, 2021). Digital transformation enables these businesses to adapt better to market demands and navigate resource limitations (Avdullahi & Hoti, 2020).

The performance of SMEs in Kosovo is influenced by a number of factors. Better business performance is favorably connected with both the use of corporate social responsibility (CSR) strategies and efficient working capital management (Bekteshi et al., 2021). Additionally, the educational background of business owners and managers plays a significant role, with higher education levels linked to better business outcomes (Terstena et al., 2023).

Access to finance remains one of the most pressing challenges for SMEs in Kosovo. This barrier limits their capacity to invest in technology and human capital essential for innovation and productivity (Draga, 2021). The COVID-19 epidemic has made these issues worse, putting more financial and operational pressure on companies (Kabashi & Kabashi, 2023). In addition, a volatile market and a lack of managerial experience add layers of complexity, discouraging possible investments and limiting prospects for expansion (Rexhepi et al., 2024).

Research emphasizes how important policy changes are in tackling these issues, especially when it comes to lowering entrance barriers and enhancing access to funding (Avdullahi & Hoti, 2020). Policymakers may create an atmosphere that supports SMEs' success by encouraging digital innovation and providing targeted assistance. Furthermore, Kosovo's entrepreneurial ecosystem may become even more competitive and position its SMEs as important catalysts for innovation and economic growth by integrating cutting-edge technologies like artificial intelligence (AI).

3.2.4 *Performance Expectancy*

The degree to which people think that utilizing a specific technology would improve their job performance is known as performance expectancy, or PE (Mensah, Wang, Gui, & Wang, 2021); (Kurniasari et al., 2023); (Aliu, 2024). As Kosovo's entrepreneurs integrate artificial intelligence (AI) and other cutting-edge technologies into their operations, this idea is particularly crucial. Strong performance expectancy has been found to have a favorable impact on technology adoption because people are more likely to accept innovations when they believe they will increase their productivity, creativity, and competitive edge.

There is little study examining how performance expectancy and technology adoption interact in developing nations like Kosovo, despite studies from industrialized economies showing a strong association between the two. The degree to which entrepreneurs believe that AI and other technologies will improve their company's performance can influence how these technologies are adopted by startups in Kosovo.

3.2.5 *Effort Expectancy*

The apparent ease of use of a certain technology is known as effort expectation. This concept highlights the difficulties entrepreneurs encounter while incorporating cutting-edge technologies into their businesses, especially in light of the lack of infrastructure and technical know-how in the context of Kosovo startups. Startups can overcome these challenges with the help of easily navigable tools and easily available training programs.

According to research, effort expectancy has a big impact on people's adoption of technology. For instance, Wichean and Sungsanit (2022) draw attention to the fact that effort expectation is a crucial component of technology adoption in agricultural contexts and is defined by users' perceptions of difficulty when utilizing technology. Similarly, authors (Sari et al., 2024) discuss the direct relationship between effort expectancy and people's expectations of how simple a system will be to use, which influences their intention to utilize it.

3.2.6 *Social Influence*

The degree to which people believe that significant others, including peers, investors, or consumers, think they should utilize a specific technology is known as social influence. International investors, development agencies, and diaspora networks are among the external stakeholders that have a significant influence on Kosovo's startup ecosystem. Understanding how these individuals influence attitudes and decisions regarding technology use is crucial to creating an environment that promotes innovation.

This concept is central to the Technology Acceptance Model (TAM) and its extensions, which emphasize how people's intentions to embrace specific technologies are influenced by social norms and other people's perspectives. For example, Cioc, Popa, Olariu et al. (2023) explain social influence as a crucial concept in the TAM framework, emphasizing how a person's behavioral intentions toward adopting technology are greatly influenced by the opinions of significant others. Similarly, Ruangkanjanases et al. (2021) observe how social impact shapes consumer pleasure and new technology recommendations, highlighting the significance of social views in technology adoption.

3.2.7 *Price Value*

Price value assesses the trade-off between a technology's perceived benefits and adoption costs. Financial limitations frequently have a significant impact on how startups in Kosovo decide whether to use new technologies. The availability of affordable solutions and the potential for large returns on investment are the main factors influencing the popularity of emerging technology. Establishing a product's economic value is crucial to fostering widespread adoption in environments with limited resources.

The significance of price value in technology adoption has been emphasized in numerous research. For instance, Dai and Cheng (2022) draw attention to the fact that consumers usually weigh the costs and benefits of new technology to estimate their whole worth. They contend that the chance of technology adoption rises when price and value are seen favorably. Similarly, authors (Mohamad et al., 2021) argue that consumers are more likely to adopt mobile commerce technologies when they perceive a good price value, supporting the notion that finding a balance between cost and utility is essential in the decision-making process.

3.3 Methodology

The qualitative approach is the methodology applied in this scientific chapter since it is more compatible with the nature of this study. Various researchers specify the advantages that this methodological approach provides. This approach is more comprehensive by helping researchers analyze the study's more complex aspects, including perceptions, behaviors, and motivations, compared to the quantitative approach, which focuses more on data numbers (Moleong, 2013; Yin, 2013). The chapter uses multiple case study forms. Therefore, Dana and Dumez (2015) argue that researchers who use this approach should apply a structured interview, a more suggested technique since quantitative data can limit the researcher. Such method has also been used by other researchers who address entrepreneurship topics (Toska et al., 2022); (Rudaku et al., 2023); (Ramadani & Ramadani, 2021); (Sadiku-Dushi, 2019) and specifically in scientific papers that address UTAUT-3 technology acceptance models in different contexts (Akbar, 2021). Authors (Williams et al., 2021) argue that qualitative data is appropriate when analyzing the acceptance of new technologies because it allows researchers to better understand respondents' perceptions. Therefore, they use qualitative data to analyze students' social media acceptance in an academic library in Belgium and South Africa, relying on the constructs of the UTAUT model. Although quantitative studies dominate technology acceptance models, other researchers have applied qualitative approaches to obtain more detailed analyses that affect respondents' acceptance of new technology (Rempel & Mellinger, 2015); (Gruzd et al., 2012).

Based on the above arguments, by the nature of the study, the structured interview has been applied in this paper, helping us to collect data from respondents, in this case, startup businesses in Kosovo. By applying this method, we manage to answer our research questions related to the constructs of the UTAUT-3 model, highlighting the motivation why Kosovar startups apply new technologies, specifically AI technology, and their benefits from using such technology.

This study used the data collection technique "snowballing," originally applied by Goodman (1961). This technique helps researchers collect data by relying on contacts established with startup businesses and obtaining information or references for other startup businesses during these contacts.

3.3.1 *Methodological Clarifications and Rigor*

Although the term "structured interviews" is used in this study, it is essential to clarify that the interviews followed a semi-structured format. While pre-specified, theory-based questions—derived from the UTAUT-3 model—were used to maintain consistency across respondents, the interview design intentionally allowed for elaboration and open-ended responses. This flexible format enabled the capture of nuanced and context-specific insights that might otherwise be overlooked in rigid interview structures. Such an approach is particularly important when investigating new and under-researched phenomena, such as the adoption of artificial intelligence in startups within institutionally fragile contexts.

The study applied a snowball sampling technique (Goodman, 1961), widely recognized as a pragmatic strategy in exploratory research—especially in settings where formal sampling frames are unavailable or difficult to construct. However, this method is not without limitations. The inherent risk of homogeneity bias—where respondents are likely to refer to individuals within similar demographic or professional circles—can reduce sample diversity and limit generalizability. Although this limitation is transparently acknowledged, its potential impact on the breadth of perspectives captured remains a concern. To mitigate this risk, conscious efforts were made to ensure heterogeneity in sectoral representation and business orientation; however, the impact of network-driven referral cannot be completely eliminated.

Data analysis followed a largely inductive logic, prioritizing thematic emergence over deductive imposition. While the UTAUT-3 model informed the initial coding structure, the analytical process remained open to patterns and categories that emerged organically from the data. This approach reinforces the sensitivity of the study to context and allows for the inclusion of findings that extend or challenge the theoretical framework. However, reliance on inductive reasoning also requires methodological vigilance to prevent overinterpretation or researcher bias. To address this, analysis was conducted through multiple iterations of coding and supported by peer validation mechanisms, thereby increasing the reliability and analytical rigor of the findings.

3.3.2 *Data collection*

Data collection focused on Kosovo startups established within the last five years. We managed to answer our research questions in this study using structured interviews. Based on the arguments that the application of new technologies is not the same in all countries (Lawalata & Yuliana, 2024); (Mazher & Tramankuti, 2024), the aim of this study is to shed light on what motives have influenced startups in Kosovo to apply new technologies in their business operations, such as AI technology. In this regard, five research questions were compiled based on the UTAUT-3 technology acceptance model. The first research question focused on obtaining information on the use of new technologies by these businesses as well as the importance, platforms, factors, and advantages that the application of AI technology has brought to the market. Other research questions were adapted to the selected constructs of the UTAUT-3 model: *Performance Expectancy, Effort Expectancy, Social Influence, and Price Value*. These constructs were chosen because they help to provide reliable results in different contexts (Rabaa'i, 2017).

In the interview, some information on the characteristics of the respondents was also collected, which is presented in Fig. 3.1. The interviews were conducted in mixed ways: direct meetings with respondents, by phone and by e-mail, using electronic tools. A total of **10 interviews** were conducted. The literature does not clearly define the number of samples. However, many researchers suggest that in scientific papers using multiple case studies, samples should be from 4 to 15 respondents because a larger number may lose the depth of the information required (Sarfo, Debrah, Gbordzoe, Afful, & Obeng, 2021). Based on this argument, in accordance with the research nature, this study has a reliable sample. The interviews were conducted in Albanian and then translated into English. All respondents agreed to have their business name mentioned. The research questions are specified below:

RQ1. **How often do you use artificial intelligence in your business?**

The following sub-questions help us to have clearer information about the first research question: Do you apply it more to daily operations or medium and long-term planning (e.g., sales planning or marketing strategies)? How do you assess the importance of AI in achieving your business goals? Which AI platforms do you currently use in your business, and what factors have influenced their choice (e.g., price, cost, functionality, technical support)? Can you share any advantages or limitations you have encountered with these platforms?

***RQ2*. Performance Expectancy from using AI:**

The following sub-question helps us clarify the second research question: How and to what extent do you think that using artificial intelligence helps you perform your tasks more efficiently, and how does this affect your personal or professional productivity?

***RQ3*. Effort Expectancy from using AI:**

The following sub-questions help us clarify the third research question: How easy do you find using artificial intelligence in your activity? Are its different aspects understandable and suitable for your business needs? Which specific features do you find most useful, and why?

***RQ4*. Social Influence of using AI:**

The following sub-questions help us clarify the fourth research question: Have you been influenced by people around you, such as close friends, to use artificial intelligence in your activity? Have social networks encouraged you to use AI? How do you think these suggestions influence your decisions to adopt artificial intelligence?

***RQ5*. Expected value (relative to price) from using AI**

The following sub-questions help us to have clearer information on the fifth research question: Do you think that using artificial intelligence provides good value for your business operations and activity? And does its simplicity justify the price and costs associated with its use?

3.4 Findings

Below we present the answers received from the respondents.

***RQ1*. How often do you use artificial intelligence in your business?**

The first part of the interview was focused on obtaining data on the characteristics of the company respondents. Now, the following questions will focus on answering our research questions and fulfilling the purpose of this study. The first research question aims to obtain information on how often AI is used in startups in Kosovo, assisted by sub-questions posed to respondents (Fig. 3.1).

Interviewed	Age	Gender	Education	Name of company	Number of employees	Place	Operation	Position	Years of operation
Case 1	28	Male	Faculty	Aced Solutions	5	Pristina	Consumer support (outsourcing)	CEO	1
Case 2	21	Male	Faculty	Acubens Clothing	3	Gjilan	Clothing Brand	CEO	2
Case 3	31	Male	Master	TMT Service	2	Gjilan	Home appliance servicing	CEO	3
Case 4	23	Male	High School	INTER Electronics Sh.P.K	5	Mitrovice	Retail sale of home appliances	CEO	2
Case 5	34	Male	PhD	Omi Kitchen	10	Gjilan	Gastronomy	CEO	5
Case 6	27	Male	Faculty	Veonteck LLC	10	Pristina	Cybersecurity	Lead Engineer	3
Case 7	24	Female	Master	Vlertech LLC	2	Gjilan	Software Development	CEO	1
Case 8	30	Male	Faculty	COURT EXPERTISE Sh.P.K	2	Gjilan	Tax and Law Advisor	Managing Partner	1
Case 9	40	Male	Master	BPOWER FINANCIAL EXPERTISE Sh.P.K.	1	Gjilan	Accounting services	CEO	2
Case 10	28	Male	Faculty	Hyper Meet Networks L.L.C.	3	Pristina	Organization of Business Conferences and Trade Fairs	Manager	1

Fig. 3.1 Characteristics of respondents. (*Source* Authors)

In the case of Aced Solutions, we have this statement:

AI is essential for our outsourcing company, which provides customer support services in the US. Its use helped us attract new customers and identify potential markets from market analyses made using this platform. AI continues to be used in our company even now for market analyses and effective marketing strategies to provide efficient services to our customers. We use platforms such as chatbots for data analyses based on machine learning. We chose them for their cost, functionality, and technical support.

Clothing Brand from another business activity states the following:

We use AI to remove backgrounds from images, an important process for creating visual materials for our brand. AI helps us design images and create posters for promotional issues in brand promotional campaigns. We also use AI to address marketing issues in the context of improving the sales process. Our company uses chatbots, and the factors that influenced us to choose them are functionality and technical support.

TMT Service:

I use artificial intelligence (AI) almost on a daily basis. I used it mostly instead of Google Search to solve equipment defects and detect equipment error codes. Chatbots are what research all the articles and bring the results much faster. This has helped us to improve customer service since we are a company that provides product servicing. I emphasize that functionality, and technical support are the factors that influenced us to adopt this technology in the company.

Veonteck LLC, as a Cybersecurity company, has this statement:

> *Due to data privacy and security concerns, our company does not use general LLM models. Instead, it relies on internal AI tools to optimize processes, which does not avoid the problem of sharing data with others. Since the company operates by providing services to our clients in data protection and privacy, these AI tools help in this purpose. We help our clients by responding proactively to potential risks through these platforms.*

Vlertech LLC:

> *Our company uses AI daily as an important tool to help us improve various aspects of programming. AI is integrated into existing systems, improving efficiency and helping us adapt to specific needs. Through AI, we can create content and automate and refine processes to ensure quality and consistency, which helps the company in long-term marketing and sales strategies in our programming services.*

In cases of Bpower Financial Expertise Sh.P.K., we have this statement:

> *We often use artificial intelligence (AI) in business, mainly for data analysis, process optimization, and the automation of administrative tasks. It helps analyze market demand, especially in exports to EU countries. We currently use ChatGPT for business analysis and strategy, Microsoft Copilot for document automation, and ERP software with artificial intelligence for stock management and production processes. The main factors in choosing them were functionality, ease of use, and technical support.*

Other respondents had similar answers. Based on the answers received from the first research question, we can conclude that AI is used on a daily basis in startup businesses in Kosovo and in different industries. Companies use AI to achieve their business goals in the context of marketing, sales, market penetration, and cybersecurity in specific companies. The use of chatbots dominates, but in specific industries, other forms of AI, such as Microsoft Copilot and those that do not include LLM models, are also used. Companies state that the factors that encouraged them to adopt AI were functionality, cost, ease of use, and technical support.

***RQ2*. Performance Expectancy from using AI?**

In the second research question, we received responses from startup businesses in Kosovo on their performance expectancy when adopting new technologies such as AI in the context of efficiency due to personal or professional productivity.

In the case of Aced Solutions, we have this statement:

> *AI has significantly impacted my efficiency as a manager, performing tasks faster and more accurately and optimizing time. Using AI, I perform real-time analysis of operations. In addition, AI automates routine tasks such as managing communications, preparing reports, and tracking financial data, increasing my and the company's productivity.*

Acubens Clothing declares as follows:

> *AI has greatly accelerated my work, improving the efficiency of design and promotional materials. It has also increased my productivity and significantly improved creative processes while contributing to the company's overall performance.*

Another answer is also specified in the case of the company Veonteck LLC:

> *AI has significantly increased work performance, especially in identifying, analyzing, and alerting to cybersecurity threats. By shortening response times, AI has enabled us to respond to such incidents proactively while achieving higher productivity and efficiency.*

Vlertech LLC:

> *Rapid data analysis by AI and its interpretation in work tasks helps us increase work efficiency and productivity in our programming industry, influencing professional and personal growth at work.*

Court Expertise Sh.P.K., states:

> *The use of AI has helped in the management of documents, contracts, and analyses, saving time and reducing human errors. By optimizing the time spent preparing documents quickly, we have increased the company's efficiency and overall performance.*

Hyper Meet Networks L.L.C:

> *In our company, AI helps save time through automation and data analysis and enables more efficient event management. It also significantly impacts marketing strategies. Consequently, it increases productivity by helping with innovation and long-term strategies.*

Based on the responses received from startup businesses in Kosovo, referring to the Performance Expectancy construct of the UTAUT-3 model, AI as new technology has significantly influenced the increase in efficiency and productivity in both the personal and professional aspects of these businesses. The findings are consistent with other studies (Aliu, 2024), which analyze the new NFC payment technology in the Kosovar context and (Camilleri, 2024); (Choudhury & Shamszare, 2024), where Performance Expectancy is specifically analyzed from the adoption of ChatGPT technology. The findings are also consistent with Greece's experience as a developed market where the authors analyze mobile banking technology (Dendrinos & Spais, 2024). Respondents argue that AI significantly improves work processes, data analysis, automation, and time optimization and eliminates human errors.

***RQ3*. Effort Expectancy from using AI?**

Respondents from startup businesses in Kosovo answered the third research question, relying on the other construct of the UTAUT-3 model, Effort Expectancy from using AI. The aim was to ask respondents how easy and understandable it is to use technology for these businesses' needs.

The case of the company Aced Solutions:

> *Using lightweight technology like AI in our business has been relatively easy, and the platforms are simple to understand. AI is suitable for our company and brings benefits such as Real-time data analysis, trend prediction, performance monitoring, and personalization of customer communications.*

In the case of the company Acubens Clothing, we have this answer:

> *Using AI is relatively easy and suitable for a clothing brand's needs. AI is also understandable and suitable for my startup, making the process faster and more efficient.*

TMT Service:

> *AI is simple for our activity and understandable if we properly formulate the request. Efficiency and productivity are the two main aspects that make AI useful by saving us time. AI satisfactorily meets our company's needs.*

Veonteck LLC declares as follows:

> *AI tools are very easy and understandable to use, making our daily tasks simpler and more efficient. For a cybersecurity company, the automated searches, search intelligence, and analytics that AI provides are extremely useful in our industry. Therefore, we conclude that it is a technology that is easy to adopt and very effective in meeting our company's needs.*

Bpower Financial Expertise Sh.P.K, we have this statement:

> *AI is easy to use in analytical and administrative aspects, but integration requires more effort for production and inventory management. The most useful features are document automation, strategic analysis, and resource optimization, which help increase efficiency and improve decision-making in my business.*

INTER Electronics Sh.P.K:

> *The use of AI is easy and understandable; it is a new technology that is easily adopted. Our activity has helped a lot by meeting business needs such as efficiency and productivity, in particular, optimizing the time to obtain new information, which are requests from customers and which in the past took us more time to come to information in specific cases.*

We emphasize that other respondents gave similar answers to the third research question. From the answers received, we can conclude that AI technology has been easily adopted in startup businesses in Kosovo, where we have empirical evidence of Effort Expectancy, being consistent with other studies conducted in other contexts (Wichean & Sungsanit, 2022) and specifically recent studies that specifically address AI technology (Tanantong & Wongras, 2024). The findings are also consistent with the experience of Greece, where the authors address the specifics of the acceptance of mobile banking technology (Dendrinos & Spais, 2024).

Respondents also specify that process automation and data analysis simplicity had a positive impact on meeting the needs of these businesses after adopting AI technology. It was also emphasized that integrating AI into complex workflows presents some challenges. However, the benefits of adopting AI technology in the businesses included in the study outweigh the difficulties.

***RQ4*. Social Influence of using AI?**

In the fourth research question, responses were obtained based on the social influence construct regarding the adoption of AI technology in startup businesses. Respondents were asked about the influences from friends, social networks, and other social factors that pushed them to adopt AI technology in their businesses.

In the case of Aced Solutions, we have this statement:

> *Since my friends and colleagues share a similar commitment to me, they influenced me to adopt AI technology in my business. From discussions with them, I became better acquainted with this technology's advantages. The influence of social networks and the like should not be overlooked.*

Acubens Clothing:

> *As a startup, we have received many suggestions from friends and colleagues on how to use AI, especially for marketing and design. Social Media has also played an important role in encouraging the use of AI, as we often see other brands using it successfully. These suggestions and examples influenced our decision to integrate AI into our business.*

In the case of TMT Service, we have this statement:

> *We have started implementing AI in our business field almost from the beginning. We have also seen excellent results and have pushed our friends and colleagues to use AI; after the launch of Chatgpt, the discussion in society and social networks has been intense, pushing us to continue using it and seeing successful results in various fields.*

INTER Electronics Sh.P.K declares as follows:

I was most influenced to use AI on social media, specifically TikTok and Facebook. There, we have seen a lot of material on how businesses benefit from using AI.

Vlertech LLC:

Before starting the business, while engaging in other projects, we followed the development of AI from the early stages. We were also involved in beta testing and experimenting with new AI technologies where we learned a lot about the potential of AI. Friends and social media played a role, but our practical curiosity significantly influenced our acceptance of this technology.

Based on the responses received and the fact that other respondents also gave similar answers, we can conclude that social influence played an important role in adopting new technologies, such as AI, in startup businesses in Kosovo. This is consistent with studies (Cioc, Popa, Olariu et al., 2023) and also from recent scientific evidence that addresses the acceptance of AI as a new technology based on the social influence construct (Kandoth & Shekhar, 2022). Similarities have also been observed in China's experience in a study addressing the adoption of blockchain technology in supply chain management, where the construct of social influence played an important role (Shahzad et al., 2024).

The responses suggest that social influence also impacted the success of these businesses; by adopting this technology, they could automate work processes and increase efficiency.

RQ5. Expected value (relative to price) from using AI?

The fifth research question was based on the constructed expected value (relative to price) from the use of AI. Respondents here answered whether the use of AI offers good value for the company's operations and activities. Their simplicity also justifies the price in relation to the cost of using this technology.

Aced Solutions:

AI offers excellent value for our company. The costs of its use are justified by the benefits we have in terms of efficiency and quality of services. Automated processes have reduced operating costs and increased productivity, which has quickly returned investment costs. On the other hand, AI does not require training since users easily learn it.

In the case of Acubens Clothing, we have this statement:

> *The price and costs associated with using AI are justified by its benefits, including the speed of creating designs and optimizing promotional campaigns.*

TMT Service:

> *AI is necessary since our activity may continuously face new problems in servicing household appliances. It helps us with quick information to solve these problems when we have specific cases. The cost of implementation is reasonable, it does not require training, and the ROI is high compared to the investment in subscribing to this platform.*

In the case of Omi Kitchen Sh.P.K., we have this statement:

> *We find that using AI provides good value in our business operations. The most important benefit is the automation of processes, which saves additional time and resources.*

Vlertech LLC:

> *The price of AI is highly reasonable, considering all the benefits it brings to the company in terms of work optimization and efficiency. These will undoubtedly improve our performance, and the price will be justifiable.*

In the case of Hyper Meet Networks L.L.C., we have this statement:

> *AI reduces operational costs by increasing productivity and efficiency. It is easy to use, and its benefits justify the costs.*

Similar responses are found among other respondents included in the study. Findings related to the fifth research question conclude that AI is justifiable regarding expected value (relative to price). Respondents argue that the benefits obtained from AI justify all its costs. Furthermore, respondents emphasize that AI is easy to use and does not require additional training costs. Therefore, AI justifies the investment made, having a good return on investment concerning the benefits companies receive from using this technology. Therefore, the last construct investigated in this study, expected value (relative to price), is confirmed by respondents of startup businesses in Kosovo, which is coherent with other studies (Dai & Cheng, 2022); (Mohamad et al., 2021).

3.5 Discussion

This study critically examines the use of artificial intelligence (AI) among startups in Kosovo through the analytical framework of the UTAUT-3 model, focusing on the key constructs of Performance Expectancy, Effort Expectancy, Social Impact, and Price Value. Empirical evidence shows that AI is widely perceived as a transformative force, enhancing operational efficiency, stimulating innovation, and increasing productivity across various sectors. However, while these findings reflect global trends in both developed and developing economies, their manifestation within the Kosovar context exposes important contextual dissonances that challenge the universal applicability of the UTAUT-3 model.

Kosovo's entrepreneurial landscape is shaped by deep structural deficiencies – most notably institutional fragility, limited financial access, and the lack of a cohesive innovation infrastructure. In this environment, formal mechanisms for technology diffusion are often replaced by informal social networks, peer influence, and diaspora engagement. These pathways, while effective in fostering trust and rapid adoption, operate outside traditional institutional channels and complicate the predictive clarity of constructs such as Social Impact or Performance Expectation. The findings suggest that applying UTAUT-3 without critical contextual calibration risks oversimplifying the socio-economic realities of fragile ecosystems, where technology adoption is less a function of individual utility and more a negotiation of structural constraints and relational capital.

Moreover, participants' enthusiasm for the benefits of AI—ranging from task automation to market expansion—is tempered by latent anxieties surrounding integration complexity, data security, and technological dependency. Particularly in sectors such as cybersecurity, the reluctance to rely on externally hosted AI platforms underscores a broader tension between technological advancement and institutional underdevelopment. These concerns are not simply operational—they reflect the deep entanglement of technology with governance gaps, infrastructure constraints, and trust deficits. Thus, any serious account of AI adoption in contexts like Kosovo must move beyond technocentric optimism to engage with the systemic vulnerabilities that condition such processes.

While Kosovo shows encouraging signs of digital engagement and entrepreneurial ambition, defining it as an "emerging innovation hotspot" requires caution. The lack of strong comparative data within the Western Balkans, coupled with persistent barriers to capital, policy coherence, and ecosystem coordination, suggests that this narrative remains aspirational rather than proven. Kosovo's potential as a regional leader in AI-driven entrepreneurship is real, but remains highly contingent – dependent not only on startup initiative, but also on structural transformation, sustained public investment, and a fundamental rethinking of how innovation ecosystems are nurtured in post-conflict and transition economies.

3.6 Theoretical and Practical Implications

3.6.1 Theoretical Implications

This study provides a critical epistemological contribution to the technology adoption literature by situating the UTAUT-3 model within the structurally fragile and institutionally constrained entrepreneurial context of Kosovo. In doing so, it goes beyond the conventional application of UTAUT-3 as a context-neutral framework and demonstrates that core constructs such as Performance Expectation and Social Impact are deeply mediated by systemic informality, resource scarcity, and asymmetric institutional development.

The findings problematize the implicit universality of models of technology adoption, revealing that in post-conflict and transitional economies, behavioral constructs are inadequate unless they are included within a broader socio-institutional and political-economic analysis. Informal networks, relational trust, and social capital, often absent from mainstream models, emerge here as crucial mediators of adoption behavior. Therefore, future theoretical extensions of UTAUT-3 should include variables that capture the quality of institutional infrastructure, the density and functionality of informal systems, as well as the cognitive dimensions of trust and risk perception in fragile economies.

Moreover, by integrating a socio-technical perspective, the study contributes to an ontological reframing of AI adoption—not as a purely instrumental or utility-maximizing act, but as a dynamic process embedded in stratified social systems, unequal power structures, and local epistemic logics. This reorientation enables a more nuanced and ecologically valid framework for interpreting technology adoption in contexts where formal institutions are weak but adaptive capacities and social embeddedness are high. In this regard, the study advances both the theoretical granularity and contextual sensitivity of contemporary technology adoption studies.

3.6.2 Practical Implications

The practical implications of this study extend beyond operational recommendations and speak to the strategic and institutional reconfigurations needed for a meaningful technological transformation in Kosovo and comparable environments. For entrepreneurs, the findings highlight that while AI technologies can significantly increase efficiency, scalability, and competitive positioning, successful adoption depends on matching technological capabilities with organizational absorptive capacity, data governance norms, and trust-based operational ecosystems. In environments marked by infrastructural and regulatory deficiencies, entrepreneurs must adopt strategic selectivity in technology sourcing and prioritize interoperability, security, and long-term sustainability over short-term utility.

For policymakers, the study highlights the necessity of abandoning "one-size-fits-all" digitalization policies in favor of context-responsive innovation governance. This includes designing institutional mechanisms that acknowledge and reinforce the functional role of informal networks, diaspora actors, and peer-to-peer knowledge flows in driving digital adoption. Policy frameworks need to move from abstract ecosystem rhetoric to tangible structural interventions: increasing access to AI through targeted subsidies, fostering localized AI competencies through integrated training programs, and integrating trust-building architectures across digital infrastructure. Furthermore, the role of the state as an orchestrator of innovation legitimacy needs to be strengthened – by providing regulatory clarity, protecting data ethics, and promoting inclusive access to technology as an enabler of development, not simply a commercial tool.

Ultimately, positioning Kosovo as a sustainable innovation ecosystem will require a paradigm shift from fragmented policy experimentation to systemic capacity building rooted in structural realism and socio-technical harmonization.

3.7 Conclusion

This chapter examined the use of new technologies, such as AI, by startup businesses in Kosovo, analyzing selected constructs of the UTAUT-3 model: *Performance Expectancy, Effort Expectancy, Social Influence, and Price Value*. This study aims to provide scientific evidence from the Kosovo perspective on the adoption of new technologies, such as AI, by startup businesses in Kosovo and their impact on business performance. Based on empirical evidence, we can conclude that startups are inclined to adopt new technologies, such as artificial intelligence, in their business activities. Businesses are encouraged to use AI by needing innovation, process improvement, time optimization, avoidance of human errors, and easier access to markets. The answers obtained based on the selected constructs also find coherence in other studies and other empirical experiences, such as in emerging markets and developing countries. (Ahmad, 2014) argues that technology acceptance models can bring different results in different cultures and contexts. Therefore, studies on the acceptance of new technologies are always in the interest of the academic and practical community. They contribute to the existing literature on Kosovo's experience as an emerging market and also bring a scientific perspective to new startup businesses on the importance of new technologies in improving business operations.

This study has some *limitations*. First, it was used with qualitative data, through case bases with a structured interview. In this study, only the constructs: *Performance Expectancy, Effort Expectancy, Social Influence, and Price Value* were analyzed. The interview sample was supported only by several cities in Kosovo. Since Kosovo is a multi-ethnic state, the study does not include perspectives of entities other than Albanians.

Further studies can focus on another methodological approach, including the quantitative methodological approach. Other studies can also analyze other constructs of the UTAUT-3 model. Other areas and cities of Kosovo, including rural areas, can also be included in the study. Other studies can also include other entities in Kosovo. It is important to bring in other scientific evidence from other emerging countries to see similarities and differences.

References

Ahmad, M. I. (2014). Unified theory of acceptance and use of technology (UTAUT): A decade of validation and development. *Proceedings of the 4th International Conference on ICT in our Lives (ISSN 2314–8942)* (pp. 1–13). Alexandria, Egypt: Information Systems and Computer Science Department, Faculty of Commerce, Alexandria University.

Akbar, M. (2021). Investigating the intentions to adopt E-learning using UTAUT-3 model: A perspective of COVID-19. In *Proceedings of the AUBH E-Learning Conference 2021: Innovative Learning & Teaching - Lessons from COVID-19* (pp. 1–10). Riffa, Bahrain: American University of Bahrain.

Aliu, F. (2024). Usage and adoption intent of NFC payment methods: An investigation based on the UTAUT-3 model and perceived risk theory. *Journal of Science and Technology Policy Management*. https://doi.org/10.1108/JSTPM-01-2024-0013

Aliu, F., & Kutllovci, E. (2025). Exploring job satisfaction's impact on turnover tendency among employees in Kosova's microfinance institutions. *International Journal of Organizational Analysis, 33*(3), 665–681. https://doi.org/10.1108/IJOA-01-2024-4200

Ananda, S., Davesh, S., & Lawati, A. M. (2020). What factors drive the adoption of digital banking? An empirical study from the perspective of Omani retail banking. *Journal of Financial Services Marketing, 25*, 14–24.

Avdullahi, A., & Hoti, A. (2020). The search for determinants of Kosovan small and medium enterprises performance. *International Journal of Economic Sciences, 9*(2), 1–22. https://doi.org/10.20472/ES.2020.9.2.001

Bekteshi, X., Alshiqi, S., & Ramushi, A. S. (2021). The impact of corporate social responsibility and working capital management on SMES performance during a pandemic. *Baltic Journal of Economic Studies, 7*(5), 18–28. https://doi.org/10.30525/2256-0742/2021-7-5-18-28

Camilleri, M. A. (2024). Factors affecting performance expectancy and intentions to use ChatGPT: Using SmartPLS to advance an information technology acceptance framework. *Technological Forecasting and Social Change*. https://doi.org/10.1016/j.techfore.2024.123247

Choudhury, A., & Shamszare, H. (2024). The impact of performance expectancy, workload, risk, and satisfaction on trust in ChatGPT: Cross-sectional survey analysis. *JMIR Human Factors*. https://doi.org/10.2196/55399

Cioc, M. M., Popa, ȘC., Olariu, A. A., Popa, C. F., & Nica, C.-B. (2023). Behavioral intentions to use energy efficiency smart solutions under the impact of social influence: an extended tam approach. *Applied Sciences, 13*(18), 10241. https://doi.org/10.3390/app131810241

Dai, Q., & Cheng, K. (2022). What drives the adoption of agricultural green production technologies? An extension of TAM in agriculture. *Sustainability, 14*(21), 14457. https://doi.org/10.3390/su142114457

Dana, L.-P., & Dumez, H. (2015). Qualitative research revisited: epistemology of a comprehensive. *International Journal of Entrepreneurship and Small Business, 26*(2), 154–170. https://doi.org/10.1504/IJESB.2015.071822

Dendrinos, K., & Spais, G. (2024). An investigation of selected UTAUT constructs and consumption values of Gen Z and Gen X for mobile banking services and behavioral intentions to facilitate the adoption of mobile apps. *Journal of Marketing Analytics, 12*(3), 492–522. https://doi.org/10.1057/s41270-023-00271-1

Draga, E. (2021). Barriers of SME'S in Kosovo. *International Journal, 47*(1), 181–186. https://doi.org/10.35120/kij4701181d

Emini, A., & Merovci, S. (2021). Do-it-yourself marketing and digital marketing adoption: Evidence from a developing country. *Business Systems Research Journal, 12*(2), 1–16. https://doi.org/10.2478/bsrj-2021-0016

Fang, J. (2023). Research on the design of business models and transformation management of new entrepreneurial ventures driven by artificial intelligence. In *7th International Conference on Economics and Management, Education, Humanities and Social Sciences (EMEHSS 2023)* (pp. Vol. 49, pp. 36–41.). Artificial Intelligence. BCP Business & Management.

Goodman, L. A. (1961). Snowball sampling. *The Annals of Mathematical Statistics, 32*(1), 148–170.

Gruzd, A., Staves, K., & Wilk, A. (2012). Connected scholars: Examining the role of social media in research practices of faculty using the UTAUT model. *Computers in Human Behavior, 28*(6), 2340–2350. https://doi.org/10.1016/j.chb.2012.07.004

Horák, J., & Turková, M. (2023). Using artificial intelligence as business opportunities on the market: An overview. *Innovative Economic Symposium 2022 – Opportunities in Post-Covid Era (IES2022)* (pp. Vol. 160, pp. 12). SHS Web of Conferences.

Kabashi, S., & Kabashi, N. (2023). The economic impact of the covid-19 pandemic on small and medium-sized enterprises in the developing market. *Corporate and Business Strategy Review, 4*(1), 158–166. https://doi.org/10.22495/cbsrv4i1art14

Kandoth, S., & Shekhar, S. K. (2022). Social influence and intention to use AI: The role of personal innovativeness and perceived trust using the parallel mediation model. *Forum Scientiae Oeconomia, 10*(3), 131–150.

Krasniqi, S., Jashari, A., & Mehmeti, I. (2022). Management's perception of the determinants that influence SMES performance: Evidence from Kosovo. *Journal of Liberty and International Affairs, 8*(3), 135–153. https://doi.org/10.47305/JLIA2283135k

Kumar, D., & Ratten, V. (2024). Artificial intelligence and family businesses: A systematic literature review. *Journal of Family Business Management*. https://doi.org/10.1108/JFBM-08-2024-0160

Kurniasari, F., Lestari, E. D., & Tannady, H. (2023). Pursuing long-term business performance: investigating the effects of financial and technological factors on digital adoption to leverage SME performance and business sustainability—Evidence from Indonesian SMEs in the traditional market. *Sustainability, 15*(16), 12668. https://doi.org/10.3390/su151612668

Lawalata, J., & Yuliana, L. (2024). The impact of international financial reporting standards on global accounting practices. *Advances in Applied Accounting Research, 2*(2), 83–93. https://doi.org/10.60079/aaar.v2i2.262

Loku, A., & Loku, N. (2020). Internal factors affecting the performance of small and medium enterprises in Kosovo. *Technium Social Sciences Journal, 11*(1), 115–127. https://doi.org/10.47577/tssj.v11i1.1376

Mazher, M. A., & Tramankuti, Y. N. (2024). Leveraging business analytics for enhanced decision-making navigating challenges and exploiting opportunities. *International Journal of Multidisciplinary: Applied Business and Education Research, 5*(10), 4062–4071. https://doi.org/10.11594/ijmaber.05.10.21

Mensah, I. K., Wang, R., Gui, L., & Wang, J. (2021). Exploring the elements influencing the behavioral adoption of e-commerce by Chinese small and medium enterprises (SMES). *Information Development, 39*(4), 679–698. https://doi.org/10.1177/02666669211048486

Mohamad, M. A., Radzi, S. M., & Hanafiah, M. H. (2021). Understanding tourist mobile hotel booking behaviour: incorporating perceived enjoyment and perceived price value in the modified technology acceptance model. *Tourism & Management Studies, 17*(1), 19–30. https://doi.org/10.18089/tms.2021.170102

Moleong, L. J. (2013). *Metodologi Penelitian Kualitatif.* Bandung: PT Remaja Rosdakarya Offset.

Obschonka, M., & Audretsch, D. B. (2020). Artificial intelligence and big data in entrepreneurship: A new era has begun. *Small Business Economics, 55*(3), 529–539.

Rabaa'i, A. (2017). The use of UTAUT to investigate the adoption of e-government in Jordan: a cultural perspective. *International Journal of Business Information Systems, 24*(3), 285–315. https://doi.org/10.1504/IJBIS.2017.082037

Ramadani, N., & Ramadani, V. (2021). Rural entrepreneurship challenges and development: the case of Albanian women entrepreneurs in North Macedonia. *World Review of Entrepreneurship, Management and Sustainable Development, 17*(4), 531–557. https://doi.org/10.1504/WREMSD.2021.116688

Ratten, V., Hasan, R., Kumar, D., Bustard, J., Ojala, A., & Salamzadeh, Y. (2024). Learning from artificial intelligence researchers about international business implications. *Thunderbird International Business Review, 66*(2), 211–219. https://doi.org/10.1002/tie.22374

Reim, W., Åström, J., & Eriksson, O. (2020). Implementation of Artificial Intelligence (AI): A roadmap for business model innovation. *AI, 1*(2), 180–191. https://doi.org/10.3390/ai1020011

Rempel, H. G., & Mellinger, M. (2015). Bibliographic management tool adoption and use: A qualitative research study using the UTAUT model. *Reference & User Services Quarterly, 54*(4), 43–53. https://doi.org/10.5860/rusq.54n4.43

Rexhepi, B. R., Mustafa, L., Berisha, B. I., Vranovci, S. H., & Sadiku, M. K. (2024). Creating a factoring service specifically designed for small and medium enterprises at pro credit bank in Kosovo. *International Journal of Religion, 5*(6), 715–740. https://doi.org/10.61707/tc834x95

Ruangkanjanases, A., Sirisrisakulchai, P., Sonata, N., & Simamora, B. H. (2021). Predicting consumer intention to adopt online grocery shopping: A comparative study between millennials in Thailand And Indonesia. *International Journal of Electronic Commerce Studies, 12*(2), 193. https://doi.org/10.7903/ijecs.1894

Rudaku, A., Toska, A., Gleason, K., & Zeqiri, J. (2023). Returned entrepreneurs and ability to generate innovations: Case of Kosovo. *International Journal of Sustainable Development & Planning, 18*(9), 2911–2921. https://doi.org/10.18280/ijsdp.180929

Ruiz-Real, J. L., Uribe-Toril, J., Torres, J. A., & Pablo, J. D. (2020). Artificial intelligence in business and economics research: Trends and future. *Journal of Business Economics and Management, 22*(1), 98–117. https://doi.org/10.3846/jbem.2020.13641

Sadiku-Dushi, N. (2019). Survival or willing? Informal ethnic entrepreneurship among ethnic Serbs in Kosovo. In V. D. Ramadani, *Informal Ethnic Entrepreneurship* (pp. 115–131). Springer.

Sarfo, J. O., Debrah, T. P., Gbordzoe, N. I., Afful, W. T., & Obeng, P. (2021). Qualitative research designs, sample size and saturation: Is enough always enough. *Journal of Advocacy, Research and Education, 8*(3), 60–65. https://doi.org/10.13187/jare.2021.3.60

Sari, N. P., Duong, M.-P.T., Li, D., Nguyen, M.-H., & Vuong, Q.-H. (2024). Rethinking the effects of performance expectancy and effort expectancy on new technology adoption: Evidence from Moroccan nursing students. *Teaching and Learning in Nursing, 19*(3), e557–e565. https://doi.org/10.1016/j.teln.2024.04.002

Shahzad, K., Zhang, Q., & Khan, M. K. (2024). Blockchain technology adoption in supply chain management: an investigation from UTAUT and information system success model. *International Journal of Shipping and Transport Logistics, 18*(2), 165–190. https://doi.org/10.1504/IJSTL.2024.137893

Shaw, N., & Sergueeva, K. (2019). The non-monetary benefits of mobile commerce: Extending UTAUT2 with perceived value. *International Journal of Information Management, 45*, 44–55.

Singh, N., & Chouhan, S. S. (2021). Role of artificial intelligence for development of intelligent business systems. In *International Symposium on Smart Electronic Systems (iSES)*. Jaipur, India: IEEE; https://doi.org/10.1109/iSES52644.2021.00092.

Souiden, N., Ladhari, R., & Chaouali, W. (2021). Mobile banking adoption: A systematic review. *International Journal of Bank Marketing, 39*(2), 214–241.

Tanantong, T., & Wongras, P. (2024). A UTAUT-based framework for analyzing users' intention to adopt artificial intelligence in human resource recruitment: a case study of Thailand. *Systems, 12*(1), 28. https://doi.org/10.3390/systems12010028

Terstena, A., Mehmeti, I., & Krasniqi, S. (2023). Examining the owners and manager's perceptions of the determinants that influence the effectiveness of SME: Evidence from Kosovo. *International Journal of Applied Economics, Finance and Accounting, 17*(1), 67–75. https://doi.org/10.33094/ijaefa.v17i1.1036

Toska, A., Ramadani, V., Dana, L.-P., Rexhepi, G., & Zeqiri, J. (2022). Family business successors' motivation and innovation capabilities: The case of Kosovo. *Journal of Family Business Management, 12*(4), 1152–1166. https://doi.org/10.1108/JFBM-11-2021-0136

Venkatesh, V., Thong, J., & Xu, X. (2012). Consumer acceptance and use of information technology: Extending the unified theory of acceptance and use of technology. *MIS Quarterly, 36*(1), 157–178.

Wichean, A., & Sungsanit, M. (2022). Factors influencing the intentions to adopt technology of the broiler farmer in livestock region 3, Thailand. *Trends in Sciences, 19*(1), 1707. https://doi.org/10.48048/tis.2022.1707

Williams, M. L., Saunderson, I., & Dhoest, A. (2021). Students' perceptions of the adoption and use of social media in academic libraries: a UTAUT study. *Communication: South African Journal of Communication Theory and Research, 47*(1), 76–94.

Wong, C.-H., Tan, G.W.-H., Loke, S.-P., & Ooi, K.-B. (2015). Adoption of mobile social networking sites for learning? *Online Information Review, 39*(6), 762–778.

Yin, R. K. (2013). *Case study research: Design and methods*. Sage Publications.

CHAPTER 4

Fostering Sustainable Growth: Integrating Responsible Innovation in Technology Startups

Apurva Verma and Anoop Singh

4.1 Introduction

The global business landscape is undergoing rapid transformation driven by technological progress, environmental concerns, and shifting societal values. Technology startups, due to their agility and innovative potential, have emerged as critical players in addressing sustainability challenges while driving economic growth. Startups face unique opportunities and challenges as they strive to embed sustainability into their core Business models while navigating competitive market conditions and financial constraints.

A. Verma (✉) · A. Singh
Department of Management Sciences, Indian Institute of Technology, Kanpur, Uttar Pradesh, India
e-mail: apurva20@iitk.ac.in

A. Singh
e-mail: anoops@iitk.ac.in

D. Kumar et al. (eds.), *Evolving Trends in Technology Entrepreneurship*, Palgrave Studies in Global Entrepreneurship,
https://doi.org/10.1007/978-981-95-7441-4_4

Sustainable growth and responsible innovation have become focal points for both business strategy and policy-making. Startups, often characterized by their lean structures and high innovation capacity, are well-positioned to drive positive change. However, balancing economic success with environmental and social responsibility presents a complex challenge. Startups must engage with stakeholders, adopt sustainable and novel Business models, and leverage advanced technologies to achieve long-term benefits while mitigating negative externalities.

This chapter explores the intersection of sustainable growth and responsible innovation in technology startups. It identifies key frameworks for embedding sustainability into Business models, including systems thinking, circular economy principles, and stakeholder engagement. The chapter also presents case studies and practical strategies, highlighting how successful startups have navigated resource limitations, adopted renewable resources, and integrated advanced technologies. Finally, it discusses the challenges faced by startups in implementing sustainable innovation and proposes future research directions to enhance understanding and practice in this emerging field.

4.2 Understanding Sustainable Growth and Responsible Innovation

Sustainable growth and responsible innovation are interconnected concepts that shape the strategic direction of technology startups. Startups must address economic, environmental, and social objectives simultaneously to create long-term value. This requires switching from conventional Business models that exclusively focus on financial performance to the alternatives that account for broader societal and environmental impacts.

4.2.1 Defining Sustainable Growth in Startups

Sustainable growth refers to a startup's ability to scale its operations and increase profitability while minimizing environmental harm and contributing positively to society. Unlike conventional growth strategies that prioritize rapid market expansion and short-term profitability, sustainable growth emphasizes long-term resilience, resource efficiency, and social impact (Carayannis et al., 2018).

Carayannis and Campbell (2010) introduced the models named *Quadruple Helix* and *Quintuple Helix*, to explain the complex dynamics of sustainable innovation. These models highlight the importance of collaboration between public and private sectors, academic institutions and civil society in fostering sustainable growth. The key components include:

- **Triple Helix:** Interaction between government, industry, and academia to drive technological innovation and economic development.
- **Quadruple Helix:** Inclusion of civil society and public opinion in shaping innovation outcomes.
- **Quintuple Helix:** Integration of environmental concerns into the innovation ecosystem.

According to Ninh and Hue (2025), startups in emerging markets face additional barriers to sustainable growth, including limited access to capital, infrastructure gaps, and weak institutional support. However, startups in these markets have shown remarkable adaptability by adopting frugal innovation models and leveraging local resources. (Dote-Pardo et al., 2025). Grameen Shakti, a social enterprise in Bangladesh, offers solar home systems, biogas systems and improved cooking stoves to rural communities, combining affordability, accessibility, and social impact. By training local technicians and creating micro-financing options, the organisation has reached over 3.5 million people, improving energy access in rural areas and reducing carbon emissions (Asif and Barua, 2011, 2019). Despite facing logistical challenges such as supply chain disruptions and inconsistent regulatory support, it has demonstrated resilience by forming strategic partnerships with local governments and NGOs. Lessons from Grameen Shakti highlight the importance of community involvement and adaptive Business models in driving sustainable impact.

4.2.2 *Importance of Responsible Innovation in Technology Startups*

Responsible innovation (RI) refers to the process of designing and implementing new technologies and Business models in a manner that anticipates and addresses ethical, social, and environmental implications. Stilgoe et al. (2013) defined RI based on four key pillars:

1. **Anticipation:** Identifying potential risks and societal impacts before launching a product or service.
2. **Reflexivity:** Encouraging self-assessment and continuous improvement.
3. **Inclusion:** Involving stakeholders in the decision-making process.
4. **Responsiveness:** Adjusting strategies based on stakeholder feedback and emerging challenges.

Veloudis et al. (2025) proposed the Social Responsibility for Startups Model (SRSM), which provides a practical framework for embedding RI into startup operations. The SRSM model emphasizes the role of executive-level ethical decision-making, incorporation of social and environmental metrics into performance evaluation of startups and establishment of formal channels for stakeholder engagement. DeepMind established an ethics board to monitor the development of its AI technologies. The deployment of AI systems in sensitive domains such as healthcare has raised important debates regarding data governance and responsible innovation (Powles & Hodson, 2017). The company engaged ethicists, scientists, and policymakers to address potential societal impacts, such as algorithmic bias and privacy concerns. The firm also faced challenges in balancing commercial goals with ethical commitments, particularly when integrating AI systems into healthcare and finance. The key learning from DeepMind is that establishing independent oversight mechanisms can help align technological innovation with societal values. These perspectives are consistent with recent evidence showing that AI-enabled green process innovation, when guided by environmentally oriented leadership, can strengthen sustainable practices and responsible innovation in technology-driven industries (Liu et al., 2025).

4.3 Frameworks for Integrating Responsible Innovation

Implementing responsible innovation requires structured frameworks that align business strategy with sustainability goals. Startups can adopt various frameworks to integrate responsible innovation into their core operations. This section provides a detailed examination of three frameworks - systems thinking, circular economy principles, and stakeholder engagement to enable startups to navigate sustainability challenges and leverage innovation for competitive advantage. A structured approach ensures that responsible innovation becomes an integral part of the business model rather than a peripheral initiative.

By embedding responsible innovation into strategic decision-making, startups can boost stakeholder trust, foresee and reduce risks, and generate long-term value. Each framework provides distinct advantages and can be modified to accommodate the unique requirements and market conditions of a startup. Systems thinking helps startups understand intricate interactions between company's operation and external systems, circular economy principles encourage minimizing waste and efficient use of resources, while stakeholder engagement ensures that innovation aligns with societal values and expectations.

4.3.1 Systems Thinking

Systems thinking provides an inclusive approach to comprehend the interconnections between business activities and broader societal and environmental systems. According to Senge (1990), systems thinking enables organizations to identify feedback loops (reinforcing or balancing mechanisms that drive systemic behavior), leverage points (strategic interventions to shift system outcomes), and unintended consequences.

Building on this perspective, research on sustainable business model innovation suggests that a systems-oriented approach enables organizations to understand the interactions between resource flows, value creation processes, and stakeholder networks, thereby supporting more informed strategic decision-making in complex environments (Bocken et al., 2014). Key tools for systems thinking include:

- **Causal Loop Diagrams (CLDs):** Visualizing cause-and-effect relationships.
- **Stock and Flow Diagrams:** Tracking resource accumulation and movement.
- **Scenario Analysis:** Simulating different strategic options.

Tesla's development of charging infrastructure alongside electric vehicles reflects a systems thinking approach. The firm recognized that consumer adoption of electric vehicles depended on the availability of charging infrastructure. By investing in a network of superchargers, it increased customer confidence and accelerated market adoption. Tesla faced initial resistance from local governments and competitors, but by adopting a vertically integrated model, the company retained control over its infrastructure and customer experience.

4.3.2 *Circular Economy*

The circular economy model fosters waste minimization and efficient use of resources using closed-loop production techniques and systems. This model serves as a critical framework for fostering sustainable growth in technology startups by aligning innovation with environmental stewardship and resource efficiency (Zaghdoud, 2025). Ellen MacArthur Foundation (2015) proposed three key principles for circular economy strategies:

- **Design out waste and pollution.**
- **Extending Product and Material Lifespans**
- **Regenerate natural systems.**

These principles enable startups to transition from linear "take-make-dispose" models to closed-loop systems that decouple economic activity from finite resource consumption. Fairphone designs modular smartphones with easily replaceable components, enabling customers to repair and upgrade their devices (Krishna and Budhiraja, 2023). Their devices also receive eight years of software updates, countering planned obsolescence and reducing replacement cycles. This approach reduces electronic waste and extends product lifespan.

4.3.3 *Stakeholder Engagement*

Integrating stakeholder engagement into technology startups is pivotal for fostering sustainable growth through responsible innovation, as it aligns business objectives with societal and environmental imperatives. Stakeholder engagement ensures that startups navigate complex socio-technical ecosystems by embedding inclusivity, transparency, and responsiveness into their innovation processes. Freeman's (1984) stakeholder theory posits that stakeholders—defined as individuals or groups influencing or influenced by organizational outcomes—are critical to long-term success.

For startups, this expands beyond shareholders to include customers, suppliers, regulators, NGOs, and local communities. Lubberink et al. (2017) outlined a stakeholder-based model for responsible innovation, emphasizing:

- **Direct engagement:** Open communication with customers, suppliers, and regulators.
- **Collaborative innovation:** Co-developing solutions with stakeholders.
- **Feedback mechanisms:** Incorporating stakeholder input into business strategy.

Unilever's Sustainable Living Plan involved direct stakeholder engagement to address environmental and social concerns and demonstrates that systemic stakeholder engagement drives both sustainability and profitability. The company worked with NGOs, governments, and local communities to reduce its environmental footprint and improve labor practices.

4.4 Sustainability Assessment in Technology Startups

Sustainability assessment allows startups to measure and track their environmental, social, and economic impacts. Unlike traditional performance metrics, sustainability assessment considers broader societal outcomes, helping businesses identify areas for improvement and align with stakeholder expectations. For startups focused on responsible innovation, robust sustainability assessment is essential for attracting impact investors, securing regulatory approvals, and maintaining consumer trust.

Startups operate in highly dynamic environments where financial and operational performance often takes precedence over sustainability goals. However, successful startups recognize that including sustainability into fundamental business strategies improves competitive advantage and resilience over the long run. The framework offered by sustainability assessment enables startups to:

- Identify environmental and social risks associated with business operations.

- Measure the effectiveness of sustainability initiatives.
- Align business practices with stakeholder expectations and regulatory requirements.

Effective sustainability assessment also enhances transparency, allowing startups to communicate their impact to investors, customers, and regulators. The following sections explore key methods for assessing sustainability performance, including Life Cycle Assessment (LCA), Social Return on Investment (SROI), and Environmental, Social, and Governance (ESG) metrics.

4.4.1 *Life Cycle Assessment (LCA)*

LCA is a systematic method for evaluating the environmental impacts of a product or service throughout its life-cycle—from raw material extraction to production, distribution, use, and end-of-life disposal. Grounded in ISO 14040 and 14,044 standards, LCA provides a structured framework to quantify resource consumption, emissions, and ecological consequences, enabling businesses to identify environmental "hotspots" and optimize design decisions for sustainability. For technology startups, integrating LCA into innovation processes is pivotal for fostering responsible growth aligned with circular economy principles and stakeholder expectations. Apple exemplifies LCA's application in reducing environmental footprints. By conducting ISO-compliant LCAs, Apple identified that aluminum production accounted for 27% of the MacBook Air's carbon footprint. In response, the company transitioned to 100% recycled aluminum enclosures, eliminating the need for virgin bauxite mining and reducing associated emissions by 72%. This shift, validated by third-party audits, aligns with its broader goal to use solely recycled or renewable materials by 2030. By emulating industry leaders like Apple and adhering to ISO standards, startups can reduce ecological footprints while enhancing market competitiveness.

4.4.2 *Social Return on Investment (SROI)*

Social Return on Investment (SROI) is an impact-assessment framework that evaluates the social value generated by an organisation relative to the resources invested. Unlike traditional financial performance measures,

SROI incorporates both economic returns and broader social and environmental outcomes, enabling organisations to communicate their overall impact to investors and other stakeholders. By assigning monetary proxies to both tangible and intangible outcomes, the SROI approach provides a more comprehensive assessment of value creation beyond conventional financial indicators. This framework is particularly relevant for startups engaged in social entrepreneurship and environmentally oriented initiatives, where demonstrating measurable societal impact is increasingly important. As impact measurement gains prominence in responsible and impact-driven investment decisions, tools such as SROI enable organisations to systematically capture and communicate the social value created through their activities (Nicholls et al., 2012; Krlev et al., 2013). This trend reflects the broader growth of impact investing, in which financial performance is evaluated alongside measurable social and environmental outcomes. In practice, SROI analysis typically involves several stages, including:

- **Identifying stakeholders** affected by business activities.
- **Mapping outcomes** to understand the impact of business operations.
- **Assigning value** to outcomes using financial proxies.
- **Calculating net present value** of outcomes relative to investment.

The "One for One" program was started by TOMS Shoes, which donates a pair of shoes for each pair that is sold. The program created both social and financial returns by increasing consumer loyalty and expanding market share. Despite initial logistical challenges related to distribution and supply chain inefficiencies, TOMS demonstrated that social impact initiatives could strengthen brand equity and drive long-term growth. Despite its success, the company faced criticism regarding unintended consequences. For instance, critics argued that distributing free shoes disrupted local economies by undermining small-scale manufacturers. In response, TOMS adapted its approach by collaborating with local suppliers in recipient countries to produce shoes locally, thereby fostering economic development alongside philanthropy.

While SROI offers significant advantages, it also presents challenges such as assigning monetary values to intangible outcomes and selection of methods. Startups can address these issues by utilizing established frameworks such as the Global Reporting Initiative (GRI) or Social Value International standards, iteratively refining their SROI calculations through stakeholder feedback and data validation or partnering with third-party evaluators to enhance credibility and transparency.

4.4.3 Environmental, Social, and Governance (ESG) Metrics

Environmental, Social, and Governance (ESG) metrics have evolved as critical tools for assessing a company's sustainability and ethical practices. These metrics assess performance in three primary domains: Environmental (e.g., Carbon footprints, waste reduction, and efficiency of resources), Social (e.g., Workforce diversity, labor law compliance, and community engagement), and Governance (e.g., diversity on the board, payouts to executives, and business ethics). For technology startups aiming to integrate responsible innovation, ESG metrics provide a structured framework to align business operations with societal values and long-term sustainability goals.

Startups are uniquely positioned to embed ESG principles into their Business models from inception, leveraging these metrics to enhance transparency, attract investment, and build resilience. Investors increasingly rely on ESG performance to evaluate business viability, with high ESG ratings correlating with lower capital costs, stronger investor confidence, and improved competitiveness. By integrating ESG frameworks early on, startups can future-proof their operations against regulatory changes while fostering trust among stakeholders.

Tesla has consistently scored high in environmental ratings due to its leadership in electric vehicles and renewable energy (Jobaaj Learnings, 2026). However, Tesla's environmental practices have faced scrutiny due to issues such as toxic wastewater leaks at its Austin factory and air pollution violations at its Fremont facility. These controversies underscore the complexity of maintaining environmental leadership while scaling operations. Few governance issues, such as labor practices and executive compensation, have also lowered its overall ESG score. Addressing these challenges is critical for sustaining investor confidence and market leadership. Tesla's experience highlights the importance of balancing all three dimensions of ESG. While excelling in one area may enhance brand equity temporarily, neglecting others can undermine long-term sustainability.

4.5 Case Studies and Practical Strategies

Startups that have effectively incorporated sustainability and responsible innovation into their business plans offer insightful information to other enterprises dealing with similar challenges. The following expanded case studies highlight strategic decisions, operational challenges, and key lessons learned.

4.5.1 Overcoming Resource Limitations

Startups often face financial and operational constraints when implementing sustainable practices. However, strategic resource allocation and external partnerships can help overcome these barriers.

Example 1: Tesla

Tesla's growth in the electric vehicle market demonstrates how strategic partnerships and government incentives can address resource limitations. The company initially benefited from a considerable amount of debt from the U.S. Department of Energy, which enabled it to scale up production and develop battery technology. Tesla also partnered with Panasonic to build a battery production facility (Gigafactory), reducing supply chain dependencies and lowering costs. Tesla faced early challenges related to production delays, supply chain disruptions, and regulatory hurdles. The company addressed these issues by vertically integrating its supply chain and investing in in-house manufacturing capabilities. Access to public funding and strategic partnerships can accelerate technological development. Vertical integration reduces reliance on external suppliers and enhances operational efficiency.

Example 2: Impossible Foods

Impossible Foods faced high production costs and limited scalability when launching its plant based meat products. The company secured funding from venture capital firms and strategic investors, including Bill Gates, to build production facilities and streamline supply chains. Impossible Foods faced criticism for the environmental impact of sourcing ingredients like soy, which contributes to deforestation in carbon-rich regions. To mitigate these concerns, the company adopted life-cycle assessments (LCAs) to quantify and reduce its environmental footprint. Consumer scepticism and regulatory hurdles regarding food safety standards posed barriers to market acceptance but transparency in product sourcing and manufacturing helped in building consumer trust. Early-stage investments in production capacity enabled scalability.

4.5.2 *Adopting Renewable Resources and Advanced Technologies*

Innovations like blockchain, artificial intelligence (AI), and the Internet of Things (IoT) have enabled startups to enhance operational efficiency and integrate sustainability into their Business models.

Example 1: Siemens

Siemens' development of smart grid technology demonstrates how AI and IoT can enhance energy efficiency. In order to optimize energy distribution and minimize waste, the company deployed AI-based energy management systems that analyze data in real time. Siemens faced technical challenges related to data security and interoperability with existing infrastructure. Technological advancement such as AI helped in enhancing grid stability and reducing operational costs. It is evident that collaboration with regulators and local utilities is essential for large-scale implementation.

Example 2: Everledger

Everledger makes the diamond supply chain transparent by utilizing blockchain technology. In order to ensure ethical sourcing and lower the risk of conflict diamonds, the company developed a platform that tracks the journey of diamonds from mining to sale. The company faced adoption barriers of limited industry awareness and resistance from traditional stakeholders, but it has proved that blockchain enhances trust and accountability in supply chains. Along with that, industry-wide adoption of blockchain technology requires collaboration with regulators and major market players.

4.6 Challenges and Limitations

Despite the success of some startups, broader adoption of responsible innovation and sustainable practices remains limited due to several key barriers.

4.6.1 *Policy and Regulatory Barriers*

Startups face complex and evolving regulations related to environmental protection, data privacy, and labor standards. Lack of incentives for sustainable practices and misaligned policies may hamper adoption. For example, electric vehicle manufacturers face inconsistent emissions standards across different countries, complicating market entry and expansion strategies. In the renewable energy sector, regulatory approval processes for new projects can be lengthy and costly.

4.6.2 *Financial Constraints*

Short-term financial gains are often given precedence over long-term sustainability objectives by investors. Startups focusing on responsible innovation often face higher capital costs and longer payback periods. Green startups frequently struggle to secure venture capital funding due to perceived risk and uncertainty regarding market demand. The lack of standardized metrics for evaluating environmental and social impact further complicates access to funding.

4.6.3 *Technological and Operational Challenges*

It takes a large initial investment and technical know-how to implement revolutionary technologies like blockchain and AI. Investing in R&D and infrastructure for sustainable technologies can strain startup budgets. Startups often lack in-house expertise to implement complex technologies. Integrating new technologies with existing systems can be challenging due to compatibility issues.

4.6.4 *Cultural and Organizational Resistance*

Organizational inertia and resistance to change can impede the adoption of responsible innovation and sustainability initiatives. Startups under pressure from investors to achieve quick returns may deprioritize long-term sustainability goals. Employees and management may lack a shared vision for sustainability, leading to fragmented efforts.

4.7 The Road Ahead

Future studies need to emphasize on addressing the gaps and challenges in the current understanding and implementation of responsible innovation and sustainable practices in startups. Developing standardized metrics for evaluating environmental and social impact is essential to enable consistent benchmarking and improve investor confidence, such as the enterprise digital technology innovation index developed using digital patent data to assess how technological innovation contributes to productivity improvement, efficient labour allocation, and more inclusive value distribution within firms (Zhang and Chen, 2025). Research into the financial impact of sustainable Business models could help startups demonstrate long-term value creation to potential investors.

Government policies, regulations, and incentive frameworks play a critical role in supporting sustainable innovation. Comparative studies across different markets could identify best practices and inform policy recommendations. Additionally, research into the role of AI, blockchain, and IoT in enhancing sustainability performance could provide actionable insights for startups and industry stakeholders.

Understanding cross-cultural variations in sustainable entrepreneurship is another key area for exploration. Differences in consumer behavior, regulatory environments, and market structures can influence the adoption of sustainable practices. Research into these variations could help startups tailor their strategies to different geographic and cultural contexts.

Finally, examining the long-term performance of sustainable startups could provide valuable insights into the financial and operational benefits of responsible innovation. Longitudinal studies tracking startup performance over time could identify the factors that contribute to business resilience and market competitiveness.

4.8 Conclusion

Technology startups have the potential to drive sustainable growth and responsible innovation by adopting systems thinking, circular economy models, and stakeholder engagement. Incorporating sustainability into their fundamental business plans allows entrepreneurs to solve environmental and societal issues while producing long-term benefits. Successful examples from renewable energy, AI, and blockchain demonstrate that sustainable Business models are not only viable but also offer long-term competitive advantages (Danil et al., 2025).

However, startups face significant challenges, including financial constraints, regulatory barriers, and technological limitations. Overcoming these obstacles requires coordinated efforts from policymakers, investors, industry leaders, and research institutions. Government incentives, standardized sustainability metrics, and increased access to impact investment capital can provide the necessary support for sustainable startups to thrive.

Future research should focus on developing practical frameworks for sustainability assessment, investigating the financial impact of responsible innovation, and exploring the potential of digital technologies in driving sustainable Business models.

References

Asif, M., & Barua, D. (2011). Salient features of the Grameen Shakti renewable energy program. *Renewable and Sustainable Energy Reviews, 15*(9), 5063–5067. https://doi.org/10.1016/j.rser.2011.07.050

Bocken, N. M. P., Short, S. W., Rana, P., & Evans, S. (2014). A literature and practice review to develop sustainable business model archetypes. *Journal of Cleaner Production, 65*, 42–56. https://doi.org/10.1016/j.jclepro.2013.11.039

Carayannis, E. G., & Campbell, D. F. J. (2010). Triple helix, quadruple helix and quintuple helix and how do knowledge, innovation and the environment relate to each other? *International Journal of Social Ecology and Sustainable Development, 1*(1), 41–69. https://doi.org/10.4018/jsesd.2010010105

Carayannis, E. G., Grigoroudis, E., Campbell, D. F. J., Meissner, D. and Stamati, D. (2018). The ecosystem as helix: an exploratory theory-building study of regional co-opetitive entrepreneurial ecosystems as Quadruple/Quintuple Helix Innovation Models. *R & D Management, 48*: 148–162. https://doi.org/10.1111/radm.12300

Danil, L., Jahroh, S., Syarief, R., & Taryana, A. (2025). Technological innovation in start-ups on a pathway to achieving Sustainable Development Goal (SDG) 8: A systematic review. *Sustainability, 17*(3), 1220. https://doi.org/10.3390/su17031220

Dote-Pardo, J., Ortiz-Cea, V., Peña-Acuña, V., Severino-González, P., Contreras-Henríquez, J. M., & Ramírez-Molina, R. I. (2025). Innovative entrepreneurship and sustainability: A bibliometric analysis in emerging countries. *Sustainability, 17*(2), 658. https://doi.org/10.3390/su17020658

Ellen MacArthur Foundation. (2015). Towards a circular economy: Business rationale for an accelerated transition. Retrieved from https://www.ellenmacarthurfoundation.org

Freeman, R. E. (1984). Strategic Management: A Stakeholder Approach. Boston, MA: Pitman Publishing.

Krishna, M., & Budhiraja, H. (2023). Fairphone: Dialing up sustainability in smartphones (Case No. W32379). Ivey Publishing. https://www.thecasecentre.org/products/view?id=192845

Jobaaj Learnings. (2026, January 27). Tesla's leadership in EVs and sustainable energy: A case study. https://www.jobaajlearnings.com/casestudies/Teslas-Leadership-in-EVs-and-Sustainable-Energy-A-Case-Study

Khatami, S., Taghvaei, A., & Karimi, S. (2022). Systems thinking and startup innovation: Understanding the feedback loops. *Journal of Business Strategy, 34*(2), 175–190. https://doi.org/10.1108/JBS-09-2021-0152

Krlev, Gorgi & Münscher, Robert & Mülbert, Katharina. (2013). Social Return on Investment (SROI): state-of-the-art and perspectives - a meta-analysis of practice in Social Return on Investment (SROI) studies published, 2002–2012.

Liu, Y., Ho, T. C. F., Omar, R., & Ning, B. (2025). Green entrepreneurial leadership and AI-driven green process innovation: Advancing environmental sustainability in the Traditional Chinese Medicine industry. *Journal of Environmental Management, 375*, Article 124438. https://doi.org/10.1016/j.jenvman.2025.124438

Lubberink, R., Blok, V., Van Ophem, J., & Omta, O. (2017). Lessons for Responsible Innovation in the Business Context: A Systematic Literature Review of Responsible, Social and Sustainable Innovation Practices. *Sustainability, 9*(5), 721. https://doi.org/10.3390/su9050721

Nicholls, J., Lawlor, E., Neitzert, E., & Goodspeed, T. (2012). A guide to social return on investment. London: The SROI Network.

Ninh, T. T. T., & Hue, T. T. (2025). Sustainable entrepreneurial ecosystems: What are the main schools of thought and topical trends? Discover Sustainability, 6, 115. https://doi.org/10.1007/s43621-025-00931-5

Powles, J., Hodson, H. Google DeepMind and healthcare in an age of algorithms. Health Technol. 7, 351–367 (2017). https://doi.org/10.1007/s12553-017-0179-1

Senge, P. M. (1990). The fifth discipline: The art and practice of the learning organization. Doubleday/Currency.

Stilgoe, J., Owen, R., & Macnaghten, P. (2013). Developing a framework for responsible innovation. *Research Policy, 42*(9), 1568–1580. https://doi.org/10.1016/j.respol.2013.05.008

Veloudis, S., Ryan, M., Ketikidi, E., & Blok, V. (2025). Responsible innovation in start-ups: Entrepreneurial perspectives and formalisation of social responsibility. *Journal of Responsible Innovation, 12*(1). https://doi.org/10.1080/23299460.2025.2453251

Zaghdoud, O. (2025). Technological progress as a catalyst for energy efficiency: A sustainable technology perspective. *Sustainable Technology and Entrepreneurship, 4*(1), Article 100084. https://doi.org/10.1016/j.stae.2024.100084

Zhang, B., & Chen, P. (2025). Digital technology innovation and common prosperity within enterprises: Destruction or creation. *Environment, Development and Sustainability*. https://doi.org/10.1007/s10668-024-05912-8

CHAPTER 5

Leveraging Blockchain Technology to Enhance Speed of Adjustment in Technology Startups: A Financial and Strategic Perspective

Neha Sharma, Mayank Arora, and Darren Henry

N. Sharma (✉)
Department of Management Studies, IIT Kanpur, Uttar Pradesh, Kanpur, India
e-mail: nehasharma20@iitk.ac.in

Department of Accounting and Management, Business School, La Trobe University, Melbourne, VIC, Australia

M. Arora
Department of Electrical Engineering IIT Kanpur, Uttar Pradesh, Kanpur, India

e-mail: marora21@iitk.ac.in

Department of Computer Science, La Trobe University, Melbourne, VIC, Australia

D. Kumar et al. (eds.), *Evolving Trends in Technology Entrepreneurship*, Palgrave Studies in Global Entrepreneurship,
https://doi.org/10.1007/978-981-95-7441-4_5

5.1 Background

In today's rapidly evolving business environment, technology startups operate in dynamic and uncertain markets that demand agility and strategic foresight.

Financial decisions, particularly those concerning capital structure, play a pivotal role in determining a startup's growth trajectory and long-term sustainability (Berger & Udell, 1998; Manigart & Khosravi, 2024). Managing capital structure effectively strikes an optimal balance between debt and equity, reducing capital costs and boosting profitability. However, achieving and maintaining an optimal capital structure is a complex task, especially for startups in the digitilization era characterized by limited financial resources, high-risk profiles, and unpredictable revenue streams. Digitalization has revolutionized finance by introducing innovative investment avenues such as crowdfunding and ICOs, fostering the rise of technology-driven investors, and reshaping the dynamics of traditional investment practices. The financial ecosystem has become more segmented with the rise of new investor types such as incubators, accelerators, family offices, impact investors, and sovereign wealth funds, expanding the range of funding options available to startups. Moreover, investors remain more oriented toward non-financial objectives, such as reducing environmental issues along with societal issues (Manigart & Khosravi, 2024).

A key aspect of managing capital structure is the speed of adjustment (SOA), which measures how quickly a company realigns its capital structure back to an optimal target following disruptions caused by internal or external shocks. The adjustment procedure depends on the level of transaction costs, market conditions, regulatory restrictions, as well as access to financing. For technology ventures, getting a high adjustment speed is essential for the sustainability of financial stability, capturing opportunities for growth, and coping with risks triggered by abrupt changes in the market (Ghaemi Asl et al., 2024). Despite its importance, many startups face challenges in maintaining an optimal capital structure and achieving

D. Henry
Department of Accounting and Management, La Trobe University, Melbourne, VIC, Australia
e-mail: D.Henry@latrobe.edu.au

faster adjustments. Traditional financial systems often impose constraints such as high borrowing costs, lengthy approval processes, and lack of access to diversified funding sources. These limitations hinder startups' ability to make timely adjustments, leaving them vulnerable to financial distress and competitive disadvantages (Haddad & Hornuf, 2021).

Recent advancements in blockchain technology present a transformative opportunity to address these challenges. Blockchain, with its core features of decentralization, transparency, immutability, and automation through smart contracts, has the potential to revolutionize financial strategies in startups. Through decentralized finance (DeFi) and tokenization, blockchain enables startups to access alternative funding mechanisms, streamline capital restructuring, and automate compliance, thereby enhancing their ability to adjust capital structures quickly and efficiently (Schär, 2021).

This chapter aims to investigate the role of blockchain technology in accelerating the adjustment speed of capital structure in technology startups. It examines theoretical foundations, practical applications, and case studies to provide insights into how blockchain can be leveraged as a financial and strategic tool. Furthermore, the chapter addresses challenges such as regulatory barriers, ethical considerations, and scalability issues, offering strategies to overcome these obstacles.

This chapter is organized as follows: Sect. 2 reviews capital structure theories and blockchain applications, incorporating case studies and empirical evidence to illustrate their practical use. Section 3 explores blockchain-driven financial adjustments, including decentralized finance and automated mechanisms. Section 4 discusses challenges and ethical considerations, followed by Sect. 5, which examines future trends and implications. Finally, Sect. 6 offers conclusions and recommendations for researchers, entrepreneurs, and policymakers. By providing a comprehensive analysis, this chapter seeks to bridge the gap between traditional financial theories and emerging technologies, demonstrating how blockchain can enhance financial flexibility and resilience in technology startups.

5.2 Background and Literature Review

5.2.1 *Theories of Capital Structure Adjustment*

Various capital structure theories explain how firms balance debt and equity to optimize their financial strategies. Among them, the trade-off theory and the pecking order theory stand out by providing key perspectives on how companies make financial decisions (Paul et al., 2007).

The trade-off theory suggests that companies try to balance the tax benefits of debt since interest payments reduce taxable income with the potential costs of financial distress. While debt offers valuable tax shields, too much debt raises bankruptcy risk and related costs. As a result, firms aim for an optimal capital structure where the added benefit of taking on more debt matches its added cost (Bradley et al., 1984; Miller, 1977). This theory implies that companies actively adjust their financing mix to maintain this balance, particularly in markets with frequent fluctuations.

The pecking order theory highlights a financing preference hierarchy (Myers, 1984a). Firms prioritize internal funds like retained earnings because they are cheaper and involve less information asymmetry. If internal resources fall short, companies turn to debt before considering new equity issuance (Myers, 1984b). This theory suggests that adjustments to capital structure are driven by the availability and cost of financing sources rather than a predefined optimal target. Startups, which often lack retained earnings, may rely heavily on debt and external funding sources, making their capital structure adjustments slower and more reactive. But sometimes startups prefer outside equity over debt, known as Reversed pecking order (Hechavarría et al., 2016; Minola et al., 2013) because Venture Capitalists and Business angels are believed to have greater knowledge and coping mechanisms with information asymmetry about the firm they invest in.

Researchers also point out that startup capital structure choices are shaped by several additional theories. Agency theory highlights conflicts between investors and entrepreneurs stemming from differing goals and information gaps, which can make investors wary of risky ventures or push them to demand higher returns (Bellavitis et al., 2017; Meckling & Jensen, 1976). Signaling theory suggests startups use financial moves, like securing well-known investors to signal quality to outsiders (Eddleston et al., 2016). Market timing theory argues that firms tend to issue equity when market conditions are favorable and rely more on debt during downturns, with these timing decisions impacting capital structure long-term due to adjustment costs (Baker & Wurgler, 2002). Lastly, path dependence theory explains how early funding choices influence later financing strategies, sometimes causing firms to become locked into specific capital structures (Samuelsson et al., 2021; Sydow et al., 2009). And finally, the financial growth life cycle model which suggests that as firms mature, their financing sources evolve from insider funding and trade credits to venture capital, bank loans, and eventually public equity, although this model oversimplifies real-world startup financing patterns (Berger & Udell, 1998).

Empirical studies on the speed of adjustment (SOA) indicate that firms exhibit varying speeds in realigning their capital structures. Large, established firms often have faster SOA due to better access to financial resources and lower transaction costs. Startups, however, face structural and operational constraints, leading to slower adjustments. Research highlights that factors such as firm size, profitability, growth opportunities, and market conditions influence SOA, with higher adjustment speeds observed in financially flexible firms (Lemma & T. et al.,., 2014; Sharma & Saurabh, 2024).

Blockchain technology has the potential to enhance SOA by reducing transaction costs, improving access to funding, and automating compliance processes. By leveraging decentralized finance, startups can overcome traditional barriers and achieve faster adjustments, aligning their capital structures with strategic goals more efficiently. The following sections will delve deeper into the integration of blockchain and its impact on financial adjustments in startups.

5.2.2 *Blockchain Technology in Financial Management*

Blockchain technology has emerged as a groundbreaking innovation in financial management, revolutionizing traditional practices by introducing enhanced efficiency, security, and transparency to a range of financial processes. At its core, blockchain operates as a decentralized system, eliminating the dependence on intermediaries such as banks or clearinghouses. This decentralization reduces transaction costs, enhances system resilience by removing single points of failure, and democratizes access to financial systems. By distributing data across a network of nodes, blockchain ensures that all participants have access to the same, up-to-date information, which is particularly valuable in mitigating risks associated with fraud or data manipulation in financial transactions (Rella, 2019). Furthermore, the technology's ability to streamline cross-border payments and settlements has positioned it as a viable solution for addressing delays and inefficiencies in global financial networks, creating a seamless and cost-effective alternative to conventional methods (Zhang, 2020).

Another defining characteristic of blockchain technology is its inherent transparency and immutability (Sharma et al., 2024). Transactions recorded on a blockchain are visible to all authorized participants in real time, fostering trust and accountability within the financial ecosystem. This visibility ensures that all parties operate with the same set of verifiable data, reducing the likelihood of disputes or discrepancies. Moreover, the immutability of blockchain data guarantees that once information is added to the ledger, it cannot be altered or deleted, safeguarding the integrity of financial records. Complementing these features are smart contracts, which are self-executing agreements with terms coded directly into the blockchain. Smart contracts automate complex financial processes such as payments, compliance checks, and settlements, eliminating the need for manual intervention and reducing the potential for human error. These attributes collectively make blockchain a cornerstone for modernizing financial systems, paving the way for greater innovation, inclusivity, and resilience in the global financial landscape (Khan et al., 2021).

Blockchain technology has found transformative applications across various financial processes, significantly enhancing efficiency and reducing costs. One prominent area is the facilitation of cross-border payments, clearing, and settlement. Traditional systems for these operations are often plagued by delays, high transaction costs, and inefficiencies, particularly in global markets. Blockchain addresses these challenges by enabling real-time processing of transactions, which reduces the time and costs associated with intermediaries. For instance, blockchain streamlines clearing and settlement procedures, ensuring faster completion of transactions while minimizing risks like counterparty defaults or settlement failures. This capability has made blockchain an attractive solution for financial institutions seeking to modernize their operations and improve service delivery (Islam et al., 2023).

Applications in Fundraising and Risk Management: Blockchain has reshaped fundraising by enabling new digital methods that allow startups to raise capital directly from investors. These models bypass traditional financial middlemen such as banks and venture capital firms, offering fresh alternatives to conventional funding processes (Campino et al., 2022;

Kondova & Simonella, 2019; Schückes & Gutmann, 2021). By leveraging blockchain, companies can reach a broader base of investors globally, increasing their chances of securing funding. Moreover, the transparency and programmability of blockchain enhance trust and compliance in fundraising activities.

Another critical application of blockchain lies in risk management. The technology's transparency and immutability enable more effective tracking of transactions and assets, playing a crucial role in detecting fraud and ensuring regulatory compliance. Smart contracts further enhance risk management by automating processes such as risk assessments and adherence to legal requirements, reducing human error and ensuring more reliable outcomes. Smart contracts have found applications in insurance company operations, enabling functions like pooling premiums, assessing risks, and distributing claims without requiring a centralized authority. While still in their early stages, platforms like Lemonade, Etherisc, and Nexus Mutual are leveraging smart contracts for parametric and pooled insurance products. These innovations have the potential to reduce operational costs and provide efficient, secure, and accurate payouts, offering significant advantages over traditional insurance models (Reuters: Is blockchain the next big thing for insurance companies Reuters, 2024). Together, these applications illustrate blockchain's potential to redefine financial ecosystems, making them more secure, efficient, and inclusive.

5.2.3 *Case Examples of Blockchain Adoption in Financial Markets*

Blockchain technology has been increasingly adopted by major financial institutions to enhance operational efficiency, reduce costs, and improve security. JPMorgan Chase created its own digital currency, JPM Coin, to enable real-time international payments for customers, showcasing how blockchain can transform conventional banking services. This initiative reflects a broader trend among financial institutions to integrate blockchain into their services to streamline processes and offer real-time transaction capabilities (Shevchenko & Lunsford, 2023).

Similarly, SIX Digital Exchange (SDX) utilizes blockchain to tokenize traditional securities, enabling faster settlement times and reduced counterparty risk, thereby enhancing the efficiency of financial markets. SDX's approach illustrates how blockchain can be leveraged to modernize financial market infrastructures, providing more secure and efficient platforms for trading and settlement (https://www.sdx.com/news/six-digital-exchangesuccessfully-tokenizes-private-shares-on-its-regulated-blockchain-based-centralsecurities-depository-in-partnership-with-f10-and-aequitec/).

In the asset management sector, firms like Janus Henderson have tokenized units of funds on a blockchain, allowing for instant trading and serving as collateral in blockchain transactions. This integration showcases the potential of blockchain to enhance liquidity and operational efficiency in asset management (Mohamed, 2021).

These examples illustrate blockchain's growing influence in financial management, offering solutions that enhance operational efficiency, provide alternative fundraising mechanisms, and improve risk management practices. As the technology matures, its adoption is expected to become more widespread, further transforming the financial landscape.

5.2.4 *Blockchain and Capital Structure Adjustments*

Blockchain technology is revolutionizing the way firms manage and adjust their capital structures by introducing innovative mechanisms that enhance flexibility, efficiency, and accessibility in financial operations. Key components facilitating these advancements include Decentralized Finance (DeFi), smart contracts, and tokenization.

5.2.5 *Role of Decentralized Finance (DeFi) in Enabling Flexible Financing Decentralized*

Finance (DeFi) represents a shift in how financial services are delivered by leveraging blockchain technology and smart contracts. It consists of various applications mostly built on platforms like Ethereum that operate without traditional middlemen such as banks. Through DeFi protocols, users can lend, borrow, and trade directly with one another, giving businesses and individuals more direct access to financial tools.

By eliminating traditional intermediaries, DeFi creates a permissionless ecosystem that democratizes access to financial resources, offering unparalleled opportunities for flexible financing options. This decentralization reduces reliance on traditional financial institutions, lowers transaction costs, and offers more flexible financing options. For instance, platforms like Aave allow users to supply and borrow cryptocurrency assets across various blockchains by posting collateral, facilitating efficient capital allocation and liquidity management (Wu & Wu, 2022).

One of DeFi's core contributions is its ability to provide programmable and automated financial services through smart contracts, which act as trustless executors of agreements. This innovation allows users to engage in borrowing, lending, and investing without relying on centralized entities. Platforms like decentralized lending protocols enable individuals to access credit by staking collateral in the form of crypto-assets, significantly reducing the barriers typically associated with traditional credit systems (Gramlich et al., 2022; Schär, 2021).

Additionally, DeFi enhances liquidity and accessibility by tokenizing traditional and novel asset classes. Through decentralized exchanges and liquidity pools, participants can trade and stake assets globally, with minimal latency and cost. Such systems are particularly valuable in underbanked regions, where traditional financial infrastructure is limited. By offering fractional ownership and innovative funding mechanisms, DeFi bridges the gap for small-scale investors and entrepreneurs seeking capital (Gramlich et al., 2022; Schär, 2021).

5.2.6 *Smart Contracts for Real-Time Execution of Financing Decisions*

Smart contracts are agreements encoded directly into software that run on blockchain networks. They automatically carry out financial transactions once specific conditions are met, removing the need for intermediaries and minimizing the risk of human error (Global, 2022). In capital structure adjustments, smart contracts can automate processes such as debt issuance, repayments, and equity distributions, ensuring timely and accurate execution of financing decisions. This automation enhances operational efficiency and allows firms to respond swiftly to changing financial needs. Blockchain-based bonds have the potential to improve the efficiency of traditional capital market operations (Crabb, 2019).

Blockchain-Enabled Tokenization for Fundraising and Debt Restructuring Tokenization involves representing physical assets as digital tokens recorded on a blockchain. This process enables fractional ownership, increased liquidity, and easier transferability of assets. In fundraising, firms can issue tokens representing equity or debt instruments to raise capital from a broad investor base without geographical limitations. Tokenization also facilitates debt restructuring by allowing existing debt to be converted into digital tokens, which can be traded or utilized in DeFi protocols for refinancing. This approach enhances market efficiency and provides firms with innovative tools for managing their capital structures. For example, the tokenization of financial assets can lead to significant operational cost savings and improved liquidity by shortening settlement cycles and enabling 24/7 market operations (Darlin et al., 2022; https://www.reuters.com/technology/abu-dhabi-firm-launch-tokenized-ustreasuries-fund-2024-10-31; Zhitomirskiy et al., 2023).

In summary, as illustrated in Fig. 5.1, the integration of DeFi, smart contracts, and tokenization into financial management practices offers firms enhanced flexibility and efficiency in adjusting their capital structures. By leveraging these blockchain-based solutions, companies can optimize their financial strategies to better navigate the complexities of modern financial markets.

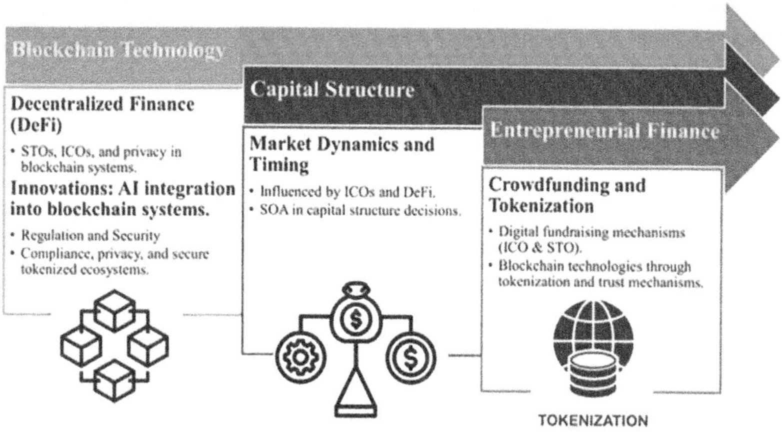

Fig. 5.1 Overview of the Synergies and Interconnections Between Blockchain Technology, Entrepreneurial Finance, and Capital Structure. (*Source* Author)

5.3 Blockchain-Driven Financial Adjustments in Startups

5.3.1 Enhancing Financial Flexibility

In the rapidly evolving landscape of technology startups, maintaining financial flexibility is crucial for adapting to market changes and seizing growth opportunities.Blockchain technology enables greater flexibility by providing real-time data access and supporting decentralized financing systems.

5.3.2 Real-Time Data and Decision-Making for Capital Adjustments

Blockchain's decentralized ledger provides startups with immediate access to accurate and transparent financial data. This real-time visibility enables informed decision-making regarding capital structure adjustments (Wang et al., 2022). For instance, the implementation of smart contracts can automate financial transactions and compliance checks, allowing startups to respond swiftly to funding needs or market shifts. The transparency inherent in blockchain technology also facilitates better risk assessment and management, as all transactions are recorded and immutable, providing a reliable basis for strategic financial decisions.

5.3.3 Decentralized Systems Reducing Delays and Costs in Financing Activities

Conventional financing typically relies on intermediaries, which can cause delays and raise costs. Blockchain removes this dependency by facilitating peer-to-peer transactions via decentralized finance (DeFi) platforms. This reduction in intermediaries accelerates the financing process and lowers associated costs, making capital more accessible to startups. For example, DeFi platforms allow startups to engage in direct lending and borrowing, providing flexible financing options without the constraints of traditional banking systems. Additionally, the automation of processes through smart contracts reduces administrative overhead, further enhancing financial efficiency (Gramlich et al., 2022; Schär, 2021; Wu & Wu, 2022).

In summary, blockchain technology empowers startups by providing real-time financial data and streamlining financing activities through decentralization. These capabilities enhance financial flexibility, enabling startups to adjust their capital structures efficiently and effectively in response to the dynamic business environment.

5.3.4 *Improving Access to Capital*

In the evolving landscape of startup financing, blockchain-based fundraising mechanisms such as Initial Coin Offerings (ICOs) and Security Token Offerings (STOs) have emerged as viable alternatives to traditional funding methods. These innovative approaches offer distinct advantages in terms of accessibility and investor participation.

5.3.5 *Initial Coin Offerings and Security Token Offerings*

Emerging Funding Alternatives Initial Coin Offerings (ICOs) have emerged as a fundraising mechanism where startups issue digital tokens to investors, typically receiving popular cryptocurrencies like Bitcoin or Ethereum in return. These tokens often grant access to platforms, services, or potential profits. The ICO concept was introduced by J.R. Willett in 2012, with Mastercoin (later renamed Omni Coin) pioneering this approach on the Bitcoin blockchain in 2013. Since then, ICOs have expanded rapidly, largely relying on Ethereum's decentralized application (dApp) platform.

By the end of 2018, the number of ICO projects surpassed 2,000, collectively raising more than $10 billion over just two years (2017–2018). This rapid growth posed a substantial challenge to traditional funding routes. For instance, during the second quarter of 2018 alone, ICOs raised roughly $9 billion, which amounted to 56% of the capital raised via U.S. initial public offerings (IPOs) in the same period, according to data from CB Insights and PwC.

Prominent ICO successes include Tezos, which raised $232 million, and Blockstack, which secured $52 million. Both ventures created decentralized ecosystems aimed at supporting dApps, underscoring ICOs' potential to transform fundraising models. While ICOs offer rapid access to capital and a broad investor base, they often face regulatory uncertainties that can expose both issuers and investors to risks (Tao et al., 2023; Wats et al., 2024).

5.3.6 *Security Token Offerings (STOs)*

STOs represent a more regulated evolution of ICOs, where the issued tokens are classified as securities and are subject to federal securities laws. These tokens are backed by tangible assets or company profits, providing investors with legal rights such as ownership, dividends, or profit sharing. STOs combine the benefits of blockchain technology with the regulatory oversight of traditional financial markets, potentially offering greater investor protection and legitimacy (Lambert et al., 2022). For many smaller companies, including startups, security token offerings (STOs) present an appealing financing option. They often provide a faster and more straightforward way to raise capital compared to traditional methods such as initial public offerings (IPOs), venture capital investments, or conventional bank financing. Following concerns over investor protection and widespread fraud in ICOs (Momtaz et al., 2019), security tokens have developed as a more reliable and regulated form of investment (Lambert et al., 2022).

5.3.7 *Lower Barriers to Financing and Increased Investor Participation*

Both Initial Coin Offerings (ICOs) and Security Token Offerings (STOs) significantly lower the barriers to entry for startups and investors alike. Traditional fundraising approaches, such as venture capital or public offerings, often demand substantial resources and access to established networks, which can be particularly challenging for early-stage startups. In contrast, ICOs and STOs enable companies to directly reach a global pool of investors, democratizing the fundraising process and expanding access to capital. Additionally, the tokenization of assets facilitates fractional ownership, allowing investors to participate with smaller capital contributions. This inclusivity not only diversifies the investor base but also enhances market liquidity. Furthermore, the integration of smart contracts automates various processes, reducing administrative overhead and accelerating the fundraising timeline. This efficiency allows startups to secure funding more quickly and cost-effectively than through conventional methods.

However, it is essential to recognize that while these methods offer significant advantages, they also come with challenges. Regulatory compliance is a critical concern, as the legal landscape surrounding ICOs and STOs continues to evolve. Additionally, market volatility poses risks for both startups and investors, while thorough due diligence is necessary to ensure sound investment decisions. These challenges highlight the importance of balancing innovation with caution in the rapidly growing tokenized fundraising ecosystem.In conclusion, ICOs and STOs provide startups with innovative avenues for capital acquisition, lowering traditional barriers and enhancing investor participation. As the regulatory environment evolves, these mechanisms may become increasingly integral to the startup financing ecosystem.

5.3.8 *Automation and Risk Mitigation*

Incorporating smart contracts into financial operations offers significant advantages in automating processes and mitigating risks, particularly in debt restructuring and compliance management.

Smart Contracts Automating Debt Restructuring and Compliance Smart contracts are agreements encoded directly into blockchain-based software that execute automatically when conditions are met. In debt restructuring, they can handle the creation and administration of debt instruments, making sure repayments and interest calculations follow the agreed terms exactly. For example, smart contracts can track whether debt covenants, like certain debt-to-equity ratios are being respected, and automatically issue alerts or take corrective steps if violations happen (Global, 2022). This level of automation cuts down on manual intervention, lowers the chance of errors, and enforces contract compliance consistently.

5.3.9 *Reducing Transaction Costs and Errors Through Programmable Systems*

Smart contracts automate processes by cutting out intermediaries, which simplifies workflows and lowers transaction costs. Without manual steps, the chance of mistakes drops, improving both the accuracy and efficiency of financial transactions. In supply chain management, for example, smart contracts have been shown to reduce administrative costs and errors by automating processes and enhancing transparency (Crabb, 2019). This efficiency is particularly beneficial in complex financial operations, where precision is crucial, and the cost of errors can be substantial.

In summary, the integration of smart contracts into financial systems facilitates automated debt restructuring and compliance monitoring, leading to reduced transaction costs and minimized errors. This technological advancement enhances the overall efficiency and reliability of financial operations.

5.4 Challenges and Ethical Considerations

5.4.1 Barriers to Blockchain Adoption: Regulatory Frameworks, Scalability, and Interoperability

Despite its transformative potential, blockchain technology faces significant challenges that impede its widespread adoption. A primary concern is the lack of clear regulatory frameworks, which creates uncertainty for businesses and investors. Without well-defined legal guidelines, companies may hesitate to implement blockchain solutions due to fears of non-compliance or future legal repercussions. This regulatory ambiguity can deter investment and slow innovation in the blockchain space. For instance, financial institutions may be reluctant to adopt blockchain without explicit guidance from regulatory bodies, leading to a cautious approach toward integration.

Scalability remains a major challenge for blockchain networks. Many existing systems have difficulty processing high transaction volumes quickly, leading to delays and increased fees during busy periods. This restricts their competitiveness against traditional centralized payment platforms capable of handling thousands of transactions per second. To overcome this, solutions like second layer protocols such as Bitcoin's Lightning Network that facilitates off-chain transactions and the transition to proof of stake consensus models, exemplified by Ethereum 2.0, aim to boost scalability and reduce energy consumption (Alghamdi et al., 2024).

Interoperability is also a critical issue. The current blockchain ecosystem is fragmented, with numerous isolated blockchains operating independently. This lack of seamless communication between different blockchain platforms limits the technology's potential for widespread application. Bridging this gap is essential for creating a more connected and efficient blockchain infrastructure. Projects like Polkadot and Cosmos are working to create blockchain ecosystems that can interoperate smoothly, enabling different blockchains to exchange information and transactions. However, widespread adoption of these solutions is still pending, and without interoperability, the blockchain ecosystem remains fragmented, which can stifle innovation and adoption (Ren et al., 2023). Addressing these challenges is crucial for the future development and integration of blockchain technology across various industries. Collaborative efforts among policymakers, industry leaders, and technologists are necessary to establish clear regulations, enhance scalability, and improve interoperability, thereby unlocking the full potential of blockchain.

5.4.2 *Ethical Concerns: Privacy, Transparency, and ESG Compliance*

Blockchain technology presents several ethical considerations, particularly concerning Privacy, Transparency, and Environmental, Social, & Governance (ESG) compliance. While the transparency inherent in blockchain ensures accountability, it can inadvertently expose sensitive information, leading to privacy concerns especially when transactions are linked to personal identities. The immutable nature of blockchain records means that once data is recorded, it cannot be altered or deleted, necessitating a careful balance between transparency and confidentiality, especially when handling personal data. This tension between openness and privacy is a critical issue in the deployment of blockchain systems (Council, 2024). Moreover, aligning blockchain operations with ESG criteria is essential for sustainable and ethical technology deployment. Blockchain can enhance ESG compliance by providing transparent and immutable records that facilitate accurate reporting and supply chain transparency. However, the energy consumption associated with some blockchain networks raises environmental concerns, highlighting the need for adopting more sustainable practices within the technology.

5.4.3 *Strategies to Overcome Barriers and Maintain Ethical Standards*

To effectively address challenges in blockchain adoption while upholding ethical standards, a multifaceted approach is essential. Engaging with regulatory bodies to establish clear guidelines is crucial for facilitating compliance and encouraging widespread adoption. Implementing scalability solutions, such as sharding and off-chain transactions, can significantly enhance performance and accommodate network growth. Developing interoperability protocols enables seamless communication between diverse blockchain platforms, thereby overcoming integration issues. Employing advanced cryptographic techniques is vital for protecting user privacy without compromising transparency. Additionally, integrating Environmental, Social, & Governance (ESG) considerations by adopting energy-efficient consensus mechanisms and ensuring ethical governance aligns blockchain operations with sustainability standards (Zhou et al., 2020).

These strategies collectively contribute to a more robust, efficient, and ethically sound blockchain ecosystem. Active regulatory engagement not only aids in compliance but also builds trust among users and stakeholders, fostering a conducive environment for innovation. Scalability solutions address the pressing issue of transaction bottlenecks, ensuring that blockchain networks can handle increased demand without compromising speed or efficiency. Interoperability protocols break down silos between different blockchain systems, facilitating a more interconnected and versatile digital infrastructure. Advanced cryptographic measures safeguard user data, striking a balance between the openness of blockchain and the necessity for confidentiality. Finally, ESG integration reflects a commitment to responsible technology deployment, ensuring that blockchain advancements contribute positively to environmental sustainability and ethical governance (Buterin et al., 2024).

By adopting these comprehensive strategies, stakeholders can navigate the complexities of blockchain technology, promoting its growth and integration across various sectors while maintaining high ethical standards.

5.5 Future Trends and Implications

5.5.1 *Advances in Blockchain, AI, and IoT Impacting Capital Structure Decisions*

The convergence of blockchain with Artificial Intelligence (AI) and the Internet of Things (IoT) is poised to transform capital structure decisions. AI can analyze vast datasets to inform optimal capital structures, while IoT devices can provide real-time data to enhance decision-making.

Blockchain ensures the security and integrity of this data, facilitating more informed and agile financial strategies (Zuo, 2024).

5.5.2 *Role of Decentralized Autonomous Organizations (DAOs) in Corporate Governance*

Decentralized Autonomous Organizations (DAOs) represent a novel approach to corporate governance, operating through smart contracts on blockchain platforms. DAOs enable stakeholder participation in decision-making processes without centralized authority, potentially leading to more democratic and transparent governance structures. This model can influence capital structure decisions by aligning them more closely with stakeholder interests (Ding et al., 2021).

5.5.3 *Policy Frameworks to Support Blockchain Adoption in Financial Systems*

Developing comprehensive policy frameworks is crucial to support blockchain adoption in financial systems. Such frameworks should address regulatory clarity, standardization, and security to foster innovation while protecting stakeholders.

Collaborative efforts between governments, industry participants, and academia are essential to create an environment conducive to the integration of blockchain technology in financial management.

5.6 Conclusion and Recommendations

5.6.1 *Summary of Findings on Blockchain's Role in Speeding Up Capital Structure Adjustments*

This study highlights the transformative potential of blockchain technology in enhancing the Speed of Adjustment (SOA) in capital structures, particularly for technology startups navigating dynamic and uncertain environments. The research underscores the role of decentralized finance (DeFi) platforms, such as Aave, which facilitate efficient capital allocation and liquidity management by offering decentralized lending and borrowing mechanisms. These platforms reduce reliance on traditional financial systems, although challenges such as regulatory ambiguities and technical vulnerabilities persist. Nevertheless, as DeFi matures, its capacity to drive financial inclusion and global innovation is expected to grow.

Another critical aspect is the automation enabled by smart contracts, which streamline financial transactions and compliance checks. This allows startups to respond swiftly to funding needs or shifts in the market, thereby enhancing financial flexibility and operational efficiency. Additionally, tokenization, which involves creating digital representations of assets, provides innovative tools for startups to raise funds and restructure debt. By enabling fractional ownership and increased liquidity, tokenization supports greater financial agility in a competitive market environment.

5.6.2 *Practical Recommendations for Entrepreneurs, Investors, and Policymakers*

Entrepreneurs should consider leveraging decentralized finance platforms to access flexible financing options, which reduces their dependence on traditional banking systems and enhances their capacity for capital adjustments. The adoption of smart contracts can further automate financial operations, ensuring timely execution of transactions and compliance with regulations, leading to cost savings and operational efficiencies. Moreover, tokenizing assets can enable startups to attract a broader investor base, thereby increasing liquidity and improving financial flexibility.

For investors, it is essential to evaluate startups based on their integration of blockchain technologies, as these can indicate enhanced operational efficiency and adaptability in managing capital structures. By diversifying their investment portfolios to include ventures that leverage blockchain for financial adjustments, investors can position themselves to benefit from the resilience and growth potential exhibited by such companies in rapidly evolving markets.

Policymakers should focus on developing clear and comprehensive regulatory frameworks to support blockchain applications in finance. These regulations should foster innovation while ensuring compliance and security, thereby creating an environment conducive to the technology's widespread adoption. Additionally, promoting education and awareness initiatives can equip stakeholders with the knowledge necessary to understand the benefits and risks associated with blockchain technology, facilitating informed decision-making and broader adoption across industries.

5.6.3 *Directions for Future Research in Blockchain-Enabled Financial Strategies*

Future research should delve into several key areas to advance understanding and application of blockchain technology in financial strategies. Longitudinal studies are needed to assess the sustained impact of blockchain technology on capital structure adjustments and overall financial performance over time. Comparative analyses of different blockchain platforms and tools can provide insights into their effectiveness in enhancing SOA, identifying best practices and areas requiring improvement. Furthermore, regulatory impact studies should explore how varying regulatory environments influence the adoption and efficacy of blockchain-enabled financial strategies, offering valuable guidance for policymakers and international stakeholders.

By addressing these research directions, scholars and practitioners can contribute to a deeper understanding of blockchain's potential in financial management. This will not only drive innovation but also support the development of strategic approaches to integrating blockchain technology in the broader financial landscape. innovation and strategic development in the field.

References

Alghamdi, T. A., Khalid, R., & Javaid, N. (2024). A survey of blockchain based systems: Scalability issues and solutions, applications and future challenges. *IEEE Access, 12*, 79626–79651. https://doi.org/10.1109/ACCESS.2024.3408868

Baker, M., & Wurgler, J. (2002). Market timing and capital structure. *The Journal of Finance, 57*(1), 1–32.

Bellavitis, C., Filatotchev, I., Kamuriwo, D.S., Vanacker, T.: Entrepreneurial finance: new frontiers of research and practice: Editorial for the special issue embracing entrepreneurial funding innovations (2017)

Berger, A. N., & Udell, G. F. (1998). The economics of small business finance: The roles of private equity and debt markets in the financial growth cycle. *Journal of Banking & Finance, 22*(6–8), 613–673.

Bradley, M., Jarrell, G. A., & Kim, E. H. (1984). On the existence of an optimal capital structure: Theory and evidence. *The Journal of Finance, 39*(3), 857–878.

Buterin, V., Illum, J., Nadler, M., Schär, F., & Soleimani, A. (2024). Blockchain privacy and regulatory compliance: Towards a practical equilibrium. *Blockchain Research and Applications, 5*(1), 100176.

Campino, J., Brochado, A., & Rosa, Á. (2022). Initial coin offerings (icos): Why do they succeed? *Financial Innovation, 8*(1), 17.

Council, F.T. (2024). Blockchain and data privacy: The future of technology compliance. *Forbes*. https://www.forbes.com/councils/forbestechcouncil/2024/02/15/blockchainand-data-privacy-the-future-of-technology-compliance, accessed: 2025-01-14

Crabb, J. (2019). Société générale blockchain issuance a sign of things to come. *International Financial Law Review*. https://www.iflr.com/article/2a638wpvv67olpsbb1gcg/societe-generaleblockchain-issuance-a-sign-of-things-to-come, accessed: 2025-01-14

Darlin, M., Palaiokrassas, G., Tassiulas, L. (2022). Debt-financed collateral and stability risks in the defi ecosystem. In *2022 4th Conference on Blockchain Research & Applications for Innovative Networks and Services (BRAINS)*. (pp. 5–12). IEEE.

Ding, W.W., Liang, X., Hou, J., Wang, G., Yuan, Y., Li, J., Wang, F.Y. (2021). Parallel governance for decentralized autonomous organizations enabled by blockchain and smart contracts. In: *2021 IEEE 1st International Conference on Digital Twins and Parallel Intelligence (DTPI)* (pp. 1–4). https://doi.org/10.1109/DTPI52967.2021.9540069

Eddleston, K. A., Ladge, J. J., Mitteness, C., & Balachandra, L. (2016). Do you see what I see? Signaling effects of gender and firm characteristics on financing entrepreneurial ventures. *Entrepreneurship Theory and Practice, 40*(3), 489–514.

Ghaemi Asl, M., Ghasemi Doudkanlou, M., Canarella, G., Miller, S.M. (2024). On the speed of adjustment (soa) toward the target financial leverage ratios and its determinants: Evidence from the capital structure of the ict sector. *Journal of Evolutionary Economics* pp. 1–38

SP Global. (2022). Smart contracts could improve efficiency and transparency in financial transactions. https://www.spglobal.com/en/research-insights/specialreports/smart-contracts-could-improve-efficiency-and-transparency-in-financialtransactions, accessed: 2025-01-14

Gramlich, V., Principato, M., Schellinger, B., Sedlmeir, J., Amend, J., Stramm,J., Zwede, T., Strüker, J., Urbach, N. (2022). Decentralized finance (defi): Foundations, applications, potentials, and challenges. *Applications, Potentials, and Challenges*.

Haddad, C., Hornuf, L. (2021). *The impact of fintech startups on financial institutions' performance and default risk.*

Hechavarría, D. M., Matthews, C. H., & Reynolds, P. D. (2016). Does start-up financing influence start-up speed? Evidence from the panel study of entrepreneurial dynamics. *Small Business Economics, 46*, 137–167.

Islam, M. M., Islam, M. K., Shahjalal, M., Chowdhury, M. Z., & Jang, Y. M. (2023). A low-cost cross-border payment system based on auditable cryptocurrency with consortium blockchain: Joint digital currency. *IEEE Transactions on Services Computing, 16*(3), 1616–1629. https://doi.org/10.1109/TSC.2022.3207224

Khan, S. N., Loukil, F., Ghedira-Guegan, C., Benkhelifa, E., & Bani-Hani, A. (2021). Blockchain smart contracts: Applications, challenges, and future trends. *Peer-to-Peer Networking and Applications, 14*, 2901–2925.

Kondova, G., & Simonella, G. (2019). Blockchain in startup financing: Icos and stos in Switzerland. *Journal of Strategic Innovation and Sustainability, 14*(6), 43–48.

Lambert, T., Liebau, D., Roosenboom, P. (2022). Security token offerings. *Small Business Economics* (pp. 1–27).

Lemma, T., & Negash, M. (2014). Determinants of the adjustment speed of capital structure: Evidence from developing economies. *Journal of Applied Accounting Research, 15*(1), 64–99.

Manigart, S., & Khosravi, S. (2024). Unanswered questions in entrepreneurial finance. *Venture Capital, 26*(1), 1–29.

Meckling, W.H., Jensen, M.C. (1976). Theory of the firm. In *Managerial Behavior, Agency Costs and Ownership Structure.*

Miller, M. H. (1977). Debt and taxes. *The Journal of Finance, 32*(2), 261–275.

Minola, T., Cassia, L., & Criaco, G. (2013). Financing patterns in new technology-based firms: An extension of the pecking order theory. *International Journal of Entrepreneurship and Small Business, 19*(2), 212–233.

Mohamed, H. (2021). Decentralizing finance via cryptocurrencies and tokenization of assets and peer-to-peer platforms. *International Journal of Islamic Economics, 3*(01), 1–16.

Momtaz, P.P., Rennertseder, K., Schröder, H. (2019). *Token offerings: A revolution incorporate finance*? Available at SSRN 3346964.

Myers, S. (1984). *Corporate financing and investment decisions when firms have information that investors do not have.*

Myers, S.C. (1984). *Capital structure puzzle.*

Paul, S., Whittam, G., & Wyper, J. (2007). The pecking order hypothesis: Does it apply to start-up firms? *Journal of Small Business and Enterprise Development, 14*(1), 8–21.

Rella, L. (2019). Blockchain technologies and remittances: From financial inclusion to correspondent banking. *Frontiers in Blockchain, 2*, 14.

Ren, K., Ho, N. M., Loghin, D., Nguyen, T. T., Ooi, B. C., Ta, Q. T., & Zhu, F. (2023). Interoperability in blockchain: A survey. *IEEE Transactions on Knowledge and Data Engineering, 35*(12), 12750–12769. https://doi.org/10.1109/TKDE.2023.3275220

Reuters: Is blockchain the next big thing for insurance companies? Reuters. (2024). https://www.reuters.com/legal/legalindustry/is-blockchain-next-bigthing-insurance-companies-2024-10-09/, accessed: 2025-01-14

Reuters: Abu Dhabi firm launches tokenized us treasuries fund. (2024). https://www.reuters.com/technology/abu-dhabi-firm-launch-tokenized-ustreasuries-fund-2024-10-31, accessed: 2025-01-14

Samuelsson, M., Söderblom, A., & McKelvie, A. (2021). Path dependence in new ventures' capital structures. *Entrepreneurship Theory and Practice, 45*(2), 319–349.

Schär, F. (2021). Decentralized finance: On blockchain-and smart contract-based financial markets. *FRB of St. Louis Review.*

Schückes, M., & Gutmann, T. (2021). Why do startups pursue initial coin offerings (icos)? The role of economic drivers and social identity on funding choice. *Small Business Economics, 57*(2), 1027–1052.

Sharma, N., Saurabh, S. (2024). *Leverage complexity quest.*

Sharma, V., Agrawal, R., & Manupati, V. K. (2024). Blockchain technology as an enabler for digital trust in supply chain: Evolution, issues and opportunities. *International Journal of System Assurance Engineering and Management, 15*(9), 4183–4209.

Shevchenko, E., Lunsford, R. (2023). Blockchain disruption in finance: JPMorgan Chase's success story and the transfer of quorum to consensys. *Journal of Finance and Accountancy 32.*

SIX Digital Exchange: Six digital exchange successfully tokenizes private shares on its regulated blockchain-based central securities depository in partnership with f10 and aequitec. (2022). https://www.sdx.com/news/six-digital-exchangesuccessfully-tokenizes-private-shares-on-its-regulated-blockchain-based-centralsecurities-depository-in-partnership-with-f10-and-aequitec/, accessed: 2025-01-13

Sydow, J., Schreyögg, G., & Koch, J. (2009). Organizational path dependence: Opening the black box. *Academy of Management Review, 34*(4), 689–709.

Tao, Z., Peng, B., & Ma, L. (2023). Optimal initial coin offering under speculative token trading. *European Journal of Operational Research, 306*(2), 632–644.

Wang, G., Li, J., Wang, X., Li, J., Yuan, Y., & Wang, F. Y. (2022). Blockchain-based cryptomanagement for reliable real-time decision-making. *IEEE Transactions on Computational Social Systems, 10*(6), 3333–3342.

Wats, S., Joshi, M., & Singh, S. (2024). Initial coin offerings: Current trends and future research directions. *Quality & Quantity, 58*(2), 1361–1387.

Wu, B., Wu, B. (2022). Decentralized finance (defi): Reinventing financial services. In *Blockchain for Teens: With Case Studies and Examples of Blockchain Across Various Industries*, (pp. 315–384). Springer

Zhang, Y. (2020). Developing cross-border blockchain financial transactions under the belt and road initiative. *The Chinese Journal of Comparative Law, 8*(1), 143–176.

Zhitomirskiy, E., Schmid, S., & Walther, M. (2023). Tokenizing assets with dividend payouts—A legally compliant and flexible design. *Digital Finance, 5*(3), 563–580.

Zhou, Q., Huang, H., Zheng, Z., & Bian, J. (2020). Solutions to scalability of blockchain: A survey. *IEEE Access, 8*, 16440–16455. https://doi.org/10.1109/ACCESS.2020.2967218

Zuo, Y. (2024). Exploring the synergy: AI enhancing blockchain, blockchain empowering AI, and their convergence across IoT applications and beyond. *IEEE Internet of Things Journal*. https://doi.org/10.1109/JIOT.2024.3507746

CHAPTER 6

AI-Based Start-Ups and Applications in the Sports Industry

Halil Erdem Akoğlu, Övünç Erdeveciler, and Kadir Yıldız

H. E. Akoğlu (✉)
Department of Sports Management, Faculty of Sports Sciences, Niğde Ömer Halisdemir University, Niğde, Türkiye
e-mail: erdemakoglu@hotmail.com

Ö. Erdeveciler
Department of Sports Management, Faculty of Sports Sciences, Ankara University, Ankara, Türkiye
e-mail: erdeveciler@ankara.edu.tr

K. Yıldız
Department of Sports Management, Faculty of Sports Sciences, Manisa Celal Bayar University, Manisa, Türkiye
e-mail: kadir.yildiz@cbu.edu.tr

D. Kumar et al. (eds.), *Evolving Trends in Technology Entrepreneurship*, Palgrave Studies in Global Entrepreneurship,
https://doi.org/10.1007/978-981-95-7441-4_6

6.1 Introduction

The sports industry has emerged as a key driver of economic growth, increasingly attracting commercial investment (Li, 2021). Its growing prominence has positioned it among the ten largest economies globally. Technological advancements play a crucial role in this ongoing expansion (Erdeveciler & Cengiz, 2024). In particular, developments associated with Industry 4.0 have accelerated the integration and visibility of artificial intelligence (AI) tools across the sector. AI enables the sports industry to collect, analyse and interpret data from diverse sources, including content creation, fan engagement and ticket sales. For instance, coaches can refine training programmes and match strategies in real time using feedback from AI-powered sensors (Tan & Ran, 2023). Furthermore, AI enhances the spectator experience by offering personalised content and product recommendations, thus creating new forms of engagement (Glebova et al., 2020). These developments have also created novel business opportunities in areas such as marketing, sales and digital media.

While the impact of AI on sports remains a subject of debate, both its advantages and limitations continue to draw significant attention from the public and the academic community. This technological transformation is reshaping the sports landscape—affecting everything from athlete training and performance to fan interaction and the communication strategies of sports organisations. Today, sports clubs, federations and businesses are actively adopting AI-driven innovations in performance analytics, fan engagement and operational processes. In response to this momentum, entrepreneurs have developed a wide range of AI-based applications tailored to the needs of the sports industry. Simultaneously, global technology giants such as Amazon, Microsoft and Google are steadily increasing their investments in these emerging ventures. This section explores some of the most widely adopted AI-driven start-ups in the sports domain.

6.2 Conceptual Framework

6.2.1 *Advantages of Big Data and Artificial Intelligence Technologies for Sports Organisations*

When considering the benefits of AI applications in the sports industry, the rapid generation, processing, delivery and storage of data are of paramount importance to all stakeholders. AI's capacity to deliver personalised information in real time enables a highly consumer-centric approach, pushing the boundaries of traditional engagement models. Through the diversification of AI applications via start-ups, companies aim to enhance both efficiency and profitability. Although AI is widely recognised as a catalyst for success, companies primarily invest in it to gain a competitive edge and expand their market share (Pottala, 2018). Globant (NYSE: GLOB), in its report on the growing influence of AI in sports and entertainment, projects that the global AI in sports market will reach $19.2 billion by 2030, underscoring the rapid acceleration of investment in AI-driven technologies within the industry.

6.2.2 *Artificial Intelligence-Supported Innovations Attract the Attention of Large Companies*

When traditional decision-making methods are employed, the reliance on limited and superficial data often results in inaccurate or misleading conclusions. The advent of artificial intelligence has significantly transformed this paradigm. AI-enabled start-ups now allow companies to process large-scale data sets, forecast market trends, enhance product and service quality, automate routine operations, and extract actionable insights. These capabilities facilitate the functioning of smart factories with minimal human intervention, particularly in areas such as production control, quality assurance and maintenance (Basri, Fahad, Veisieh, Ouaissa, & Ouaissa, 2025). As a result, the number of AI-driven applications is expanding rapidly, benefiting both business operations and the broader sports industry.

In the context of marketing, AI-powered recommendation systems have been shown to increase the likelihood of consumers purchasing products aligned with their preferences. Sales departments can leverage AI to identify who is most likely to buy, what they are likely to purchase, and the optimal timing for engagement. For sports organisations, this level of insight enables more effective consumer interaction and supports the development of targeted sponsorship strategies (Pottala, 2018).

Meanwhile, the sports betting sector has experienced substantial growth, with AI becoming a key tool for enhancing predictive accuracy. Rather than relying solely on personal expertise or intuition, bettors are increasingly turning to AI-based models to improve their odds of success. Multi-layer perceptron (MLP) networks, for instance, are frequently cited as highly effective in forecasting football match outcomes (Kollár, 2021).

The enhanced accuracy of these systems has fuelled the growth of betting participation and drawn significant interest from betting companies. The U.S. sports betting market was valued at USD 13.76 billion in 2023 and is projected to grow at a compound annual growth rate (CAGR) of 10.5% from 2024 to 2030. Similarly, the European market, estimated at USD 33.75 billion in 2023, is expected to grow at a CAGR of 9.9% over the same period (Grand View Research, 2023).

Another critical area of AI integration is wearable sports technology. Advanced sensors such as three-axis gyroscopes, accelerometers and optical heart rate monitors now enable the effective tracking of various physiological and locational data during physical activity (Wang, 2017). The market for AI-integrated wearables continues to expand, with global projections reaching $152 billion by 2030 (Markets & Markets, 2025).

Enhancing athletic performance and preventing injuries remain top priorities for sports clubs. The loss of a high-profile athlete—due to injury or underperformance—can result in significant financial and reputational setbacks, including decreased fan loyalty, diminished brand value and sponsorship losses. Consequently, clubs are increasingly investing in AI-based solutions to optimise athlete preparedness. AI is widely applied in sports medicine for injury prevention, performance enhancement, rehabilitation and recovery (Guelmami et al., 2023). The most common AI applications in this area are outlined below:

Injury prevention: Through the use of AI, the aim is to prevent potential injuries based on information gathered from player data, biomechanical and physiological parameters.

Training Optimization: Thanks to AI applications, it is becoming increasingly popular to apply appropriate training methods adapted from personalised data to athletes. There is a process evolving from the classical times when everyone used the same training methods to individualised training.

Rehabilitation and Recovery: Thanks to simultaneous data sets, the use of AI tools in the creation of appropriate programmes for the rehabilitation of the athlete can produce more accurate results in decision-making and treatment initiation.

Performance Development: Image processing through AI, evaluation of physiological parameters, nutrition programmes, etc., are among the most common areas of use to support athlete development in technical and tactical terms with appropriate analysis.

6.2.3 *The Contribution of Artificial Intelligence in Fan Engagement and Media Management*

In the media industry, artificial intelligence has emerged as an increasingly critical business tool and strategic capability. While AI's transformative effects are evident across numerous sectors, its influence is becoming particularly pronounced in the media. AI-driven platforms now span a wide array of communication channels, encompassing both traditional outlets—such as television, radio and print—and digital environments including online publications, social media networks and streaming services (Govindaraj et al., 2023). A European market study revealed that 80% of media professionals anticipate a significant impact of AI on their sector, with 62% believing it will enhance decision-making processes and 47% expecting improvements in productivity (Shields, 2018).

As the integration of AI in media deepens, the interaction between sports fans and content continues to evolve. The concept of fandom is undergoing a transformation, where fans increasingly share real-time excitement through technological devices and digital platforms rather than attending live events in person. The global adoption of AI in fan engagement and sports broadcasting has facilitated the development of interactive and personalised viewing experiences (Xu & Baghaei, 2025). For instance, WSC Sports offers AI-personalised content formats and tailored viewing channels, enhancing the fan experience. Similarly, the sports platform is positioning itself as a comprehensive provider of sports content, delivering services across 15 sports to clients worldwide.

6.3 Cluster-Based Classification of AI Start-Ups in Sports Industry

Before presenting detailed examples of AI-based start-ups across various sports domains, Table 6.1 clusters these start-ups based on their core technological focus. This classification enhances the clarity and readability of the following sections by grouping similar innovations under common technological frameworks.

Table 6.1 Cluster-based classification of AI start-ups in the sports industry

Cluster	*Technology base*	*Start-up examples*	*Application area*
Sensor-Based	Wearable sensors	Supersapiens, Whoop, Zone7	Performance tracking, glucose monitoring, fatigue management
Computer Vision	Image processing, 3D analysis	Uplift Labs, Sportsbox AI, HomeCourt	Biomechanical analysis, skill development
Predictive Analytics	Machine learning, forecasting	Probility AI, Field Vision, SciSports	Injury prediction, match outcome forecasting, scouting
Natural Language-Based	Text processing/chatbot	Gambly	Betting recommendations
Data Aggregation & IoT	IoT integration, data consolidation	Second Spectrum, Perch, Talnets	Performance, tactical analysis, talent identification

6.4 Artificial Intelligence Applications in the Sports Industry

Artificial intelligence applications in the sports industry are concentrated in different areas. These applications can be examined in seven main categories: wearable technologies, disability and rehabilitation, performance analytics, training systems, fan experience and media, betting and match prediction and transfer and talent discovery. These application areas and examples of start-ups in each category are summarised in Fig. 6.1.

6.4.1 Wearable Technologies and Performance Tracking

Wearables refer to electronic technologies or devices that are integrated into items designed to be comfortably worn on the body. These devices typically include motion sensors capable of capturing real-time data, which is synchronised with mobile devices or computers for monitoring purposes. While wearable technology encompasses a range of devices, activity trackers and smartwatches remain the most widely adopted (Chawla, 2020). Additionally, more invasive forms of wearables—such as implantable microchips or smart tattoos—are gaining attention for their advanced data collection capabilities (Ometov et al., 2021).

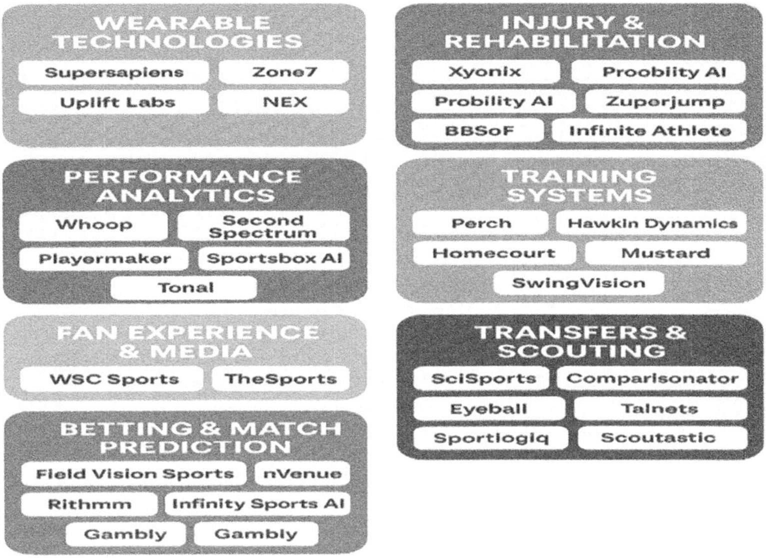

Fig. 6.1 Artificial intelligence applications in the sports industry and examples of start-ups

With the integration of artificial intelligence, wearable technologies are gradually replacing traditional cloud-based systems. This transition is expected to significantly reduce the latency between data collection and interpretation. Furthermore, although cloud technologies are susceptible to various security vulnerabilities, AI-driven wearable devices are considered to offer lower risks of data breaches (Gaffar & Gearhart, 2024).

AI is also increasingly utilised for performance tracking in sports. By analysing a broad spectrum of parameters—such as player metrics, travel schedules and sleep patterns—AI systems can generate personalised recommendations to optimise athletic performance (Calleja-Gonzalez et al., 2020).

The following section presents selected start-ups operating in the AI-enabled wearable technology and performance tracking domain within the sports industry (Table 6.2).

Table 6.2 Examples of AI-enabled wearable technology and performance monitoring start-ups

Start-ups	*Description*
NEX	NEX is an AI-driven eSports start-up that offers a platform called *Playground*, designed to enhance player performance and engagement through personalised coaching and data-based insights. The platform provides features such as skill assessment, performance monitoring, and goal setting, enabling users to track their development and maintain motivation. https://www.nex.inc/who-we-are
Zone7	Zone7 leverages AI to optimise human performance and reduce injury risk in high-performance sports environments. Its platform delivers data-driven insights for injury prediction, stress management, and performance enhancement across disciplines such as football, basketball and American football. https://zone7.ai/
Uplift Labs	Uplift Labs utilises AI-powered technology to deliver detailed 3D movement analysis for athletes using only two iPhones or iPads. The platform offers performance insights aimed at injury prevention and also enhances sports broadcasting by integrating biomechanical data. https://www.uplift.ai/
Supersapiens	Founded in 2020 and based in Atlanta, Supersapiens is a sports technology start-up that offers real-time glucose monitoring through wearable biosensors, powered by Abbott's Libre Sense Glucose Sports Biosensor. https://www.supersapiens.com/
ZYGO	ZYGO provides app-based swimming lessons for users of all levels, supported by partnerships with swim schools and instructors. Its core product, ZYGO Solo, includes a wireless headset, transmitter and goggles. The company generates revenue through both hardware sales and subscription-based premium content. https://www.zygo.com/
Tempo	Tempo is an AI-powered home fitness system that uses 3D sensors to provide real-time feedback and adapt workout intensity based on user performance. By analysing data from each session, it personalises future workouts to match the user's evolving strength and endurance levels

Source Created by the authors

6.4.2 Artificial Intelligence Supported Athlete Health and Rehabilitation

Another significant application of artificial intelligence in sports lies in injury prevention and the enhancement of rehabilitation processes following injuries (Biró et al., 2022; Taghian et al., 2023). By leveraging data and advanced analytics, AI facilitates the prediction of potential risks, accelerates diagnostic procedures and personalises recovery protocols.

Wearable technologies and smart sensors contribute to injury prevention by continuously monitoring athletes' movements and environmental conditions, while AI-powered imaging systems enable more accurate and timely diagnoses. During rehabilitation, AI adapts treatment strategies to the individual needs of athletes, thereby ensuring more effective and efficient recovery outcomes (Elkhamisy, 2025). Table 6.3 presents several start-ups that have emerged in the field of AI-supported athlete rehabilitation.

Table 6.3 Examples of AI-enabled athlete rehabilitation start-ups

Start-ups	*Description*
Xyonix	Xyonix applies AI technologies to sports and rehabilitation therapy, focusing on injury prediction, prevention and progress monitoring to enhance efficiency and reduce treatment costs. https://www.xyonix.com/industries/health/sports-and-rehabilitation-therapy
Spark	Spark Emerging Technologies is at the forefront of this innovation, delivering advanced AI solutions that revolutionise injury prevention. https://sparkemtech.co.uk/blog/injury-prevention-ai-revolutionising-athlete-safety
Probility AI, Inc	Probability ARC is an AI-powered analytics platform that forecasts athlete availability, reliability and performance. Leveraging 26 AI models, it evaluates injury risk and performance metrics across seasonal and career timelines, offering behavioural insights to enhance longevity and effectiveness. https://probility.ai/
Zuperjump	Zuperjump provides neuromuscular fatigue analysis to help coaches and athletes detect early signs of performance decline—often observable in the nervous system before changes in heart rate—through strength and speed testing. http://www.zuperjump.com/
BBSoF	BBSoF, in collaboration with the University of Padua, offers a patented AI powered screening method (ACL Quick Check®) for on-field assessment of ACL injury risk. Its markerless motion capture system combines computer vision and deep learning to deliver comprehensive biomechanical analyses. https://www.bb-sof.com/
Infinite Athlete	Infinite Athlete develops integrated technology infrastructure for major sports by aggregating data from multiple sources. Its key products, including AI Injury Detection and the Game Operations Dashboard™, support injury prevention and enhance fan engagement through real-time tracking and personalised visual overlays. https://infiniteathlete.ai/

Source Created by the authors

Artificial intelligence has become a pivotal tool in the development and continuous enhancement of innovative technologies that have transformed modern sports training. By simulating human learning, cognition, and decision-making processes through advanced algorithms, AI can analyse vast amounts of data to increase the efficiency and effectiveness of training regimes (Roll & Wylie, 2016; Wei et al., 2021). These capabilities assist coaches and athletes in enhancing performance, providing guidance at any time and place and reducing the risk of injury.

AI applications in sports training generally fall into two primary categories: (1) strength and conditioning programmes aimed at optimising physical performance, and (2) coaching support systems designed for sport-specific technical training (Chu et al., 2019). Notably, Artificial Intelligence of Things (AIoT) technologies further enhance movement analysis by integrating big data, cloud computing and Internet of Things (IoT) infrastructures. For instance, AI-driven motion sensors used in weight training can assess athletes' form in real time, thus helping to prevent injuries (Chu et al., 2019).

Numerous AI-powered start-ups have emerged in this domain, offering cutting-edge solutions to elevate athletic performance. Some of these are outlined below (Table 6.3):

6.4.3 *Artificial Intelligence Applications in Training Processes and Start-Ups*

Artificial intelligence has become a pivotal tool in the development and continuous enhancement of innovative technologies that have transformed modern sports training. By simulating human learning, cognition and decision-making processes through advanced algorithms, AI can analyse vast amounts of data to increase the efficiency and effectiveness of training regimes (Roll & Wylie, 2016; Wei et al., 2021). These capabilities assist coaches and athletes in enhancing performance, providing guidance at any time and place and reducing the risk of injury.

AI applications in sports training generally fall into two primary categories: (1) strength and conditioning programmes aimed at optimising physical performance, and (2) coaching support systems designed for sport-specific technical training (Chu et al., 2019). Notably, Artificial Intelligence of Things (AIoT) technologies further enhance movement analysis by integrating big data, cloud computing and Internet of Things (IoT) infrastructures. For instance, AI-driven motion sensors used in weight training can assess athletes' form in real time, thus helping to prevent injuries (Chu et al., 2019).

Numerous AI-powered start-ups have emerged in this domain, offering cutting-edge solutions to elevate athletic performance. Some of these are outlined below (Table 6.4):

In addition to these systems, AI-based solutions for tactical analysis in team sports are also advancing rapidly. One notable example is SportVU, an advanced tracking system used in the NBA, which monitors player movements to analyse passing patterns, shooting behaviour and defensive strategies (Wei et al., 2021). These AI-powered analytics enable teams to optimise training approaches and enhance decision-making during games.

In summary, AI-supported training systems play a pivotal role in enhancing athletic performance. From strength conditioning to tactical analysis, AI technologies contribute significantly to modern sports science by equipping coaches and athletes with data-driven insights for more effective decision-making. Start-up-driven innovations in this domain are expected to assume an even greater role in the future of sports performance analysis and training methodologies.

6.4.4 *Artificial Intelligence Applications and Start-Ups in Betting and Match Predictions*

In sports betting, wagers are placed on the outcomes of specific events, with each possible result assigned a probability and corresponding profit margin determined by the bookmaker. If the bettor's prediction is accurate, the original stake is returned along with the associated profit; otherwise, the stake is forfeited (Hubáček et al., 2019). Globally, individuals engage in betting across various sports categories, with football being the most prominent (Stübinger et al., 2019). To capitalise on the widespread appeal of this activity, entrepreneurs have developed advanced tools to enhance predictive accuracy in sports outcomes. Among the most commonly employed machine learning techniques are artificial neural networks (ANNs) and support vector machines (SVMs), which have been widely adopted to forecast match results. Several start-ups are leveraging these technologies to offer innovative solutions in the domain of sports betting and match prediction.

Below are examples of start-up applications that utilise ANNs and SVMs for developing match prediction systems (Table 6.5):

Table 6.4 Example start-ups supported by artificial intelligence in training applications

Start-ups	*Description*
Perch	Founded in 2017 by MIT graduates, Perch is an AI-powered system that uses IoT-enabled cameras and sensors to monitor athletes during weight training, providing real-time feedback and strength analytics for coaches. https://perch.fit
Hawkin Dynamics	Founded in the U.S. in 2017, this start-up developed an AI-based ground force platform that assesses athletes' jumping ability, detects fatigue and injury risk and delivers personalised training programmes. https://www.hawkindynamics.com
Playermaker	Founded in Israel in 2016, Playermaker is an AI system that uses ankle-mounted IoT sensors to analyse footballers' movements and generate personalised development plans based on metrics such as passing, shooting and speed. https://www.playermaker.com
Whoop	Founded in 2012 by Will Ahmed, Whoop is a wearable tech start-up that monitors biometric data to optimise athletes' sleep, stress and recovery, aiming to enhance overall training efficiency. https://www.whoop.com
Second Spectrum	Founded in 2013 by Rajiv Maheswaran and Yu-Han Chang, Second Spectrum is an AI-driven tracking system used by major leagues like the NBA and Premier League to analyse athlete movements and support tactical decision-making. https://www.secondspectrum.com
Tonal	Founded in 2015 by Aly Orady, Tonal is an AI-powered smart fitness system that personalises resistance training using motion sensors to analyse muscle engagement and deliver real-time feedback on form. https://www.tonal.com
Homecourt	HomeCourt is an AI-powered basketball training app that provides personalised exercises based on player skill level and progress. Its system analyses performance data to recommend targeted workouts, offering a freemium model with advanced features through subscription. https://www.homecourt.ai/
Sportsbox AI	Founded by Jeehae Lee in 2020, Sportsbox AI develops mobile coaching apps using patent-pending 3D motion analysis and kinematic AI technology. Its flagship product, Sportsbox 3D Golf, enables 3D swing analysis from a single 2D video and provides real-time corrective feedback, offering a cost-effective alternative to traditional motion capture systems. https://www.sportsbox.ai/

(continued)

Table 6.4 (continued)

Start-ups	*Description*
SwingVision	Founded by Swupnil Sahai, SwingVision is an AI-driven tennis app that delivers real-time video analytics via iOS. Using computer vision algorithms, it tracks match and practice metrics to provide performance insights, making professional-level analysis accessible to all players. https://swing.vision/
Mustard	Founded in 2020 by Tom House and Jason Goldsmith, Mustard is an AI-powered coaching app that analyses athlete-recorded videos to assess and improve technique. Focused on golf and baseball, it leverages computer vision to deliver personalised feedback based on movement analysis. https://teammstrd.com/

Source Created by the authors

Table 6.5 Example start-ups developing match prediction systems with artificial neural networks

Start-ups	*Description*
Field Vision Sports	Field Vision, a Portland-based start-up, offers an AI-powered mobile app that provides game and player-level predictions to support informed betting decisions. It was founded by former NFL executive Scott Bouska and Stanford PhD Cameron Taylor https://www.fieldvisionsports.com/
nVenue	nVenue is an AI-powered platform that enables real-time micro-betting during live sports events. It delivers live odds and predictions across leagues such as MLB, NFL, NBA and NASCAR, and collaborates with media and betting partners, including Apple TV + Friday Night Baseball. https://www.nvenue.com/
Rithmm	Rithmm is a sports betting app that uses AI to generate personalised match and player performance predictions across leagues such as the NFL, NBA, NCAAF, NCAAM, WNBA and Golf. It aims to support faster, data-driven betting decisions. https://www.rithmm.com/
Infinity Sports AI	Infinity Sports AI develops machine learning tools for sports betting, offering high-accuracy predictions for match outcomes and player performance in leagues like the NBA and MLB. The platform delivers data-driven insights to enhance users' strategic decision-making and profit potential. https://infinitysports.ai/
Gambly	Gambly is an AI-powered betting assistant that processes natural language input to help users easily search and select betting options. It distinguishes itself through an intuitive interface and an accessible, text-based approach to betting. https://gambly.com/

Source Created by the authors

These start-ups are revolutionising sports betting and match prediction using advanced machine learning techniques such as artificial neural networks and support vector machines. Each is redefining the sports betting experience and helping sports fans make more informed and strategic betting decisions.

6.4.5 *Artificial Intelligence Applications and Start-Ups in Athlete Transfers and Talent Scouting*

The primary objective of player recruitment is to identify individuals who can positively influence a team's performance. To achieve this, clubs must evaluate multiple players and estimate their potential impact based on various performance metrics (Akoğlu & Doğaner, 2023). This process is often time-consuming and labour-intensive. However, AI-enabled applications have introduced new opportunities for clubs and managers by streamlining talent identification and evaluation. Entrepreneurs have developed platforms that facilitate player discovery, assessment and performance tracking—particularly valuable in a high-stakes, financially intensive domain such as player transfers. Moreover, AI models can forecast transfer fees by analysing player performance data, thereby assisting clubs in avoiding overvaluation and identifying undervalued talent (Sulimov, 2024). The integration of AI into transfer operations yields considerable benefits, offering both strategic recruitment advantages and financial efficiency.

Several start-ups exemplify these applications and are outlined below (Table 6.6):

These applications are some of the popular ones in the big pool. However, with constantly updated technology, new ones of these start-ups are constantly being added.

6.4.6 *Regional Dynamics of AI Start-Ups in the Sports Industry: A Comparative Perspective*

While the global AI wave in sports is largely powered by tech giants like Amazon, Google and Microsoft, a closer look at regional AI start-up ecosystems reveals distinct strategic orientations shaped by local markets.

Table 6.6 Example start-ups supported by artificial intelligence in athlete transfers and talent scouting

Start-ups	*Description*
SciSports	Founded in 2012 in the Netherlands, SciSports is a leading sports analytics company providing AI-driven insights for professional football organisations. Its services include transfer, match and performance analysis, with clients such as Ajax, KNVB and Go Ahead Eagles. https://www.scisports.com/
Comparisonator	Founded in 2020 by Erdal Kibaroğlu, Comparisonator is an AI-based analytics platform that enables performance comparisons of football players across 271 leagues. It supports data-driven decision-making in scouting and transfer processes by allowing cross-league player and team analysis. https://comparisonator.com/tr
Eyeball	Founded in 2019 by Mats Meersman, Eyeball is a digital scouting company that tracks the performance of approximately 180,000 young footballers worldwide using video and automated tracking systems. It collaborates with Premier League and other elite clubs to identify and recruit emerging talent. https://www.eyeball.club/
Talnets	Founded in 2021 by former England footballer Sol Campbell, Talnets is an AI-based scouting platform that tracks young players in countries such as South Africa, Ghana, Ivory Coast and Senegal. It collects performance data, supports talent discovery and monitors player development to maximise potential. https://talnets.ch/
Sportlogiq	Founded in 2015 in Montreal by Craig Buntin and Mehrsan Javan, Sportlogiq uses patented computer vision and machine learning technologies to capture in-game data beyond human observation. It provides real-time analytics to teams, leagues and media in sports such as hockey, soccer and American football, supporting performance improvement and strategic decision-making. https://www.sportlogiq.com/

(continued)

Table 6.6 (continued)

Start-ups	*Description*
ProZone-MatchViewer	Founded in 1998 in England by Andy O'Boyle and acquired by STATS LLC in 2015, ProZone is a performance analytics platform for football. Its MatchViewer tool delivers real-time analysis of metrics such as running distances, passing accuracy, and ball possession. Widely used in top leagues like the Premier League, La Liga and Bundesliga, it supports teams, coaches and analysts with in-depth performance insights
Scoutastic	Founded in 2020 by Roland Becker, Scoutastic is a German AI start-up that identifies undervalued talent in European football leagues. By combining machine learning and real-time performance tracking, it provides predictive analytics to help clubs target players with high resale potential. The platform is used by teams in the Bundesliga, La Liga and other top leagues. https://scoutastic.com/en/

Source Created by the authors

US United States: Start-ups in the U.S. mainly drive performance analytics, real-time tracking and fan monetisation, reflecting the commercialised sports model (e.g. NFL, NBA). Companies such as Second Spectrum and Whoop exemplify this trend (Xu & Baghaei, 2025).

EU Europe: European ventures emphasise athlete health, injury prevention and biomechanics, aligned with the player welfare models in football-centric organisations. Notable examples include Zone7 and BBSoF (Elkhamisy, 2025; Guelmami et al., 2023).

IN India: According to Tracxn (2025), India hosts over 55 sports-focused AI start-ups, with 12 venture-backed and 5 at Series A + level, accumulating around $7.6 M in funding. Additionally, ventures like Footrax, KIBI Sports and Stupa Sports Analytics provide wearable tracking, real-time data collection and AR/VR-enhanced fan experience (Inc42, 2022; Times of India, 2025). India's AI sport ecosystem prioritises accessibility, mobile scalability and cost-efficiency, frequently supported by government-funded incubators and local innovation networks (IMARC Group, 2025). These traits distinguish India's AI approach from the health-focused models of Europe and the performance analytics orientation of the U.S. These trends highlight that AI applications in sport are not uniformly distributed but are strategically shaped by regional market conditions. Understanding these dynamics is critical for both investors and policymakers seeking to support context-relevant technological innovation.

6.5 Growth and Investment Trends of Artificial Intelligence Start-Ups

Artificial intelligence (AI) has emerged as a transformative technology in recent years, driving substantial investment across multiple sectors, including sports, healthcare, finance, automotive and retail. The surge in AI adoption has led to a significant increase in global funding. Investments in AI-related companies reached $55.6 billion in 2023 and are projected to surpass $100 billion—an increase of over 80%. Approximately one-third of all global venture capital is expected to be allocated to AI ventures (Glaser & Yao, 2025). According to Statista (2023), the global AI market exceeded €130 billion in 2023 and is forecast to grow to approximately €1.9 trillion by 2030 (Thormundsson, 2024). The majority of these investments are privately funded, with the United States accounting for €62.5 billion and China €7.3 billion in 2023 (Stanford University, 2024).

Among the most prominent investors is Amazon, whose total investment in AI-focused companies has reportedly reached $8 billion (The Guardian, 2024). Amazon Web Services (AWS) supports various AI and machine learning applications in sports, offering data analytics, real-time performance evaluation and fan engagement tools to organisations such as the NFL, Formula 1 and MLS. Moreover, Amazon leverages AI to optimise logistics and manage large-scale data flows during live events. On the consumer side, Amazon Prime Video enhances viewer experience with AI-driven personalised recommendations, real-time statistics and interactive features. Additionally, AI is integrated into Amazon's smart home products, such as Alexa, enabling voice-based access to sports scores, news and tailored updates.

Microsoft has also made considerable investments, spending $64.5 billion in capital expenditures in 2024, with plans to allocate $80 billion to AI-powered data centres in 2025 (Soni, 2025). In the sports domain, Microsoft's Azure AI cloud platform underpins real-time analytics systems like NBA Stats, which assist coaches and analysts in making data-informed decisions. Furthermore, Microsoft's Azure and Xbox AI tools are employed in performance analysis and player monitoring within the gaming and e-sports sectors, enhancing gameplay through sophisticated data collection and in-game analysis.

Google, meanwhile, announced a $75 billion AI investment strategy for 2025 (Levy, 2025). As the owner of YouTube, Google utilises AI algorithms to recommend sports content—such as match highlights and live streams—based on user behaviour. These systems aim to elevate user engagement by providing real-time sports analytics and personalised content delivery.

6.6 Conclusion

This chapter examines the multifaceted applications of artificial intelligence (AI) in various areas of the sports industry, including wearable technologies, injury prevention, performance analysis, training systems, fan engagement, betting and talent scouting. The information detailed above demonstrates that AI-focused start-ups not only offer innovative solutions but also reshape traditional decision-making mechanisms by providing real-time data analysis, predictive modelling and personalized solutions.

From an industry perspective, the integration of AI into sports enhances operational efficiency, improves athlete health and performance and transforms the fan experience. Policymakers and industry leaders should support AI innovation through regulatory frameworks that address data privacy, algorithmic transparency and equitable access to AI-based resources in both elite and grassroots sports contexts.

For future research, scholars should investigate the long-term impacts of AI on coaching strategies, athlete development and sport integrity. Comparative studies between AI adoption levels in professional versus amateur sports, and the sociocultural implications of AI-enhanced fan engagement, also represent valuable areas of inquiry. As the AI ecosystem continues to evolve, sustained academic attention is needed to guide responsible and impactful AI integration within the global sports landscape.

References

Akoğlu, H. E., & Doğaner, S. (2023). Spor endüstrisinde yapay zeka uygulamaları. In N. Dinçer, & M. Dalkılıç (Eds.), *Spor bilimlerinde ileri ve çağdaş çalışmalar* 2. İzmir: Duvar Pub., (pp. 140–155). (**In Turkish**)

Basri, T., Fahad, M., Veisieh, D., Ouaissa, M., & Ouaissa, M. (2025). Artificial intelligence for startups and innovation. In I. U. Khan, H. Taherdoost, M. Madanchian, M. Ouaissa, S. E. Hajjami, & H. Rahman (Eds.), *Future tech startups and innovation in the age of AI* (pp. 1–20). Cham: Taylor & Francis.

Biro, A., Jánosi-Rancz, K. T., Szilagyi, L., Cuesta-Vargas, A. I., Martín-Martín, J., & Szilágyi, S. M. (2022). Visual object detection with DETR to support video-diagnosis using conference tools. *Applied Sciences, 12*(12), 5977. https://doi.org/10.3390/app12125977

Calleja-Gonzalez, J., Marques-Jimenez, D., Jones, M., Huyghe, T., Navarro, F., Delextrat, A., & Terrados, N. (2020). What are we doing wrong when athletes report higher levels of fatigue from traveling than from training or competition? *Frontiers in Psychology, 11*, 194. https://doi.org/10.3389/fpsyg.2020.00194

Chawla, N. (2020). AI, IOT and wearable technology for smart healthcare. A review. *International Journal of Recent Research Aspects, 7*(1), 9–13.

Chu, W. C. C., Shih, C., Chou, W. Y., Ahamed, S. I., & Hsiung, P. A. (2019). Artificial intelligence of things in sports science: Weight training as an example. *Computer, 52*(11), 52–61. https://doi.org/10.1109/MC.2019.2933772

Economic Times. (2024). *Sportstech startup Str8bat raises $3.5 million from Exfinity Venture Partners*. https://economictimes.indiatimes.com/tech/funding/sportstech-startup-str8bat-raises-3-5-million-from-exfinity-venture-partners/articleshow/104183919.cms

Elkhamisy, Y. K. (2025). Applications of artificial intelligence in sport medicine: A review. *Translational Health Sciences, 1*(1), 52–62. https://doi.org/10.21608/ths.2025.345621.1005

Erdeveciler, Ö., &Cengiz C. (2024). Siber güvenlik tehditlerinin spor ekonomisine etkileri. In H. Şahan, & Y. Er (Eds.), *Spor Bilimlerinde Yenilikçi Çalışmalar* – 12. İzmir: Duvar Pub., (pp. 114–128). (**In Turkish**)

Gaffar, S., & Gearhart, A. (2024). Artificial intelligence and wearable technology. In A. C. Chang, & A. Limon (Eds), *Intelligence-based cardiology and cardiac surgery*. Academic Press. (pp. 351–356). https://doi.org/10.1016/B978-0-323-90534-3.00056-1

Glaser, J. D., & Yao, K. M. (2025). *The state of the funding market for AI companies: A 2024–2025 outlook*. The National Law Review. Retrieved February 25, 2025, from https://natlawreview.com/article/state-funding-market-ai-companies-2024-2025-outlook

Glebova, E., Desbordes, M., & Geczi, G. (2020). Relocations of sports spectators' customer experiences—A sporteseményt nézők vásárlói élményeinek áthelyeződése. *Testnevelés, Sport, Tudomány, 5*(1–2), 44–49. https://doi.org/10.21846/TST.2020.1-2.4

Govindaraj, M., Gnanasekaran, C., Sivakulanthay, T., Gnanamanickam, S. V., & Khan, P. (2023). Role of artificial ıntelligence across various media platforms: A quantitative ınvestigation of media expert's opinion. *Journal of Law and Sustainable Development, 11*(5), e1175. https://doi.org/10.55908/sdgs.v11i5.1175

Grand View Research. (2023). *Europe sports betting market size, share & trends analysis report by type, by platform, by sports type (football, basketball, baseball, horse racing, cricket, hockey, others), by country, and segment forecasts, 2024–2030.* Retrieved February 22, 2025, from https://www.grandviewresearch.com/industry-analysis/europe-sports-betting-market-report

Guelmami, N., Fekih-Romdhane, F., Mechraoui, O., & Bragazzi, N. L. (2023). Injury prevention, optimized training and rehabilitation: How is AI reshaping the field of sports medicine. *New Asian Journal of Medicine, 1*(1), 30–34.

HAI. (2024). *AI Index 2024 annual report.* Stanford University, Human-Centered Artificial Intelligence. Retrieved February 26, 2025, from https://aiindex.stanford.edu/report/

Hubáček, O., Šourek, G., & Železný, F. (2019). Exploiting sports-betting market using machine learning. *International Journal of Forecasting, 35*(2), 783–796. https://doi.org/10.1016/j.ijforecast.2019.01.001

IMARC Group. (2025). *India sports technology market: Industry trends, share, size, growth, opportunity and forecast 2025–2030.* https://www.imarcgroup.com/india-sports-technology-market

Inc42. (2022). *Meet the startups scoring big on the Indian sports tech pitch.* https://inc42.com/startups/indian-sports-tech-startups/

Kollár, A. (2021). *Betting models using AI: A review on ANN, SVM, and Markov Chain* (MPRA Paper No. 106821). Munich Personal RePEc Archive. https://mpra.ub.uni-muenchen.de/106821/

Levy, A. (2025). *Alphabet will spend $75 billion on artificial intelligence (AI) in 2025, but it spent $69 billion on something else entirely in 2024 that makes it worth buying and holding forever.* Nasdaq. Retrieved February 25, 2025, from https://www.nasdaq.com/articles/alphabet-will-spend-75-billion-artificial-intelligence-ai-2025-it-spent-69-billion

Li, J. (2021). Development trend of the integration of artificial intelligence and sports industry. *Journal of Physics: Conference Series, 1744*(3), 032023. https://doi.org/10.1088/1742-6596/1744/3/032023

Markets and Markets. (2025). *Wearable technology market size, share & industry trends report.* Retrieved February 20, 2025, from https://www.marketsandmarkets.com/Market-Reports/wearable-electronics-market-983.html

Ometov, A., Shubina, V., Klus, L., Skibińska, J., Saafi, S., Pascacio, P., & Lohan, E. S. (2021). A survey on wearable technology: History, state-of-the-art and current challenges. *Computer Networks, 193*, Article 108074. https://doi.org/10.1016/j.comnet.2021.108074

Pottala, M. (2018). *Artificial intelligence: Artificial intelligence in sports* (Master's thesis, Centria University of Applied Sciences, Kokkola, Finland).
Roll, I., & Wylie, R. (2016). Evolution and revolution in artificial intelligence in education. *International Journal of Artificial Intelligence in Education, 26*, 582–599. https://doi.org/10.1007/s40593-016-0110-3
Sennaar, K. (2019). *Artificial intelligence in sports – Current and future applications*. Emerj Artificial Intelligence Research. Retrieved February 19, 2025, from https://emerj.com/ai-sector-overviews/artificial-intelligence-in-sports/
Shields, R. (2018). *What the media industry really thinks about the impact of AI*. The Drum. Retrieved February 16, 2025, from https://www.thedrum.com/news/2018/07/06/what-the-mediaindustry-really-thinks-about-the-impact-ai
Soni, A. (2025). *Microsoft data center leases slowing, analysts say, raising investor attention*. Retrieved 19.02.2025 from https://www.reuters.com/technology/microsoft-shelves-ai-data-center-deals-sign-potential-oversupply-analyst-says-2025-02-24/
Stübinger, J., Mangold, B., & Knoll, J. (2019). Machine learning in football betting: Prediction of match results based on player characteristics. *Applied Sciences, 10*(1), 46. https://doi.org/10.3390/app10010046
Sulimov, D. (2024). *Performance insights-based AI-driven football transfer fee prediction* (arXiv preprint arXiv:2401.16795). arXiv. https://doi.org/10.48550/arXiv.2401.16795
Taghian, A., Abo-Zahhad, M., Sayed, M. S., & Abd El-Malek, A. H. (2023). Virtual and augmented reality in biomedical engineering. *Biomedical Engineering Online, 22*(1), 76. https://doi.org/10.1186/s12938-023-01138-3
Tan, L., & Ran, N. (2023). Applying artificial intelligence technology to analyze the athletes' training under sports training monitoring system. *International Journal of Humanoid Robotics, 20*(06), 2250017. https://doi.org/10.1142/S0219843622500177
The Guardian. (2024). *Amazon doubles down on AI startup Anthropic with $4bn investment*. Retrieved February 14, 2025, from https://www.theguardian.com/technology/2024/nov/22/amazon-anthropic-ai-investment
Thormundsson, B. (2024). *Artificial intelligence (AI) market size worldwide from 2020 to 2030*. Statista. Retrieved February 21, 2025, from https://www.statista.com/forecasts/1474143/global-ai-market-size
Times of India. (2025). *How Indian sports tech startups like Footrax and KIBI are bringing AI to grassroots*. https://timesofindia.indiatimes.com/business/startups/how-indian-sports-tech-startups-are-bringing-ai-to-grassroots/articleshow/110234598.cms
Tracxn. (2025). *Artificial Intelligence startups in Sports Tech in India*. https://tracxn.com/d/artificial-intelligence/ai-startups-in-sports-tech-in-india

Xu, T., & Baghaei, S. (2025). Reshaping the future of sports with artificial intelligence: Challenges and opportunities in performance enhancement, fan engagement, and strategic decision-making. *Engineering Applications of Artificial Intelligence, 142*, Article 109912. https://doi.org/10.1016/j.engappai.2024.109912

Wang, Z., Yang, Z., & Dong, T. (2017). A review of wearable technologies for elderly care that can accurately track indoor position, recognize physical activities and monitor vital signs in real time. *Sensors, 17*(2), 341. https://doi.org/10.3390/s17020341

Wei, S., Huang, P., Li, R., Liu, Z., & Zou, Y. (2021). Exploring the application of artificial intelligence in sports training: A case study approach. *Complexity, 2021*(1), 4658937. https://doi.org/10.1155/2021/4658937

CHAPTER 7

Transforming Entertainment and Recreation: The Impact of Changing Technology on Work and Workers

Tolga Beşikçi and Ezgi Abay Beşikçi

7.1 Introduction

In retelling the compelling and captivating story of the contemporary hyper pace of technological change and its profound effect on work and workers, it is undeniably tempting to characterize this remarkable era as an unprecedented and exhilarating time of immense challenge and opportunity. Reflecting upon the not-so-distant past, when the Internet was merely an academic curiosity and email was considered a cutting-edge technology, one cannot help but marvel at the astonishing progress we have made. As we venture forth into the present day, and eagerly

T. Beşikçi (✉) · E. Abay Beşikçi
Department of Recreation, Faculty of Sport Sciences, Manisa Celal Bayar University, Manisa, Türkiye
e-mail: tolga.besyo@hotmail.com; tolga.besikci@cbu.edu.tr

E. Abay Beşikçi
e-mail: ezgi.abay@cbu.edu.tr

D. Kumar et al. (eds.), *Evolving Trends in Technology Entrepreneurship*, Palgrave Studies in Global Entrepreneurship,
https://doi.org/10.1007/978-981-95-7441-4_7

gaze into the future, it becomes increasingly evident that we now find ourselves immersed in a period of unparalleled significance, characterized by both complex challenges and promising opportunities. The boundless potential of humanity's creative prowess and inventiveness seems to know no bounds, as we witness the constant evolution of technology and its ever-expanding impact on our lives. We are experiencing a period in which rapid technological progress is reshaping the fundamental structure of work and everyday life. The convergence of emerging technologies and society's continuous pursuit of advancement is generating significant developments that challenge established norms and create new opportunities for innovation. As we navigate the intricate web of possibilities and challenges that this era presents, we must embrace the exhilarating uncertainty that comes hand in hand with progress, forging ahead with an unwavering determination to shape our destinies amidst the ever-shifting tides of change. In this exciting age of perpetual innovation, the fusion of human potential and cutting-edge technology opens doors to uncharted territories and unimagined opportunities. It is an era that demands adaptability and resilience, propelling us toward new horizons of knowledge and understanding. As we contemplate the significance of this momentous epoch, we are reminded of the indomitable spirit of humanity, forever driven by curiosity and our continued interest in exploring emerging technological possibilities. Together, let us embrace the challenges and seize the opportunities that await us on this extraordinary journey, fueling our aspirations and cultivating a future rooted in unlimited possibilities.

Although the multifaceted nature of the challenges and opportunities posed by today's technological advancements may seem unprecedented in their complexity, scope, speed, and profound effects, it is essential to acknowledge that humanity's responses throughout history, often marked by confusion and hesitation, have exhibited a remarkable consistency. What sets this era apart from previous periods, however, is the extraordinary speed and transformative power of the changes unfolding before us. Long-standing traditions, deeply rooted institutions, established professions, education systems, welfare structures, and nearly every familiar and assumed aspect of modern life now face relentless challenges, demanding adaptation and revaluation.

Advocates of a simpler lifestyle often propose curbing or restraining technological advancements. However, upon closer examination, it becomes clear that such an approach is neither feasible nor practical in our contemporary reality—if it ever truly was. Modern economies are deeply and irreversibly interwoven with technology, serving as the primary catalyst for progress at an unparalleled pace. The dynamic interplay between technology and society has created an environment where innovation is not merely an option but an essential component of development. In today's interconnected world, the relentless global competition to harness the latest advancements spans a wide array of domains, including entertainment, recreation, biotechnology, finance, information services, business strategy, and manufacturing. These sectors thrive on technological breakthroughs, which fuel growth, enhance efficiency, and redefine the boundaries of human capability. As a result, embracing technological change has become an imperative, driving forward the evolution of modern economies and societies (Bingaman, 2023; Matyushok et al., 2021).

7.1.1 *Background and Significance*

Over the past two decades, waves of rapidly advancing and constantly evolving technology have immensely and significantly impacted the nature and structure of work, profoundly shaping worker satisfaction and distress. Science and technology, in particular, have exerted an immense influence on work within the United States, a country that has steadily transitioned from an agrarian society and an industrial base to a vibrant and thriving information- and service-providing economy. As this transformation continues to unfold, it is accompanied by massive and profound changes within workplaces that will undoubtedly reverberate through organizations and significantly impact on the lives of workers.

New and innovative tools are continuously emerging, along with novel and ground-breaking behaviors that are revolutionizing industry, agriculture, and the service sector. These technological advancements are not limited solely to these areas, as they also permeate the realms of entertainment, recreation, and the home, transforming and enhancing these aspects of our lives in remarkable ways. This chapter meticulously examines and scrutinizes some of the most recent and influential effects of technology on these various facets.

Specifically, this comprehensive analysis delves into how changing technology is shaping the very foundation of entertainment, revolutionizing the way we perceive and experience recreation, and dramatically influencing the fundamental nature of work and the resulting products of the leisure industries. By providing both short-term and long-term perspectives, this chapter elucidates the profound implications of these technological influences on a highly industrialized society, shedding light on how these advancements will continue to shape our world in ways previously unimaginable.

From technological inventions to transformative shifts in societal dynamics, the profound influence of technology is undeniable. As we navigate the uncharted territories of this ever-evolving landscape, it is imperative to grasp the multifaceted impacts of technology on both individuals and society as a whole. This chapter serves as a comprehensive and thought-provoking exploration of these influences, illuminating the path forward for a society that is intricately intertwined with technology (Hurd et al., 2021; Marion & Fixson, 2021).

Recreation and entertainment have changed so significantly in contemporary society that we frequently fail to identify sufficiently with our forebears to fully comprehend their forms of leisure activity, or to understand work activities that were embedded within play. However, the primary purpose and product of workers in this era did not differ significantly from our contemporary challenges. The surge of economic activity generated during the first two decades of the twentieth century took half of the American workers' time. Researchers have documented the extensive working hours, limited vacation periods, and general aging of the workforce during that period. Working literally from cradle to grave, the American worker invested considerably less time for leisure, recreation, and entertainment. Today, Americans have ample resources, highly developed tools, and constantly improving and changing technology as the basis of work to afford far more leisure and play. This chapter focuses on how the changing and emerging entertainment and recreation technologies affect work and workers in the leisure industries (Parker, 2021; Tribe, 2020).

In conclusion, the interplay between technological advancements and the evolving nature of work has profound implications for worker satisfaction and distress. As organizations navigate this complex landscape, it is crucial to prioritize the well-being of employees by investing in both technological infrastructure and mental health resources. The future of work will undoubtedly continue to be shaped by these advancements, necessitating a proactive approach to managing their impacts on individuals and society as a whole.

7.1.2 Purpose and Scope

This section aims to explore the intricate relationship between technology, work, recreation, and entertainment by examining their evolving nature and associated demands. The discussion is structured to achieve two primary objectives:

High-Level Overview of Work in Entertainment and Recreation: This section provides a comprehensive overview of work related to entertainment and recreational activities. By offering a high-level aggregation, it establishes a foundation for understanding the broader landscape. It identifies potential users and constraints, evaluates strategies guiding technological evolution, and highlights the societal contributions of these advancements.

Analysis of Technological Advancements and Trends: A detailed examination of the state of the art and emerging trends in technology is conducted, focusing on how these developments align with the defined needs and objectives of various entertainment and recreational tasks. This analysis considers critical economic and social factors that influence the pace and direction of technological progress in these fields.

Special attention is given to the implications of technological advancements on vocational training, employment opportunities, and job satisfaction. Additionally, the economic benefits to workers and society are assessed, alongside the inherent capabilities and limitations of these technologies. These considerations aim to ensure the efficient and effective integration of technology into entertainment and recreation, resulting in societal impacts that are both beneficial and widely acceptable.

Ultimately, this discussion seeks to establish a framework for actionable strategies that support the development and implementation of technology in a manner that maximizes its positive contributions to society while addressing potential challenges.

7.2 Historical Evolution of Entertainment and Recreation

It is of utmost significance for individuals residing in the current era, which harbors a plethora of ground-breaking technological advancements, to acknowledge that this particular juncture in history does not mark the maiden occasion when technology has revolutionized labor, and the skill set requisite for individuals involved in social production. Our focus in this segment is centered around comprehending the historical alterations in the realm of entertainment and recreation technology, as well as the types of workers enlisted in this domain. Despite persisting even in contemporary post-industrial societies, these forms of employment are imperative, albeit representing a minute fraction of the overall social production. The creation of television sets, production of films, acting in broadcast shows, stocking video stores, and the management and screening of films in theaters demand diligent labor, just as the milking of cows, the transformation of milk into cheese, the supervision and contribution to grocery stores, and the establishment of restaurants where individuals can indulge in delectable nourishment, revel in music, and be catered to by waitstaff, necessitate dedicated efforts (Cowan, 2008).

Before the development of telecommunications and electronic information storage and retrieval devices, the only methods of storing and transmitting information that humans had were all physical in nature: human memory, cloth, paper, parchment, wood, stone, metal, and silk. All physical storage of information took up space, and physical means were required to store, transmit, and retrieve such information. The need for physical transportation to reach a location where other people could deliver food, music, entertainers, and provide settings for entertainment and pastime was fulfilled by humans and sometimes animals with human guidance. Finally, the skills that were required for the creation and presentation of entertainment and information were generally exceptional versions of universal human skills: oral and physical communication, specific physical dexterity such as handwriting, and the ability through dance, music, story, or mimicry to evoke emotions in other human beings, the ultimate transfer of information. As a result, employment in the entertainment and recreation trades showed no unusual degree of professionalization. While the payment to entertainers could be extravagant, the payment to the mass of people who organized buildings for the presentation of entertainers or contributed toward creating the performance was modest.

This Table 7.1 outlines the historical progression of major technologies in the entertainment and recreation industries. It highlights how different time periods brought specific innovations that not only influenced audience experiences but also redefined job structures and labor demands in the sector.

In this era preceding the advent of telecommunications and electronic information storage and retrieval devices, the range of techniques

Table 7.1 Timeline of key technological developments in entertainment and recreation

Period	*Key technologies*	*Impact on entertainment and work*
Pre-1900s	Printing press, live performances	Manual labor in physical venues; local, community-based leisure
1900s–1950s	Radio, cinema, phonograph	Rise of mass entertainment; new roles in production and broadcasting
1960s–1980s	Television, videotapes, arcade machines	Home-based entertainment grows; expansion of technical support jobs
1990s	Internet, CD-ROM, cable TV	Digital transformation begins; online platforms and content distribution
2000s	Streaming, MMO games, mobile devices	Global reach; user-generated content and remote leisure participation
2010s–2020s	VR, AR, AI, ML, cloud gaming	Immersive and personalized experiences; emergence of new creative roles

Source Created by the authors

available to store and transmit data was limited to physical mediums. These mediums included human memory, cloth, paper, parchment, wood, stone, metal, and silk. Each of these physical storage options occupied a tangible space and necessitated physical means for storage, transmission, and retrieval. To meet the requirement of transporting goods, music, entertainers, and creating an environment for leisure and enjoyment, humans and at times, animals under human guidance, played the role of transporters. Moreover, the skills essential for crafting and delivering entertainment and information were chiefly extraordinary versions of universal human skills: oral and physical communication, exquisite physical dexterity like handwriting, and the ability to elicit emotions in fellow humans through dance, music, storytelling, or mimicry—the ultimate transmission of information. Consequently, the professionalization of the entertainment and recreation industries did not witness any exceptional degree. While entertainers were sometimes bestowed with extravagant payments, the remuneration for the majority involved in organizing venues for entertainment or contributing to the creation of performances remained modest. (Chai, 2011; Lanza et al., 2022).

7.3 Technological Innovations in Entertainment and Recreation

The rapid advancement of technology in recent decades has profoundly reshaped the domains of entertainment and recreation, mirroring its transformative impact across numerous sectors of society. This evolution is most evident in the advent and widespread adoption of pioneering technologies such as cable television, video cassettes, video games, satellites, computers, and laser discs. These innovations have not only revolutionized how individuals experience leisure but have also accelerated shifts in the nature of work and workforce dynamics. Particularly within the entertainment and recreation industries, this transformation challenges traditional conventions and redefines long-standing perceptions of work, blending playfulness with professional engagement in unprecedented ways (Lopez et al., 2021). The integration of digital technologies into the domestic sphere has also had a profound impact on leisure and entertainment. The increasing penetration of information and communication technologies (ICTs) into the home has transformed the way individuals and families engage with media and entertainment, blurring the boundaries between the public and private spheres (Asakitikpi et al., 2018; Sosale, 2011).

The electronic and computer revolutions have fundamentally redefined leisure experiences through the integration of interconnected systems and devices. From the introduction of magnetically recorded home video programming to the ubiquitous presence of cable television and compact home satellite systems, these advancements have reimagined the possibilities of recreation. Additionally, the emergence of video games and electronic amusement machines has inaugurated a new era of interactive entertainment, offering endless opportunities for engagement and enjoyment. Additionally, the emergence of video games and electronic amusement machines has inaugurated a new era of interactive entertainment, offering endless opportunities for engagement and enjoyment (Cheok et al., 2006). These technological innovations have not only transformed how individuals experience leisure but also accelerated shifts in the nature of work and workforce dynamics within the entertainment and recreation industries (Roshan, 2023).

As these ground-breaking technologies reshape the landscape of entertainment, they have disrupted established norms while simultaneously creating myriad new opportunities for employment. Their impact is evident not only in the methods by which entertainment is consumed but also in the generation of diverse job roles within the industry. This ripple effect demonstrates the sector's responsiveness to innovation and foreshadows further transformative shifts driven by creative minds introducing novel technological advancements.

Understanding and harnessing the potential of these developments pose both a challenge and an opportunity. It is essential to evaluate these innovations within broader economic, social, and employment contexts. By carefully examining their implications, we can strategically navigate the evolving landscape of entertainment and recreation, ensuring that these advancements are leveraged effectively to maximize societal and economic benefits.

In conclusion, the scope of recent and emerging technological innovations in entertainment and recreation is vast and transformative. These advancements have already had an indelible impact on the way individuals' work and experience leisure, and their influence is expected to grow. Embracing these changes with a forward-thinking and proactive approach will enable the creation of a future where the intersection of work, recreation, and technology thrives. With thoughtful integration, this field can continue to evolve as a vibrant and fulfilling domain amidst the dynamic challenges of a technologically driven world (Ahuja, 2021).

7.3.1 Virtual Reality and Augmented Reality

The increasing integration of advanced technology into the realm of entertainment is poised to yield transformative effects, reshaping conventional experiences into entirely novel forms. Among the most profound innovations is the advent of virtual reality (VR), which offers users the ability to transcend their physical environment and immerse themselves in alternate, fully interactive worlds. Virtual reality operates through the mathematical simulation of reality, achieved by processing data inputs via computers that control video and audio outputs, often enhanced by specialized hardware such as optical devices. This technology enables multisensory experiences, encompassing sight, sound, touch, and even olfaction. Current research and development efforts explore diverse applications of VR, including industrial and medical training, education, telepresence, entertainment, and adult experiences (Hidayat & Wardat, 2024; Shu & Huang, 2021; Smith et al., 2023).

Similarly, augmented reality (AR) represents a significant evolution in information-rich environments, transforming everyday phenomena into immersive experiences of entertainment, amusement, and engagement. AR enhances human perception by integrating virtual elements into the real world, engaging all five senses to deliver a seamless blend of physical and digital experiences. This advanced technological interface refines sensory and semantic data, amplifying human capabilities and decision-making processes. As societies evolve beyond industrial paradigms, priorities shift, particularly in education and service delivery to elite sectors, revealing both the immense potential and the societal costs of unrestricted access to such transformative technologies. The potential benefits of AR span a wide array of domains, addressing critical needs while raising significant ethical and practical considerations (Martins et al., 2022).

As societies transition beyond industrial paradigms, the landscape of entertainment and recreation is undergoing a significant transformation. Priorities are shifting toward creating immersive, accessible, and innovative experiences, particularly in catering to the evolving expectations of modern audiences. Augmented reality (AR) and virtual reality (VR) hold immense potential in reshaping entertainment by offering cutting-edge opportunities for personalized and interactive engagement. However, alongside these advancements come challenges that demand careful consideration, such as the ethical implications of unrestricted access to these transformative technologies and their broader societal impacts.

Despite their promise, the integration of AR and VR into entertainment and recreation is not without obstacles. Common issues include technical barriers such as network disruptions, user experience limitations, and the demand for more adaptable and engaging content. These challenges highlight the need for continuous innovation and the refinement of these systems to meet the dynamic needs of users. Addressing these hurdles will be pivotal in unlocking the full potential of AR and VR, ensuring their seamless adoption in creating ground-breaking experiences that captivate and inspire audiences (Saudagar, 2024).

7.3.2 Artificial Intelligence and Machine Learning

Artificial Intelligence (AI) refers to the conceptualization, design, and creation of systems that emulate human-like capabilities. In recent years, AI research and development have witnessed rapid advancements, emerging as a pivotal force across various industries. In the realm of filmmaking, AI is driving the innovation of immersive park attractions, enabling creators to offer visitors unparalleled and engaging experiences. Similarly, within the hospitality sector, AI has become indispensable as hoteliers seek to leverage its transformative potential to elevate the quality and personalization of guest services. Moreover, educators are increasingly recognizing the critical importance of thoughtfully integrating AI technologies into their pedagogical approaches. By harnessing these advancements, they aim to lay a robust foundation for the development of future entertainment and recreation content, ensuring it aligns seamlessly with the possibilities presented by emerging AI capabilities.

The domain of artificial intelligence (AI) encompasses an expansive array of interdisciplinary fields, each contributing to its remarkable advancements. Among these, the dynamic field of machine learning stands out for its transformative potential, continuously redefining the boundaries of technological capability. Machine learning algorithms, inspired by the cognitive mechanisms of the human mind, empower systems to enhance their performance incrementally by acquiring and applying knowledge through experience. Equally significant is the concept of embodied cognition, which delves into the ways intelligent systems can actively engage with their environments. This approach emphasizes a holistic interaction, mirroring the manner in which humans perceive and respond to the world. Furthermore, neural networks, a cornerstone of AI research, strive to emulate the intricate web of interconnected neurons in the human brain. This design enables machines to process and analyze vast amounts of information with remarkable efficiency, further advancing our understanding of intelligent systems.

In the field of artificial intelligence (AI), several critical challenges demand thoughtful analysis and innovative solutions. One prominent issue is the development of optimal strategies to harmonize AI and human cognitive processes, enabling seamless interaction and fostering collaborative efforts to enhance overall efficiency. To achieve meaningful synergy, it is essential to explore how AI can effectively complement human abilities, leveraging strengths to boost productivity and improve problem-solving capabilities. For AI systems to fulfill their potential, they must be designed with the capacity to perceive and interpret their environment accurately. They should possess the ability to understand and respond to human communication in a natural and intuitive manner, adapt by acquiring new knowledge, and refine their existing skills over time. Furthermore, AI systems should demonstrate physical agility and precision in manipulating objects as needed and execute tasks competently in alignment with their intended functions. These capabilities are integral to the advancement of AI as a tool that enriches human endeavors across various domains.

The rise of artificial intelligence (AI) has ushered in a new era of innovative developers leading this transformative intellectual movement. At the forefront of these advancements are the designers and creators of digital assistants and robots, which have seamlessly integrated into daily life, enhancing our interactions with technology and making them more efficient. Furthermore, AI-based learning systems have evolved to actively engage users, exemplified by the development of chatbots designed specifically for children. These systems not only offer personalized support but also promote cognitive development and social interaction. By doing so, they are reshaping educational paradigms and fostering the intellectual growth of young minds in an increasingly interconnected and technology-driven world (Datta & Goswami, 2021; Goralski & Tan, 2020).

Machine Learning (ML), a subset of artificial intelligence (AI), is characterized by the development of algorithms capable of identifying patterns in data through training processes rather than relying on explicit programming. Modern advancements in ML emphasize the optimization of network nodes and the strategic placement of layers within neural networks. Key methodologies include supervised learning, reinforcement learning, unsupervised learning, and deep learning. ML shares conceptual ties with fields such as information processing, computational modeling of intelligence, computer simulations of natural phenomena, decision science, formal reasoning, knowledge management, natural language processing, and robotics. These interconnected disciplines continue to shape the evolution of AI. Early conceptualizations of logical systems aimed at creating engaging and interactive experiences have laid the groundwork for current efforts to expand ML's capabilities, leveraging its growing capacity for more complex applications. An iterative access-and-extend loop, incorporating set property and functor transformations, has been proposed as a framework to unify theoretical and practical

Table 7.2 Comparison of emerging technologies in entertainment and recreation

Technology	*Primary use cases*	*Key benefits*	*Challenges*
Virtual Reality (VR)	Immersive gaming, training simulations	Full sensory immersion, user engagement	High cost, technical limitations, content development
Augmented Reality (AR)	Interactive events, live experiences	Real-world integration, broader accessibility	Device dependency, user interface challenges
Artificial Intelligence (AI)	Content recommendation, automation	Efficiency, personalization	Data privacy, algorithmic bias
Machine Learning (ML)	Game design, behavioral analytics	Predictive modeling, adaptive experiences	Requires large datasets, complexity of interpretation

Source Created by the authors

approaches across traditionally siloed domains. This iterative process not only aids in advancing theoretical understanding of ML but also offers practical insights into developing user-centered experiences, grounded in models of human cognition. The proliferation of remote work technologies has significantly influenced the ML field, enabling research and development from virtually anywhere. This trend is anticipated to accelerate further democratizing access to ML innovation and fostering new opportunities for interdisciplinary collaboration (Itam & Warrier, 2024) (Table 7.2).

This matrix compares four major emerging technologies based on their primary applications, advantages, and limitations within entertainment and recreation. It helps clarify their distinct roles, overlapping potentials, and operational constraints in shaping the user experience and the labor market.

7.4 Digital Distribution Platforms

Digital technology has profoundly transformed the realms of entertainment, media, and recreation by introducing innovative channels for the distribution of media content. Among the earliest and most significant developments was the commercialization of the World Wide Web, a milestone facilitated by the advent of the Mosaic web browser and the establishment of viable Business models in the mid-1990s. The World Wide Web has since become a dynamic platform, offering seamless access to a wide variety of content with just a single click. This digital medium serves as a vital resource, supporting the dissemination of information, the promotion of media performances, and the delivery of advertising. It further provides an interactive environment for the consumption of diverse media forms, including text, graphics, audio, and video. (Dolega et al., 2021).

The advent of the internet and the rapid evolution of digital technologies have fundamentally reshaped the landscape of leisure and recreation, profoundly influencing how individuals engage with entertainment and information. In the early stages of the web's development, visionaries foresaw a transformation in the distribution of motion pictures, driven by the burgeoning demand for broadband capacity. For example, viewers could stream halftime performances in real-time or reduce the "release window" between a film's theatrical debut and its availability for rental by a day or more, revolutionizing traditional media consumption.

Internet search companies emerged as pivotal players in this shift, leveraging advanced interconnection and searching technologies to manage the timely distribution of vast quantities of information. Unlike earlier models, where content was predominantly stored on personal devices, these companies introduced centralized systems capable of aggregating and delivering massive datasets efficiently. This innovation laid the foundation for pricing strategies that positioned certain platforms as monopolistic "black holes" of internet information, analogous to the dominance of Hollywood in the motion picture industry (Mishra & Tyagi, 2022; Ratchford et al., 2022).

However, as computing technology continues to advance, with powerful and user-friendly devices becoming increasingly accessible, the concentration of information and control within specific platforms or industries may diminish. This democratization of access holds the potential to decentralize content distribution, empowering individuals and smaller entities to create and share information on their own terms.

The implications of these changes extend beyond the realms of leisure and recreation, influencing work dynamics and the relationship between employees and their professional environments. As technology enables new forms of engagement and interaction, the boundaries between work and leisure blur, necessitating a reevaluation of traditional notions of productivity, creativity, and well-being. In this evolving landscape, the interplay between technological advancement and human adaptability will continue to redefine the ways in which individuals navigate the complex intersections of work, leisure, and recreation.

7.4.1 Streaming Services

The advent of streaming services has profoundly transformed the landscape of television. The practice of binge-watching entire series has become so deeply ingrained in modern life that it is difficult to imagine a time, not long ago, when subscribers in the United States averaged fewer than two episodes of a series per week. Today, streaming platforms have revolutionized both the creation and consumption of television, reshaping narrative structures and viewing habits. These platforms wield significant cultural and, in some cases, political influence by controlling vast audiences and substantial revenue streams. But how have these streaming giants established their dominance, and what is the extent of their power? (Lotz, 2022).

Consumers were drawn to streaming services not merely for their affordability and convenience but for the immersive experience of watching entire series in one sitting, a phenomenon that has given rise to the colloquial term "couch potato" in the United States. To capitalize on this behavior, television series adopted intricate narratives and suspenseful plot devices designed to captivate audiences and compel them to continue watching episode after episode. This strategy would have been unsustainable within the constraints of traditional weekly free-to-air broadcasts. However, streaming services upended this model entirely.

These platforms prioritized subscriber acquisition to such an extent that they collectively invested over $8 billion annually in content. Leveraging sophisticated algorithms, they curated seamless viewing experiences, guiding audiences from one program to the next, hour after hour. This strategic approach fostered high levels of viewer retention. As subscriptions grew, the substantial content costs were transformed into multibillion-dollar gross operating surpluses. Streaming services reinvested these profits into producing new content, fueling rapid subscription growth and ensuring their continued dominance in the entertainment industry (Budzinski et al., 2021; Climent & Haftor, 2021).

7.4.2 Online Gaming Platforms

The extraordinary success of the early Massively Multiplayer Online (MMO) games heralded an exciting future for the dynamic and ever-evolving realm of online gaming. Web-based games, whether designed for solo players or multiplayer experiences, provided a vast array of gaming opportunities, seamlessly blending traditional formats with innovative concepts uniquely suited to the internet. A hallmark of many of these games was their social component, which enabled unprecedented levels of interaction and connection among players. For casual gamers—those not devoted to a specific genre or gaming style—major online gaming platforms offered extensive catalogs featuring diverse web-based games. Interestingly, approximately half of the users subscribed to these platforms engaged primarily with these games. Despite generating no direct revenue from these casual users, their activity significantly boosted page views, which became a critical driver of advertising revenue. Notably, a substantial portion of this revenue stemmed from banner advertisements, which, during that period, were highly profitable. The pricing of web-based games for advertisers was predominantly based on the volume of page views rather than click-through rates, underscoring the importance of audience engagement in this burgeoning digital ecosystem (Gouriou, 2020).

In many massively multiplayer online (MMO) games, participants—often referred to as inhabitants, users, or entrants—were required to purchase game time with real-world currency. This time allowed them to immerse themselves in intricately crafted fantasy worlds, where they adopted and developed virtual personas. Players dedicated their time to honing skills, amassing goods, and interacting with others in diverse and meaningful ways. To sustain their presence in these digital environments, participants paid a recurring fee for game time, effectively "renting" their existence within these virtual spaces. A cornerstone of innovation within the MMO industry was the development of advanced software capable of managing the complexities of these expansive virtual worlds. This included establishing dynamic marketplaces for virtual goods and services, where players could engage in buying, selling, and trading. Additionally, MMOs offer customizable and evolving experiences, allowing the tone and nature of gameplay to adapt based on the decisions and actions of their inhabitants. Developers also enriched these games with features that kept the world dynamic and engaging, such as introducing new quests, adventures, and unexplored territories. These continual updates ensured that players experienced a vibrant and ever-evolving digital universe. (Zendle et al., 2020).

Moreover, the motivations behind online gaming are multifaceted. Research indicates that social motives significantly influence the time spent on gaming, with players often seeking social connections and community engagement as primary drivers for their gaming activities. The interplay between gaming motives and psychological factors, such as social anxiety and impulsivity, further complicates the landscape of online gaming, highlighting the need for a nuanced understanding of player behavior. As the gaming industry continues to grow, the implications of these dynamics on player engagement and the overall health of the gaming ecosystem remain critical areas for ongoing research (Billieux et al., 2014; Kuss & Griffiths, 2011; Rho et al., 2017).

In conclusion, the landscape of online gaming platforms, particularly through MMOs, illustrates a complex interplay of social interaction, economic models, and player motivations. The success of these platforms hinges on their ability to engage a diverse user base, particularly casual gamers, while continuously evolving to meet the demands of an ever-changing digital environment.

7.5 Impact on Work in the Entertainment Industry

Work in the entertainment sector provides significant creative and emotional value to performers, audiences, and others involved in production. Workers on the technical and support side of the industry also have challenges that make their jobs different from those of workers in other sectors. The special problems of work in the technical and support fields are mainly a result of the industry producing not goods but moments in time. Irrational demand, which leads either to increased sizes or decreased work hours, is the core of the sub optimization problem for production managers. A second problem stems from the varying quality of work within a given job classification and the communication problems that develop as workers move from one job to another. To some extent, these problems are similar to those of long production lines in other industries. A third feature modernizes these problems in the technical aspect of entertainment: technological change (Alojaiman, 2023).

The title discusses the significance of employing ground-breaking methods within the realm of performing arts, coupled with the distinctive financial hurdles encountered by professionals within this field. Official labor organizations serve an essential function in guaranteeing equitable allocation of exceedingly precarious positions, notwithstanding the prevailing uncertainty surrounding economic models. Consequently, this enables an economic evaluation that remains closely aligned with conventional theory, even in light of the industry's inherently unpredictable nature.

7.5.1 Changes in Production Processes

The ability to encode and store vast amounts of data digitally has enabled exciting and ground-breaking applications in various forms of media like music, television, film, electronic media, and even the flourishing industry of electronic games. This technological revolution has brought about unprecedented opportunities and possibilities. However, it is important for us to not be solely enchanted by the wonders of change, as it also entails certain costs that should not be overlooked or underestimated. When analyzing the entertainment and recreation industries, it becomes crucial to devote meticulous attention to the intricate processes that go into producing these products. This includes acknowledging and valuing the invaluable contributions made by the multitude of talented individuals who tirelessly work within these vibrant and thriving sectors.

We often think of the entertainment industry as one where the product is created on an individual-by-individual basis. After all, each person listens to his or her own music, watches television programs, plays the occasional electronic game, or reads music via digital file downloads. But the entertainment product involves a number of team inputs, all acting more or less simultaneously or consecutively. For popular music, the process usually involves composition, songwriting, lyric writing, performances, and recording, with possible contributions from many engineers, mixers, producers, and arrangers. Animated movies and video games require the collaboration of people with numerous special skills who work in multifunctional teams (Lindtner, 2011).

This Table 7.3 contrasts typical job roles before and after the widespread integration of digital technologies in the entertainment industry. It illustrates how new technical demands have created emerging positions while transforming or replacing traditional occupations.

Table 7.3 Technological shifts in job roles within the entertainment industry

Category	*Pre-1990s Job Roles*	*Post-2020 Job Roles*
Content Creation	Cameramen, sound engineers	VR designers, AI content developers
Distribution	Media duplicators, delivery agents	Streaming engineers, cloud system architects
Marketing	Print advertising coordinators	Data-driven algorithm specialists, platform marketers
Technical Support	Set builders, projectionists	XR developers, motion-capture technicians

Source Created by the authors

7.5.2 New Job Opportunities

Digital prepress technicians, photo-compositors, scanning operators, color prepress scanners, and digital prepress specialists are all emerging job titles within the ever-growing field of electronic support for the printing process. These occupations may not be widely recognized by the general public, but they play a crucial and significant role in the efficient and cost-effective completion of small to large-scale printing projects. With the advancements in technology and the increasing demand for high-quality printed materials, the need for skilled professionals in these areas is rapidly expanding, opening up ample opportunities for job training, career advancement, and job security.

In the field of digital prepress, technicians and scanning operators play a pivotal role in analyzing and processing original artwork, offering valuable insights and recommendations to clients and colleagues. Their responsibilities encompass evaluating various critical factors that influence the final quality of a document, such as resolution, contrast, and other technical parameters. To ensure accurate capture and preservation of visual information, these professionals utilize sophisticated digital scanners or digital camera backs. Through a meticulous process known as digitization, these advanced devices transform original artwork into high resolution digital image files, which are then displayed on monitors for further refinement using specialized prepress software.

Operators managing prepress system software hold a central role in optimizing digital files to achieve superior output quality. They undertake a series of precise adjustments, including selecting appropriate light sources, fine-tuning contrast to enhance image clarity, and adjusting colors to ensure faithful representation. Once these digital files are perfected, they are transmitted to a computer-to-film (CTF) recorder—a highly specialized device that generates negatives essential for subsequent stages in the printing process. This intricate workflow demands a high degree of precision, technical expertise, and attention to detail, underscoring the importance of skilled professionals in this domain.

The field of digital prepress represents a dynamic and rewarding career path for individuals keen on leveraging cutting-edge technology to advance the printing industry. As technological innovations continue to reshape the industry, the demand for adept professionals in digital prepress grows steadily. Expertise in this area offers substantial opportunities for career advancement and stability in an ever-evolving job market. To excel, professionals must stay abreast of emerging trends and technological advancements by engaging in specialized training programs. By continuously updating their knowledge and skills, practitioners can remain competitive and well-positioned for success in this exciting and rapidly developing field (Kenwright, 2022).

7.6 Impact on Workers in the Entertainment Industry

Technological advances have not only made workers in the entertainment industry exponentially more productive but also made their jobs infinitely more interesting, engaging, and captivating (Christopherson, 2008). Gone are the days when simply pressing a button was enough to achieve success in this competitive field. Instead, these highly skilled workers have transformed into the epitome of information generators, meticulously crafting ground-breaking scripts that not only captivate audiences but also elevate the overall quality of the audience experience to unparalleled heights.

The rapid expansion of job opportunities in the entertainment industry is both significant and well-documented, as evidenced by a variety of sources including unemployment insurance records, union membership data, and extensive private sector surveys. These indicators collectively point to a singular conclusion: the entertainment sector has witnessed an unparalleled increase in employment. This growth is largely driven by remarkable technological advancements, which have broadened the scope for potential employers (Ochiva, 2016). With more industry leaders now possessing substantial resources, their capacity to recruit and support creative professionals has markedly improved. As a result, these developments have significantly reduced risks for workers, enhanced income stability, and provided a greater sense of security and well-being.

The entertainment industry is inherently defined by its dynamic nature, marked by a continual flow of ideas and an unrelenting wave of innovation. In this era of rapid progress, professionals within the sector need not fear competition from low-cost producers. Instead, the industry benefits from a sophisticated content evaluation framework that naturally distinguishes superior productions from mediocre ones. As a result, the United States, with its reservoir of exceptional creative talent and unparalleled expertise, occupies a distinctive position to excel on the global stage, maintaining its leadership and influence in a highly competitive landscape (De-la-Calle-Durán & Rodríguez-Sánchez, 2021; Nhamo et al., 2020).

However, the new technologies pose significant challenges for industry workers, ranging from finding work to intellectual property protection. More technical skills and greater competition make getting hired harder. Then, too, the type of compensation—wages and profit shares—often poses a problem. The new compensation contracts emerge because of the important role that promotion and distribution play in entertainment industry success, but determining how these new compensation contracts will impact all the workers involved in the creative process is an unresolved issue. Format wars over production and distribution standards in music and video industries have tended to reward established parties, such as the recording industry and movie studios, by making it more difficult for new participants to achieve success. However, these roadblocks are not insurmountable since garage bands, independents, and newcomers do overcome these hurdles in order to be successful.

7.6.1 Skill Requirements and Training Needs

Not only are occupational employment requirements changing, so too are the requirements for both workers and the training systems that prepare them for the workforce. Before the arrival of cables, satellites, broadcast television, and its supporting industries—studios, recording, and large theater chains—there was a small, concentrated cluster. The bulk of occupations were mostly professional, with a few high-skill, semi-skilled, and unskilled positions. These operations were organized in various ways: production, distribution, theater exhibition, radio, cable, network broadcasting, and affiliated services. Specialized production concerns included lighting, scoring, props, film cameras, sound recording, audio mixing, animation, and editing. Professional and novice workers are often career-bound and acquire on-the-job training. The arrival of concert arenas, stadiums, theme parks, gaming camps, and the internet, along with its explosion in programming and special effects, has significantly expanded the reach of entertainment and increased consumer choices. Consequently, the range and number of special effects have increased exponentially in many fields. As for games, their "ultimate" experiences seem to lend themselves to being produced in this way; it also offers the advantages of economies of scale. Worker production conditions, however, are no longer hierarchical, as the range of occupations in these industries is far more horizontal. As a result, workers are now characterized by a blend of production skills and are hired for them. To illustrate this reality, the wide range of industry clusters requires players to do their best to get hired. In effect, secondary and post-secondary training systems have been linked.

7.6.2 Work–Life Balance

Technology serves as both a reflection of society and a catalyst for its transformation. It mirrors our ideals, aspirations, and cherished hopes while exposing the fissures in our beliefs and dreams. This dual nature—illuminating progress and revealing imperfections—positions technology as a profound agent of change. It challenges established norms, disrupts traditions, and transcends cultural prohibitions, pushing humanity toward uncharted possibilities.

As a symbol of progress, technology not only portrays society but profoundly shapes it. It influences our values, redefines our aspirations, and provides a framework for envisioning an ideal future. Each technological breakthrough sends ripples of change across society, reaching dimensions far removed from its immediate application. Among these, the emergence of telecommunication technologies is set to redefine foundational concepts such as work and professional activity.

In the near future, the traditional understanding of work as a fixed physical location will undergo a transformative shift. The tethering of work to specific spaces, machines, or resources will give way to a more fluid and adaptable paradigm. Work will evolve into a dynamic concept, unbound by geography, enabling individuals to contribute irrespective of their location. However, this transformation will not occur without resistance. It will disrupt entrenched norms and challenge existing structures, prompting companies to adopt innovative work arrangements that prioritize flexibility and adaptability.

Organizations are gradually recognizing the necessity of providing employees with the freedom to balance professional responsibilities with personal commitments. This shift will foster the development of dynamic teams, uniting individuals with diverse skills and backgrounds in collaborative, location-independent environments. The reimagining of work will also ripple through societal constructs such as family. Traditional roles will evolve: wives will balance dual responsibilities as professionals and homemakers, while retired specialists will contribute their wealth of knowledge as grandparents and active members of the workforce. The integration of remote technologies and flexible work arrangements has increasingly blurred boundaries between personal and professional spheres, reshaping traditional labor norms (Kossek et al., 2023).

Ultimately, technology is not merely an external force acting upon society but an intrinsic part of it, interwoven with its cultural and social fabric. It embodies the collective values, desires, and aspirations of humanity, shaping our shared future while reflecting our present realities. With each wave of technological advancement, society is presented with the opportunity to redefine itself, embracing growth, innovation, and change. The future, no longer constrained by traditional norms, emerges as an open canvas, a space for creativity, imagination, and the transformative power of technology (Fang et al., 2022; Rossner et al., 2021).

7.7 Conclusion

Employees in the entertainment and recreation industries, including those who install and maintain their equipment, are engaged in occupations that are relatively insulated from the direct effects of the rapidly changing technology. They are, however, greatly affected by the rate and structure of consumer demand and consequently by the economy's overall rate of growth and the share of income spent on leisure. In addition to the direct occupational contributions, employment prospects in the industries are greatly impacted by the other three employment defining influences: the market structure and technology of the industry and other institutions that regulate work.

The market structure plays a vital role in shaping employment prospects for individuals in the entertainment and recreation industries. The level of competition, market saturation, and industry dynamics all contribute to the availability of jobs and the stability of employment. As the industry evolves, new opportunities arise, creating a need for skilled workers who can adapt to changing demands. This necessitates continuous learning and development to stay relevant and competitive in the job market.

Technological advancements not only impact the equipment used in entertainment and recreation but also the way these industries operate. From online ticketing systems to virtual reality experiences, technology has transformed the way people consume entertainment and leisure activities. As a result, employees must keep pace with these changes, acquiring new skills to navigate digital platforms and utilize advanced tools. This technological aspect also opens up new avenues for innovative job roles and entrepreneurship within the industry.

Furthermore, institutions that regulate work, such as labor laws and government policies, can significantly influence employment opportunities in the entertainment and recreation sectors. These regulations ensure fair treatment, safety standards, and create a level playing field for both employees and businesses. Additionally, the support and incentives provided by governments and organizations further shape the health of the industry and the availability of jobs. By fostering a favorable environment, these institutions contribute to sustainable growth and employment stability.

Overall, the employment landscape in the entertainment and recreation industries is shaped by the interplay of market structure, technology, and institutional regulations. While the direct impact of rapidly changing technology may be minimal, other factors such as consumer demand, economic growth, and income distribution play pivotal roles. By understanding these influences and adapting to the evolving nature of the industry, individuals can seize opportunities and thrive in this exciting sector. (Abulibdeh et al., 2024).

Recent technological developments have had almost no direct impact on the occupations of entertainers and recreation workers, although technological advances will undoubtedly affect these occupations in the future. Many entertainers, especially actors, can achieve a substantial improvement in the quality of their output by converting their craft activities into a more capital-intensive and technologically advanced process.

The chief obstacle that has hindered this progress thus far has been the exorbitant capital costs associated with creating technological alternatives to live performances. However, there is great potential for these costs to be significantly reduced by developing less expensive equipment and by empowering workers to finance their investment by selling directly to consumers. Over time, as these technological alternatives become more accessible, the range and variety of leisure opportunities available to the public would expand exponentially, considerably surpassing the current output. The mix and quantity of services that could be enjoyed by individuals would expand as well, enabling a more diverse and immersive entertainment experience for all.

This chapter has explored how rapidly evolving technologies—such as VR, AR, AI, ML, streaming, and gaming platforms—are transforming the nature of entertainment, recreation, and the work associated with them. Four major insights emerge:

- Technology is redefining job structures across entertainment and recreation, creating new occupations while displacing others, especially in content creation, distribution, and marketing.
- Workers face shifting skill requirements, with success increasingly dependent on digital fluency, creative adaptability, and cross-functional collaboration.
- Workplace norms are changing, especially as telepresence, remote collaboration, and digital production environments challenge traditional notions of work–life boundaries.
- Technological access is uneven, and the benefits of innovation are not equally distributed. New models of inclusion and support are essential to ensure equitable participation across all demographics.

Based on these insights, several practical and policy-oriented implications arise. Educators should prioritize curricula that combine technical training with creativity and ethics, preparing students for fluid, multidisciplinary roles. Labor planners and policymakers must forecast and support reskilling efforts, ensuring workers can transition into emerging job categories. Technology companies must invest in user-centered design and equitable access, acknowledging their influence on labor patterns and social well-being. Together, these efforts will be crucial in shaping an inclusive, dynamic, and sustainable future for entertainment and recreation work.

References

Abulibdeh, A., Zaidan, E., & Abulibdeh, R. (2024). Navigating the confluence of artificial intelligence and education for sustainable development in the era of industry 4.0: challenges, opportunities, and ethical dimensions. *Journal of Cleaner Production, 437*(1), 1–15. https://doi.org/10.1016/j.jclepro.2023.140527

Ahuja, V. (2021). Transforming the media and entertainment industry: cases from the social media marketing world. *Journal of Cases on Information Technology, 3*(4), 1–17. https://doi.org/10.1186/s12889-023-17028-1

Alojaiman, B. (2023). Technological modernizations in the industry 5.0 era: a descriptive analysis and future research directions. *Processes, 11*(5), 1318. https://doi.org/10.3390/pr11051318

Asakitikpi, A., Aderogba, A., & Nnamani, J. A. (2018). Socialization through leisure: A case study of nickelodeon cable television. *International Journal of the Sociology of Leisure, 1*(1), 99–115. https://doi.org/10.1007/s41978-018-0008-8

Billieux, J., Deleuze, J., Griffiths, M. D., & Kuss, D. J. (2014). Internet gaming addiction: the case of massively multiplayer online role-playing games. In: N. el-Guebaly, M. Galanter and G. Carrà (Eds.), *Textbook of Addiction Treatment: International Perspectives* (pp. 1515–1525). Milan: Springer. https://https://doi.org/10.1007/978-88-470-5322-9105

Bingaman, K. A. (2023). Religion in the digital age: an irreversible process. *Religions, 14*(1), 108. https://doi.org/10.3390/rel14010108

Budzinski, O., Gaenssle, S., & Lindstädt-Dreusicke, N. (2021). The battle of YouTube, TV and Netflix: an empirical analysis of competition in audiovisual media markets. *SN Business & Economics, 1*(9), 116. https://doi.org/10.1007/s43546-021-00122-0

Chai, A. (2011). Consumer specialization and the romantic transformation of the British grand tour of Europe. *Journal of Bioeconomics, 13*(3), 181–203. https://doi.org/10.1007/s10818-011-9110-4

Cheok, A. D., Teh, K. S., Nguyen, T. H. D., Qui, T. C. T., Lee, S. P., Liu, W., et al. (2006). Social and physical interactive paradigms for mixed-reality entertainment. *Computers in Entertainment, 4*(2), 5. https://doi.org/10.1145/1129006.1129015

Christopherson, S. (2008). Beyond the self-expressive creative worker: An industry perspective on entertainment media. *Theory, Culture & Society, 25*(7–8), 73–95. https://doi.org/10.1177/0263276408097797

Climent, R. C., & Haftor, D. M. (2021). Value creation through the evolution of business model themes. *Journal of Business Research, 122*(2), 353–361. https://doi.org/10.1016/j.jbusres.2020.09.007

Cowan, R. S. (2008). *More work for mother: The ironies of household technology from the open hearth to the microwave*. Basic Books.

Datta, A., & Goswami, R. (2021). The film industry leaps into artificial intelligence: scope and challenges by the filmmakers. In: V. S. Rathore, N. Dey, V. Piuri, R. Babo, Z. Polkowski, & J. M. R. S. Tavares (Eds.) *Rising threats in expert applications and solutions. Advances in Intelligent Systems and Computing, vol 1187* (pp. 860–869). Singapore: Springer. https://doi.org/10.1007/978-981-15-6014-9_80

De-la-Calle-Durán, M. C., & Rodríguez-Sánchez, J. L. (2021). Employee engagement and wellbeing in times of COVID-19: a proposal of the 5Cs model. *International Journal of Environmental Research and Public Health, 18*(10), 5470. https://doi.org/10.3390/ijerph18105470

Dolega, L., Rowe, F., & Branagan, E. (2021). Going digital? The impact of social media marketing on retail website traffic, orders and sales. *Journal of Retailing and Consumer Services, 60*, 102501. https://doi.org/10.1016/j.jretconser.2021.102501

Fang, C., Wang, W., Qiu, C., Hu, S., MacRae, G. A., & Eatherton, M. R. (2022). Seismic resilient steel structures: a review of research, practice, challenges and opportunities. *Journal of Constructional Steel Research, 191*, 107172. https://doi.org/10.1016/j.jcsr.2022.107172

Goralski, M. A., & Tan, T. K. (2020). Artificial intelligence and sustainable development. *The International Journal of Management Education, 18*(1), 100330. https://doi.org/10.1016/j.ijme.2019.100330

Gouriou, M. (2020). *Influence of virtual communities of companies in the gaming industry: a case study of mmo games*. Master's thesis, Copenhagen Business School, Copenhagen.

Hidayat, R., & Wardat, Y. (2024). A systematic review of augmented reality in science, technology, engineering and mathematics education. *Education and Information Technologies, 29*, 9257–9282. https://doi.org/10.1007/s10639-023-12157 x

Hurd, A., Anderson, D. M., & Mainieri, T. (2021). *Kraus' recreation and leisure in modern society* (12th ed.). Jones & Bartlett Learning.

Itam, U. J., & Warrier, U. (2024). Future of work from everywhere: A systematic review. *International Journal of Manpower, 45*(1), 12–48. https://doi.org/10.1108/IJM-06-2022-0288

Kenwright, B. (2022). *The hard truth about soft skills in game development*. Retrieved February 20, 2025, from https://arxiv.org/abs/2205.07875.

Kossek, E. E., Perrigino, M. B., & Lautsch, B. A. (2023). Work-life flexibility policies from a boundary control and implementation perspective: A review and research framework. *Journal of Management, 49*(6), 2062–2108. https://doi.org/10.1177/01492063221140354

Kuss, D. J., & Griffiths, M. D. (2011). Internet gaming addiction: A systematic review of empirical research. *International Journal of Mental Health and Addiction, 10*(2), 278–296. https://doi.org/10.1007/s11469-011-9318-5

Lanza, M., Sebastian, A., Lü, W., Gallo, M. L., Chang, M., Akinwande, D., et al. (2022). Memristive technologies for data storage, computation, encryption, and radio-frequency communication. *Science*. https://doi.org/10.1126/science.abj9979

Lindtner, S. (2011). The promise of play: a new approach to productive play. *Games and Culture, 6*(5), 453–478. https://doi.org/10.1177/1555412011402678

Lopez, K. J., Tong, C., Whate, A., & Boger, J. (2021). "It's a whole new way of doing things": the digital divide and leisure as resistance in a time of physical distance. *World Leisure Journal, 63*(3), 281–300. https://doi.org/10.1080/16078055.2021.1973553

Lotz, A. (2022). *Netflix and streaming video: The business of subscriber-funded video on demand* (1st ed.). Polity Press.

Marion, T. J., & Fixson, S. K. (2021). The transformation of the innovation process: How digital tools are changing work, collaboration, and organizations in new product development. *Journal of Product Innovation Management, 38*(1), 192–215. https://doi.org/10.1111/jpim.12547

Martins, N. C., Marques, B., Alves, J., Araújo, T., Dias, P., & Santos, B. S. (2022). Augmented reality situated visualization in decision-making. *Multimedia Tools and Applications, 81*(11), 14749–14772. https://doi.org/10.1007/s11042-021-10971-4

Matyushok, V., Krasavina, V., Berezin, A., & García, J. S. (2021). The global economy in technological transformation conditions: A review of modern trends. *Economic Research-Ekonomska Istraživanja, 34*(1), 1471–1497. https://doi.org/10.1080/1331677X.2020.1844030

Mishra, S., & Tyagi, A. K. (2022). The role of machine learning techniques in internet of things-based cloud applications. In: S. Pal, D. De, & R. Buyya (Eds.) *Artificial intelligence-based internet of things systems. Internet of Things* (pp. 63–82). Cham: Springer. https://doi.org/10.1007/978-3-030-87059-1_4

Nhamo, G., Dube, K., & Chikodzi, D. (2020). Implications of COVID-19 on gaming, leisure and entertainment industry. *In: Counting the Cost of COVID-19 on the Global Tourism Industry* (pp. 177–197). Cham: Springer. https:// https://doi.org/10.1007/978-3-030-56231-1_12

Ochiva, D. (2016). Entertainment technologies: past, present and future. In *The Movie Business Book* (pp. 543–581). Routledge.

Parker, S. (2021). *The sociology of leisure (1st ed.)*. London: Routledge. https://doi.org/10.4324/9781003213567

Ratchford, B., Soysal, G., Zentner, A., & Gauri, D. K. (2022). Online and offline retailing: What we know and directions for future research. *Journal of Retailing, 98*(1), 152–177. https://doi.org/10.1016/j.jretai.2022.02.007

Rho, M. J., Lee, H., Lee, T., Cho, H., Jung, D. J., Kim, D., & Choi, I. Y. (2017). Risk factors for internet gaming disorder: Psychological factors and internet gaming characteristics. *International Journal of Environmental Research and Public Health, 15*(1), 40. https://doi.org/10.3390/ijerph15010040

Roshan, F. S., Alhani, F., Zareiyan, A., & Kazemnejad, A. (2023). Development and psychometric properties of Iranian women's quality of life instrument (IWQOLI): Mixed exploratory study. *BMC Public Health*. https://doi.org/10.1186/s12889-023-17028-1

Rossner, M., Tait, D., & McCurdy, M. (2021). Justice reimagined: Challenges and opportunities with implementing virtual courts. *Current Issues in Criminal Justice, 33*(1), 94–110. https://doi.org/10.1080/10345329.2020.1859968

Saudagar, A. K. J., Kumar, A., & Khan, M. B. (2024). Mediverse beyond boundaries: a comprehensive analysis of AR and VR integration in medical education for diverse abilities. *Journal of Disability Research, 3*(1), 1–15. https://doi.org/10.57197/jdr-2023-0066

Shu, Y., & Huang, T. C. (2021). Identifying the potential roles of virtual reality and STEM in maker education. *The Journal of Educational Research, 114*(2), 108–118. https://doi.org/10.1080/00220671.2021.1887067

Smith, J. R., Snapp, B., Madar, S., Brown, J. R., Fowler, J., Andersen, M., et al. (2023). A smartphone-based virtual reality plotting system for STEM education. *Primus, 33*(1), 1–15. https://doi.org/10.1080/10511970.2021.2006378

Sosale, S. (2011). The knowledge economy and the domestic sphere. *Journal of International Communication, 17*(1), 3–20. https://doi.org/10.1080/13216597.2011.558003

Tribe, J. (2020). *The economics of recreation, leisure and tourism (6th ed.)*. London: Routledge. https://doi.org/10.4324/9780429278259

Zendle, D., Meyer, R., & Ballou, N. (2020). The changing face of desktop video game monetisation: an exploration of exposure to loot boxes, pay to win, and cosmetic microtransactions in the most-played Steam games of 2010–2019. *PLoS ONE, 15*(5), 1–13. https://doi.org/10.1371/journal.pone.0232780

CHAPTER 8

Navigating Tech Startup Financing: A Critical Review of Models, Challenges, and Future Trends

Ananthi Rajayya, Smarty P. Mukundan, and Fezeena Khadir

8.1 Introduction

Technology startups are leading the charge on innovation, economic development, and disruption across industries. Startups are bringing innovative solutions to the marketplace in important sectors such as software, artificial intelligence (AI), biotechnology, renewable energy, and

A. Rajayya (✉)
Amrita School of Business, Amrita Vishwa Vidyapeetham, Kochi, Kerala, India
e-mail: r_ananthi@asb.kochi.amrita.edu

S. P. Mukundan · F. Khadir
School of Management Studies, Cochin University of Science and Technology, Kochi, Kerala, India
e-mail: smarty123@cusat.ac.in

F. Khadir
e-mail: fezeena@cusat.ac.in

D. Kumar et al. (eds.), *Evolving Trends in Technology Entrepreneurship*, Palgrave Studies in Global Entrepreneurship,
https://doi.org/10.1007/978-981-95-7441-4_8

financial technology (FinTech). All of these innovations will have an impact on many other industries. (Mohammadi Lanbaran et al., 2024). Technology startups are catalyzing a shift in the global economy. They are pioneering new technologies and spearheading digital transformation. They are advancing artificial intelligence, blockchain technology, cybersecurity, biotechnology, and sustainable energy solutions. They are developing disruptive Business models, including subscription-based services, platform economies, and decentralized finance (DeFi) (Ballard, n.d.). When startups reach scale, they are creating jobs in engineering, marketing, finance, and operations. The startup ecosystem is able to attract and develop talent and skills. Many startups flourish as training campuses for future entrepreneurs, resulting in constant business creation. Startups are fostering competition by challenging traditional market-leading companies, driving up efficiency and productivity (Ballard, n.d.). They are democratizing access to technology by giving small businesses and consumers the opportunity to benefit from technology innovation. Industry leaders are often collaborating with or acquiring startups to outpace industry innovation. Successful startups can scale up globally, increasing the opportunities for cross-border trade and investment (Khuan et al., 2023). Governments have also recognized technology startups as engines of growth and are creating policy incentives, grants, and regulations to help their success. The expansion of the high-growth startups is creating a rich venture capital (VC) ecosystem (*The Role of Government Initiatives in Boosting Startups*, n.d.).

Tech startups exhibit distinct financial needs and challenges, unlike conventional businesses, in light of their intense growth trajectory and long development cycles coupled with ambiguous revenue streams (Singh & Bala Subrahmanya, 2022). Access to adequate capital is arguably the most influential factor on the success of a tech startup. Capital is important for R&D, product development and commercialization, scaling, and other matters relating to entry into markets, competition, and regulation. According to Resource Dependency Theory, startups are dependent on external resources to overcome their internal limitations, which shapes their strategic choices and relationships with financiers. This dependence on external capital creates power asymmetries that influence decision-making, governance structures, and funding negotiations.

Financial requirements of startups evolve as they grow, which necessitates varying financial sources at different stages (Pardo-del-Val et al., 2024). In line with the theory, as startups progress from seed to growth and expansion stages, their increasing resource needs heighten their dependence on external investors, thereby influencing their bargaining power and strategic autonomy. Early-stage investors, large businesses such as Angel investors or growth stage investors, CVC or Private Equity (PE) investors, are typically the most important sources of funding (Hegeman et al., 2024). CVC is the process of individual service firms making minority investments in entrepreneurial firms with set objectives that may reflect either financial or strategic objectives. CVC has also been identified as one potential avenue to facilitate ambidexterity, whereby the minority investment in a startup enhances either the internal exploitative capabilities of established firms or their ability to explore new markets and technologies (Pinkow & Iversen, 2020). Startups strategically choose among these funding sources to not only obtain financial resources but also to access complementary strategic assets such as market networks, technological expertise, and institutional legitimacy needed to reduce environmental uncertainties and enhance survival prospects. Governments and investors are dependent and essential for financing startups; they can provide funding and policy frameworks in exercise of their influence to stimulate the growth of startups through financing (*The Role of Government Initiatives in Boosting Startups*, n.d.). Venture capital, followed by public offerings, is traditional, but private equity is increasingly used for growth funding. Besides collaborations with large corporations and participation in tech hubs like Silicon Valley, foster innovation and provide startups with the necessary resources and knowledge (Ahluwalia & Kassicieh, 2024).

Acquiring sufficient capital at the right moment can be challenging due to several financing strategies, each with distinct advantages, dangers, and trade-offs. Various funding mechanisms for entrepreneurial initiatives have emerged in recent years, including incubators, startup accelerators, family investment funds, social impact investors, and state-owned sovereign wealth funds, which enable new enterprises to access a wider range of financial sources and types (Manigart & Khosravi, 2024). High uncertainty and information asymmetries make it difficult for startups to secure early-stage financing. This is particularly challenging in markets like India, where first-time entrepreneurs struggle with product-market fit and valuation (*Major Challenges Facing Startups in India and How to Overcome Them, Startup Challenges, India Startups, Overcoming Obstacles*, n.d.). Startups need to manage human, research, and social capital effectively. The choice of financial source often depends on these needs.

Effective policies and government interventions can play a crucial role in fostering technological innovations and supporting startups (*Major Challenges Facing Startups in India and How to Overcome Them, Startup Challenges, India Startups, Overcoming Obstacles*, n.d.).

This systematic literature review focuses on both traditional and new financing models for tech startups, representing an important gap in understanding their utilization across different technology sectors. In focusing on the key factors associated with the choice of financing models across various technology sectors, the review also explores the key challenges tech-driven startups experience in raising funding at different intervals of development. The review concludes by providing potential research paths to further develop research in this area. More specifically, the subsequent research questions (RQs) have been formulated to systematically review the literature on financing mechanisms for tech startups.

RQ1: What key factors determine the choice of financing models for startups across different technology sectors?

RQ2: What are the key challenges technology-driven startups face in securing funding across different stages of development?

8.2 Methodology

This research adopts a systematic literature review (SLR) methodology to investigate financing frameworks, identify challenges, and explore emerging trends in the funding of technology startups. This review was undertaken using the Preferred Reporting Items for Systematic Reviews and Meta-Analyses (PRISMA) protocol (Page et al., 2021). It provides comprehensive guidelines for conducting transparent, rigorous, and reproducible systematic reviews and meta-analyses. The methodical process used for article selection in compliance with the PRISMA protocol is described in Fig. 8.1.

The method follows a transparent process for identifying, screening, and assessing relevant academic literature through Scopus, one of the largest citation databases of peer-reviewed research. A Boolean search strategy was executed using the query: (technology OR tech) AND (startup OR venture OR "tech-based enterprise") AND (financing OR funding OR investment) to ensure a comprehensive consideration of studies discussing financing mechanisms and challenges in select technology sectors. The query was used in the title, abstract, and keywords

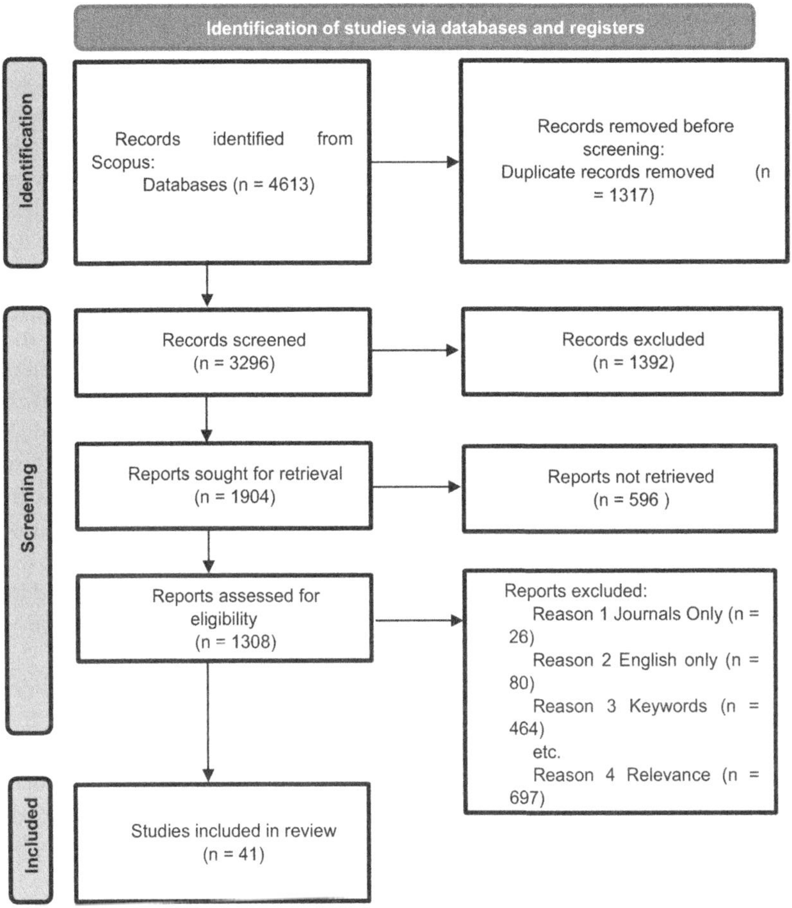

Fig. 8.1 PRISMA flow diagram illustrating article selection. (*Database searched*: Scopus)

fields for the searches to maximize relevancy. Following the initial analysis of results, additional filters by subject were applied, including Management, Business Studies, and Financial Accounting; Economic Sciences, Econometric Analysis, and Financial Studies; Clean Energy and Green Tech Startups; Biochemistry, Genetics, and Molecular Biology for Biotech Startups; Medicine for HealthTech Startups; Environmental Science for

Sustainability and Impact Investing; and Social Sciences for policy, regulation and entrepreneurship.

In order to maintain relevance and rigor, specific inclusion and exclusion criteria were established for the paper. Full-text articles and conference papers published in peer-reviewed journals indexed in Scopus and published between 2015 and 2025 were included to obtain relevant up-to-date articles. Peer-reviewed studies focused on funding models, challenges, and financing trends for tech startups were eligible for inclusion. In addition, studies that offered empirical data on startup financing, considering theoretical research, were included as well. Articles specifically on emerging financing trends, such as digital financing and blockchain-based investments, were also considered for inclusion. There were also strict exclusion criteria. First, articles that were not related to financing startups and solely focused on large companies were excluded. Second, book chapters were excluded, and any articles published in other languages were excluded. Studies that were not published in peer-reviewed journals, editorials, or articles that offered limited data or anecdotal evidence were excluded.

Key funding sources for tech startups were identified through data extraction and analysis. These included venture capital, angel investment, crowdfunding, and government grants. The data extraction and analysis also examined some of the challenges associated with these funding sources, including challenges of valuations, equity dilution, and regulatory barriers, as well as emerging trends, especially with respect to digital financing, revenue-based funding, and decentralized finance. Geographical perspectives were offered in the data extraction and analysis to demonstrate some of the discrepancies in funding ecosystems by place. Lastly, both qualitative and quantitative analysis techniques were employed to determine findings across the reviewed literature and to inform the research questions in relation to the determinants and challenges of financing tech startups. During the data extraction and analysis, multiple researchers validated each of the pieces of literature selected for the study. Nonetheless, limitations to the methodology were noted when reporting the findings.

One limitation of the limitations is that the database was limited to Scopus, excluding potentially relevant studies in alternatives such as Web of Science and Google Scholar. Second, the focus was on the period of 2015–2025, excluding all potentially relevant studies by virtue of their publication date, regardless of ethical integrity. There was also the potential for the method to exhibit industry-specific bias and not adequately represent niche industries. The validity of methodology was also improved by drawing from solely peer-reviewed materials, although this could result in the omission of valuable literature in industry reports or non-conclusions. Despite these limitations, this is a robust methodology for reviewing literature regarding tech startup financing that identifies important funding models, challenges, and suggests future avenues for research. In the following section, the findings and their broader implications from the reviewed studies will be analyzed.

8.3 Results and Discussion

Startups in many technology areas encounter distinct fundraising constraints and possibilities influenced by factors such as capital intensity, revenue models, risk profiles, and regulatory obstacles (Junada Sulillari, 2023). Comprehending the determinants that influence financial model selections is crucial for entrepreneurs, investors, and governments aiming to optimize funding mechanisms and augment the likelihood of startup success (Junada Sulillari, 2023). Moreover, pursuing finance at various developmental phases—from seed capital to late-stage expansion—poses distinct hurdles, including securing venture capital, assessing financial viability, and adhering to regulatory requirements (Pinkow & Iversen, 2020). This literature study analyzes the principal elements influencing financing decisions for startups within technology industries and identifies critical challenges that startups encounter in securing funding at various growth stages.

8.3.1 Tech Startup Financing Models Across Different Sectors

The choice of financing strategies for startups in different technology areas is influenced by a blend of sector-specific factors, startup-specific characteristics, and ecosystem conditions. Resource dependency theory suggests that startups actively seek to minimize dependencies that can threaten their autonomy, often preferring financing models that offer strategic resources alongside capital, such as knowledge, networks, and legitimacy. For example, corporate venture capital not only provides funds but also reduces environmental uncertainty through strategic support, thus becoming attractive despite ownership dilution. Figure 8.2 illustrates the framework for determining the choice of financing models for startups across technology sectors.

Startups in capital-intensive industries, including deep tech, biotech, and cleantech, necessitate substantial finance due to prolonged R&D cycles, regulatory obligations, and commercialization challenges (Nguyen et al., 2024). Consequently, these sectors generally fund innovation

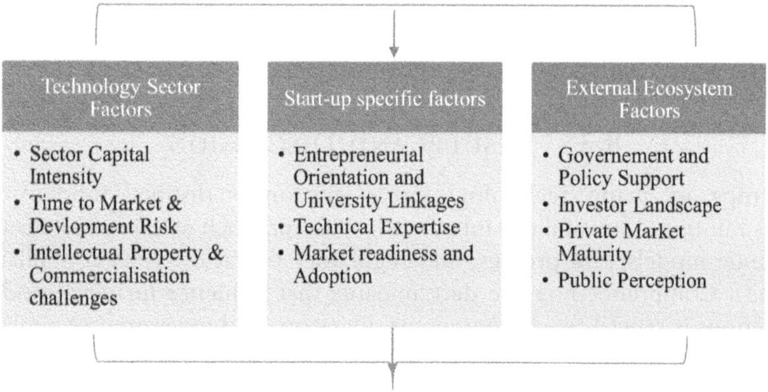

Suitable Financing Models across different technology sectors	
Technology Sector	**Primary Financing Models**
Deep Tech Sectors like AI, Quantum, Robotics	Venture Capital, Governement Grants, Corporate Partnerships
Biotech & Healthcare	Governement Funding, Venture Capital and Corporate R&D partnerships
FinTech & RegTech	Angel Investors, Corporate Funding, VC, Private Equity
CleanTech and ClimateTech	Impact Investors, Green Bonds, VC, Carbon Credit Financing
SaaS & Consumer Tech	Bootstrapping, Crowdfunding, Angel Investment, Revenue based Financing
AgriTech & FoodTech	University Grants, Funding from Technology Transfer Organisations, Government Subsidies, Impact Investors

Fig. 8.2 Framework for determining the choice of financing models for startups across technology sectors, compiled by the authors

via venture capital, government grants, and collaborations with corporate research and development. Conversely, digital and SaaS firms that necessitate lower capital investment and possess shorter market timelines frequently utilize bootstrapping, angel financing, or crowdfunding as their funding mechanism (*How to Get SaaS Funding for Your Startup in 6 Steps*, n.d.). Crowdfunding platforms that employ equity provide investors the opportunity to become shareholders by acquiring minor ownership interests in novel innovative enterprises (Cicchiello & Kazemikhasragh, 2022). Startups are able to access financial resources through investor networks which were developed via crowdfunding. Organizational challenges like gaps in resources and trust issues, and information asymmetry often obstruct success. Emerging strategies for overcoming such organizational barriers include investor mapping, establishing proactive communication plans, and crowd stratifying (Pietro et al., 2021). The complexities of contemporary major challenges and the focus on public awareness have propelled business endeavors into the realm of ESG (Environmental, Social, and Governance) issues. Entrepreneurial universities have begun to acknowledge this transition toward ESG in their efforts to commercialize through technology transfer and the involvement of academic spin-offs. Government initiatives that facilitate startup financing, such as Germany's EXIST program, have recently encouraged this shift toward impact entrepreneurship with sustainable momentum as a means of economic development (Lehmann et al., 2024). Collaboration with technology transfer offices, corporate and industry experts, and strategic partners is crucial to support academic inventors in navigating the complex commercialization process (Eidlisz et al., 2024). High-tech companies are prospering in knowledge economies by means of creative goods, utilization of intellectual property (IP), and commercialization techniques. Academic institutions are integral to this ecosystem, regarded as the origin of research, technological transfer, and entrepreneurial assistance (Yetisen et al., 2015). Technological advancements are typically seen as effective for reducing the environmental implications of economic activities. However, for organizations, especially SMEs, achieving innovation success depends on securing appropriate external financing (Demirel & Parris, 2015). Impact Tech Startups (ITSs) are a burgeoning organizational category that employs new ways to tackle societal and environmental challenges while operating under a for-profit framework, often supported by private financing (Gidron et al., 2021).

Elements specific to startups, in conjunction with industry features, are essential for identifying the most suitable funding method, including resources and support, given that nascent companies depend on financial resources for legitimacy during the startup and scale-up phases (Lange et al., 2024). Startups affiliated with universities will have access to additional financing resources, including research grants and incubator help, whereas independent startups typically pursue angel investments or accelerator funding (*Accelerator-Mediated Access to Investors among Early-Stage Start-Ups | Annals of Operations Research*, n.d.). Corporate angels are considered a vital provider of seed funding and early-stage funding for technology startups because of their comparable technological expertise and industry experience, as well as their proactive involvement in the investment and development of these enterprises (Hegeman et al., 2024). Investments by corporate angels will also result in additional kinds of investor knowledge inflows into the corporate angel firm, enhancing the organizational and cultural processes of the firm (Hegeman et al., 2024). Moreover, firms possessing commercialization ability and seasoned business leaders are likely to attract venture capital investment (*Accelerator-Mediated Access to Investors among Early-Stage Start-Ups | Annals of Operations Research*, n.d.). Entities founded predominantly by technical entrepreneurs may pursue equity via strategic alliances for commercialization and expansion in ventures or venture builders (*Accelerator-Mediated Access to Investors among Early-Stage Start-Ups | Annals of Operations Research*, n.d.). Barriers to adoption specific to regulated areas such as healthcare and fintech necessitate affluent finance sources that offer patient capital to adhere to bureaucratic funding systems, hence restricting startups. Innovations in consumer interaction, as observed in e-commerce and SaaS, facilitate the market entry of consumer innovations via crowdfunding and revenue-based financing, enabling scalable capital (Dey, 2024).

Finally, the wider external ecosystem, encompassing government legislation, the investor landscape, and public perception, influences the financing alternatives accessible to a company. Countries with robust national innovation policies, such as Thailand's "Thailand 4.0" effort and the EU's Green Tech initiatives, typically provide targeted assistance through grants and subsidies, leading to non-dilutive financing alternatives for emerging businesses. In advanced venture ecosystems like the U.S. and Europe, venture capital and private equity prevail, but emerging markets generally depend on other funding mechanisms such as microfinance and loan financing. Project initiators contemplating alternative funding models, including equity-based crowdfunding, peer lending, and incentive-based funding platforms, must recognize both the challenges and opportunities involved in raising awareness for their projects and securing financing from crowd investors (Camilleri & Bresciani, 2024). Moreover, social proof and public perception influence fundraising; consumer-oriented startups can showcase their market potential through crowdfunding platforms, whereas B2B startups must establish legitimacy and credibility through institutional partnerships and strategic investors (Camilleri & Bresciani, 2024). FoodTech and Agri companies invest in technology-driven transformations to enhance their primary operations, implement defensive strategies against technological threats to the core operations, and formulate portfolio strategies that leverage profit opportunities, thereby securing increased financial support from corporate venture capital investors (Mac Clay et al., 2024).

By aligning funding options with sector needs, startup maturity, and funding availability, entrepreneurs can optimize the financial landscape to serve their growth and impact.

Furthermore, comparative analyses reveal that while venture capital is predominant in the United States due to robust investor networks and favorable tax structures, in contrast, countries like Germany and Japan rely more on bank loans and government-backed funds owing to conservative risk cultures and strong banking systems (*Financing SMEs and Entrepreneurs 2020*, 2020). Integrating these international differences deepens the understanding of how financing models operate within specific regulatory and cultural environments.

Recent scholarship by Collinson (2025) expanded this typology beyond advanced economies to include emerging and developing regions. In contexts across Asia, Latin America, and Africa, institutional frameworks—ranging from regulatory quality to venture readiness—fundamentally shape the configuration and effectiveness of startup financing models. As such, a more inclusive varieties-of-capitalism approach is essential for understanding how capital-intensive innovation ecosystems emerge globally under distinctive institutional constraints.

8.3.2 Challenges in Securing Funding Across Different Stages of Development

Securing funding for startups across different technology sectors presents distinct challenges at various stages of development. Figure 8.3 depicts the framework for challenges in securing funding across different stages of development. In the early stage, where ideas are still being conceptualized and research is ongoing, startups face high risks and uncertainty, making it difficult to attract institutional investors. A major barrier for early-stage companies is the shortage of venture capital combined with inadequate entrepreneurial experimentation needed for growth (Corsatea, 2014; Jones, 2014). Many rely on government grants, university spin-off funds, and crowdfunding to support initial development. For example, the scarcity of private funding for technology transfer activities significantly hampers the commercialization of university-developed technologies (Munari et al., 2018). Internal gap funding from universities would significantly facilitate the translation of academic technologies into the marketplace (Munari et al., 2018). Regulatory hurdles, particularly in healthcare, fintech, and deep tech, further complicate early-stage financing. To overcome these barriers, startups must establish credibility through proof-of-concept demonstrations, partnerships with research institutions, or early customer validation. The financial gap impacts environmental SMEs that are engaged in early-stage and less applicable research initiatives. It becomes essential for these SMEs to participate in creative activities and advocate for enhanced government intervention to help innovative SMEs with early-stage projects, thereby instilling trust in private investors through the demonstration of long-term commitment (Demirel & Parris, 2015). Women-led startups face challenges such as deep-rooted cultural attitudes, societal pressures, lack of exposure, and financial constraints in their early stages (Alateeg & Al-Ayed, 2024; Sylla & Uzor, 2023). Battery companies face challenges stemming from substantial funding requirements and protracted commercialization processes, which hinder their ability to develop financially sustainable products (Hanson et al., 2017). The development of sustainable startups relies significantly on venture capital investment (Bocken, 2015).

As startups move into the growth stage, they require significant capital to develop prototypes, navigate regulatory approvals, and establish market entry strategies. Under Resource Dependency Theory, their financing decisions at this stage are driven by the need to access critical

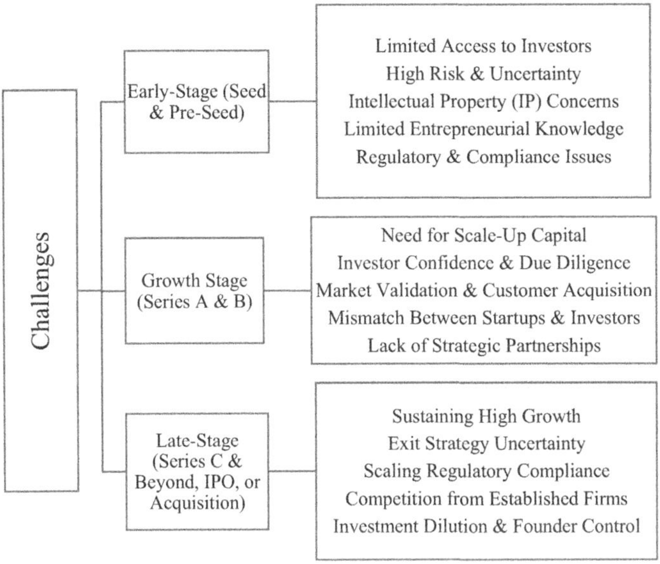

Fig. 8.3 Framework for challenges in securing funding across different stages of development, compiled by the authors

external resources while managing dependency risks that could compromise their strategic direction or innovation focus. This phase demands funding from venture capital firms, strategic industry partnerships, and debt financing for asset-heavy sectors like manufacturing or cleantech. However, attracting investors at this stage necessitates a clear commercialization plan and an ability to demonstrate scalability. Many technology-driven startups face difficulties in aligning their growth plans with investor expectations, often struggling with infrastructure expansion, competitive market positioning, and securing industry-specific accelerators that can provide both capital and strategic guidance. Healthtech startups face significant hurdles in acquiring venture capital due to high risks, complex regulations, and the need for substantial funding, making it challenging to secure investment and scale their operations (Shaw & Glover, 2024; Skolkovo Foundation, Moscow, Russia & Khodova, 2017). Clean energy financing is transitioning from early-stage venture capital to mainstream investment, driven by increasing government policies, corporate commitments, and investor demand for sustainable assets (Temmes et al., 2021).

Startups encounter adoption obstacles like elevated prices, cybersecurity threats, and a demand for proficient personnel. Surmounting these obstacles can facilitate business-to-business investments, local and international market prospects, and enhancements in industry-wide efficiency (Kamalapuram & Choudhury, 2024).

During the expansion stage, startups focus on scaling operations, expanding into new markets, and competing with well-funded industry players. Investor expectations are high, with venture capital firms and private equity investors seeking strong financial performance and defined exit strategies. Following regulatory compliances due diligently would facilitate the Tech startups to get adequate funding. Incentive programs like HITECH[1] can catalyze innovation in regulated industries, resulting in greater investment in seed-stage healthcare IT firms (Lite et al., 2020; Winkler et al., 2016).

Funding options at this stage include private equity investments, IPOs for high-growth companies, and revenue-based financing models for subscription-driven businesses like SaaS. Startups must also navigate global market challenges, including regulatory compliance and operational risks. To succeed in this phase, companies must optimize their financial strategies, secure long-term partnerships, and position themselves for potential mergers, acquisitions, or public listings to ensure sustained growth.

8.4 Conclusion

The literature underscores that financing decisions are highly sector-specific, shaped by factors such as capital intensity, scalability, revenue models, risk levels, regulatory considerations, and exit strategies. The influence of venture capital on SME growth is positive but not significant (Schweickart et al., 2023). While VC funding remains dominant in high-growth sectors, alternative financing models, including revenue-based financing, crowdfunding, and strategic partnerships, are gaining prominence in sectors with stable cash flows or longer development cycles (Cumming et al., 2023). Additionally, securing funding at different

[1] The Health Information Technology for Economic and Clinical Health (HITECH) Act was enacted in 2009 as part of the American Recovery and Reinvestment Act (ARRA). It aimed to promote the adoption and meaningful use of electronic health records (EHRs) and enhance healthcare IT infrastructure in the United States.

startup stages presents unique challenges, from the initial struggle to validate business models to investor concerns over growth sustainability (Junada Sulillari, 2023).

The literature also reveals that securing funding remains one of the most significant challenges for technology-driven startups, evolving across different stages of development. While seed-stage startups struggle with market validation and limited funding sources, early-stage ventures face regulatory barriers and due diligence requirements. Growth-stage startups encounter stiff competition for capital and scalability risks, whereas late-stage firms must navigate investor expectations, macroeconomic risks, and regulatory scrutiny. Startups need to take appropriate measures, like enhancing the influx of unrestricted funding for creative companies and augmenting both the quantity and quality of advanced projects to meet investor expectations (Kulanov et al., 2020). Addressing these challenges requires tailored financial strategies, policy interventions, and innovative funding mechanisms to support startup ecosystems globally. Applying Resource Dependency Theory further underscores the importance of designing financing structures that balance startups' dependence on external resources with their need for strategic autonomy, ensuring that capital inflows do not compromise long-term innovation goals and organizational mission. There is a need for flexible policy frameworks that can support startups in overcoming challenges associated with financing, regulation, and market integration. A strong policy framework must foster innovation, be accessible with funding, with limited regulatory burden for startups during the initial stages—enabling growth and scaling, and engaging in global best practices to encourage an innovative ecosystem that supports a startup's entire life cycle (Sudaryana et al., 2025).

While this research provides valuable knowledge of the financial strategies and general challenges technology-focused firms contend with in the development life cycle, there are some limitations. The results can be better understood in the context of these limitations, also indicating areas for further examination and enhancements in future research. The study was limited to works that were listed in the Scopus database. This could have excluded relevant sources from other databases such as Web of Science or Google Scholar, which might feature more telling articles. The study analyzed articles from 2015 to 2025, altogether dismissing any prior literature that could have provided useful background information or historical context. The methodology may also contain bias toward general or well-covered technology sectors which are generally disregarded for more niche or emerging industries. Future research may be conducted around how emerging financial technologies like blockchain-based funding and DeFi—decentralized finance can revolutionize the startup funding landscape.

References

Accelerator-mediated access to investors among early-stage start-ups/Annals of Operations Research. (n.d.). Retrieved March 31, 2025, from https://doi.org/10.1007/s10479-023-05583-0

Ahluwalia, S., & Kassicieh, S. (2024). Pathways to success: The interplay of industry and venture capital clusters in entrepreneurial company exits. *Journal of Risk and Financial Management, 17*(4), 4. https://doi.org/10.3390/jrfm17040159

Alateeg, S., & Al-Ayed, S. (2024). Exploring the role of artificial intelligence technology in empowering women-led startups. *Knowledge and Performance Management, 8*(2), 28–38. https://doi.org/10.21511/kpm.08(2).2024.03

Ballard, M. (n.d.). *Tech Startups to Watch in 2024: Innovations and Breakthroughs*. Slashdev.Io—Hire Freelance Software Engineers. Retrieved March 31, 2025, from https://slashdev.io/-tech-startups-to-watch-in-2024-innovations-and-breakthroughs

Bocken, N. M. P. (2015). Sustainable venture capital–catalyst for sustainable start-up success? *Journal of Cleaner Production, 108*, 647–658. https://doi.org/10.1016/j.jclepro.2015.05.079

Camilleri, M. A., & Bresciani, S. (2024). Crowdfunding small businesses and startups: A systematic review, an appraisal of theoretical insights and future research directions. *European Journal of Innovation Management, 27*(7), 2183–2209. https://doi.org/10.1108/EJIM-02-2022-0060

Cicchiello, A. F. F., & Kazemikhasragh, A. (2022). Tackling gender bias in equity crowdfunding: An exploratory study of investment behaviour of Latin American investors. *European Business Review, 34*(3), 370–395. https://doi.org/10.1108/EBR-08-2021-0187

Collinson, S. (2025). Towards more inclusive varieties of capitalism. *Elements in Reinventing Capitalism*. https://doi.org/10.1017/9781009513616

Corsatea, T. D. (2014). Increasing synergies between institutions and technology developers: Lessons from marine energy. *Energy Policy, 74*, 682–696. https://doi.org/10.1016/j.enpol.2014.07.006

Cumming, D., Kumar, S., Lim, W. M., & Pandey, N. (2023). Mapping the venture capital and private equity research: A bibliometric review and future research agenda. *Small Business Economics, 61*(1), 173–221. https://doi.org/10.1007/s11187-022-00684-9

Demirel, P., & Parris, S. (2015). Access to finance for innovators in the UK's environmental sector. *Technology Analysis & Strategic Management, 27*(7), 782–808. https://doi.org/10.1080/09537325.2015.1019849

Dey, A. (2024). The emergence of alternative financing models: An in-depth analysis of revenue-based financing. *Journal of Global Economy, Business and Finance, 6*(12), 1–6. https://doi.org/10.53469/jgebf.2024.06(12).01

Eidlisz, J., Von Simson, I., & Gold-von Simson, G. (2024). Exploring the current state of technology transfer in the United States: Perspectives and improvement strategies from the experts. *Frontiers in Research Metrics and Analytics, 9*, 1376185. https://doi.org/10.3389/frma.2024.1376185

Financing SMEs and Entrepreneurs 2020. (2020). OECD. https://www.oecd.org/en/publications/financing-smes-and-entrepreneurs-2020_061fe03d-en.html

Gidron, B., Israel-Cohen, Y., Bar, K., Silberstein, D., Lustig, M., & Kandel, D. (2021). Impact tech startups: A conceptual framework, machine-learning-based methodology and future research directions. *Sustainability, 13*(18), 10048. https://doi.org/10.3390/su131810048

Hanson, E. D., Mayekar, S., & Dravid, V. P. (2017). Applying insights from the pharma innovation model to battery commercialization—Pros, cons, and pitfalls. *MRS Energy & Sustainability, 4*(1), 10. https://doi.org/10.1557/mre.2017.12

Hegeman, P. D., Sørheim, R., Landström, H., & Saether, E. A. (2024). Corporate angels: A new breed of investors in the funding landscape for technology-based start-ups. *Technovation, 134*, Article 103016. https://doi.org/10.1016/j.technovation.2024.103016

How to Get SaaS Funding for Your Startup in 6 Steps. (n.d.). Retrieved March 31, 2025, from https://payproglobal.com/how-to/get-saas-funding/

Jones, C. H. (2014). Canadian venture capital—Unlocking the funding challenge. *Journal of Commercial Biotechnology*. https://doi.org/10.5912/jcb649

Junada Sulillari, Ph. D. C. (2023). An analysis of the funding challenges that a start-up has to deal with and the impact that it can have on the future of the company. In *Proceedings of The 6th International Conference on Management, Economics and Finance*. The 6th International Conference on Management, Economics and Finance. https://doi.org/10.33422/6th.icmef.2023.03.001

Kamalapuram, S. K., & Choudhury, D. (2024). Industry 4.0 technologies for cultivated meat manufacturing. *Food Bioengineering, 3*(1), 14–28. https://doi.org/10.1002/fbe2.12080

Khuan, H., Andriani, E., & Rukmana, A. Y. (2023). The role of technology in fostering innovation and growth in start-up businesses. *West Science Journal*

Economic and Entrepreneurship, 1(03), 124–133. https://doi.org/10.58812/wsjee.v1i03.151

Kulanov, A., Issakhova, A., Koshkina, O., Issakhova, P., & Karshalova, A. (2020). Venture financing and the fuel and energy complex: Investing in alternative energy. *International Journal of Energy Economics and Policy, 10*(5), 531–538. https://doi.org/10.32479/ijeep.9963

Lange, J., Rezepa, S., & Zatrochová, M. (2024). The role of business angels in the early-stage financing of startups: A systematic literature review. *Administrative Sciences, 14*(10), 10. https://doi.org/10.3390/admsci14100247

Lehmann, E. E., Otto, J. M., & Wirsching, K. (2024). Entrepreneurial universities and the third mission paradigm shift from economic performance to impact entrepreneurship: Germany's EXIST program and ESG orientation. *The Journal of Technology Transfer, 49*(6), 2184–2199.

Lite, S., Gordon, W. J., & Stern, A. D. (2020). Association of the meaningful use electronic health record incentive program with health information technology venture capital funding. *JAMA Network Open, 3*(3), Article e201402. https://doi.org/10.1001/jamanetworkopen.2020.1402

Mac Clay, P., Feeney, R., & Sellare, J. (2024). Technology-driven transformations in agri-food global value chains: The role of incumbent firms from a corporate venture capital perspective. *Food Policy, 127*, Article 102684. https://doi.org/10.1016/j.foodpol.2024.102684

Major Challenges Facing Startups in India and How to Overcome Them, Startup Challenges, India Startups, Overcoming Obstacles. (n.d.). Retrieved March 31, 2025, from https://www.corpzo.com/major-challenges-facing-startups-in-india-and-how-to-overcome-them

Manigart, S., & Khosravi, S. (2024). Unanswered questions in entrepreneurial finance. *Venture Capital, 26*(1), 1–29. https://doi.org/10.1080/13691066.2023.2178349

Mohammadi Lanbaran, N., Naujokaitis, D., Kairaitis, G., Jenciūtė, G., & Radziukynienė, N. (2024). Overview of startups developing artificial intelligence for the energy sector. *Applied Sciences, 14*(18), 18. https://doi.org/10.3390/app14188294

Munari, F., Sobrero, M., & Toschi, L. (2018). The university as a venture capitalist? Gap funding instruments for technology transfer. *Technological Forecasting and Social Change, 127*, 70–84. https://doi.org/10.1016/j.techfore.2017.07.024

Nguyen, N. T. H., Kowalski, A. M., & Dzienis, A. M. (2024). Sustainable entrepreneurial process in the deep-tech industry. *Sustainability, 16*(19), 19. https://doi.org/10.3390/su16198714

Page, M. J., McKenzie, J. E., Bossuyt, P. M., Boutron, I., Hoffmann, T. C., Mulrow, C. D., Shamseer, L., Tetzlaff, J. M., Akl, E. A., Brennan, S. E., Chou, R., Glanville, J., Grimshaw, J. M., Hróbjartsson, A., Lalu, M. M., Li,

T., Loder, E. W., Mayo-Wilson, E., McDonald, S., & Moher, D. (2021). The PRISMA 2020 statement: An updated guideline for reporting systematic reviews. *Systematic Reviews, 10*(1), 89. https://doi.org/10.1186/s13643-021-01626-4

Pardo-del-Val, M., Cerver-Romero, E., Martinez-Perez, J. F., & Mohedano-Suanes, A. (2024). From startup to scaleup: Public policies for emerging entrepreneurial ecosystems. *Journal of the Knowledge Economy*. https://doi.org/10.1007/s13132-024-02175-6

Pietro, F. D., Bogers, M. L. A. M., & Prencipe, A. (2021). Organisational barriers and bridges to crowd openness in equity crowdfunding. *Technological Forecasting and Social Change, 162*, Article 120388. https://doi.org/10.1016/j.techfore.2020.120388

Pinkow, F., & Iversen, J. (2020). Strategic objectives of corporate venture capital as a tool for open innovation. *Journal of Open Innovation: Technology, Market, and Complexity, 6*(4), 157. https://doi.org/10.3390/joitmc6040157

Schweickart, T., Hill-Whilton, Z., Chitale, S., Cobos, D., Gilon-Yanai, M., Achuonjei, J., Vizgan, G., Gillespie, C., & Gold-von Simson, G. (2023). The biomedical entrepreneurship skills development program for the advancement of research translation: Foundations of biomedical startups course, metrics, and impact. *Journal of Clinical and Translational Science, 7*(1), Article e77. https://doi.org/10.1017/cts.2023.25

Shaw, J., & Glover, W. (2024). The political economy of digital health equity: Structural analysis. *Journal of Medical Internet Research, 26*, Article e46971. https://doi.org/10.2196/46971

Singh, S., & Bala Subrahmanya, M. H. (2022). The financial requirements of tech startups over its lifecycle in Bangalore: An analysis of why and how do they differ? *International Journal of Finance & Economics, 27*(4), 4123–4141. https://doi.org/10.1002/ijfe.2362

Skolkovo Foundation, Moscow, Russia, & Khodova, K. A. (2017). Genome games: Market challenges, investment opportunities and patent battles. *Cellular Therapy and Transplantation, 6*(1), 44–47. https://doi.org/10.18620/ctt-1866-8836-2017-6-1-44-47

Sudaryana, S. H., Wirjodirdjo, B., & Windrarto, A. (2025). A systematic literature review of digital startup business dynamics and policy interventions. *Cogent Business & Management, 12*(1), 2440636. https://doi.org/10.1080/23311975.2024.2440636

Sylla, P., & Uzor, N. (2023). Women, surgeons, and the innovation pipeline. *Clinics in Colon and Rectal Surgery, 36*(05), 342–346. https://doi.org/10.1055/s-0043-1764238

Temmes, A., Heiskanen, E., Matschoss, K., & Lovio, R. (2021). Mobilising mainstream finance for a future clean energy transition: The case of Finland.

Journal of Cleaner Production, 319, Article 128797. https://doi.org/10.1016/j.jclepro.2021.128797

The Role of Government Initiatives in Boosting Startups. (n.d.). Retrieved March 31, 2025, from https://www.investindia.gov.in/blogs/role-government-initiatives-boosting-startups

Winkler, T. J., Ozturk, P., & Brown, C. V. (2016). Sustainability strategies for regional health information organization startups. *Health Policy and Technology, 5*(4), 341–349. https://doi.org/10.1016/j.hlpt.2016.07.002

Yetisen, A. K., Volpatti, L. R., Coskun, A. F., Cho, S., Kamrani, E., Butt, H., Khademhosseini, A., & Yun, S. H. (2015). Entrepreneurship. *Lab on a Chip, 15*(18), 3638–3660. https://doi.org/10.1039/C5LC00577A

CHAPTER 9

"Tech for Good" as a Catalyst for Social Entrepreneurship: Revealing Research Topics with Unsupervised Topic Modeling with Latent Dirichlet Allocation (LDA)

Richa Goyal and Swati Garg

9.1 Introduction

An emerging phenomenon of Socio-tech entrepreneurship aligns with the United Nations' Sustainable Development Goals (SDGs). These entrepreneurs are leveraging technology to address social problems by maintaining economic sustainability. Social-tech entrepreneurship is essential for framing policies for society and industry, as this entrepreneurship aims to "develop and deploy technology-driven solutions to address

R. Goyal (✉) · S. Garg
Department of Business Administration, National Institute of Technology, Kurukshetra, Haryana, India
e-mail: 62300003@nitkkr.ac.in

S. Garg
e-mail: 62310029@nitkkr.ac.in

D. Kumar et al. (eds.), *Evolving Trends in Technology Entrepreneurship*, Palgrave Studies in Global Entrepreneurship,
https://doi.org/10.1007/978-981-95-7441-4_9

social needs" (Sargent & Ahmed, 2017), and is comparatively different from high-tech companies. These conceptions shift the behavior at organizational and individual levels for the people and the planet benefits. Though the availability of literature related to technology-oriented social entrepreneurship is in its nascent stage, there is an intervening need for academicians to assist social entrepreneurs in effectively and efficiently meeting their societal objectives. This study pertains to address this gap by scientifically mapping the trending themes related to the Socio-tech entrepreneurship aspect, targeting future researchers for further research development over technology-driven social entrepreneurship. 1,168 abstracts were systematically studied on "Social Entrepreneurship," "Technology Entrepreneurship," and "Socio-Tech," which were published during the year 2010 to January 2025. Descriptive and content analysis methods were employed to conceptualize STE as a standalone theme under the entrepreneurship conceptualization.

The conceptual framework of literature distinguishes the "Socio-Tech Entrepreneurship" from "Social Entrepreneurship" and "Technology Entrepreneurship," legitimating it as an autonomous research topic. The Social Entrepreneurship (SE) addresses the social problems, whereas the Technology Entrepreneurship (TE) emphasizes extracting value from technical and innovative capabilities (Bailetti et al., 2012). The Socio-Tech Entrepreneurship (STE) has integrated these two concepts as STE are ventures that inherently combine technological innovation with the explicit aim of generating social value and are not merely technologically driven or socially motivated in isolation (Desa & Kotha, 2006). STE as a standalone category where technological capabilities are leveraged explicitly for social betterment rather than the commercial gain alone. The global priorities reflect dominance of themes like digital technology and frugal innovation in STE (Zahra et al., 2023). Though this focus has been overshadowed by governance, ethical tensions, and cross-cultural dynamics (Grassi and Toschi, 2024). These underexplored dimensions highlight the need for deeper theoretical engagement to advance the field (Poonamallee et al., 2020).

The comprehensive assessment of the literature unveils latent topics, particularly for "Technology or Social Entrepreneurship" and topics like "socio-technology entrepreneurship" are yet to be addressed as potential future research opportunities. Moreover, this study has extracted and visualized the latent themes for the "Socio-tech entrepreneurship" available academic literature through the topic modeling technique (LDA).

The findings of this study revealed the five major related themes, namely, (1) Entrepreneurial Learning for Shaping Sustainable Futures, (2) Designing and Modernizing Social Entrepreneurship, (3) Tech-Driven Entrepreneurship, (4) Social Entrepreneurship and its Resource Mobilization, and (5) Longitudinal Effects of Social Entrepreneurship. "Socio-tech entrepreneurship" research has a significant impact on business and other disciplines, including management, social sciences, engineering, and mathematics. This study aims to introduce the relevant socio-tech entrepreneurship themes with an appropriate methodology of topic modeling, for contributing toward the following research question:

RQ1: What are the majorly discussed themes of scholarly interest in the field of Socio-Tech Entrepreneurship?

9.2 Review of Literature

9.2.1 Socio-tech entrepreneurship (STE)

The mission and concept of the businesses are explored by STE entrepreneurs. It makes it essential to investigate whether the specific individual or behavioral characteristics of STEs are identified in the literature or not. In the earlier studies, STE is narrated with TPB, HCT, and AT theories, and is aligned with the SN, PBC, work experience, EE, and cognitive and psychological traits dimensions.

The subjective norms are about collectively shaping STEs' vision for stakeholder commitment (Ariza-Montes & Muniz, 2013). PBC helps STEs in overcoming limitations and obstacles with creative solutions (Linna, 2013). Work experience ensures competence to handle dynamic business challenges (Scillitoe et al., 2018a, 2018b). EE is the specialized expertise of the founding members or entrepreneurs (Austin & Leonard, 2008). Finally, cognitive and psychological traits include self-confidence in their skills to motivate them to achieve their work mission (Linna, 2013) and support them in their operational work (Scillitoe et al., 2018a, 2018b).

Several scholars have explored socio-tech entrepreneurship (STE) and related fields through diverse theoretical lenses and qualitative approaches. Chou and Lin (2024) adopted IDT, TPB, and CAT, employing a qualitative methodology supported by meta-analysis. Diaz Gonzalez and Dentchev (2021), while not explicitly grounded in theory, conducted a qualitative literature review to explore themes within the field. Farinha et al. (2020) utilized IT, TAT, IST, ET, actor-network theory, and SMT for bibliometric analysis. Gupta et al. (2020) brought in theories such as servant leadership, institutional complexities, social movement, social learning and self-efficacy, paradox, and resource dependency theories, using a systematic literature review (SLR) approach. Mor Barak (2020) contributed to the discourse theory SCT, employing a theoretical and conceptual research methodology to develop a framework. Finally, Spicer et al. (2019) used a mixed-method approach rooted in the theory of social change and field theory, combining descriptive statistics with qualitative content analysis and secondary data analysis. Together, these studies demonstrate a strong theoretical foundation and methodological pluralism, though they also highlight a gap in incorporating perspectives from development studies, ethics, and feminist theory.

9.3 Methodology

9.3.1 Data Collection

Scopus, one of the most important sources of scientific databases, was used in this study to determine Socio-tech entrepreneurship-related topics. To search for literature related to "Socio-tech entrepreneurship," we used a standard search in Scopus. We defined the search query as, "Social Entrepreneurship" OR "Technology Entrepreneurship" OR "Socio-Tech Entrepreneurship." To make it more specific, 1,168 abstracts were retrieved on 10th January 2025.

Next, we applied LDA- topic modeling (Gatti et al., 2015) to quantify the variation of topics across abstracts related to Socio-tech entrepreneurship (STE).

9.3.2 Text pre-processing

In the second place, to pre-process the obtained data, "quanteda package was used for tokenization, lemmatization, n-grams identification, and stop word removal to develop corpus as an output (Heydt et al., 2018; Kirilenko et al., 2023; Laureate et al., 2023; Maier et al., 2018; Manning et al., 2008; V′ azquez et al., 2022)," and the following steps were followed:

Text pre-processing ensures a more reliable and accurate text analysis. Firstly, the tokens having fewer than four or more than twenty-five words are excluded. Secondly, the non-textual elements, such as hashtags, numbers, URLs, and punctuation, are removed. Thirdly, the words are converted into lowercase after adjusting for the Spanish language. Subsequently, the stop-words were eliminated by using the tm package over R (Laureate et al., 2023). This process enhances consistency to avoid the discriminativeness of topic modeling.

9.3.3 Topic Modeling

To explore the thematic dimensions of socio-tech entrepreneurship by analyzing abstracts from Scopus-indexed publications, this study has used LDA package, introduced by Blei et al. (2003). LDA is conceptualized as a generative probabilistic model for identifying the latent themes and topics by following the classical pLSA model by Hofmann (1999). This data-driven exploratory approach is used particularly for analyzing the large and unstructured text to identify emerging themes without prior labeling or manual intervention (Maier et al., 2018).

LDA offers an automated and objective method for identifying latent patterns within the text as compared to manual thematic content analysis (Jia, 2020), making it more suitable for research domains requiring the analysis of extensive datasets, such as innovation studies, business analytics, and interdisciplinary fields like socio-tech entrepreneurship. This algorithm iteratively assigns topics to words in the corpus, refines topic-word probabilities, and stabilizes these assignments to uncover meaningful thematic patterns (Blei et al., 2003) (Fig. 9.1).

Its application could be accessed in literature where LDA was used for identifying innovation trends (Kakatkar et al., 2020), understanding consumer behavior in business marketing, and analyzing narratives in the travel and hospitality sector. Thus, authors have used this technique to uncover themes related to entrepreneurial processes, technological advancements, and societal impacts with the help of the obtained Scopus-based abstracts. LDA is widely used for analyzing patterns in genetic

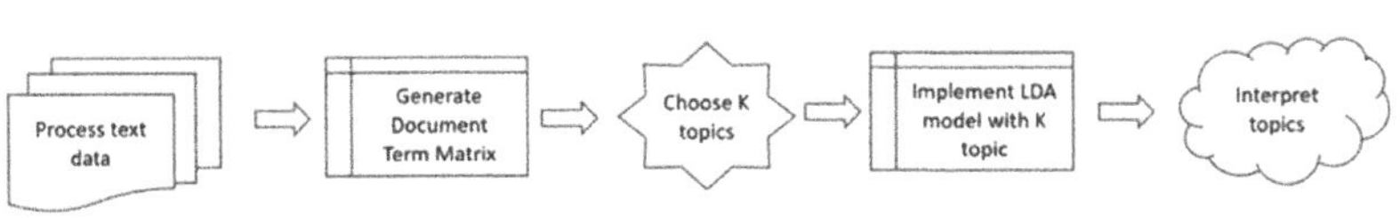

Fig. 9.1 Steps for LDA topic modeling

research, visual content, and social interaction platforms (Blei, 2012). In this study, the integration of LDA into the analysis of socio-tech entrepreneurship provides a robust framework to explore the multi-faceted.

9.4 Results

The study has used LDA for thematic analysis for a transparent and unbiased thematic mapping of the data. A word cloud showcasing the key relevant terms (Fig. 9.2) visually captures the concise and predominant themes in the database. Furthermore, in Fig. 9.3, the optimal number of topics was determined to be five topics according to the sum function of the four monitored metrics, i.e., Griffiths and Steyvers (2004) represented in circle, Cao et al. (2009) represented in triangle, Arun et al. (2010) represented in square, and Deveaud et al. (2014) represented with " + " symbol. The better-defined topics are indicated by their higher, lower, and higher values, respectively. After extracting the topics, the data were visualized and interpreted.

9.4.1 *Identified research topics*

Theme 1: Entrepreneurial Learning for Shaping Sustainable Futures

Terms like "student," "business," and "sustainability" indicate that entrepreneurial education prepares learners to account for global SDGs such as climate change and inequality. Adding sustainability principles to the existing academic syllabus would prepare learners with the tools to create innovative, ethical, and impactful solutions. To develop practical strategies for sustainable business practices, case studies, and simulation methods would be of great help. A systemic change and improved alignment with the United Nations Sustainable Development Goals is being argued in the literature that integrates sustainability into entrepreneurship education.

Theme 2: Designing and Modernizing Social Entrepreneurship

This topic emphasizes the importance of rigorous research and methodology for modernizing social entrepreneurship. Key terms such as "research," "design," and "implication" reflect the need for empirical studies that inform the development of socio-tech entrepreneurial solutions. Research frameworks increasingly integrate interdisciplinary approaches, such as the usage of artificial intelligence for entrepreneurial

Fig. 9.2 Word Cloud

practices could benefit the operational and managerial conduct (Dees, 1998; Zahra et al., 2009).

Theme 3: Tech-driven entrepreneurship

This topic explores the pivotal role of technology and innovation in socio-tech entrepreneurship for integrating digital inclusion with healthcare accessibility, through "technology," "innovation," and "impact" keywords. Researchers have emphasized leveraging technology to foster economic growth and enhance the adaptability of entrepreneurial ventures in dynamic markets (Audretsch et al., 2020; Autio et al., 2014). Moreover, socio-tech entrepreneurship bridges the gap between innovation and societal value creation, enabling entrepreneurs to address complex social issues effectively.

Theme 4: Social entrepreneurship and their Resource Mobilization

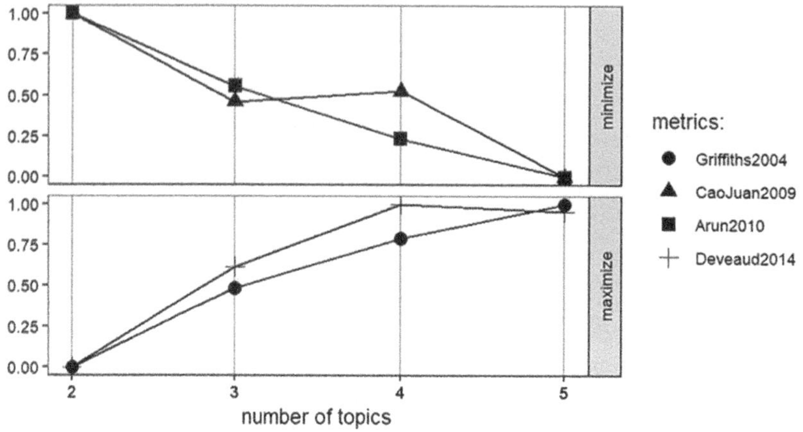

Fig. 9.3 Selection of the number of topics for LDA modeling

This topic highlights the role of community resources and institutional frameworks in supporting social enterprises through the "community," "resource," and "institutional" terms. This theme underlines the need for effective resource mobilization strategies to sustain entrepreneurial ventures through partnerships, funding, and capacity building. Institutional support, including incubation programs and policy incentives, fosters innovation and scalability while maintaining the social mission of these enterprises (Mair and Martí, 2006). Such collaborative efforts between institutions and entrepreneurs are critical for addressing socio-economic challenges.

Theme 5: Longitudinal Effects of Social Entrepreneurship

Keywords "impact," "performance," and "relationship" reflect the growing significance of Social Return on Investment (SROI) to quantify societal benefits. This topic addresses the need to assess the social impact of entrepreneurial activities and performances. Researchers highlight the need to examine how entrepreneurial intentions translate into measurable impacts and long-term societal outcomes. Strategic partnerships and community engagement play a vital role in enhancing the effectiveness and sustainability of socio-tech entrepreneurship (Austin, 2006; Nicholls, 2009).

Moreover, the probability of each word of the identified themes is shown in Fig. 9.4. LDAvis is used for graphically presenting the predominant themes of topic modeling (Sievert and Shirley, 2014) (Fig. 9.5). LDAvis is an advanced visualization tool to explore the in-depth topic significance and inter-topic relationships with its two interface panels. The left interface panel highlights the topic similarity with circles, where the size of the circle hints toward the dominating themes of the corpus.

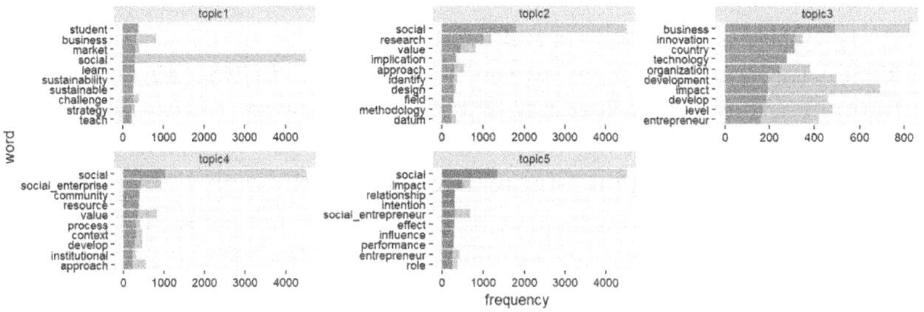

Fig. 9.4 The topic-by-word distributions for each of the five topics

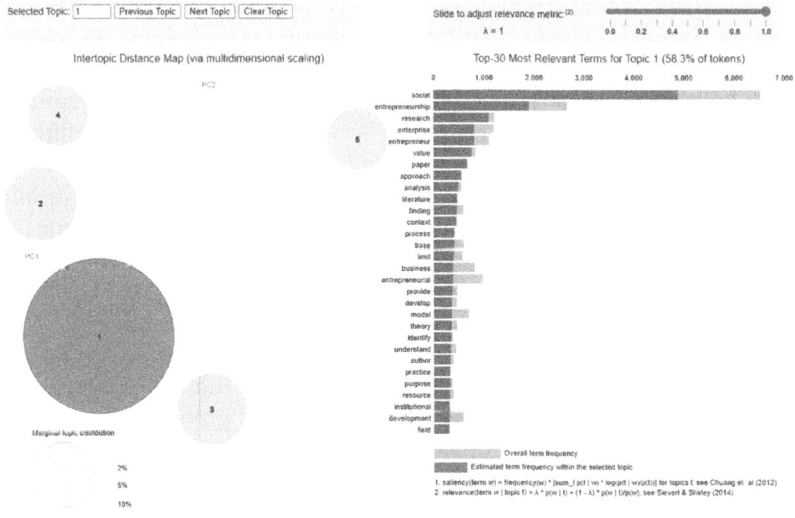

Fig. 9.5 Topic visualization with LDAvis

The right panel presents a horizontal bar chart highlighting the most salient terms for a selected topic, including term frequency and relevance metrics. The graphical representation highlights separated topics in the topic modeling framework, suggesting a well-structured and coherent LDA model. This separation indicates that the topics are uniquely defined, minimizing thematic overlap and enhancing interpretability.

9.5 Implications of the Study

This study also unveils several implications.

First, the previously unexplored thematic clusters in socio-tech entrepreneurship are explored with the application of LDA. These findings could enrich existing theoretical frameworks with the emerging constructs, such as Shaping Sustainable Futures through Entrepreneurial Learning, Advancing Research in Social Entrepreneurship, Tech-Driven Entrepreneurship, Resource Mobilization for Social Enterprises, and Measuring Impact on Social Entrepreneurship, as critical dimensions of socio-tech entrepreneurship.

Second, the integration of technology management, social innovation, and sustainability is examined as the significant interdisciplinary linkages for transcending disciplinary silos, incorporating insights from social sciences, business management and accounting, psychology, sociology, engineering, and organizational behavior. Such integration can offer a more holistic understanding of how socio-tech entrepreneurial ventures navigate their complex ecosystems. However, the analysis also highlights the need to consider potential unintended consequences, including power asymmetries and implementation failures. Future research should critically examine when and how STE produces equitable outcomes, ensuring its impact aligns with broader societal goals (Winner, 1980).

Third, established entrepreneurs are advised to focus on enhancing social impact while ensuring financial sustainability to identify strategic areas for scaling their ventures. For instance, crowdfunding and resource mobilization can guide them in diversifying their funding sources and expanding outreach to vulnerable and critical social groups.

Lastly, addressing societal challenges—especially those affecting vulnerable groups—this research highlights the importance of supporting STE ventures as drivers of socio-technical innovation and sustainable economic growth. Policies could be designed by taking care of funding schemes, tax incentives, and support to address emerging societal problems.

Overall, this study acts as a catalyst for advancing theoretical and practical knowledge in the domain. Academicians can use the obtained themes to identify unexplored research areas and frame novel research questions.

9.6 Limitations and Future Research Directions

The current research possesses some limitations that can be addressed in future research work. *Firstly*, a key limitation of this study is the reliance on abstracts rather than full-text articles for semantic analysis. While abstracts provide accessible and standardized summaries, they may not capture the original studies' full conceptual depth and methodological detail (Yanshan et al., 2016). Nonetheless, previous research supports using abstracts as reliable proxies for full texts in large-scale semantic and bibliometric analyses due to their consistent structure and broad availability (Boyack & Klavans, 2010; Jurgens et al., 2018). Future studies should consider leveraging full-text data where feasible to enhance the depth and accuracy of semantic insights.

Secondly, the study used LDA to extract topics. Though it is a robust model, it still does not capture themes related to sentiment, ethical dimensions, or context-specific challenges. Future researchers could advance these text-mining techniques by incorporating STM, LSA, or sentiment analysis to extend the insights of the semantic and emotional aspects of STE.

Lastly, this study does not account for the demographic characteristics or geographic context of the research contributions analyzed which have significant influence over the thematic focus. Also, the interdisciplinary patterns are overlooked, which might be addressed as a research gap. Thus, the future researchers could examine the influence of demographic or regional variations in STE research to uncover potential biases or region-specific trends, providing more actionable insights for global stakeholders.

9.7 Conclusion

In this paper, five themes related to Socio-tech entrepreneurship were examined with the help of topic modeling research. In detail, the authors have applied topic modeling (LDA) over abstract data of the past 15 years. We focused on 25 reputed journals included in the ABDC list, Web of Science, and ABS under the categories "Journal of Business Ethics" and "Journal of Business Research," respectively. LDA-obtained topics purely result from the statistical structure of the abstract text and do not require any prior knowledge, being an unsupervised learning algorithm. This study has leveraged the posterior document-topic and topic-word distribution to examine the context and its interdisciplinary variation. While the interdisciplinary nature of STE is acknowledged, future research should draw more explicitly on development studies, ethics, and feminist theory to critically examine power structures, equity implications, and inclusive innovation processes (Poonamallee et al., 2020; Grassi and Toschi, 2024). These perspectives are essential to deepen understanding of how technological innovation interacts with social justice and marginalization in STE contexts. This study could be beneficial for the research community, including the editors of journals, the publishing houses, the organizers of conferences, along with the funding agencies. The study could directly facilitate conference themes for Socio-tech entrepreneurship conferences.

One of the study's potential future directions is to examine the research topic from an evolutionary and dynamic standpoint by incorporating data from other sources, like Science Direct, to analyze the evolution and upcoming variation in the research content. To gain more insights, RTM (Chang & Blei, 2009) and author topic models (Rosen-Zvi et al., 2012) could be used in the future.

References

Ariza-Montes, J. A., & Muniz, N. M. (2013). Virtual ecosystems in social business incubation. *Journal of Electronic Commerce in Organizations (JECO), 11*(3), 27–45.

Arun, R., Suresh, V., Veni Madhavan, C. E., & Narasimha Murthy, M. N. (2010, June). On finding the natural number of topics with latent dirichlet allocation: Some observations. In *Pacific-Asia conference on knowledge discovery and data mining*, (pp. 391–402). Springer Berlin Heidelberg.

Audretsch, D. B., Siegel, D. S., & Terjesen, S. (2020). Entrepreneurship in the public and nonprofit sectors. *Public Administration Review, 80*, 468.

Austin, J. (2006). Social and commercial entrepreneurship: Same, different, or both. *Entrepreneurship Theory and Practice.*

Austin, J. E., & Leonard, H. B. D. (2008). Can the virtuous mouse and the wealthy elephant live happily ever after? *California Management Review, 51*(1), 77–102.

Autio, E., Kenney, M., Mustar, P., Siegel, D., & Wright, M. (2014). Entrepreneurial innovation: The importance of context. *Research Policy, 43*(7), 1097–1108.

Bailetti, T., Bot, S. D., Duxbury, T., Hudson, D., McPhee, C., Muegge, S., & Westerlund, M. (2012). An overview of four issues on technology entrepreneurship in the TIM Review. *Technology Innovation Management Review, 2*(5).

Blei, D. M. (2012). Probabilistic topic models. *Communications of the ACM, 55*(4), 77–84.

Blei, D. M., Ng, A. Y., & Jordan, M. I. (2003). Latent Dirichlet Allocation. *Journal of Machine Learning Research, 3*, 993–1022.

Boyack, K. W., & Klavans, R. (2010). Co-citation analysis, bibliographic coupling, and direct citation: Which citation approach represents the research front most accurately? *Journal of the American Society for Information Science and Technology, 61*(12), 2389–2404. https://doi.org/10.1002/asi.21419

Cao, J., Xia, T., Li, J., Zhang, Y., & Tang, S. (2009). A density-based method for adaptive LDA model selection. *Neurocomputing, 72*(7–9), 1775–1781.

Chang, J., & Blei, D. (2009, April). Relational topic models for document networks. In *Artificial intelligence and statistics* (pp. 81–88). PMLR.

Chou, D. C., & Lin, B. (2024). Social entrepreneurship success: Relevance to social mediating technologies. *Journal of Computer Information Systems, 64*(3), 329–341.

Dees, J. G. (1998). The Meaning of Social Entrepreneurship. *Kauffman Foundation and Stanford University.*

Desa, G., & Kotha, S. (2006). Ownership, mission and environment: An exploratory analysis into the evolution of a technology social venture. *Social entrepreneurship* (pp. 155–179). Palgrave Macmillan UK.

Deveaud, R., SanJuan, E., & Bellot, P. (2014). Accurate and effective latent concept modeling for ad hoc information retrieval. *Document numérique, 17*(1), 61–84.

Diaz Gonzalez, A., & Dentchev, N. A. (2021). Ecosystems in support of social entrepreneurs: A literature review. *Social Enterprise Journal, 17*(3), 329–360.

Farinha, L., Sebastião, J. R., Sampaio, C., & Lopes, J. (2020). Social innovation and social entrepreneurship: Discovering origins, exploring current and future trends. *International Review on Public and Nonprofit Marketing, 17*(1), 77–96.

Gatti, C. J., Brooks, J. D., & Nurre, S. G. (2015). A historical analysis of the field of OR/MS using topic models. *arXiv preprint* arXiv:1510.05154.

Grassi, E., & Toschi, L. (2024). A systematic literature review of technology social ventures: State of the art and directions for future research at the micro-, meso- and macro-level. *Journal of Social Entrepreneurship, 15*(3), 833–865.

Griffiths, T. L., & Steyvers, M. (2004). Finding scientific topics. *Proceedings of the National academy of Sciences, 101*(suppl_1), 5228–5235.

Gupta, P., Chauhan, S., Paul, J., & Jaiswal, M. P. (2020). Social entrepreneurship research: A review and future research agenda. *Journal of Business Research, 113*, 209–229.

Heydt, Q., Larrue, C., Saland, E., Bertoli, S., Sarry, J. E., Besson, A., & Mas, M. D. (2018). Oncogenic FLT3-ITD supports autophagy via ATF4 in acute myeloid leukemia. *Oncogene, 37*(6), 787–797.

Hofmann, T. (1999). Probabilistic latent semantic analysis. In *UAI* (Vol. 99, pp. 289–296).

Jia, S. (2020). Toward a better fitness club: Evidence from exerciser online rating and review using latent Dirichlet allocation and support vector machine. *International Journal of Market Research, 61*(1), 64–76.

Jurgens, D., Kumar, S., Hoover, R., McFarland, D., & Jurafsky, D. (2018). Measuring the evolution of a scientific field through citation frames. *Transactions of the Association for Computational Linguistics, 6*, 391–406. https://doi.org/10.1162/tacl_a_00028

Kakatkar, C., Bilgram, V., & Füller, J. (2020). Innovation analytics: Leveraging artificial intelligence in the innovation process. *Business Horizons, 63*(2), 171–181.

Kirilenko, P., Najmi, M. A., Ma, B., Shushanian, A., Velazquez-Rizo, M., Iida, D., & Ohkawa, K. (2023). High crystallinity N-polar InGaN layers grown on cleaved ScAlMgO4 substrates. *AIP Advances, 13*(4).

Laureate, C. D. P., Buntine, W., & Linger, H. (2023). A systematic review of the use of topic models for short text social media analysis. *Artificial Intelligence Review, 56*(12), 14223–14255.

Linna, P. (2013). Bricolage as a means of innovating in a resource-scarce environment: A study of innovator-entrepreneurs at the BOP. *Journal of Developmental Entrepreneurship, 18*(03), 1350015.

Maier, L., Pruteanu, M., Kuhn, M., Zeller, G., Telzerow, A., Anderson, E. E., & Typas, A. (2018). Extensive impact of non-antibiotic drugs on human gut bacteria. *Nature, 555*(7698), 623–628.

Mair, J., & Marti, I. (2006). Social entrepreneurship research: A source of explanation, prediction, and delight. *Journal of World Business, 41*(1), 36–44.

Manning, C., Raghavan, P., & Schutze, H. (2008). Term weighting, and the vector space model. In *Introduction to information retrieval* (pp. 109–133).

Mor Barak, M. E. (2020). The practice and science of social good: Emerging paths to positive social impact. *Research on Social Work Practice, 30*(2), 139–150.

Nicholls, A. (2009). 'We do good things, don't we?': 'Blended Value Accounting'in social entrepreneurship. *Accounting, Organizations and Society, 34*(6–7), 755–769.

Poonamallee, L., Scillitoe, J., & Joy, S. (Eds.). (2020). *Socio-tech innovation: Harnessing technology for social good*. Springer Nature.

Rosen-Zvi, M., Griffiths, T., Steyvers, M., & Smyth, P. (2012). The author-topic model for authors and documents. *arXiv preprint* arXiv:1207.4169.

Sargent, J., & Ahmed, A. (2017). What is IT for social impact? A review of literature and practices. *IEEE Technology and Society Magazine, 36*(4), 62–72.

Scillitoe, J. L., Poonamallee, L., & Joy, S. (2018a). Balancing market versus social strategic orientations in socio-tech ventures as part of the technology innovation adoption process–examples from the global healthcare sector. *Journal of Social Entrepreneurship, 9*(3), 257–287.

Scillitoe, J. L., Poonamallee, L., & Joy, S. (2018, August). Technological innovation investments influence on the strategic orientation of socio-tech ventures. In *2018 Portland International Conference on Management of Engineering and Technology (PICMET)* (pp. 1–10). IEEE.

Sievert, C., & Shirley, K. (2014, June). LDAvis: A method for visualizing and interpreting topics. In *Proceedings of the workshop on interactive language learning, visualization, and interfaces* (pp. 63–70).

Spicer, J., Kay, T., & Ganz, M. (2019). Social entrepreneurship as field encroachment: How a neoliberal social movement constructed a new field. *Socio-Economic Review, 17*(1), 195–227.

V´ azquez, M. A., Pereira-Delgado, J., Cid-Sueiro, J., & Arenas-Garcia, J. (2022). Validation of scientific topic models using graph analysis and corpus metadata. *Scientometrics, 127*(9), 5441–5458.

Winner, L. (1980). Do artifacts have politics? *Daedalus*, 109(1), 121–136. https://www.jstor.org/stable/20024652

Yanshan, W., Sohn, S., Liu, S., Shen, F., Wang, Y., & Liu, H. (2016). Clinical information extraction applications: A literature review. *Journal of Biomedical Informatics, 77*, 34–49. https://doi.org/10.1016/j.jbi.2017.11.011

Zahra, S. A., Gedajlovic, E., Neubaum, D. O., & Shulman, J. M. (2009). A typology of social entrepreneurs: Motives, search processes and ethical challenges. *Journal of Business Venturing, 24*(5), 519–532.

Zahra, S. A., Liu, W., & Si, S. (2023). How digital technology promotes entrepreneurship in ecosystems. *Technovation, 119*, Article 102457.

CHAPTER 10

Education for Sustainable Technology Entrepreneurship

Usha Shree Rathod and M. Rajyalaxmi

10.1 Introduction

In the rapidly changing world today, two of the most imperative challenges that face us are the continuous speed of technological development and the necessity of sustainable development (Tavares et al., 2022). As much as technology has no doubt transformed sectors, economies, and daily existence, its footprint on society and the environment is no longer debatable (Rees, 2008). From natural resource depletion to the expanding digital divide, these challenges underscore the imperatives of an even balance that leverages innovation for both people and planet. This slippery slope leads us to the paradigm of Sustainable Technology Entrepreneurship, a dynamic synthesis of innovation, ethics, and

U. S. Rathod (✉) · M. Rajyalaxmi
School of Business, SR University, Warangal, Telangana 506371, India
e-mail: ushashreerathod1234@gmail.com

M. Rajyalaxmi
e-mail: Laxmi.gunna@gmail.com

D. Kumar et al. (eds.), *Evolving Trends in Technology Entrepreneurship*, Palgrave Studies in Global Entrepreneurship,
https://doi.org/10.1007/978-981-95-7441-4_10

ecological awareness (Johnson et al., 2016). At the center of this revolution is education. It is no longer enough for education systems to merely provide technical skills or entrepreneurial knowledge in a vacuum. Rather, contemporary education must serve as a force for developing future entrepreneurs who are not just technologically sophisticated but also passionately devoted to sustainable practices. This transformation calls for a change of mind—a change in which students are empowered with the knowledge, skills, and ethical frameworks that enable them to develop ventures addressing global issues such as climate change, resource shortage, and social inequality (Kwauk & Casey, 2022).

10.1.1 The Dual Crisis: Technology and Sustainability

The world stands at a juncture, with technological advancement reaching new heights while the planet struggles with environmental degradation (Hornborg, 2001). Artificial intelligence, blockchain, and renewable energy technologies have created new avenues for innovation, but the question is: Are these innovations sustainable (Boppana, 2018)? For instance, AI models need enormous computing power, which can use lots of energy. Similarly, blockchain technology, as transparent as it vows to be, has been faulted for its carbon price (Schinckus, 2020). Such paradoxes highlight the need for technology entrepreneurs to adopt sustainable methods from the onset. Sustainability is not a "nice-to-have" but a necessity for the building of resilient economies and societies (Rigolon et al., 2022). And that is where education fits in. By integrating sustainability and technology entrepreneurship, education can guide students toward creating solutions that balance economic development with environmental and social sustainability (Kozma, 2005).

10.1.2 Education as Catalyst

Education is also at the forefront of shaping how next generation entrepreneurs will think, act, and innovate (Ma et al., 2020). It is the foundation for developing what can be called a sustainable entrepreneurial attitude, a blend of creativity, problem-solving, and making ethical choices (Ahmad et al., 2023). Students today are tomorrow's leaders, and future leaders' capacity to see technology not just as a money-maker but as a force for good is dependent to a great extent on what they study (Waddock & Post, 2000).

10.1.3 The Rise of Conscious Entrepreneurship

One of the most notable concepts covered under this chapter is conscious entrepreneurship where responsibility and innovation intersect (Schaltegger & Wagner, 2011). Contrary to traditional entrepreneurship models where the goal is profiting generation, conscious entrepreneurs seek to establish enterprises that provide solutions for society while keeping sustainability goals in mind (Haldar, 2019). This concept challenges students to prioritize greater long-term impact and lesser short-term profit, connecting their Business models to the United Nations' SDGs. For instance, consider entrepreneurs creating AI-driven platforms for carbon footprint tracking or blockchain platforms for fair-trade operations. These projects utilize not only cutting-edge technology but also incorporate sustainability as part of their purpose. Education must challenge students to embrace this new thinking, blending entrepreneurial enthusiasm with a deep sense of global responsibility.

10.1.4 Bridging The Gap: From Theory to Practice

But to equip the students in a manner that will equip them for sustainable technology entrepreneurship, there has to be something more than traditional classroom instruction (Lans et al., 2014). There has to be experience, there has to be engaging, practical training that is as close to real problems as possible. They encompass activities like hackathons, design thinking labs, and corporate collaborations where students can test their ideas, address real-world problems, and create tangible solutions (McGowan, 2019). Additionally, interdisciplinarity in environmental science, business management, and technology gives a comprehensive view to students. For instance, a sustainable entrepreneurship course can encompass green startups case studies, climate modeling through the deployment of AI, and policy analysis of renewable energy bills. Among the key concepts elaborated in this chapter is conscious entrepreneurship when responsibility is paired with innovation. As opposed to conventional profit-oriented entrepreneurship education, socially entrepreneurial students aim to establish businesses that solve social issues and pursue social sustainability aims (Shepherd & Patzelt, 2011). The concept provokes students to think beyond short-term money-making and long-term philanthropy and directs their business toward the United Nations' SDGs. For example, think of AI-based tools to track the carbon footprint or blockchain technologies to maintain fair-trade practices. These organizations adopt the most advanced technologies but prioritize sustainability at the center of their mission statements (Amiri, 2023). The school system itself needs to inspire the adoption of this transformation among students and merge an entrepreneurial attitude with an enlightened sense of world citizenship.

10.1.5 *Objectives*

Considering these concepts, this chapter will:

1. Emphasize the role of education in developing sustainable technology entrepreneurship.
2. Investigate how cross-disciplinary curricula and hands-on learning prepare students.
3. Discuss the concept of conscious entrepreneurship and its influence on responsible innovators.
4. Analyze the disruptive technologies leading to sustainable solutions.
5. Outline the responsibilities of educators, policymakers, and industry leaders in establishing a conducive environment.

While integration between entrepreneurship and sustainability has been tried in previous studies, this chapter proposes a novel approach by placing these words in an educational framework that prioritizes ethical innovation, interdisciplinary education, and experiential experience. By introducing the "conscious entrepreneurship" framework (Shukla et al., 2024) and aligning pedagogical approaches with the United Nations Sustainable Development Goals (SDGs), this methodology is differentiated from traditional entrepreneurship education that does not have an overt ethical and sustainability-driven paradigm. Moreover, it emphasizes the operationally engaged role of education systems in generating socially conscious entrepreneurs who are technologically literate and answerable, an aspect for which literature is scarce.

10.2 Methodological Approach

This chapter takes a conceptual and narrative approach, combining understanding from scholarly literature and policy blueprints in education, sustainability, and entrepreneurship. Instead of using empirical data gathering or quantitative studies, it capitalizes on a theoretical reconciliation of interdisciplinary insights to conceptualize a holistic education framework for sustainable technology entrepreneurship. The arguments made are based on a wide literature review covering peer-reviewed scholarly research, international policy reports (e.g., SDGs, UNESCO ESD guidelines), and actual cases from schools and tech companies. This is in line with previous conceptual studies in education and management studies, where new areas do not have common empirical datasets but need intellectual scaffolding to support future empirical research. Although the chapter does not empirically test hypotheses or measure outcomes, it offers a critical synthesis and theoretical model that can be used to inform curriculum development, policy design, and future empirical research. The limitations of this narrative approach are recognized, such as the absence of field validation, but its strength is in providing foundational directions for incorporating sustainability and entrepreneurship into education.

10.2.1 The Intersection of Education, Technology, And Sustainability

In the twenty-first century, the intersection of education, technology, and sustainability has become a potent paradigm for propelling innovative solutions to global problems (Rahimi & Oh, 2024). This intersection is the basis for sustainable technology entrepreneurship, an arena where knowledge acquisition, technological innovation, and environmental awareness intersect. Knowing how these three pillars are linked is important to develop a generation of entrepreneurs who not only innovate innovative solutions but do so in a responsible manner, providing long-term gains for the economy and the world (Voegtlin & Scherer, 2017).

10.2.2 Key concepts

In order to completely understand the connection between education, technology, and sustainability, we first need to deconstruct these terminologies:

Figure 10.1. illustrates the interconnected relationship between Education, Sustainability, and Technology, with Conscious Entrepreneurship at the center. Education empowers learners with digital tools for innovation and growth, while sustainability instills ethical responsibility for a greener future. Technology, however, is a driver of harnessing innovation to address environmental and social issues. The intersectionality of the three areas (Fig. 10.1) promotes conscious entrepreneurship, whereby enterprises and people bring together learning, ethics, and technological innovation for sustainable and ethically oriented innovation (Dreyer et al., 2017). The integrated approach emphasizes aligning knowledge, ethical duty, and innovation to cause significant social impact.

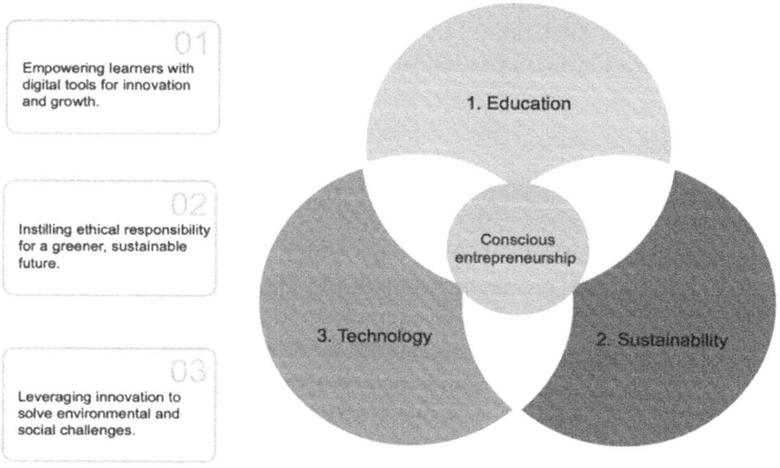

Fig. 10.1 Intersection of education, technology, and sustainability

10.2.3 Deepening the Theoretical Foundations: Sustainability and Entrepreneurship

To make one use sustainability and entrepreneurship in learning in a meaningful way, there is a necessity to demystify these terms practically, theoretically, and philosophically. The definition of sustainability as having a connection with environmental stability primarily has been transformed from a parameter to encompass "triple bottom line" by John Elkington (1994) (Zaharia et al., 2021), which focuses on environmental integrity, social equity, and economic prosperity. This strategy resists conventional growth-oriented paradigms by emphasizing long-term planetary health, ethical leadership, and shared development. Sustainability philosophers contend that sustainability entails intergenerational justice, ensuring that present activities do not jeopardize future generations' capacity to fulfill their own needs. Likewise, entrepreneurship is not merely founding a firm or seeking profit. As per the economic thought, entrepreneurship is hypothesized as a process of creative destruction—initiating innovation that reshapes existing systems. This has evolved over time into various forms, such as social entrepreneurship, which is value creation for society, and sustainable entrepreneurship, which combines economic innovation with environmental and societal objectives. Contemporary theory, such as "conscious entrepreneurship," is educating purposeful business that is ethically right and ecologically sound. These new meanings recognize that entrepreneurship is not merely a managerial or technical act but also a civic and moral practice, contextual, intentional, and system aware. In a reference to such theoretical perspectives, this chapter opens the door for an education model that empowers students not merely with innovation literacy but also critical thinking and moral direction so they can ride out the dynamics of sustainability entrepreneurialism.

10.2.4 Education For Sustainable Development (ESD)

ESD is a learning approach for empowering learners to gain knowledge, skills, and values to deal with global problems such as climate change, poverty, and inequality. UNESCO identifies ESD as empowering learners to make informed choices and take responsible action for environmental sustainability, economic development, and social justice. For entrepreneurship, ESD introduces students to critical reflection on how their entrepreneurial ideas impact the world and harmonizes their innovations with the UN's SDGs (Mohanty et al., 2024).

10.2.5 *Technology Entrepreneurship*

This encompasses the process of discovering, creating, and bringing innovative technologies to the market to generate value. It is not only concerned with making profits but also addresses actual problems using technological innovation. For instance, natural disaster prediction AI algorithms, blockchain for open supply chains, or IoT devices for intelligent energy grids all come under this category. Technology entrepreneurship extends the frontiers of what can be done, fostering audacious ideas and risk-taking.

10.2.6 *Sustainability*

Sustainability involves environment, society, and economy—commonly called the "triple bottom line (Arowoshegbe et al., 2016)." It calls for satisfying current demands without undermining the capacity of coming generations to meet their own requirements. Sustainable entrepreneurship in technology hence aims for reconciling economic expansion, conservation, and social equity. It eschews "growth at any cost" in favor of supporting innovation that recognizes planetary limits (Castle, 2022). The intersection of technology, education, and sustainability is not just theoretical but has practical applications as well. Education forms the foundation for sustainable technological innovations through thinking critically and being creative, enabling students to devise solutions for the problems of the world (Steiner & Posch, 2006). Technology also enables the provision of education on sustainability through online platforms, AI-driven learning solutions, and experiential tools like virtual reality simulations (Shirazi et al., 2024). At the same time, sustainability influences entrepreneurial mentality by infusing ethical and environmental concerns into technological innovation so that development comes in harmony with long-term ecological and social health. Various real-life instances, including solar energy training schemes of Grameen Shakti, solar-powered food preservation units of Wakati, and AI-based waste management systems of Ecolife Recycling, demonstrate how these three aspects not only overlap but also complement one another. Without education, these technological fixes might never happen; without technology, sustainability goals might be beyond reach; and without sustainability, technological progress could be purchased in the form of environmental costs (Fuchs, 2008).

10.2.7 The Need for an Integrated Approach

In spite of the obvious synergies, there remains a disconnect between how these ideas are being taught and implemented. Most education systems address sustainability, technology, and entrepreneurship as distinct subjects, hardly ever emphasizing their interdependence (Fiet, 2001). To bridge this, schools need to embrace an integrated approach by:

10.2.8 Building Interdisciplinary Courses

Courses that integrate environmental science, business administration, and technological innovation encourage end-to-end thinking (Ng et al., 2010). For instance, a course on "Sustainable Tech Startups" can have modules on AI solutions for climate action, green Business models, and policy advocacy.

10.2.9 Encouraging Project-Based Learning

Hands-on project work in which students address real-world issues like developing a low-energy AI algorithm or designing a biodegradable package prototype serves to close the gap between theory and practice (James et al., 2022).

10.2.10 Establishing Innovation Centers

Universities can have centers where students collaborate on sustainable technology solutions under the support of industry collaboration and mentorship (Whitmer et al., 2010).

10.2.11 Integrating Sustainability into Entrepreneurial Education

Incubators for businesses need to promote "conscious entrepreneurship," leading startups to quantify success not only in terms of revenue but also in terms of positive environmental and social contributions (Hartmann, 2024).

10.3 Cultivating an Entrepreneurial Mindset with Sustainable Goals

In an era where technological innovation has emerged as the driver of change, imparting entrepreneurial inclination based on sustainability is imperative to the core (Hameed et al., 2016). Entrepreneurial mindset refers to a thought process that possesses creativity, risk-taking, problem-solving, and innovating aspects that are all cardinal to creating game-changing solutions. The additional element of sustainability, however, is the one that ensures not just financial returns but social responsibility as well as environmentally friendly operations. This part of the paper addresses how education can make such a mindset possible, how embedding sustainability in entrepreneurial mindset should be sought, and what the overall implications for technology entrepreneurship are (Hermann & Bossle, 2020).

10.3.1 Understanding The Entrepreneurial Mindset

Entrepreneurial mindset is not just (Zahra & Nambisan, 2012) starting a business, it is all about being able to see opportunities, being critical, and taking initiative to solve problems. It requires tenacity, adaptability, and a future orientation. Entrepreneurs perceive problems as opportunities and work tirelessly to bring their ideas to life. In the current polycrisis environment, entrepreneurs are facing multidimensional risks emerging from technology disruption, economic uncertainty, poor climatic conditions, and geopolitical issues. Identifying sustainable business ideas in these situations becomes very challenging for entrepreneurs. But traditional entrepreneurship is focused on money without necessarily considering the environmental or social aspect. This is where sustainable entrepreneurship comes into play. Sustainable entrepreneurship seeks to establish innovative business solutions in harmony with economic development, environmental, and social welfare. It is concerned with the establishment of ventures that tackle pressing global concerns like climate change, natural resource degradation, and social inequities. For example, an AI technology firm developing models for reducing energy consumption in buildings is entrepreneurial, innovative, and sustainable (Lee et al., 2019).

In order to foster such thinking, business schools must look beyond conventional business school education and integrate sustainability values into entrepreneurial training. This entails integrating interdisciplinary learning, practice in critical thinking, and solving real-world problems in the curriculum.

10.3.2 The Role of Education in Shaping a Sustainable Entrepreneurial Mindset

Learning takes a transformatory function in fostering entrepreneurs who value sustainability (Bapoo et al., 2022). Formal education enables students to acquire the intellectual and practical knowledge to create responsibly. But this involves a departure from conventional didactic approaches and toward more adaptive, interactive learning processes.

10.3.3 Interdisciplinary Curricula

One of the finest means of seeding a sustainable entrepreneurial spirit is through interdisciplinary curricula (Kazakeviciute et al., 2016). The curricula combine environmental studies, business management, technology, and social sciences to give the students a broad vision of how their entrepreneurial endeavors will help society and the world at large. An illustration of the same is in a course that can be labeled as "Sustainable Technology Entrepreneurship" would encompass the following themes:

- Green Business models and circular economies.
- AI and IoT for environmental monitoring.
- Renewable energy technologies and market prospects.
- Moral implications of technology-based projects.

These programs enable students to realize that sustainability and technology are not conflicting elements but complementary powers shaping contemporary business.

10.3.4 Experiential learning

Experiential learning that engages students in actual projects, simulations, and case studies is essential in building hands-on entrepreneurial competencies (Rao et al., 2024). Lectures are not sufficient to cause the creativity and adaptability required for sustainable innovation. Universities can utilize hackathons, design sprints, and sustainability challenges where students work in teams to create solutions to environmental problems using technology. For instance, a hackathon might challenge students to create a mobile app that tracks carbon footprints or a blockchain system for an open supply chain. Such activities condition students to think on their feet, collaborate in teams, and test their ideas in actual settings.

10.3.5 Collaboration With Industry

Partnering with technology firms, environmental groups, and government agencies can open students up to actual sustainability problems (Rondinelli & London, 2003). Industry partnerships enable students to develop live projects, receive guidance from experienced entrepreneurs, and validate their innovations in real-world contexts. For instance, a renewable energy firm might collaborate with a university business incubator to create and sell low-cost solar panels for villages. Such cooperation fosters entrepreneurial thinking while enforcing the value of coupling technological innovation with sustainability goals.

10.3.6 Embedding Sustainability into Entrepreneurial Thinking

It is not enough to develop an entrepreneurial spirit; it must be rooted in values of sustainability. To achieve this, education must:

10.3.7 Instill Ethical Awareness

Entrepreneurs must be reminded of the ethical implications of their innovations. Technological innovations can cure many problems, but they can also exacerbate social disparities or the environment if not utilized appropriately. Education must emphasize "conscious entrepreneurship," a philosophy where business success is not measured solely by profit margins but also by social and environmental gains. Examples of successful businesses like Patagonia (focusing on sustainable fashion) or

Tesla (revolutionizing clean energy transport) can be added to course content. These are examples that demonstrate how sustainability and innovation are not mutually exclusive.

10.3.8 Teach Systems Thinking

Systems thinking instructs students to view their companies as part of a larger ecosystem. It enables entrepreneurs to understand how their business decisions impact supply chains, communities, and the environment (Gonzales, 2020). For example, an AI-based irrigation system company must consider not only the technology's efficiency but also its impact on water resources, farming practices, and local economies. Courses can involve system mapping exercises where learners chart the ripple effects of their innovations and monitor positive and negative impacts. Through this, they are pushed to adopt a forward-looking perspective to long-term consequences rather than mere short-term gains.

10.3.9 Encourage Green Innovation

Green technology is about building technologies that do the least amount of harm to the environment, such as solar and wind technologies, biodegradable goods, and smart resource management systems (Heidari et al., 2024). Educators can ask students to think about how their concepts for tech can lead the circular economy, creating things with minimal or no waste, promoting recycling, and getting good use out of resources repeatedly. A practical solution would be to have students create prototypes of sustainable technology products, such as green packaging from algae-based bioplastics or AI-based software that optimizes energy consumption in factories. These projects embed sustainability into the very core of entrepreneurial problem-solving. Fostering entrepreneurial thinking with sustainable objectives is not only a requirement but an imperative priority in our contemporary world. As technology advances, education must empower students with ethical innovation skills. This is to develop multidisciplinary curriculums, adopt experiential learning processes, create partnerships with industry, and include sustainability in every facet of entrepreneurial studies.

10.4 Integrating Transformative Technologies for Sustainable Innovation

The integration of radical technologies (Lescrauwaet et al., 2022) into sustainable innovation has emerged as a determinant factor for overcoming the issues in the world. In a world gripped by climate change, resources depletion, and inequity, technology presents unprecedented possibilities for creating solutions that are not just effective but also sustainable. This chapter discusses how pioneering transforming technologies like Artificial Intelligence (AI), Blockchain, Renewable Energy Technologies, and the Internet of Things (IoT) are transforming sustainable innovation and how education can equip future entrepreneurs to employ these technologies ethically.

10.4.1 The Intersection of Technology and Sustainability

Technological innovation and sustainability (Winarto & Wisesa, 2024) are no longer separate realms; they converge to create an unstoppable alliance committed to shaping a greener, more equitable world. Sustainable innovation is about designing products, processes, and Business models that support economic growth as well as environmental footprint reduction and social welfare. Breakthrough technologies are at the heart of accelerating these innovations through making them efficient, transparent, and scalable. But it is up to how well the future entrepreneurs learn and implement them that these technologies prove effective. Utilizing AI just for the purpose of innovation is not sufficient; the concern should be how AI can make renewable energy systems more optimal, lower carbon emissions, and end social injustices. Education thus needs to focus not just on technical skills but also on the ethical and sustainable uses of these technologies.

10.5 Major Transformative Technologies to Support Sustainable Innovation

10.5.1 Artificial Intelligence (AI)

Technology has become a major force behind economic development, especially in emerging markets where innovation can potentially play a transformative role (Adeniyi et al., 2024) and Artificial intelligence is a trendsetter in sustainable innovation. Its capacity to handle large volumes of information, recognize patterns, and make decisions instantaneously makes it priceless for solving intricate environmental and social problems. Climate Modeling and Prediction: AI models are employed to forecast extreme weather, simulate climate change scenarios, and recommend mitigation methods. Organizations such as Google's DeepMind have created AI to maximize energy use in data centers, cutting power consumption by 40%.

10.5.1.1 Smart Agriculture

Agriculture is a backbone for the human race (Balyan et al., 2024). AI-based systems assist farmers in optimizing irrigation, identifying crop diseases, and resource management. Blue River Technology is one such platform that utilizes AI to detect weeds and apply herbicides only where necessary, minimizing the use of chemicals and maintaining soil health.

10.5.1.2 Sustainable Supply Chains

AI promotes transparency in supply chains by monitoring products' carbon impact and proposing greener routes of logistics. IBM's AI systems, for instance, assist in enabling businesses to track their supply chains against green compliance.

10.5.1.3 Educational Implications

Universities need to prepare the next generation of entrepreneurs with courses on AI ethics, sustainable use of AI, and machine learning models for environmental protection. AI projects for renewable energy optimization, carbon monitoring systems, and smart city technologies must be included.

10.5.2 Blockchain Technology

Blockchain is the game-changer of sustainable innovation by ensuring transparency, security, and decentralization. Its irreversible ledgers ensure traceability and authentication of transactions, which is important in establishing trust in sustainable activities.

10.5.2.1 Supply Chain Transparency

Blockchain is an advanced mechanism (Zhong, 2024) that enables businesses to map the path of raw materials from origin to end product, guaranteeing that products are ethically and sustainably sourced. For example, Provenance, a blockchain business, assists brands in highlighting their supply chain information, enabling consumers to make better-informed decisions.

10.5.2.2 Carbon Credits and Emissions Trading

Blockchain technology enables open trading of carbon credits, where companies are prompted to balance out their carbon footprints. The CarbonX platform leverages blockchain to convert carbon offsets into tradeable tokens that incentivize eco-friendly behavior.

10.5.2.3 Renewable Energy Markets

Blockchain facilitates peer-to-peer trading of energy, enabling solar-equipped households to sell surplus energy to their neighbors. Power Ledger's platform in Australia is the best example of the decentralized energy grid.

10.5.2.4 Educational Implications

Blockchain training should be incorporated into courses in sustainability. Projects to be done include designing transparent supply chains, creating blockchain-enabled carbon credit systems, and building decentralized models of renewable energy.

10.5.3 Renewable Energy Technologies

Renewable energy technologies play a crucial role in solving global energy and environmental issues (Prokopenko et al., 2023). Renewable energy technologies like solar, wind, and hydroelectricity are the backbone of sustainable innovation. These technologies are designed to decrease the use of fossil fuels, combat climate change, and develop energy-efficient systems.

10.5.3.1 Solar Innovations

Improvements in photovoltaic technology in recent years have made solar panels more efficient, cheaper, and more available. Tesla's Solar Roof and others incorporate solar cells into roofing tiles so homes can produce clean power effortlessly.

10.5.3.2 Wind Energy Solutions

Intelligent wind turbines with AI sensors maximize their yield by varying blade angles according to wind patterns. GE Renewable Energy employs AI to forecast wind speeds and optimize electricity production.

10.5.3.3 Energy Storage Systems

Sustainable business also targets energy storage systems to counter intermittency in renewable energy. Technologies such as Tesla's Powerwall store solar energy for consumption on cloudy days or peak periods, making energy reliable.

10.5.3.4 Educational Implications

Universities may provide renewable energy entrepreneurship education, where students are motivated to come up with solar-powered devices, prototype wind energy solutions, and conceptualize Business models for energy storage technologies. Hackathons on clean energy innovations can be a source of hands-on experience.

10.5.4 Internet of Things (IoT)

IoT networks devices and sensors to the Internet (Bertino et al., 2016), allowing data to be captured and analyzed in real time. IoT is at the center of sustainable innovation, streamlining the use of resources and improving the monitoring of the environment.

10.5.4.1 Smart Cities

IoT networks traffic control, air quality monitoring, and street lighting management, minimizing waste of energy. Amsterdam utilizes IoT to streamline public transport routes, reducing carbon footprint.

10.5.4.2 Water Management

IoT sensors monitor water use in agriculture and cities, identifying leaks and avoiding wastage. The SWAMP project in Brazil employs IoT to control irrigation in smart farms, saving water.

10.5.4.3 *Waste Management*

Intelligent bins with IoT sensors alert authorities once they are filled, making waste collection more efficient and reducing landfill overflows. For instance, the Bigbelly intelligent bin system is implemented in cities such as New York for litter reduction and recycling improvement.

10.5.4.4 *Educational Implications*

IoT must be incorporated into sustainability-oriented curricula, with assignments that compel students to develop smart farming systems, construct environmental monitoring networks, and design IoT solutions for urban sustainability.

10.6 Challenges In Implementing Emerging Technologies in Education

Though emerging technologies like blockchain and AI have tremendous power to drive sustainable education and enterprise, integrating them into low-income schools is particularly challenging and should not be avoided.

Blockchain technology, highly praised for its security and openness (Mahmood et al., 2022), is hard to implement in low-resource environments because of infrastructural constraints and expense. Blockchain requires a consistent source of power supply, quality computing equipment, secure internet, and very competent technical personnel, factors not necessarily readily available in developing nations or rural areas. Additionally, blockchain validation and mining are energy-intensive, often incompatible with sustainable objectives, particularly in regions that have poor or unstable power supplies. Digital divide, particularly in administrative or pedagogical technical capacity, further serves as a bottleneck to application in practice to education governance or certification schemes.

Similarly, AI-based learning technologies have certain technical, social, and ethical limitations. AI, although it may personalize education and make content delivery more efficient, is reliant on large data that dissolves privacy and surveillance, especially in educational settings where data protection laws are weak (Mukhamediev et al., 2022). Moreover, AI systems can perpetuate or amplify biases in their training data, leading to unequal access to learning. From a socio-economic perspective, most poor schools and universities lack the digital setup, e.g., internet connectivity or devices, necessary to maintain AI-powered platforms. Furthermore, there are not enough trained teachers who can read and utilize AI insights within the classroom. These issues underpin the necessity of context-sensitive planning and open-innovation approaches. The incorporation of such technologies should not be viewed as a ubiquitous solution. Rather, initiatives must be anchored in locality-based capacity development, digital infrastructure investment, and the creation of low-bandwidth open-source tools to which marginalized school communities have access.

10.7 The Educational Role in Integrating the Transformative Technologies

Table 10.1 highlights key educational strategies (Astutik et al., 2024) for integrating transformative technologies into sustainability-focused learning. Interdisciplinary programs blend technology, entrepreneurship, and sustainability, offering courses like "AI for Climate Solutions." Project-based learning enables students to apply emerging technologies (Table 10.1) to real-world challenges. Industry collaborations provide hands-on experience through internships in AI, blockchain, and renewable energy firms. Hackathons and innovation labs foster creativity in green technology solutions. Policy and ethics integration ensures responsible tech implementation. Community engagement encourages real-world sustainability impact, while emerging learning technologies like AR, VR, and AI-driven simulations enhance understanding. This holistic approach prepares students for sustainable innovation.

10.8 Mindfulness Leadership

In the evolving business and technology landscape, a new paradigm is emerging conscious entrepreneurship, one that recalibrates success by integrating profit-making, innovation, and ethical accountability. Entrepreneurship has long been driven by making money and competing in the marketplace. However, the imperative of the world's climate emergency, natural resource depletion, and social inequality demands a shift toward a more sustainable and ethically oriented model of business. Conscious entrepreneurship integrates economic growth with an acute sense of responsibility to humanity and the planet. It is aware that business enterprises not only generate wealth but also contribute toward the creation of a larger good. This chapter explores the concept of conscious

Table 10.1 Key strategies to integrate technology

Key Strategy	*Description*	*Examples of implementation*
Interdisciplinary Programs	Integrating sustainability with technology and entrepreneurship to provide holistic education	Courses like "AI for Climate Solutions," "Blockchain for Green Business," and "IoT for Smart Cities."
Project-Based Learning	Encouraging hands-on experience with real-world sustainability challenges	Students working on AI-driven renewable energy solutions, blockchain-enabled supply chains, and IoT-based water conservation systems
Collaborations with Industry	Partnering with technology firms, environmental organizations, and government bodies for practical exposure	Internships at AI research labs, blockchain startups for carbon tracking, and renewable energy firms
Hackathons and Innovation Labs	Creating platforms for students to develop sustainable technology solutions through competition and experimentation	Green-tech hackathons, university innovation labs with AI software, IoT sensors, and renewable energy kits
Policy and Ethics Integration	Teaching the ethical implications and regulatory aspects of emerging technologies in sustainability	Courses on "Ethical AI and Sustainability" and "Green Tech Policy and Governance."
Community Engagement and Outreach	Encouraging students to apply their knowledge for local and global sustainability impact	Conducting workshops on digital solutions for rural sustainability and community-driven climate action projects
Use of Emerging Learning Technologies	Leveraging AR, VR, and AI-driven simulations to enhance learning	Virtual labs for climate modeling, AI-powered sustainability analytics, and VR-based environmental impact simulations

entrepreneurship, the importance of ethical usage of technology, and how education can foster entrepreneurs who are sensitive to sustainability and social responsibility. Through developing an entrepreneurial culture of ethics, sustainability, and innovation, we are able to generate leaders who establish positive transformation and provide long-term business sustainability.

10.9 Conscious Entrepreneurship

Sustainable entrepreneurship is a central driver in today's business environment (Oluwadamilare et al., 2023) beyond the conventional business mindset and encompasses three fundamental pillars: profitability, innovation, and ethical responsibility. While profitability remains an important factor, aware entrepreneurs know that long-term success is based on balancing financial ambitions with social and ecological well-being. Conscious entrepreneurship, in its core, is purpose-driven Business models generating value beyond economic success. It involves developing products, services, and technologies to address global challenges, such as climate change, energy sustainability, poverty alleviation, and social justice. In contrast to traditional businesses that habitually project their eyes on near-term gains, conscious entrepreneurs operate on a triple bottom line of people, planet, and profit in which economic success is balanced with environmental and social influence. In addition, conscious entrepreneurship is deeply rooted in stakeholder capitalism, in which companies put the interests of all the stakeholders—employees, customers, communities, and the environment—on equal footing with that of the shareholders. Firms such as Patagonia, Tesla, and Unilever have achieved a successful combination of sustainability within their Business models, demonstrating that ethical entrepreneurship is not only good for profitability but also for societal transformation. As technology is changing rapidly, aware entrepreneurs also work toward responsible innovation. They see to it that those technological innovations, whether in AI, biotechnology, or online platforms, are invented and utilized so that they sustain high ethical standards, respect privacy, and enhance inclusivity.

10.10 The Significance of Ethical Technology Use

With technology so integral to all facets of life, the ethical concerns of technological (Mâță & Boghian, 2019) growth cannot be overlooked. Responsible entrepreneurship requires careful growth and deployment of technology to ensure that it works for society, not against it. Another essential focus for sustainable technology entrepreneurship is the ethical application of artificial intelligence (AI). While AI has the capability of transforming sectors, it also presents fears of privacy infringements, discriminatory decision-making, and the displacement of jobs. Ethical businesspersons are responsible for ensuring that AI solutions are equitable, transparent, and fair. Companies like Google DeepMind and OpenAI are working toward building ethical paradigms of AI that prevent discrimination and ensure user rights. Similarly, blockchain technology which is traditionally labeled as transparent and secure can be utilized ethically or unethically. Ethical entrepreneurs use blockchain to enhance supply chain transparency, validate carbon offsetting projects, and promote fair trade. Companies like Provenance use blockchain to track ethically sourced products so consumers can see verified sustainability claims. The renewable energy sector also presents an excellent opportunity for ethical technology application. As smart grids and solar power as well as wind power become the trend, progressive entrepreneurs are crafting solutions that decrease carbon footprints and increase energy independence. One such firm that has spearheaded the electric automobile and battery pack revolution is Tesla, making eco-friendly transportation accessible to the mass market.

10.10.1 How Education Forms Conscious Entrepreneurs

Education plays an essential part in forming conscious entrepreneurs by infusing ethical values, leadership capabilities, and social consciousness. The classical education system has primarily been devoted to success markers of businesses in terms of income growth, marketplace supremacy, and rivalry. Nonetheless, for development of sustainable tech entrepreneurship, institutes of learning are required to advance beyond the orthodox business schooling by integrating ethical making of choices, awareness of societal impact, and environmental guardianship.

10.10.2 Cultivating Empathy and Ethical Sensitivity

Empathy is a vital characteristic of self-aware entrepreneurs, which allows them to realize the requirements of society and develop solutions that actually solve significant issues (Fig. 10.2). Learning can develop empathy through service-learning classes, social entrepreneurship ventures, and practical case studies. For instance, schools that introduce Design Thinking methods into their curricula allow students to

Fig. 10.2 Role of education in shaping conscious entrepreneurs (*Source* author)

solve problems by focusing on human needs, and the result is more moral and meaningful innovations. Besides this, business ethics, CSR, and sustainable development courses enable the students to learn a moral system of decision-making. Global problems like climate change, income disparity, and abuse of human rights are exposed through coursework and dialogue, making students ready to implement ethics in their entrepreneurial activities.

10.10.3 Leadership and Entrepreneurial Mindset Development

Leadership is the other key ingredient of conscious entrepreneurship. Experiential learning, mentorship, and entrepreneurship incubators should be provided by universities and business schools to build ethical leadership. (Fig. 10.2) Hackathons and Social Innovation Challenges: Platforms that challenge students to create technology-based solutions to environmental and social problems. Collaborations with Sustainable Enterprises: Partnerships with purpose-driven companies that enable students to learn hands-on about ethical business practices.

Impact Investment and Ethical Finance Courses: Educating students to learn how businesses can raise money while keeping their ethical core strong. More institutions are now developing specialized courses in social entrepreneurship, sustainability management, and impact-driven Business models. For instance, Stanford University's business school embeds sustainability concepts in entrepreneurship training, while Harvard Business School has introduced initiatives around climate resilience and ethical AI development.

10.10.4 Developing Moral Decision-Making Capabilities

Conscious entrepreneurship demands that people make tough moral choices under conditions of complexity and high risk. Schools can foster (Fig. 10.2) critical thinking and moral reasoning through the inclusion of case-based learning, ethical dilemmas, and simulations in their instructional design. For example, students can go through role-playing exercises in which they have to face ethical dilemmas, e.g., reconciling profit interests with ecological concerns or choosing to consider shareholder interests at the expense of community welfare. Behavioral ethics and corporate governance courses can provide students with an understanding of the long-term rewards of ethical business behavior compared to short-term monetary rewards. Additionally, creating a learning culture where students question traditional Business models and think beyond conventional profit-based strategies fuels innovation based on sustainability.

10.10.5 Encouraging Policies Favorable to Sustainable Startups

Table 10.2 highlights key initiatives that foster sustainable startups through policy support, research funding, industry partnerships, and global collaborations. Governments can drive sustainability by offering grants, subsidies, and tax relief for green enterprises while simplifying regulations to ease business operations. Investments in R&D through national innovation funds and public–private partnerships (PPPs) further accelerate technological advancements in sustainability. Collaboration between academia and industry is essential, where corporate-university alliances, student projects, and sustainability-focused internships bridge the gap between research and real-world applications. Financial mechanisms such as green bonds and social impact funds support eco-friendly businesses, while corporate mentorship programs and commercialization support help startups scale. On a global level, institutions like UNDP and

Ashoka provide incubation programs, and NGOs facilitate cross-border collaborations and social innovation labs. Furthermore, awareness initiatives promoting ethical business practices, sustainability reporting, and public engagement campaigns ensure responsible entrepreneurship. These combined efforts create a thriving ecosystem for sustainable business innovation.

10.11 Proposed Educational Strategies

Although this chapter does not provide empirical findings, it provides a conceptually based framework drawn from an intensive review of research literature, policy suggestions, and cutting-edge best practices in education, sustainability, and entrepreneurship. These results provide a narrative integration of ideas to inform future educational strategies that promote sustainable technology entrepreneurs. The subsequent key elements comprise the proposed educational framework:

10.11.1 Interdisciplinary Curricula

Contemporary global challenges need more than just conventional academic disciplinarity answers. Interdisciplinary studies like the integration (Ye et al., 2023) of environmental science, business administration, and technological innovation challenge students to whole person learning. For instance, a "Sustainable Technology Entrepreneurship" study program can feature modules on renewable energy systems, green finance, startup innovation, and ethics of technology development. This allows students to consider entrepreneurial activities with the same intensity of concern for the environment, society, and economy.

10.11.2 Project-Based Learning Models

To connect practice to theory, learning must prioritize experiential, hands-on education. Formats such as design sprints, hackathons, and live case projects enable students to address real-life sustainability issues via technology (Chang et al., 2022). Learning environments foster critical thinking, innovation, collaboration, and flexibility essentials for twenty-first-century entrepreneurs. For instance, student competitions in developing low-cost solar substitutes or carbon footprint monitoring apps can simulate actual innovation environments.

Table 10.2 Key policy interventions

Category	*Initiatives*	*Description*
Encouraging Policies for Sustainable Startups	Grants and Subsidies	Financial support for clean energy, sustainable agriculture, and climate action startups
	Tax Relief for Sustainable Enterprises	Incentives for businesses adopting eco-friendly operations and carbon neutrality
	Simplified Business Rules	Reducing bureaucratic hurdles for sustainable startups
Funding R&D in Sustainable Technologies	National Innovation Funds	Financial support for research on green technology, AI-driven environmental solutions
	Public–Private Partnerships (PPPs)	Joint industry-government investment in sustainability projects
	Sustainability Competitions and Grants	Innovation challenges funding high-impact sustainability ideas
Industry-Academia Collaborations	Corporate-University Alliances	Partnerships in renewable energy, sustainable finance, and smart manufacturing
	Industry-Backed Student Projects	Sponsorship of student-led sustainability projects by corporations
	Internships in Sustainability Fields	Hands-on experience for students in sustainability-driven companies
Fostering Impact Investment & Sustainable Business models	Green Bonds and Social Impact Funds	Investment avenues supporting environmental and social causes
	Corporate Mentorship Programs	Guidance from industry leaders for sustainable entrepreneurship

10.11.3 Industry-Academia Collaborations

University-industry alliances are key to bridging educational objectives with reality within the marketplace (Zhang et al., 2022). Collaboration with technology companies, green companies, and policy research organizations gives students exposure to today's sustainability issues and future trends in tech. Industry-sponsored student projects, clean-tech internships, and mentorship by sustainable entrepreneurs can add value and influence entrepreneurial education extensively.

10.11.4 Integration of Ethics and Values

Entrepreneurship education needs to transcend profit-oriented paradigms to instill moral responsibility, empathy, and world citizenship. Education in business ethics, SDGs, and CSR enables students to critically examine the social impacts of their ventures. With the use of instruments like ethical dilemma simulations and impact analysis tools, students are taught to adopt conscious entrepreneurship where innovation goes hand in hand with integrity.

These theoretical proposals draw on contemporary global trends and institutional models. For instance, Stanford University's school offers courses that blend entrepreneurship and sustainability via human-centered design, and Power Ledger, an Australian blockchain technology company, collaborates with universities and government departments to further decentralized energy trading, a tangible instance of sustainable innovation. While this model is not empirically generalizable, it provides a strategic blueprint for curriculum development, institutional planning, and policy discussion. Pilot projects and subsequent studies can experiment with and refine these strategies, effectively bridging the gap between conceptual idealism and educational excellence.

10.12 Future Directions and Recommendations

The need for sustainable development and the quick pace of technology progress necessitates a revolution in the education of future entrepreneurs. Entrepreneurship and sustainability are not fads but necessities to deal with the world's most serious issues, such as climate change, natural resource deficits, and social inequality. This chapter highlights the main future trends and recommendations for increasing sustainable technology entrepreneurship education. By incorporating sustainability in key programs, promoting lifelong learning, encouraging cross-country collaborations, and adopting recommendations on policy interventions, actors and organizations can help design an educational curriculum that inspires responsible innovation. Incorporating Sustainability into Core Curricula in equipping students with the facts on sustainable technology entrepreneurship, concepts in sustainability and SDGs should be integrated into the main educational courses. This will help future business leaders think about environmental, social, and economic effects in their business strategies.

10.12.1 Implications for Research, Practice, and Society

Table 10.3 summarizes the primary implications of this chapter across three domains. These implications aim to guide curriculum developers, researchers, and institutional leaders in operationalizing the proposed educational framework for sustainable technology entrepreneurship (Fuerst et al., 2023).

Table 10.3 Primary implications across domains

Domain	*Key implications*	*Applications*
Research	Provides a conceptual framework for empirical validation	Study impact of interdisciplinary curricula on sustainable ventures, and compare implementation across socio-economic contexts
Educational practices	Offers a pedagogical model combining ethics, experiential learning, and sustainability	Modular courses for low-resource contexts, Interdisciplinary co-teaching models, Local problem-based learning activities
Society	Promotes socially responsible, tech-savvy entrepreneurs addressing real-world challenges	Community-focused startups, Youth-led green innovation, Sustainable job creation in underserved areas

10.12.2 Incorporating SDGs in Entrepreneurial Education

Redefining Business and Technology Courses: Business and technology courses should encompass sustainability-oriented material like green business strategies, circular economy principles, and climate-conscious innovation. Case Study-Based Learning: Using actual real-world case studies of successful sustainable tech startups exposes students to the ways in which sustainability can become a source of competitive strength. Project-Based Assignments: Engaging students to develop startup ideas based on sustainability and present them in competitions can spur applied learning. Fostering Interdisciplinary Learning. Entrepreneurship in sustainability needs education in multiple fields, such as engineering, environmental science, business, and social sciences. The institutions need to: Provide dual degree offerings in Sustainable Technology Entrepreneurship combining technology, business, and environmental science. Establish interdisciplinary courses in which students across various faculties work together on green innovation projects. Incorporate ethics and corporate responsibility education so that students will think like conscious entrepreneurs. With the integration of sustainability principles in learning, the students will learn better to formulate solutions that support economic growth as well as ecological and social wellness. Fostering Lifelong Learning Technology and sustainability are dynamic areas. To remain competitive, professionals and entrepreneurs need to be engaged in lifelong learning and upskilling on sustainable technologies and business practices.

10.12.3 Ongoing Upskilling in Sustainable Technologies

The rate of technology change demands lifelong learning to keep entrepreneurs competitive. Institutions and organizations need to: Create online learning courses and micro-credentials in renewable energy, AI for sustainability, blockchain for transparency, and impact-driven Business models. Promote certifications in green technology entrepreneurship to drive credibility and competency. Provide access to industry-driven training programs where students and entrepreneurs learn directly from the leaders in sustainability and technology experts. Developing a Culture of Ongoing Learning.

10.12.4 Learning Must Not End at Graduation

Alumni mentorship initiatives whereby successful entrepreneurs' mentor the next generation. Subscription-based learning systems where experts get frequent updates on upcoming sustainability trends. Promoting engagement in sustainability forums and conferences to expose learners to new information and international best practices. By promoting lifelong learning, institutions can guarantee that sustainability-driven entrepreneurs stay nimble and adaptive to new challenges. Strengthening Global Collaborations in this age of globalization, sustainable innovation is no longer a regional or national phenomenon. International cooperation and exchange of knowledge are critical to making a broad-based impact.

10.12.5 Seizing Opportunities Through Online Platforms for Cross-Border Innovation

Through technology, it is now easier than ever before for entrepreneurs and students across the world to unite and work together. To build global partnerships, institutions must: Establish international exchange programs through which students collaborate on shared sustainability projects with other countries' students. Support engagement in global hackathons and sustainability challenges to create cross-border solutions to problems such as climate resilience and access to renewable energy. Use online platforms for virtual networking by AI-based networking tools to connect sustainability-focused entrepreneurs globally. Establishing International Partnerships for Sustainable Entrepreneurship Universities must create partnerships with international institutions to provide joint sustainability courses and research activities. NGOs and international agencies may hold multi-country incubation programs so that entrepreneurs may test sustainability solutions in different locations. University-orchestrated sustainability projects must be supported by multinational corporations through funding and mentorship. Through promoting global collaborations, students and entrepreneurs can be exposed to increased exposure, global market access, and collaborative opportunities that multiply impact. Policy Recommendations Governments and policymakers play a pivotal role in ensuring the necessary support systems, financing, and infrastructure to facilitate sustainable technology entrepreneurship.

Strategic policies can foster innovation, lower capital hurdles, and facilitate long-term sustainability programs.

10.12.6 Financing Sustainable Student Startups

Securing initial funding is one of the largest hurdles for young entrepreneurs to overcome in converting ideas into Business models. Governments and institutions need to: Offer seed capital for green startup companies in the form of grants, low-interest loans, and impact investment funds. Implement tax breaks for green startups that deal with environmental sustainability and social responsibility. Create special research and development (R&D) grants for renewable energy, climate resilience, and circular economy models-related projects. Through financial support to student entrepreneurs, governments can empower the next generation of sustainability leaders.

10.12.7 Establishing Incubation Centers for Green Tech

A robust startup ecosystem calls for committed spaces where students may nurture, pilot, and upscale their sustainability-oriented innovations. The policymakers should: Create government-funded green tech incubators and accelerators in universities. Promote public–private collaborations to finance incubation centers focused on sustainable technologies. Provide business development training, mentorship, and networking opportunities to student entrepreneurs in these centers. Embedding Sustainability Standards in Entrepreneurship.

10.12.8 Mandate Sustainability

To ensure that sustainability is the heart of business activities, policymakers should require sustainability reporting by startups and SMEs to monitor their environmental and social footprint. Promote circular economy practices, including waste minimization, resource optimization, and responsible supply chains, among businesses. Regulate new technologies like AI and blockchain to ensure they are created and utilized ethically for sustainability purposes. Through these policy actions, governments can promote a long-term focus on sustainable entrepreneurship and technological innovation.

10.13 Conclusion

The future of sustainable technology entrepreneurship hinges on education, lifelong learning, global collaboration, and enabling policies. To ensure that the future generation of entrepreneurs grows innovations that are sustainable, ethical, and impactful, institutions and stakeholders need to: Integrate values of sustainability into mainstream education curricula to make responsible innovators. Encourage lifelong learning and frequent upskilling to maintain pace with the velocity of emerging technologies. Develop global partnerships and leverage online spaces for global sustainability initiatives. Establish international policy guidelines offering funding and incubation facilities to green innovations and startups. Through these positive initiatives, we will be in a position to transform the world into something where sustainability and innovation support one another and build a robust and responsible future. The education system, enterprises, policymakers, and international networks have to collaborate in order to guarantee the next generation of entrepreneurs takes the lead by purpose, vision, and dedication to sustainable development. In contrast to traditional strategies that address sustainability and entrepreneurship as distinct themes, this chapter presents an integrated, education-driven blueprint for developing responsible innovation. The originality of the suggested framework resides in its convergence of disruptive technologies, sustainability values, and pedagogical approaches into a cohesive framework for equipping future entrepreneurs with ethically based ventures. This contribution is especially useful for policymakers, curriculum developers, and institutions of higher education who want to make entrepreneurship education socially responsible and globally relevant.

References

Adeniyi, A., Akashaba, B., Aiyenuro, O., & Abiola, O. (2024). Framework for strategic investments in technology to enhance sustainable economic development in emerging markets. *International Journal of Innovative Science and Research Technology (IJISRT).*

Ahmad, M. I. S., Idrus, M. I., & Rijal, S. (2023). The role of education in fostering entrepreneurial spirit in the young generation. *Journal of Contemporary Administration and Management (ADMAN)*, *1*(2), 93–100. https://doi.org/10.61100/adman.v1i2.28

Amiri, M. S. (2023). *Unveiling the dynamics of startups* (Doctoral dissertation, Higher School of Management and Digital Economy). http://localhost:8080/xmlui/handle/123456789/329.

Arowoshegbe, A. O., Emmanuel, U., & Gina, A. (2016). Sustainability and triple bottom line: An overview of two interrelated concepts. *Igbinedion University Journal of Accounting, 2*(16), 88–126.

Astutik, I., Widiati, U., Ratri, D.P., Jonathans, P. M., Nurkamilah, N., Devanti, Y. M., & Harfal, Z. (2024). Transformative practices: Integrating automated writing evaluation in higher education writing classrooms—A systematic review. *Indonesian Journal on Learning and Advanced Education (IJOLAE).*

Balyan, S., Jangir, H., Tripathi, S. N., Tripathi, A., Jhang, T., & Pandey, P. (2024). Seeding a sustainable future: Navigating the digital horizon of smart agriculture. *Sustainability.*

Bapoo, M. A., Tehseen, S., Haider, S. A., Yusof, M., & Motaghi, H. (2022). Sustainability orientation and sustainable entrepreneurship intention: The mediating role of entrepreneurial opportunity recognition. *Academy of Entrepreneurship Journal, 28*(2), 1–23.

Bertino, E., Choo, K., Georgakopoulos, D., & Nepal, S. (2016). Internet of Things (IoT). *ACM Transactions on Internet Technology (TOIT), 16*, 1–7.

Boppana, V. (2018). Emerging technologies: shaping the future of innovation. *Global Research Review in Business and Economics [GRRBE]*. https://doi.org/10.56805/grrbe

Castle, N. (2022). Food futures: Food, foodways, and environmental crisis in contemporary science fiction (Doctoral dissertation, University of Warwick). http://webcat.warwick.ac.uk/record=b3913156

Chang, T. S., Wang, H. C., Haynes, A. M., Song, M. M., Lai, S. Y., & Hsieh, S. H. (2022). Enhancing student creativity through an interdisciplinary, project-oriented problem-based learning undergraduate curriculum. *Thinking Skills and Creativity, 46*, Article 101173. https://doi.org/10.1016/j.tsc.2022.101173

Dreyer, M., Chefneux, L., Goldberg, A., Heimburg, J. V., Patrignani, N., Schofield, M., & Shilling, C. (2017). Responsible innovation: A complementary view from industry with proposals for bridging different perspectives. *Sustainability, 9*(10), 1719. https://doi.org/10.3390/su9101719

Fiet, J. O. (2001). The theoretical side of teaching entrepreneurship. *Journal of Business Venturing, 16*(1), 1–24. https://doi.org/10.1016/S0883-9026(99)00041-5

Fuchs, C. (2008). The implications of new information and communication technologies for sustainability. *Environment, Development and Sustainability, 10*, 291–309. https://doi.org/10.1007/s10668-006-9065-0

Fuerst, S., Sanchez-Dominguez, O., & Rodriguez-Montes, M. A. (2023). The role of digital technology within the business model of sustainable entrepreneurship. *Sustainability, 15*(14), 10923. https://doi.org/10.3390/su151410923

Gonzales, M. (2020). Systems thinking for supporting students with special needs and disabilities. *Springer Publishing, 10*, 978–981. https://doi.org/10.1007/978-981-33-4558-4_1

Haldar, S. (2019). Towards a conceptual understanding of sustainability-driven entrepreneurship. *Corporate Social Responsibility and Environmental Management, 26*(6), 1157–1170. https://doi.org/10.1002/csr.1763

Hameed, I., Khan, M. B., Shahab, A., Hameed, I., & Qadeer, F. (2016). Science, technology and innovation through entrepreneurship education in the United Arab Emirates (UAE). *Sustainability, 8*(12), 1280. https://doi.org/10.3390/su8121280

Hartmann, C. (2024). *Exploring the potential of business incubators in fostering sustainability transitions—A Case Study of Urban Tech Helsinki*. https://urn.fi/URN:NBN:fi:aalto-202409016068

Heidari, M., Thangavel, S., Al Naamani, E., & Khashehchi, M. (2024). Emerging trends in smart green building technologies. *Sustainable Technologies for Energy Efficient Buildings*. https://doi.org/10.1201/9781003496656

Hermann, R. R., & Bossle, M. B. (2020). Bringing an entrepreneurial focus to sustainability education: A teaching framework based on content analysis. *Journal of Cleaner Production, 246*, Article 119038. https://doi.org/10.1016/j.jclepro.2019.119038

Hornborg, A. (2001). *The power of the machine: Global inequalities of economy, technology, and environment* (Vol. 1). Rowman Altamira.

James, A., Seth, A., & Mukhopadhyay, S. C. (2022). IoT System Design. In *Smart Sensors, Measurement and Instrumentation*, vol 41. Springer, Cham. https://doi.org/10.1007/978-3-030-85863-6_1

Johnson, J. T., Howitt, R., Cajete, G., Berkes, F., Louis, R. P., & Kliskey, A. (2016). Weaving Indigenous and sustainability sciences to diversify our methods. *Sustainability Science, 11*, 1–11. https://doi.org/10.1007/s11625-015-0349-x

Kazakeviciute, A., Urbone, R., & Petraite, M. (2016). Curriculum development for technology-based entrepreneurship education: A cross-disciplinary and cross-cultural approach. *Industry and Higher Education, 30*(3), 202–214. https://doi.org/10.1177/0950422216656050

Kozma, R. (2005). National policies that connect ICT-based education reform to economic and social development. *Human Technology, 1*(2), 117–156. https://doi.org/10.17011/ht/urn.2005355

Kwauk, C. T., & Casey, O. M. (2022). A green skills framework for climate action, gender empowerment, and climate justice. *Development Policy Review, 40*, Article e12624. https://doi.org/10.1111/dpr.12624

Lans, T., Blok, V., & Wesselink, R. (2014). Learning apart and together: Towards an integrated competence framework for sustainable entrepreneurship in higher education. *Journal of Cleaner Production, 62*, 37–47. https://doi.org/10.1016/j.jclepro.2013.03.036

Lee, J., Suh, T., Roy, D., & Baucus, M. (2019). Emerging technology and business model innovation: The case of artificial intelligence. *Journal of Open Innovation: Technology, Market, and Complexity, 5*(3), 44. https://doi.org/10.3390/joitmc5030044

Lescrauwaet, L., Wagner, H., Yoon, C., & Shukla, S. (2022). Adaptive legal frameworks and economic dynamics in emerging technologies: Navigating the intersection for responsible innovation. *Law and Economics, 16*(3), 202–220.

Ma, L., Lan, Z., & Tan, R. (2020). Influencing factors of innovation and entrepreneurship education based on the theory of planned behavior. *International Journal of Emerging Technologies in Learning (iJET), 15*(13), 190–206. https://doi.org/10.3991/ijet.v15i13.15345

Mahmood, S., Chadhar, M., & Firmin, S. (2022). Cybersecurity challenges in blockchain technology: A scoping review. *Human Behavior and Emerging Technologies, 2022*(1), 7384000. https://doi.org/10.1155/2022/7384000

Mâță, L., & Boghian, I. (2019). Perception of teachers in higher education towards ethical issues of information technology use. *Revista Romaneasca pentru Educatie Multidimensionala*.

McGowan, B. (2019). The role of the university library in creating inclusive healthcare hackathons: A case study with design-thinking processes. *IFLA Journal, 45*(3), 246–253. https://doi.org/10.1177/0340035219854214

Mohanty, A., Alam, A., & Mohanty, A. (2024). Education for sustainable development (ESD) and global citizenship for India. *Journal of Education for Sustainable Development Studies, 1*(2), 134–159. https://doi.org/10.70232/jesds.v1i2.17

Mukhamediev, R. I., Popova, Y., Kuchin, Y., Zaitseva, E., Kalimoldayev, A., Symagulov, A., & Yelis, M. (2022). Review of artificial intelligence and machine learning technologies: Classification, restrictions, opportunities and challenges. *Mathematics, 10*(15), 2552. https://doi.org/10.3390/math10152552

Ng, J. W., Azarmi, N., Leida, M., Saffre, F., Afzal, A., & Yoo, P. D. (2010, July). The intelligent campus (iCampus): end-to-end learning lifecycle of a knowledge ecosystem. In *2010 sixth International Conference on intelligent environments* (pp. 332–337). IEEE. https://doi.org/10.1109/IE.2010.68

Oluwadamilare, F., Usman, Odeyemi, O., Mhlongo, N. Z., Elufioye, O. A., & Ugochukwu, C. (2023). Sustainable entrepreneurship: A review of green business practices and environmental impact. *World Journal of Advanced Research and Reviews*.

Prokopenko, O., Kurbatova, T., Khalilova, M., Zerkal, A., Prause, G. K., Binda, J., Berdiyorov, T., Klapkiv, Y., Sanetra-Półgrabi, S., & Komarnitskyi, I. (2023). Impact of investments and R&D costs in renewable energy technologies on companies' profitability indicators: Assessment and forecast. *Energies*.

Rahimi, R. A., & Oh, G. S. (2024). Rethinking the role of educators in the 21st century: Navigating globalization, technology, and pandemics. *Journal of Marketing Analytics, 12*(2), 182–197. https://doi.org/10.1057/s41270-024-00303-4

Rao, S. P., Sekhar, S. C., Yadav, T. C., Kumar, V. P., & Haran, B. H. (2024). Implementing experiential learning strategies for enhanced business education in India: Challenges and opportunities. *Journal of Informatics Education and Research, 4*(3).

Rees, W. E. (2008). Human nature, eco-footprints and environmental injustice. *Local Environment, 13*(8), 685–701. https://doi.org/10.1080/13549830802475609

Rigolon, A., Yañez, E., Aboelata, M. J., & Bennett, R. (2022). "A park is not just a park": Toward counter-narratives to advance equitable green space policy in the United States. *Cities, 128*, Article 103792. https://doi.org/10.1016/j.cities.2022.103792

Rondinelli, D. A., & London, T. (2003). How corporations and environmental groups cooperate: Assessing cross-sector alliances and collaborations. *Academy of Management Perspectives, 17*(1), 61–76. https://doi.org/10.5465/ame.2003.9474812

Schaltegger, S., & Wagner, M. (2011). Sustainable entrepreneurship and sustainability innovation: Categories and interactions. *Business Strategy and the Environment, 20*(4), 222–237. https://doi.org/10.1002/bse.682

Schinckus, C. (2020). The good, the bad and the ugly: An overview of the sustainability of blockchain technology. *Energy Research & Social Science, 69*, Article 101614. https://doi.org/10.1016/j.erss.2020.101614

Shepherd, D. A., & Patzelt, H. (2011). The new field of sustainable entrepreneurship: Studying entrepreneurial action linking "what is to be sustained" with "what is to be developed." *Entrepreneurship Theory and Practice, 35*(1), 137–163. https://doi.org/10.1111/j.1540-6520.2010.00426.x

Shirazi, B. N., Safavi, A. A., Aftabi, E., & Salimi, G. (2024, February). The integration of virtual reality and artificial intelligence in educational paradigms. In *2024 11th International and the 17th National Conference on E-Learning and E-Teaching (ICeLeT)* (pp. 1–6). IEEE. https://doi.org/10.1109/ICeLeT62507.2024.10493089.

Shukla, K., Kaur, M., Mukherjee, M., Pranjal, P., & Sarkar, S. (2024). Conscious entrepreneurship: An authentic narrative for entrepreneurial ventures. In

Compelling Storytelling Narratives for Sustainable Branding (pp. 92–115). IGI Global. https://doi.org/10.4018/979-8-3693-3326-6.ch006

Steiner, G., & Posch, A. (2006). Higher education for sustainability by means of transdisciplinary case studies: An innovative approach for solving complex, real-world problems. *Journal of Cleaner Production, 14*(9–11), 877–890. https://doi.org/10.1016/j.jclepro.2005.11.054

Tavares, M. C., Azevedo, G., & Marques, R. P. (2022). The challenges and opportunities of era 5.0 for a more humanistic and sustainable society—A literature review. *Societies, 12*(6), 149.

Voegtlin, C., & Scherer, A. G. (2017). Responsible innovation and the innovation of responsibility: Governing sustainable development in a globalized world. *Journal of Business Ethics, 143*, 227–243.

Waddock, S., & Post, J. (2000). Transforming management education: The role of service-learning. In *Working for the common good* (pp. 43–54). Routledge.

Whitmer, A., Ogden, L., Lawton, J., Sturner, P., Groffman, P. M., Schneider, L., & Killilea, M. (2010). The engaged university: Providing a platform for research that transforms society. *Frontiers in Ecology and the Environment, 8*(6), 314–321. https://doi.org/10.1890/090241

Winarto, L., & Wisesa, A. (2024). Analyzing the impact of artificial intelligence and sustainability on Gen Z consumer purchase intentions: A case study of L'Oréal cosmetics Indonesia. *European Journal of Business and Management Research.*

Ye, P., & Xu, X. (2023). A case study of interdisciplinary thematic learning curriculum to cultivate "4C skills." *Frontiers in Psychology, 14*, 1080811. https://doi.org/10.3389/fpsyg.2023.1080811

Zaharia, R. M., & Zaharia, R. (2021). Triple bottom line. *The Palgrave Handbook of Corporate Social Responsibility*. https://doi.org/10.1007/978-3-030-42465-7_2

Zahra, S. A., & Nambisan, S. (2012). Entrepreneurship and strategic thinking in business ecosystems. *Business Horizons, 55*(3), 219–229. https://doi.org/10.1016/j.bushor.2011.12.004

Zhang, Y., Yuan, C., & Zhang, S. (2022). Influences of university-industry alliance portfolio depth and breadth on growth of new technology-based firms: Evidence from China. *Industrial Marketing Management, 102*, 190–204. https://doi.org/10.1016/j.indmarman.2022.01.018

Zhong, J. (2024). The influence of block-chain technology in Chinese smart logistics. *Highlights in Business, Economics and Management.*

CHAPTER 11

Opportunities, Challenges, and Strategies and Educational Approaches for Advancing Sustainable Technology Entrepreneurship Education

Anojan Vickneswaran

11.1 Introduction

In recent decades, stakeholders' concerns have increased regarding sustainable business practices. Stakeholders, especially regulators, policymakers, and investors, are more concerned about the firms' business practices, with a key concern on the four key dimensions: economy, environment, society, and governance (Eccles et al., 2014; Friede et al., 2015; Kolk, 2016; Schramade, 2016). Firms' business practices may have

A. Vickneswaran (✉)
School of Business and Creative Industries, University of the Sunshine Coast, Sippy Downs, QLD, Australia
e-mail: v_a017@student.usc.edu.au; anojanv@univ.jfn.ac.lk

Department of Accounting, Faculty of Management Studies and Commerce, University of Jaffna, Jaffna, Northern Province, Sri Lanka

D. Kumar et al. (eds.), *Evolving Trends in Technology Entrepreneurship*, Palgrave Studies in Global Entrepreneurship,
https://doi.org/10.1007/978-981-95-7441-4_11

both positive and negative effects on these dimensions (Bansal & Roth, 2000; Friede et al., 2015; Gunningham et al., 2004; Hart & Milstein, 2003). The increasing adverse impact of business practices on the environment, society, and governance highlights the importance of sustainable business practices and increases the demand for them (Ahmad et al., 2024; He et al., 2023; Shmelev & Gilardi, 2025; Treepongkaruna & Suttipun, 2024; Zopounidis & Lemonakis, 2024). Notably, shareholders' attention and actions have increased in terms of sustainability practices, including sustainable technology entrepreneurship, since the UN introduced Sustainable Development Goals (SDGs) 17 in 2015.

Firms, including large, medium-sized, and small-scale businesses, should adopt sustainable practices to ensure their long-term sustainability. A large number of global businesses are entrepreneurial. These significantly contribute to the national and global economy in numerous ways, including economic growth, fostering innovation, creating jobs, and improving living standards by introducing new technologies (e.g., AI, blockchain, and IoT) while also contributing to national income (Bağış, Kamacı, Adıgüzel, & Peçe, 2025; Esmail et al., 2025; Neumann, 2021; Nițu-Antonie et al., 2017; Ordeñana et al., 2024; Si et al., 2023). Notably, globally, nations are working to achieve UN SDGs 17 by 2030 (Fig. 11.1).

Many SDGs are directly and indirectly connected with entrepreneurship; for example, SDG 1: no poverty; SDG 2: zero hunger; SDG 3: Good health and well-being; SDG 4: quality education; SDG 6: clean water and sanitation; SDG 7: affordable and clean energy; SDG 8: decent work and economic growth; SDG 9: industry, innovation, and infrastructure; SDG 10: reduced inequalities; SDG 11: sustainable cities and communities; SDG: Climate action; SDG 12: responsible consumption and production; SDG 15: Life on land; and SDG 17: partnership for the goals. These underscore the importance of entrepreneurship and increase attention on sustainable entrepreneurship education, including technology entrepreneurship.

This chapter explores the importance, opportunities, challenges, and strategies and approaches for sustainable technology entrepreneurship education. The remaining sections of the chapter are (2) background, (3) importance, (4) opportunities, (5) challenges, (6) strategies and approaches, and (7) summary.

Fig. 11.1 United Nations Sustainable Development Goals

11.2 Background

Sustainable entrepreneurship refers to the process of starting and managing businesses aligned with the Triple Bottom Line (TBL) approach (Elkington, 1997; Gu et al., 2022; Majid & Koe, 2012; Watson et al., 2023). The TBL focuses on three dimensions: people, planet, and profit. It underscores that sustainable entrepreneurship not only seeks financial profitability but also prioritizes two other dimensions, such as people and planet. It integrates sustainability principles into business strategies to create long-term value for society, the environment, and future generations. Stakeholders are more likely to demand sustainable development, not stand alone development, in recent decades due to the potential adverse effects of business practices on society and the environment (Awa et al., 2024; Haleem et al., 2022; Nonet et al., 2022; Sun, Sulemana, & Agyemang, 2025). Sustainable development is related to the balance of economic, environmental, social, and governance outcomes to reduce disadvantages and provide benefits to stakeholders, including the general public, investors, regulators, policymakers, and other lives on land and at sea (Elkington & Rowlands, 1999; Lourenço et al., 2013). Existing literature suggests and reorganizes that entrepreneurial education is crucial in sustainable business practices, including sustainable technology (Arya et al., 2024; Hall et al., 2010; Joensuu-Salo et al., 2022; Kuckertz & Wagner, 2010; Lindner, 2018; Lourenço et al., 2013; Rosário & Raimundo, 2023; Sharma et al., 2021; Zahrani, 2022). Entrepreneurship is defined broadly. The definition of entrepreneurship may differ based on many aspects (e.g., differences in economies).

Entrepreneurship education refers to developing independent thinking and acquiring adequate individual skills and abilities related to entrepreneurship. Emancipatory approaches highlight their social and pedagogical significance in shaping society (Lindner, 2018). Entrepreneurship education is more likely extends the cultural legacy of the age of enlightenment. Existing literature shows less evidence on the definition of sustainable entrepreneurship education. Sustainable entrepreneurship education refers to developing independent thinking and acquiring adequate individual skills and abilities related to the sustainable aspects (economy, environment, social, and governance) of entrepreneurship based on the definition of entrepreneurship education and the scope of sustainability.

The scope of sustainable entrepreneurship education is broader than entrepreneurship education. Sustainable entrepreneurship education is more likely to involve rapid changes at regular intervals due to internal and external business environmental changes, including environmental, social, economic, and governance factors. Sustainable entrepreneurship education is more likely to provide benefits and reduce issues related to the sustainable aspects of the economy, environment, society, and governance (Diepolder et al., 2025; Valencia-Arias et al., 2025; Mawardi, Noor, Edityastono, 'Atikah Zulkiffli, & Mashahadi, 2025; Rosário et al., 2024; Sharma et al., 2021; Suguna et al., 2024; Karabetyan et al., 2023; Reimers, 2024). Stakeholders' attention has increased on sustainable entrepreneurship education rather than entrepreneurship education. Sustainable entrepreneurship education is more likely to be considered as a part of sustainable development. Notably, sustainable technology entrepreneurship education is a part of sustainable entrepreneurship education and sustainable development.

11.3 Importance of Sustainable Technology Entrepreneurship Education

Businesses operate in an ever-changing business environment where technology has grown rapidly over the last few decades (Calderon-Monge & Ribeiro-Soriano, 2024; Li et al., 2022; Yawson & Lewis, 2025). Technology (technological advancements) provides many benefits to the economy, society, and environment. Stakeholders demand sustainable business practices, including technology entrepreneurship, globally. The growing demand for new technologies, sustainability practices, and modern lifestyles is more likely to increase technology-related entrepreneurship. Importantly, technology is a part of day-to-day business and individual activities. Sustainable technology entrepreneurship is more likely to help achieve many SDGs because sustainable technology entrepreneurship is more likely to develop environmentally friendly technologies that help to protect the environment and increase good health and well-being. Sustainable technology entrepreneurship is helpful in treacle climate change, resource depletion, and pollution by integrating sustainability into technology advancements (George et al., 2021; Sambargi & Shubha, 2024; Truong, 2022; Hällerstrand et al., 2023; Gao et al., 2024; Shabir et al., 2023; Nguyen, Kowalski, & Dzienis, 2024a, 2024b). Sustainable technology entrepreneurship is more likely to contribute to long-term economic growth by creating sustainable job opportunities and fostering green industries. Businesses operate in an ever-changing and competitive business environment where sustainable technology is more likely to help achieve a competitive advantage. Achieving competitive advantage helps them attract investors, customers, and regulatory support, ensuring long-term success. Customers prefer sustainable products and services; therefore, sustainable technology is more likely to meet modern customers' preferences. Regulators (government and international institutions) implement sustainability-related regulations (Liao & Xiao, 2025; Jiang, Leng, Jiang, & Xu, 2025; Xin & Liu, 2025); therefore, sustainability technology is crucially important. Technologies are useful for many sectors, including education, health care, and finance. Notably, technology was helpful during the COVID-19 pandemic in teaching and assessments at all levels of educational programs. In addition, modern education programs (learning management systems, conferences, workshops, training programs, research collaborations, research, online degree programs, and distance learning programs) and healthcare services (medical testing) significantly depend on technologies. These underscore the importance of sustainable technology.

On the other hand, technological advancements may cause some adverse effects, especially on the economy, environment, and society (Islam, H., 2025; Celik, Yilmaz, Kahveci, & Yilmaz, 2025; Huang, 2021; Acemoglu & Restrepo, 2018; Zuboff, 2019). For example, certain technological developments harm land life, such as affecting birds' habitats and fertility. Some technological advancements are also used in cybercrime activities, and others facilitate academic and research fraud. Furthermore, technology entrepreneurship faces many challenges related to sustainability due to the constantly changing business environment, including advancements in technology and regulations governing their development and use. For instance, some nations ban certain technologies and related products and services. For example, "India imposed a nationwide ban on TikTok in June 2020" (Germain, 2024). Furthermore, technology entrepreneurship exists at different scales, such as large, medium, and small. As a result, small and medium-scale ventures are more likely to encounter numerous issues, like high competition and long-term sustainability concerns, than large-scale enterprises. Even large technology-related firms have failed (e.g., Nokia). Technology plays a crucial role in the economy, society, and environment. Because it offers many benefits alongside some negative effects. Education focused on sustainable technology entrepreneurship is critically important for sustainability.

11.4 Opportunities for Sustainable Technology Entrepreneurship Education

There are several opportunities for sustainable technology entrepreneurship education in line with its significant contribution to the economy, environment, and society. This section discusses some potential opportunities for sustainable technology entrepreneurship education.

11.4.1 Global Awareness

Stakeholders believe that technological advancements are crucial for sustainability. They understand the importance of technology and the lower probability of achieving sustainability without technology. Because technology contributes significantly to day-to-day human and business activities. On the other hand, they are also aware of the potential negative effects of technology, important to the economy, environment, and society. Regulators and international institutions are more likely to suggest/ recommend sustainable entrepreneurship, including technology entrepreneurship. This emerging awareness demands sustainable technology entrepreneurship education.

11.4.2 Cost and Time Savings

Based on economic theory, resources are scarce. Technology-related literature highlights that technology is more likely to save costs and time (Fähndrich, 2023; Kokina & Blanchette, 2019; Littlewood et al., 2024; Ong et al., 2025; Pearce, 2020; Santoro, Jabeen, & Troise, 2025). Not surprisingly, businesses and individuals are more likely to adopt technologies to save costs and time (Bettiol et al., 2024; Faiz et al., 2024; Ali & Maelah, 2025; Dang et al., 2025; Jackson & Allen, 2024; Nawaz et al., 2024; Featherman, Jia, Califf, & Hajli, N. (2021)). Furthermore, they are more likely to prefer sustainable technologies to ensure sustainability. Potential cost and time reductions through sustainable technologies underscore potential opportunities for sustainable technology entrepreneurship education.

11.4.3 Research and Development

Research and development offer new theories in literature and solutions for problems, including sustainability-related issues. Technology, entrepreneurship, technology entrepreneurship, and sustainability-related literature suggest that technology entrepreneurship is more likely to provide several benefits to businesses and individuals, including sustainability (Fernandes et al., 2022; George et al., 2021; Holzmann & Gregori, 2023; Kraus et al., 2019; Xu et al., 2022). These studies highlight the importance of sustainable technology entrepreneurship/ digital entrepreneurship. Notably, existing, especially recent findings on sustainable technology significantly contribute to sustainable technology entrepreneurship-related curricula. Furthermore, higher education institutions are more interested in clean energy, climate tech, and sustainable agriculture-related research as well as some prior studies highlight the need for a comprehensive approach to higher education research that integrates social sustainability to foster a more holistic and enduring form of sustainability in the future (Tafese et al., 2025; Bimo, Sulistyaningsih, & Inderawati, 2024; Osman et al., 2025; Salvia, & Brandli, 2019; Gamage et al., 2024; Li et al., 2024; Bathaei et al., 2023). Stakeholders are more likely to demand sustainable technology entrepreneurship-related research to ensure sustainability. This research, development, interests, and potential demands underscore the need for sustainable technology entrepreneurship education.

11.4.4 Collaborations and Engagements

Stakeholders are more likely to motivate higher education institutions to conduct sustainable technology-related research and academic programs to enhance the innovative ideas, skills, and abilities to create new sustainable technology entrepreneurship and boost the existing technology entrepreneurship toward sustainability. For example, the government and industries are more likely to provide funds (e.g., grants and scholarships) to develop sustainable technology entrepreneurship-related curricula and other potential research and development in these areas (e.g., scholarships for PhD students and grants for sustainable technology). Importantly, youth are more interested in the new technologies and their advancements. They are more likely to develop/use new technologies with a key focus on sustainability. Notably, the community is also more likely to support/demand sustainable technologies. These collaborations and engagements toward sustainability technology and technology-related courses and degree programs signal the need for sustainable technology entrepreneurship education.

11.4.5 Skills' Development

The future generation is expected to live in an interconnected technological environment (Forkosh Baruch & Erstad, 2018; Guttieres, 2019; Nakawake & Kobayashi, 2024; Rasa & Laherto, 2022; Reis et al., 2021). Stakeholders, particularly governments and international institutions, are more likely to motivate skills development for the development and usage of sustainable technologies in line with the national and global sustainability-related goals. They are more likely to provide skills development programs and hands-on training on sustainable technologies in every sector, for example, vocational training in solar panel installation, green construction, and circular economy practices, workshops on design thinking and business modeling for sustainable innovation, and certification programs in environment, social, and governance (ESG) and green finance. These skill development actions underscore the need for sustainable technology entrepreneurship education.

11.4.6 Modern Business Environment, Lifestyle, and Technology Advancements

We live in a globalized modern business environment. Businesses operate with interconnected technological systems. In addition, our modern lifestyle is more closely interconnected with technologies and significant technological advancements than the traditional lifestyle. Technology-related factors are external environment factors of the business environment. Technology-related factors in the external environment are crucial for the business's sustainability. Firms ought to be more aware of changes in the technology-related factors that are connected with them. If they fail to respond properly to the technological advancements/changes in the external environment, they are more likely to face negative consequences, including a reduction in customers and profits. In the modern business environment and lifestyle, technology is growing rapidly. Ever-changing internal and external business environments, lifestyles, and advancements underscore the need for sustainable technology entrepreneurship education.

11.4.7 Regular Curriculum Revision

Educational institutions, including academic and professional institutions, are more likely to revise their curricula at regular intervals (e.g., once every 5 years) due to internal and external environmental changes and demands. The importance and need for sustainable technology have increased over the years; therefore, revision of the academic curriculum is more likely to accommodate educational programs and courses on sustainable technology entrepreneurship. For example, universities are more likely to introduce technology-related courses and academic programs. The regular revision of academic programs is more likely to advance sustainable technology entrepreneurship education.

11.5 Challenges for Sustainable Technology Entrepreneurship Education

Sustainable technology entrepreneurship education is important for ensuring that present and future entrepreneurs with the adequate skills and mindset essential for sustainable ventures. However, advancing sustainable technology entrepreneurship education is subject to some potential limitations similar to other fields of education. This section lists and discusses some important potential challenges for sustainable technology entrepreneurship education.

11.5.1 Limited Resources and Support

Adequate resources and support are the two fundamental aspects that contribute significantly to every educational program, including sustainable technology entrepreneurship. Resources and support are more required, like sustainable technology entrepreneurship education, because it is interconnected with both theoretical and practical aspects. Sustainable technology entrepreneurship study programs are more likely to require trained and expert staff with recent innovation and technological advancements. However, education providers are more likely to have academic, professional, and research staff in well-established disciplines rather than in emerging academic programs, including sustainable technology entrepreneurship. These institutions may have limited expertise in sustainable technology entrepreneurship because it is an emerging and rapidly growing. Existing technology entrepreneurship and technology-related teaching and research staff are more likely to have less expertise in sustainable technology entrepreneurship. Traditional technology entrepreneurship educators mainly focus on technology entrepreneurship, making it challenging to shift toward a sustainability-focused teaching and learning environment. Further, these institutions are more likely to have limited teaching resources, including textbooks, case studies, digital tools related to sustainable technology development, and other physical facilities, including laboratory facilities. Curriculum development on sustainability technology is more likely to consume more time and money for other resources, including experts' fees. Further, they are more likely to need a huge amount of investment for new technology-oriented academic programs, especially for tangible (e.g., lab) and intangible assets (e.g., patents, copyrights). These institutions faced several difficulties and negative consequences, including low cash inflow during the COVID-19 pandemic. They are now strategically moving forward during the post-pandemic era. They have limited resources; importantly, financial constraints, lack of expertise, inadequate teaching resources, time limitations, and resistance to change are significant challenges in education for sustainable technology education.

Furthermore, global economies belong to different economic scales. Importantly, they are mainly categorized as low, middle, and upper-income nations. Government and stakeholders' support for sustainable technology entrepreneurship education in low and middle-income nations is more likely to be lower than in upper-income nations. Therefore, differences in economies, especially resource and financial capacity, are a key challenge for sustainable technology entrepreneurship education across the globe. Further, countries differ in policies related to environmental, social, and governance aspects (sustainability). Further, they may follow different legal traditions and economic agendas. For example, some nations (e.g., some African nations) struggle to fulfill the basic needs of their people. In these nations, they are less likely to give priority to sustainable technology entrepreneurship education because they are unable to fulfill their basic needs. Therefore, these potential differences among economies are more likely to be key challenges in sustainable technology entrepreneurship education.

11.5.2 Rapidly Evolving Technologies

The technology sector is a rapidly evolving sector. So, we are unable to use the same technology-oriented courses and academic programs for the long term, like other disciplines. Even education providers are unable to use or offer the same software-related certificate courses due to the rapid advancements in the same software, in addition to that, potential innovation and introduction of some new software with additional features and benefits. Academic programs related to sustainable technology entrepreneurship are more likely to require more resources, including a huge amount of investment. However, rapid changes and advancements in technologies are more likely to question and reduce academic programs related to sustainable technology entrepreneurship. Therefore, rapid advancements and growth of technologies are one of the key challenges in sustainable technology entrepreneurship education.

11.5.3 A Lack of an Interdisciplinary Approach

Today, technology is interconnected with many disciplines. For example, the accounting profession uses technology, and the agriculture profession uses technology. However, they use different technologies for each profession as per their purpose. So, technology developments depend on its need. These needs are more likely to differ among industries and disciplines. Traditional teaching and learning approaches are based on discipline. Traditional education systems often compartmentalize subjects, making it difficult to integrate entrepreneurship, sustainability, and technology into a cohesive curriculum. For example, collaboration between business, engineering, and environmental studies is limited in many institutions. Furthermore, traditional culture, norms, and values are less likely to encourage an interdisciplinary approach. Historically, we created some values for each major discipline, so the different levels of values for each discipline and profession are less likely to prefer an interdisciplinary approach. Notably, there are very few interdisciplinary courses in higher education institutions. Further, corporate firms also have different categories called industries, so they prefer to work within the industry and a similar industry. This lack of an interdisciplinary approach is one of the key challenges for sustainable technology entrepreneurship education.

11.6 Strategies and Educational Approaches

Based on the importance, opportunities, and challenges for sustainable technology entrepreneurship education, as responsible stakeholders, strategies and educational approaches are crucial for capitalizing on opportunities, overcoming challenges, and meeting global demand. This section first discusses some strategies and then discusses the educational approaches to overcome challenges and capitalize on opportunities for sustainable technology entrepreneurship education.

11.6.1 Strategies

In the globalized modern business environment and lifestyle, many opportunities exist to enhance sustainable technology entrepreneurship education. However, some factors challenge the sustainable technology entrepreneurship education. In this crucial situation, strategies are more likely to capitalize on the opportunities and overcome challenges for sustainable technology entrepreneurship education. Stakeholders, including the government, international bodies, and universities, should increase public awareness about sustainability and its importance for the present and future generations. Collaborations among universities, professional institutions, governments, international bodies, and industries are more likely to help sustainable technology entrepreneurship education because they are responsible parties who should ensure the sustainable technology-related education and its viability.

11.6.2 Educational Approaches

In the modern teaching and learning environment, the traditional teaching and learning approaches are less suitable due to advancements in technologies and lifestyle. Notably, traditional teaching and learning approaches are less suitable for sustainable technology entrepreneurship because technology entrepreneurship differs from other theoretical and practice-oriented disciplines. Furthermore, educators and learners in sustainable technology entrepreneurship education are more likely to differ from others. Teachers are more interested in cultivating ideas and developing skills related to sustainable entrepreneurship in education for sustainable technology entrepreneurship. Similarly, entrepreneurship students are more interested in acquiring adequate and appropriate ideas and skills related to sustainable technology entrepreneurship. Therefore, sustainable technology entrepreneurship education approaches are more likely to differ from the traditional ones. Integrated teaching and learning approaches, team learning, case studies, internships, project studies, action research, experimental studies, research projects, active learning, practical learning environments, problem-based learning, and simulation based learning toward sustainable technology entrepreneurship are more likely to contribute to sustainability (Leal Filho et al., 2018; Sharma et al., 2021; Blankesteijn, 2024; Cocu, Pecheanu, Susnea, Dingli,, Istrate, & Tudorie, 2025; Awotunde, & Aregbeshola, 2024; Hsu et al., 2023; Mitchell et al., 2025; Nguyen, Cleveland, Nguyen, & Joyce, 2024a, 2024b; Bhullar, & Aggarwal, 2022).

11.7 Summary

Sustainable technology demand has increased over the years due to concerns about sustainability. This growing demand underscores the importance of sustainable technology entrepreneurship education. Sustainable technology entrepreneurship is more likely to contribute to sustainable development goals related to the economy, environment, and society. There are some opportunities and challenges in sustainable technology entrepreneurship education, and these opportunities and challenges are more likely to be moderated by some key stakeholders, such as government/policy makers, regulators, standard-setters, global agencies, enterprises (for-profit and non-profit), and the general public. Some strategies and educational approaches are useful for sustainable technology entrepreneurship education, including increasing public awareness, creating collaborations among stakeholders, integrated teaching and learning, team learning, case studies, internships, project studies, action research, experimental studies, research projects, active learning, practical learning environments, problem-based learning, and simulation-based learning. Figure 11.2 summarizes the challenges, opportunities, strategies, and approaches for sustainable technology entrepreneurship education discussed in this chapter.

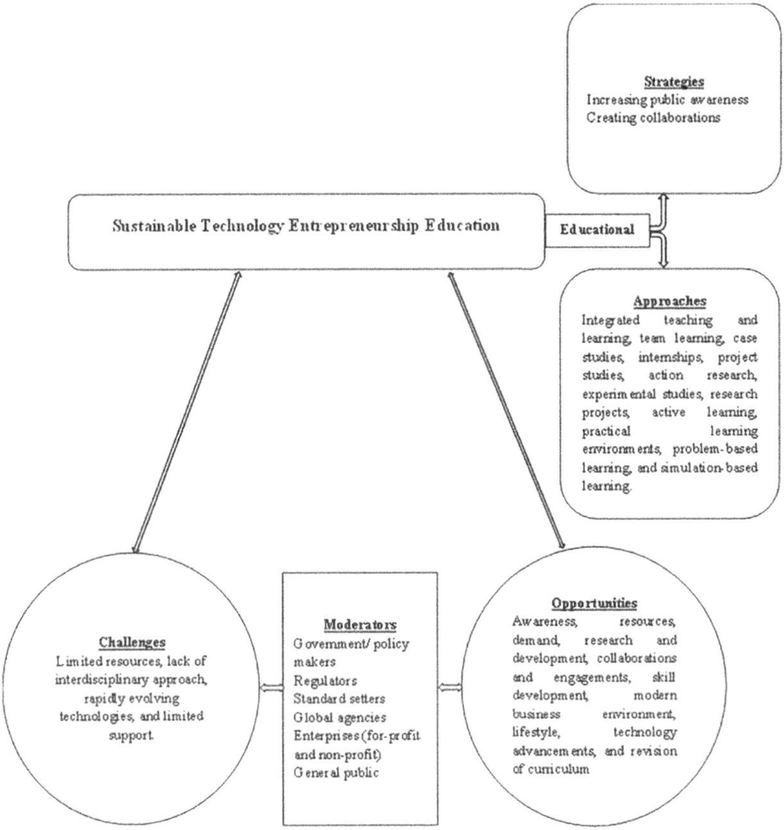

Fig. 11.2 Challenges, opportunities, strategies, and approaches for sustainable technology entrepreneurship education

References

Acemoglu, D., & Restrepo, P. (2018). Artificial intelligence, automation, and work. In *The economics of artificial intelligence: An agenda* (pp. 197–236). University of Chicago Press.

Ahmad, H., Yaqub, M., & Lee, S. H. (2024). Environmental-, social-, and governance-related factors for business investment and sustainability: A scientometric review of global trends. *Environment, Development and Sustainability, 26*(2), 2965–2987.

Ali, A. S., & Maelah, R. (2025). Technological innovation and sustainability of shared service: Insights from industry players. *Heliyon, 11*(4).

Arya, V., Gaurav, A., Gupta, B. B., & Chui, K. T. (2024). A bibliometric analysis of environmental education and sustainable entrepreneurship development in a global perspective. *Sustainable Technology and Entrepreneurship, 3*(3), Article 100080.

Awa, H. O., Etim, W., & Ogbonda, E. (2024). Stakeholders, stakeholder theory and corporate social responsibility (CSR). *International Journal of Corporate Social Responsibility, 9*(1), 11.

Awotunde, O. M., & Aregbeshola, A. R. (2024). Systemic action learning action research and entrepreneurship momentum development. *Action Learning: Research and Practice*, 1–19.

Bağış, M., Kamacı, A., Adıgüzel, Z., & Peçe, M. A. (2025). The effects of entrepreneurial ecosystems and macroeconomic indicators on high job creation expectations and the business services sector. *Journal of Enterprising Communities: People and Places in the Global Economy.*

Bansal, P., & Roth, K. (2000). Why companies go green: A model of ecological responsiveness. *Academy of Management Journal, 43*(4), 717–736.

Bathaei, A., & Štreimikienė, D. (2023). Renewable energy and sustainable agriculture: Review of indicators. *Sustainability, 15*(19), 14307.

Bettiol, M., Capestro, M., Di Maria, E., & Ganau, R. (2024). Is this time different? How industry 40 affects firms' labor productivity. *Small Business Economics, 62*(4), 1449–1467.

Bhullar, P. S., & Aggarwal, M. (2022). Simulation-based teaching pedagogy and entrepreneurship education: a bibliometric analysis. *Technology and Entrepreneurship Education: Adopting Creative Digital Approaches to Learning and Teaching* (pp. 133–157).

Bimo, I. D., Sulistyaningsih, E., & Inderawati, M. M. W. (2024). Quantifying the presence of sustainability education and climate change in higher education: a bibliometric study. *International Journal of Sustainability in Higher Education.*

Blankesteijn, M. L. M. (2024). Towards transformative experiential learning in science-and technology-based entrepreneurship education for sustainable technological innovation. *Journal of Innovation & Knowledge, 9*(3), Article 100544.

Calderon-Monge, E., & Ribeiro-Soriano, D. (2024). The role of digitalization in business and management: A systematic literature review. *Review of Managerial Science, 18*(2), 449–491.

Celik, A., Yilmaz, E. G., Kahveci, S., & Yilmaz, G. (2025). Do technological advances promote ecological sustainability? Evidence from panel causality analysis for the dirtiest and cleanest countries. *Journal of the Knowledge Economy*, 1–36.

Cocu, A., Pecheanu, E., Susnea, I., Dingli, S., Istrate, A., & Tudorie, C. (2025). Technology-enabled learning for green and sustainable entrepreneurship education. *Administrative Sciences, 15*(2), 45.

Dang, S., Quach, S., & Roberts, R. E. (2025). How time fuels AI device adoption: A contextual model enriched by machine learning. *Technological Forecasting and Social Change, 212*, Article 123975.

Diepolder, C. S., Huwer, J., & Weitzel, H. (2025). Effects of competence-based sustainable entrepreneurship education on secondary school students' sustainable entrepreneurial intention. *Sustainable Technology and Entrepreneurship, 4*(2), Article 100103.

Eccles, R. G., Ioannou, I., & Serafeim, G. (2014). The impact of corporate sustainability on organizational processes and performance. *Management Science, 60*(11), 2835–2857.

Elkington, J. (1997). The triple bottom line. *Environmental Management: Readings and Cases, 2*(1997), 49–66.

Elkington, J., & Rowlands, I. H. (1999). Cannibals with forks: The triple bottom line of 21st century business. *Alternatives Journal, 25*(4), 42.

Esmail, H. A. H., Wani, M. J. G., Attia, O. N. Y., & Galal, H. E. (2025). Entrepreneurial dynamics and their impact on economic development in Saudi Arabia. *Future Business Journal, 11*(1), 99.

Fähndrich, J. (2023). A literature review on the impact of digitalisation on management control. *Journal of Management Control, 34*(1), 9–65.

Faiz, F., Le, V., & Masli, E. K. (2024). Determinants of digital technology adoption in innovative SMEs. *Journal of Innovation & Knowledge, 9*(4), Article 100610.

Featherman, M., Jia, S. J., Califf, C. B., & Hajli, N. (2021). The impact of new technologies on consumers' beliefs: Reducing the perceived risks of electric vehicle adoption. *Technological Forecasting and Social Change, 169*, Article 120847.

Fernandes, C., Pires, R., & Gaspar Alves, M. C. (2022). Digital entrepreneurship and sustainability: The state of the art and research agenda. *Economies, 11*(1), 3.

Forkosh Baruch, A., & Erstad, O. (2018). Upbringing in a digital world: Opportunities and possibilities. *Technology, Knowledge and Learning, 23*(3), 377–390.

Friede, G., Busch, T., & Bassen, A. (2015). ESG and financial performance: Aggregated evidence from more than 2000 empirical studies. *Journal of Sustainable Finance & Investment, 5*(4), 210–233.

Gamage, A., Gangahagedara, R., Subasinghe, S., Gamage, J., Guruge, C., Senaratne, S., & Merah, O. (2024). Advancing sustainability: The impact of emerging technologies in agriculture. *Current Plant Biology, 40*, Article 100420.

Gao, F., Xin, B., Peng, W., & Gonzalez, E. D. S. (2024). Accelerating decarbonized economic growth through net-zero entrepreneurship: Low-carbon economic development perspective. *Journal of Environmental Management, 370*, Article 122684.

George, G., Merrill, R. K., & Schillebeeckx, S. J. (2021). Digital sustainability and entrepreneurship: How digital innovations are helping tackle climate change and sustainable development. *Entrepreneurship Theory and Practice, 45*(5), 999–1027.

Germain, T. (2024). *The ghosts of India's TikTok: What happens when a social media app is banned*. https://www.bbc.com/future/article/20240426-the-ghosts-of-indias-tiktok-social-media-ban

Gu, W., Pan, H., Hu, Z., & Liu, Z. (2022). The triple bottom line of sustainable entrepreneurship and economic policy uncertainty: An empirical evidence from 22 countries. *International Journal of Environmental Research and Public Health, 19*(13), 7758.

Gunningham, N., Kagan, R. A., & Thornton, D. (2004). Social license and environmental protection: Why businesses go beyond compliance. *Law & Social Inquiry, 29*(2), 307–341.

Guttieres, D. (2019). An intra-and inter-generational lens into rapid technological change. *Development, 62*(1), 37–42.

Haleem, F., Farooq, S., Cheng, Y., & Waehrens, B. V. (2022). Sustainable management practices and stakeholder pressure: A systematic literature review. *Sustainability, 14*(4), 1967.

Hall, J. K., Daneke, G. A., & Lenox, M. J. (2010). Sustainable development and entrepreneurship: Past contributions and future directions. *Journal of Business Venturing, 25*(5), 439–448.

Hällerstrand, L., Reim, W., & Malmström, M. (2023). Dynamic capabilities in environmental entrepreneurship: A framework for commercializing green innovations. *Journal of Cleaner Production, 402*, Article 136692.

Hart, S. L., & Milstein, M. B. (2003). Creating sustainable value. *Academy of Management Perspectives, 17*(2), 56–67.

He, G., Liu, Y., & Chen, F. (2023). Research on the impact of environment, society, and governance (ESG) on firm risk: An explanation from a financing constraints perspective. *Finance Research Letters, 58*, Article 104038.

Holzmann, P., & Gregori, P. (2023). The promise of digital technologies for sustainable entrepreneurship: A systematic literature review and research agenda. *International Journal of Information Management, 68*, Article 102593.

Hsu, C. Y., & Wu, T. T. (2023). Application of business simulation games in flipped classrooms to facilitate student engagement and higher-order thinking skills for sustainable learning practices. *Sustainability, 15*(24), 16867.

Huang, Y. (2021). Technology innovation and sustainability: Challenges and research needs. *Clean Technologies and Environmental Policy, 23*(6), 1663–1664.

Islam, H. (2025). Nexus of economic, social, and environmental factors on sustainable development goals: The moderating role of technological advancement and green innovation. *Innovation and Green Development, 4*(1), Article 100183.

Jackson, D., & Allen, C. (2024). Enablers, barriers and strategies for adopting new technology in accounting. *International Journal of Accounting Information Systems, 52*, Article 100666.

Jiang, K., Leng, M., Jiang, Y., & Xu, L. (2025). From penalties to profits: how government regulation and cost-revenue trade-offs shape green production and marketing: Jiang et al. *Environment, Development and Sustainability*, 1–37.

Joensuu-Salo, S., Viljamaa, A., & Varamäki, E. (2022). Sustainable entrepreneurs of the future: The interplay between educational context, sustainable entrepreneurship competence, and entrepreneurial intentions. *Administrative Sciences, 12*(1), 23.

Karabetyan, L., & Sart, G. (2023). The impact of entrepreneurship and education on the ecological footprint: Insights from the G-20 states. *Sustainability, 16*(1), 97.

Kokina, J., & Blanchette, S. (2019). Early evidence of digital labor in accounting: Innovation with Robotic Process Automation. *International Journal of Accounting Information Systems, 35*, Article 100431.

Kolk, A. (2016). The social responsibility of international business: From ethics and the environment to CSR and sustainable development. *Journal of World Business, 51*(1), 23–34.

Kraus, S., Palmer, C., Kailer, N., Kallinger, F. L., & Spitzer, J. (2019). Digital entrepreneurship: A research agenda on new Business models for the twenty-first century. *International Journal of Entrepreneurial Behavior & Research, 25*(2), 353–375.

Kuckertz, A., & Wagner, M. (2010). The influence of sustainability orientation on entrepreneurial intentions—Investigating the role of business experience. *Journal of Business Venturing, 25*(5), 524–539.

Leal Filho, W., Raath, S., Lazzarini, B., Vargas, V. R., de Souza, L., Anholon, R., & Orlovic, V. L. (2018). The role of transformation in learning and education for sustainability. *Journal of Cleaner Production, 199*, 286–295.

Li, C., Yao, H., Li, Z., Wu, F., Liu, B., Wu, Y., & Xu, Y. (2024). A bibliometric analysis of global research on climate change and agriculture from 1985 to 2023. *Agronomy, 14*(11), 2729.

Li, L., Tong, Y., Wei, L., & Yang, S. (2022). Digital technology-enabled dynamic capabilities and their impacts on firm performance: Evidence from the COVID-19 pandemic. *Information & Management, 59*(8), Article 103689.

Liao, Z., & Xiao, L. (2025). Government environmental regulation, media attention, and corporate green innovation. *International Review of Economics & Finance, 97*, Article 103751.

Lindner, J. (2018). Entrepreneurship education for a sustainable future. *Discourse and Communication for Sustainable Education, 9*(1), 115–127.

Littlewood, A., McCool, R., Edwards, M., & di Ruffano, L. F. (2024). PP19 time and cost savings of machine learning and artificial intelligence (AI) in systematic reviews: A case study. *International Journal of Technology Assessment in Health Care, 40*(S1), S61–S61.

Lourenço, F., Jones, O., & Jayawarna, D. (2013). Promoting sustainable development: The role of entrepreneurship education. *International Small Business Journal, 31*(8), 841–865.

Majid, I. A., & Koe, W. L. (2012). Sustainable entrepreneurship (SE): A revised model based on triple bottom line (TBL). *International Journal of Academic Research in Business and Social Sciences, 2*(6), 293.

Mawardi, M. K., Noor, A. Y. M., Edityastono, L., 'Atikah Zulkiffli, S. N., & Mashahadi, F. (2025). Green entrepreneurship in the era of sustainability: the relationship between intent, institutional support, and student behavior. *Cogent Business & Management*, *12*(1), 2460625.

Mitchell, K., Canham, R., Hughes, K., & Tallentire, V. R. (2025). Simulation-based education and sustainability: Creating a bridge to action. *Advances in Simulation, 10*(1), 27.

Nakawake, Y., & Kobayashi, Y. (2024). Exploring new technologies for the future generation: Exploration–exploitation trade-off in an intergenerational framework. *Royal Society Open Science, 11*(5), Article 231108.

Nawaz, N., Arunachalam, H., Pathi, B. K., & Gajenderan, V. (2024). The adoption of artificial intelligence in human resources management practices. *International Journal of Information Management Data Insights, 4*(1), Article 100208.

Neumann, T. (2021). The impact of entrepreneurship on economic, social and environmental welfare and its determinants: A systematic review. *Management Review Quarterly, 71*(3), 553–584.

Nguyen, L. T. V., Cleveland, D., Nguyen, C. T. M., & Joyce, C. (2024a). Problem-based learning and the integration of sustainable development goals. *Journal of Work-Applied Management, 16*(2), 218–234.

Nguyen, N. T. H., Kowalski, A. M., & Dzienis, A. M. (2024b). Sustainable entrepreneurial process in the deep-tech industry. *Sustainability, 16*(19), 8714.

Niţu-Antonie, R. D., Feder, E. S., & Munteanu, V. P. (2017). Macroeconomic effects of entrepreneurship from an international perspective. *Sustainability, 9*(7), 1159.

Nonet, G. A. H., Gössling, T., Van Tulder, R., & Bryson, J. M. (2022). Multi-stakeholder engagement for the sustainable development goals: Introduction to the special issue. *Journal of Business Ethics, 180*(4), 945–957.

Ong, C. Y., Ng, A. J. J., Ang, S. Y. J., & Lee, J. M. H. (2025). Savings through telemedicine: Initial data from a hospital-at-home program. *Value in Health Regional Issues, 45*, Article 101046.

Ordeñana, X., Vera-Gilces, P., Zambrano-Vera, J., & Jiménez, A. (2024). The effect of high-growth and innovative entrepreneurship on economic growth. *Journal of Business Research, 171*, Article 114243.

Osman, M. A., Sheikh Farah, A. A., & Abdi, A. I. (2025). A bibliometric analysis of sustainable development research in higher education institutions (HEIs): Key trends, global collaborations and influential contributions (2015–2023). *Cogent Education, 12*(1), 2490436.

Pearce, J. M. (2020). Economic savings for scientific free and open source technology: A review. *HardwareX, 8*, Article e00139.

Rasa, T., & Laherto, A. (2022). Young people's technological images of the future: Implications for science and technology education. *European Journal of Futures Research, 10*(1), 4.

Reimers, F. M. (2024). Entrepreneurship education to improve the world: The role of the sustainable development goals to stimulate innovation in higher education. *Entrepreneurship Education, 7*(3), 203–217.

Reis, L., Mercer, K., & Boger, J. (2021). Technologies for fostering intergenerational connectivity and relationships: Scoping review and emergent concepts. *Technology in Society, 64*, Article 101494.

Rosário, A. T., & Raimundo, R. (2023). Sustainable entrepreneurship education: A literature review. *Preprints (Basel), 1*, 1–20.

Rosário, A. T., & Raimundo, R. (2024). Sustainable entrepreneurship education: A systematic bibliometric literature review. *Sustainability, 16*(2), 784.

Salvia, A. L., & Brandli, L. L. (2019). Energy sustainability at universities and its contribution to SDG 7: A systematic literature review. *Universities as living labs for sustainable development: supporting the implementation of the sustainable development goals*, 29–45.

Sambargi, S., & Shubha, N. S. (2024). Technology and sustainability: Opportunities and challenges. *Nudging Green: Behavioral Economics and Environmental Sustainability*, 189–205.

Santoro, G., Jabeen, F., & Troise, C. (2025). How do platform-based Business models create competitive advantages by saving time for users?. *EuroMed Journal of Business*.

Schramade, W. (2016). Bridging sustainability and finance: The value driver adjustment approach. *Journal of Applied Corporate Finance, 28*(2), 17–28.

Shabir, M., Hussain, I., Işık, Ö., Razzaq, K., & Mehroush, I. (2023). The role of innovation in environmental-related technologies and institutional quality to drive environmental sustainability. *Frontiers in Environmental Science, 11*, 1174827.

Sharma, S., Goyal, D. P., & Singh, A. (2021). Systematic review on sustainable entrepreneurship education (SEE): A framework and analysis. *World Journal of Entrepreneurship, Management and Sustainable Development, 17*(3), 372–395.

Shmelev, S. E., & Gilardi, E. (2025). Corporate environmental, social, and governance performance: The impacts on financial returns, business model innovation, and social transformation. *Sustainability, 17*(3), 1286.

Si, S., Hall, J., Suddaby, R., Ahlstrom, D., & Wei, J. (2023). Technology, entrepreneurship, innovation and social change in digital economics. *Technovation, 119*, Article 102484.

Suguna, M., Sreenivasan, A., Ravi, L., Devarajan, M., Suresh, M., Almazyad, A. S., & Mohamed, A. W. (2024). Entrepreneurial education and its role in fostering sustainable communities. *Scientific Reports, 14*(1), 7588.

Sun, G., Sulemana, I., & Agyemang, A. O. (2025). Examining the impact of stakeholders' pressures on sustainability practices. *Management Decision*.

Tafese, M. B., & Kopp, E. (2025). Education for sustainable development: Analyzing research trends in higher education for sustainable development goals through bibliometric analysis. *Discover Sustainability, 6*(1), 51.

Treepongkaruna, S., & Suttipun, M. (2024). The impact of environmental, social and governance (ESG) reporting on corporate profitability: evidence from Thailand. *Journal of Financial Reporting and Accounting*, (ahead-of-print).

Truong, T. C. (2022). The impact of digital transformation on environmental sustainability. *Advances in Multimedia, 2022*(1), 6324325.

Valencia-Arias, A., Londoño-Celis, W., Moya, L. P., Iparraguirre Sanchez, G. K., Cardona-Acevedo, S., & Rodríguez-Correa, P. A. (2025). Sustainable entrepreneurial intention in undergraduates: The influence of entrepreneurship education. *Discover Sustainability, 6*(1), 588.

Watson, R., Nielsen, K. R., Wilson, H. N., Macdonald, E. K., Mera, C., & Reisch, L. (2023). Policy for sustainable entrepreneurship: A crowdsourced framework. *Journal of Cleaner Production, 383*, Article 135234.

Xin, Z., & Liu, C. (2025). Does environmental regulations boost corporate sustainability? A perspective of environmental strategy. *Journal of Environmental Management, 385*, Article 125625.

Xu, G., Hou, G., & Zhang, J. (2022). Digital Sustainable Entrepreneurship: A digital capability perspective through digital innovation orientation for social and environmental value creation. *Sustainability, 14*(18), 11222.

Yawson, R. M., & Lewis, V. J. (2025). Navigating contemporary issues in business and management. *Organization Management Journal, 22*(1), 2–9.

Zahrani, A. A. (2022). Promoting sustainable entrepreneurship in training and education: The role of entrepreneurial culture. *Frontiers in Environmental Science, 10*, Article 963549.

Zopounidis, C., & Lemonakis, C. (2024). The company of the future: Integrating sustainability, growth, and profitability in contemporary Business models. *Development and Sustainability in Economics and Finance, 1*, Article 100003.

Zuboff, S. (2019). *The age of surveillance capitalism: The fight for a human future at the new frontier of power, edn.* PublicAffairs.

CHAPTER 12

The Intersection of Sports and Technology Entrepreneurship

Esra Emir and Kadir Yıldız

12.1 Introduction

In recent years, rapid technological advancements that have profoundly influenced societal life have also led to a fundamental transformation in the sports industry. This transformation has not only enhanced athletes' training and performance processes but has also reshaped the operations of sports organizations, fan engagement, and media consumption habits. Technological innovations have introduced new Business models and opportunities in the sports industry, with cutting-edge tools such as wearable devices, data analytics, artificial intelligence (AI), and digital platforms redefining every aspect of sports (Tang et al., 2023, 2025; Wilson,

E. Emir
Department of Coaching Education, Faculty of Sport Sciences, İstanbul Aydın University, İstanbul, Türkiye

K. Yıldız (✉)
Department of Sport Management, Faculty of Sport Sciences, Manisa Celal Bayar University, Manisa, Türkiye
e-mail: kadir.yildiz@cbu.edu.tr

D. Kumar et al. (eds.), *Evolving Trends in Technology Entrepreneurship*, Palgrave Studies in Global Entrepreneurship,
https://doi.org/10.1007/978-981-95-7441-4_12

2020). This shift has created significant opportunities at the intersection of sports and technology entrepreneurship, further accelerating the growth of the sector.

Wearable technologies have revolutionized the sports world in recent years. Devices such as smartwatches, fitness trackers, and biomechanical sensors enable athletes to monitor their performance in real time. These devices collect and analyze training data, providing athletes with recommendations to optimize their performance (Mohammed et al., 2024; Smith & Johnson, 2022; Tang et al., 2023, 2025). Major sports organizations, in particular, utilize these technologies to monitor athletes' health, assess injury risks, enhance training programs, and improve overall performance. For instance, in leagues such as the NBA and NFL, wearable devices provide valuable insights into athletes' heart rate, muscle mobility, and overall physical condition, contributing to a more efficient training process (Lewis, 2004).

Data analytics has become one of the most crucial tools in the sports industry. Beyond assessing individual athlete performance, it is widely utilized in various areas, including game strategies, match analysis, and player evaluations. For instance, Major League Baseball (MLB) has adopted advanced data analytics techniques known as Sabermetrics to enhance decision-making processes, from player selection to game strategies (Lewis, 2004). Similarly, in other team sports, data analytics is employed to optimize game strategies and more accurately evaluate player performances. These advancements have enabled teams to enhance their gameplay efficiency and have introduced a new paradigm of strategic thinking. Moreover, in sports such as football, data analytics plays a critical role in player recruitment, in-game strategy development, and overall performance optimization (O'Brien & Lyman, 2021).

Artificial intelligence (AI) has gained significant prominence in the sports industry in recent years. AI algorithms are employed in various domains, including match analysis, player performance tracking, and team strategy development (Pisaniello, 2024). For instance, in football matches, Video Assistant Referee (VAR) systems utilize AI-powered tools to review referee decisions. Similarly, in team sports such as basketball and football, AI algorithms assist in player selection and the formulation of game strategies (Foster, 2021; Held et al., 2024). These technologies enhance decision-making processes, making games fairer and more accurate. Additionally, sports teams and organizations leverage AI to predict player performance and optimize their game plans.

Technology has also significantly transformed fan engagement within the sports industry. Digital platforms, live streaming services, and social media tools enable fans to interact with their favorite teams and athletes in unprecedented ways. These technologies allow sports organizations to reach a global audience and expand their fan base more effectively (Achenbach, 2020). Additionally, innovations such as augmented reality (AR) and virtual reality (VR) have made the fan experience more interactive and immersive. For example, some stadiums offer fans the opportunity to watch matches from different perspectives through VR headsets. Such technologies enhance the overall sports experience, increasing engagement among both in-stadium spectators and those watching from home (Eichhorn, 2022). As a result, the integration of sports and technology has driven a profound transformation that extends beyond athletes to include fans as well.

With this transformation, sports technology entrepreneurship has been rapidly growing, presenting significant opportunities. Entrepreneurs are not only developing innovative technologies to enhance athlete performance but also providing solutions that improve the efficiency of sports organizations' operational processes. By leveraging the latest technological advancements, these ventures are reshaping traditional Business models within the sports industry. For instance, companies such as WHOOP and Fitbit utilize wearable technologies to provide athletes with health and performance data, optimizing their training and recovery processes (Smith & Johnson, 2022). Additionally, these enterprises assist sports teams in making strategic decisions by integrating artificial intelligence and data analytics into their operations.

In conclusion, the intersection of sports and technology entrepreneurship has created significant opportunities within the sports industry, with innovative solutions driving transformation across the sector. Advancements such as wearable devices, data analytics, artificial intelligence, and digital platforms enhance athlete performance, strengthen fan engagement, and improve the operational efficiency of sports organizations. With the accelerating pace of digitalization in the twenty-first century, the sports industry has evolved beyond being solely performance-oriented and has positioned itself at the intersection of technology, entrepreneurship, and data-driven innovation. This transformation spanning from wearable technologies and AI-based analytical systems to digital platforms that redefine fan engagement and the growing ecosystem of sports entrepreneurship has reshaped both the internal dynamics of athletic performance and the broader organizational and commercial dimensions of sport. At this intersection, innovative practices not only enhance athlete performance but also influence management strategies of sports organizations, enrich fan experiences, diversify investment approaches, and expand the societal impact of sports. This chapter aims to provide a multidimensional perspective on the evolving sports ecosystem by examining the key components of this transformation through conceptual, technological, and entrepreneurial lenses. Accordingly, it explores the role of sports technologies, performance tracking systems, data analytics and artificial intelligence applications, sports entrepreneurship and investment opportunities, as well as fan engagement analyzing each theme in depth based on both academic literature and contemporary practices.

12.2 Conceptual Framework

12.2.1 The Role of Technology in Sports

Technology in sports is not a new concept. Over the years, innovations such as the invention of synthetic surfaces, advanced equipment design, and video analysis have become integral parts of the sports world (Wilson, 2020). However, the rise of digital technologies, data analytics, artificial intelligence (AI), and wearable technologies has accelerated this transformation, enabling athletes and teams to reach levels of performance, precision, and efficiency that were previously unimaginable. Particularly in recent years, the role of technology in the sports world has undergone a profound transformation. This change has not only improved athlete performance but has also led to significant shifts across various areas, from sports organization management to fan engagement. Innovations such as wearable technologies, data analytics, and AI have become key elements reshaping the dynamics of the sports industry. In particular, wearable devices are making athletes' training processes, performance, and recovery times more efficient, while data analytics and AI systems, used to develop team strategies, are guiding the future of sports.

Wearable technologies have rapidly spread throughout the sports world, allowing athletes to monitor their physical performance in real time. Devices such as smartwatches, fitness trackers, and biomechanical sensors measure athletes' speed, endurance, heart rate, and other physiological data. These devices not only track athletes' performance but also provide coaches with individualized insights into each athlete's development process. Professional athletes, in particular, can enhance the efficiency of their training and take necessary precautions to prevent injuries thanks to these devices (Smith & Johnson, 2022; Tang et al., 2025). For example, brands like WHOOP and Garmin play a significant role in optimizing post-training recovery processes by collecting health data to provide athletes with better training routines. These advancements have not only improved athletes' physical performance but also attracted the attention of technology-driven entrepreneurs within the sports industry, leading to the emergence of new Business models in this area.

The data-driven transformation of the sports industry plays a crucial role not only in shaping athletes' performance but also in influencing team strategies and game analysis. Advanced data analytics help teams use more objective and effective methods when making decisions in areas ranging from player selection to in-game strategies. Organizations like Major League Baseball (MLB) utilize statistical analysis techniques such as Sabermetrics to assess player values and team strategies (Lewis, 2004). Such analyses not only improve individual player performance but also enhance the tactical decisions teams make during games. For example, in sports such as football and basketball, advanced data analytics enable teams to evaluate players' positional effectiveness and identify the roles in which they perform most efficiently. As a result, sports organizations are increasingly making data-driven strategic decisions, leading to improved outcomes on the field.

In addition to these advancements, technologies such as artificial intelligence (AI) and machine learning have also sparked a significant transformation in the sports world. AI-based algorithms track athletes' performance while also enabling more accurate team strategies and game analyses. For example, in football matches, the Video Assistant Referee (VAR) system uses AI-based video analysis technologies to verify referee decisions, ensuring more accurate and fair game management. AI also provides insights into which strategies are most effective by analyzing game performance to optimize team outcomes. These technologies help teams understand how even small changes in gameplay can create substantial differences (Foster, 2021; Held et al., 2024; Karafil, 2023). Additionally, AI-based systems analyze players' in-game movements, identifying areas for improvement and allowing coaches to use this data to develop more targeted training processes. Consequently, athletes are able to deliver stronger performances both physically and strategically. Another significant area at the intersection of sports and technology is fan engagement. Technological innovation has fundamentally transformed the nature of fan engagement with sporting events, representing one of the most significant developments in the modern sport industry. Digital platforms, social media, and live streaming services enable fans to closely follow their favorite teams and athletes. Social media allows sports organizations and athletes to reach a global audience, while also providing an interactive and participatory experience for fans. This digital interaction not only allows fans to watch events but also enables them to contribute, comment, and communicate with other fans (Achenbach, 2020). Furthermore, technologies like augmented reality (AR) and virtual reality (VR) enhance the stadium experience by offering fans the opportunity to engage with matches from different angles. These technologies not only provide a visual experience for in-stadium spectators but also create a more interactive viewing experience by granting access to real-time statistics during the game.

In conclusion, the relationship between sports and technology has not only enhanced athlete performance but has also transformed the experiences of sports organizations and fans. Wearable technologies, data analytics, artificial intelligence, and digital interaction tools are impacting every aspect of sports, and this transformation is shaping the future of the industry. These technological advancements in the sports world offer sports organizations more efficient operations and innovative Business models, while also creating significant opportunities for entrepreneurs. This shift suggests that the future of sports will feature greater technology integration and higher levels of digital engagement. The impact of technology on the sports world will not only shape today's experience but will also define the sports experience of the future.

12.2.2 Performance Tracking and Wearable Technology

In recent years, the importance of performance tracking in the sports world has steadily increased. The integration of technology with sports allows athletes to manage their training, game performance, and recovery processes in a more scientific and data-driven manner. One of the most notable aspects of this transformation is the use of wearable technologies. Wearable devices enable athletes to monitor their physical data in real time, allowing them to make more informed decisions during training, while coaches can develop more accurate strategies (Smith & Johnson, 2022). Wearable technology not only tracks athletes' performance but also provides data-driven insights into the functioning of the sport, making decision-making within sports organizations more efficient.

Wearable devices are at the forefront of technologies used to track athlete performance (Tang, 2025). Smartwatches, fitness trackers, biomechanical sensors, and similar tools can measure athletes' speed, heart rate, muscle activity, and other biological parameters in real time. This data provides immediate feedback on athletes' physical conditions and enable coaches to guide athletes more effectively. For example, wearable devices like WHOOP and Garmin collect data on athletes' sleep patterns, heart rate, and other physiological metrics to optimize recovery times and enhance training efficiency (Smith & Johnson, 2022). While monitoring overall health, these devices also help athletes optimize rest and recovery periods necessary to prevent injuries.

In addition, the impact of wearable technologies on performance analysis is considerable. Coaches can analyze athletes' data to identify which training regimens are more effective and which physical parameters need improvement. Data-driven decisions are far more precise and reliable than traditional observation methods. For instance, in sports like football and basketball, players' movements and performance on the field are tracked through wearable devices. The resulting data helps to generate insights into which strategies are likely to be more successful. Moreover, this data not only shapes individual performance but can also influence the overall strategy of the team (Foster, 2021). Wearable technologies allow coaches to develop the most efficient strategies by tracking players' positions and activities during team sports. The opportunities that wearable technologies offer to athletes also provide significant advantages to sports organizations. By utilizing data from wearable devices, sports organizations can monitor the overall health of players and predict potential injuries in advance. Moreover, this data can serve as a valuable source of analysis for sponsors. For example, brands can analyze athletes' performance data to plan sponsorship deals in a more targeted and effective manner. This leads to an increase in athletes' sponsorship revenue, while also enabling sports organizations to make more informed and data-driven decisions (Achenbach, 2020). Additionally, players' performance data offers media companies valuable content and creates new opportunities for fan engagement. Wearable technologies, beyond individual training and performance tracking, also help professional teams and federations improve their game strategies. In sports like football, where team coordination is key, wearable devices track the movements of the entire team, and this data is used to shape the game strategy. With the help of wearable devices, coaches can analyze players' speed, reactions to the ball, and even their body language, enabling them to make strategic adjustments that enhance the team's on-field performance (Lewis, 2004). These technologies not only facilitate the monitoring of physical data but also allow for tactical analyses related to the game.

All these advancements demonstrate that the impact of wearable technologies in the sports world goes beyond just tracking individual performance. These technologies, which contribute significantly to areas such as monitoring athletes' health, reducing injury risks, enhancing training efficiency, and developing game strategies, are also transforming the overall functioning of the sports industry. Wearable devices not only provide the data necessary for athletes to showcase their optimal performance but also allow for the optimization of a team's overall strategy. This transformation in the sports world signals that wearable technologies will continue to gain importance in the future and be more widely integrated across all areas of sports. As a result, wearable technologies continue to revolutionize every aspect of the sports industry. With their advantages in tracking athletes' individual performance, reducing injury risks, and optimizing team strategies, these technologies play a significant role in the sports world. It is evident that wearable technologies offer opportunities not only for athletes and teams but also for sports organizations, media companies, and sponsorship deals. The development of these technologies will shape the future of sports and enable a more efficient, healthier, and strategically driven sports culture.

12.2.3 Data Analytics and Artificial Intelligence

Data analytics and artificial intelligence (AI) have become two transformative technological advancements in the sports industry in recent years (Mohammed et al., 2024; Rahmani et al., 2024). Sports organizations and professional teams are leveraging these technologies to enhance athletes' performance, develop game strategies, and improve fan experiences. Data analytics has transformed performance monitoring in sports from a mere numerical process into a deeper and more strategic analysis, while artificial intelligence is making these processes smarter.

AI, combined with data analytics, enables sports organizations to make real-time decisions and predict future possibilities (Williams, 2019).

Data analytics has become a powerful tool for evaluating athletes' performance, developing game strategies, and minimizing injury risks. Especially in professional sports like football, basketball, baseball, and American football, every movement of players on the field is digitally recorded, and this data is subsequently analyzed. These analyses, which cover players' speed, distance, heart rate, and other biometric data, enable a deeper understanding of each athlete's physical condition (Lewis, 2018). Thanks to data analytics, coaches can identify players' strengths and weaknesses, adjust strategies accordingly, and manage the game more consciously. For example, organizations like Major League Baseball (MLB) use statistical analysis methods known as Sabermetrics to measure player value and determine team strategies (Klein, 2020).

Moreover, artificial intelligence (AI) adds an advanced dimension to the data analytics process. AI-based systems provide algorithms that analyze players' and teams' performance. These systems process in-game data and have the capacity to predict future possibilities, not just assess the current state. For instance, AI algorithms can use historical game data to predict a player's next move, allowing coaches to adopt a more proactive approach (Brynjolfsson & McAfee, 2017). AI also analyzes biometric data to predict players' injury risks. Such analyses help monitor the condition of players who have experienced long-term injuries and accelerate their recovery processes (Müller, 2019). Teams and sports organizations can use AI to optimize tactical decisions during games and personalize training processes. Another important application of combining data analytics and artificial intelligence (AI) is match analysis and strategic planning. Coaches can analyze every aspect of their team's performance during a game using data and AI, allowing them to determine which strategies are more effective. These analyses not only provide insights into the overall performance of the team but also help understand the strategies of the opposing team. With the help of AI and data analytics, it is possible to identify in which situations athletes perform best or which strategies are most effective against opposing teams. This application is particularly valuable in sports like football and basketball, where coaches can make strategic decisions both before and during the match (Sokolov, 2020). Moreover, these technologies allow for in-depth video analyses of games, where individual players' positions, reaction times, and decision-making processes can be examined in greater detail.

Fan engagement is another important innovation enabled by data analytics and AI in sports. Emerging technologies allow sports organizations to personalize the fan experience. AI, combined with big data analytics, can analyze each fan's preferences, interests, and viewing habits. With this data, sports organizations can offer personalized content, fostering a deeper connection with fans. For example, a football club could analyze fans' past match-viewing history and social media interactions to offer personalized promotions or content. Additionally, AI-powered chatbots and smart assistants can efficiently respond to fans' inquiries, providing faster and more effective service (Gustafsson, 2021).

Another crucial aspect of data analytics and artificial intelligence (AI) applications is athlete health and injury management. Biometric data collected through wearable technologies enables coaches and healthcare professionals to monitor players' physical condition and potential injury risks. This data plays a significant role in optimizing training loads and accelerating recovery processes for athletes. AI can make predictions based on this data, helping to identify signs of overtraining or potential injuries in advance. Moreover, AI-powered health systems can enhance the efficiency of recovery processes post-injury, ensuring that players can return to play faster and with less risk of re-injury (Vanderbilt & Gibson, 2020). Such advancements allow for the optimization of athlete health and help ensure career longevity, making it possible to take important steps toward managing athlete well-being. In conclusion, data analytics and AI have emerged as two key technological innovations that are transforming the sports industry. These technologies not only enhance the monitoring and improvement of athlete performance but also revolutionize areas such as optimizing game strategies, personalizing fan experiences, and managing athlete health. Sports organizations and professional teams are leveraging these technologies to make more informed, data-driven decisions, creating a more efficient and effective sports experience. This transformation is shaping the future of sports, laying the foundation for a more innovative and strategic sports culture.

12.2.4 Sports Entrepreneurship and Innovation

Sports entrepreneurship and innovation have emerged as rapidly growing and evolving fields, significantly transforming the dynamics of the sports industry in recent years. The sports sector, moving beyond traditional Business models, is generating new opportunities shaped by factors such as technology, digitalization, and global markets. This transformation holds the potential to reshape the future of sports by enabling entrepreneurs to introduce new Business models, innovative products, and services. Sports entrepreneurship not only transcends the sports industry as a commercial sector but also deepens the societal impacts of sports (Hassan & McKeown, 2019). This article will explore how sports entrepreneurship and innovation have evolved, the opportunities and challenges faced in this field, and future trends.

Sports entrepreneurship goes beyond creating economic value in the sports field, encompassing significant aspects such as societal impacts and individual participation. Traditional sports clubs and organizations are known for their functional competencies and high performance, while the new generation of sports entrepreneurs utilizes tools such as digitalization and technology to provide more dynamic and accessible sports experiences. This shift has fostered entrepreneurship in emerging fields such as digital media and e-sports, transformed traditional sports disciplines, and created new markets. For example, e-sports has evolved into a large industry with competitive structures, sponsorship deals, and mass audiences, similar to traditional sports organizations (Hamari, Koivisto, & Sarsa, 2017). These innovative sectors are redefining not only entertainment in the sports industry but also Business models, revenue distribution, and social interaction.

Sports entrepreneurship also reflects the critical role of technology in sports. Technological innovations offer great potential for enhancing athletes' performance and improving efficiency within sports organizations. Advances in wearable technologies, data analytics, artificial intelligence, and virtual reality have created new business opportunities for sports organizations and investment prospects for entrepreneurs. For instance, wearable devices used to monitor athletes' health and optimize their performance present valuable opportunities for both users and the sports industry (Albrecht, 2020). The integration of technology with sports enables entrepreneurs to create more interactive and personalized experiences not only for athletes but also for fans. This has led to significant opportunities in fields such as digital marketing, mobile applications, and live streaming. However, one of the biggest challenges facing sports entrepreneurship is the intense competition within the sector. In an environment where technological advancements are rapidly spreading, entrepreneurs must possess innovative and differentiated Business models to survive in the market. In this context, it is crucial for entrepreneurs to understand traditional sports culture while rapidly adopting the changes brought about by digitalization and globalization. Moreover, as the sports industry requires substantial financial resources and infrastructure, it is essential for entrepreneurs to collaborate with the right investors to overcome these barriers (Funk & Pizzo, 2019). Sports entrepreneurship largely requires the dynamic management of innovation and business development processes, which may make it challenging for entrepreneurs to adapt to rapidly changing market conditions. Another important factor in sports entrepreneurship is the growing emphasis on sustainability and ethical issues. At every intersection of sport and commerce, environmental impacts, social responsibility, and ethical questions come to the forefront. Sustainability encompasses not only environmental impacts but also the responsibility of sports organizations to fulfill their societal duties. When sports entrepreneurs consider these aspects in their operations, they not only gain a competitive advantage but also set an example in implementing socially responsible and environmentally friendly strategies. For instance, some sports organizations and entrepreneurs contribute to making the sports industry greener by developing environmentally conscious products and sustainable Business models (Mason, 2018).

Another aspect of sports entrepreneurship is its relationship with globalization. Global sports markets, particularly through television broadcasts, digital content, and sponsorship deals, create vast opportunities. Entrepreneurs are now able to operate not only in local markets but also on a global scale. This global perspective encourages the growth of sports not only in physical spaces but also in digital and virtual arenas (Anderson & Cross, 2017). For example, sports brands and media companies have focused on content distribution through digital platforms in the global market, thereby increasing the international reach of sports. This process has allowed sport to become a universal language and helped entrepreneurs transcend the cultural and geographical boundaries of sports. As a result, sports entrepreneurship is reshaping the sports industry across a broad spectrum, from technological innovations to global opportunities. The globalization of sport, coupled with elements such as digitalization and sustainability, has made sports entrepreneurship a dynamic and rapidly evolving field. Entrepreneurs can leverage these opportunities with innovative products and services while adopting a strategic approach to navigate the competitive and ethical challenges in the sector. These dynamics, combined with the opportunities offered by technology and global market growth, will shape the future of sports and provide entrepreneurs with a wide area for innovation.

12.2.5 Sports Entrepreneurship and Investment Opportunities

Sports entrepreneurship and investment opportunities play a significant role in the dynamics of today's sports industry. The global growth and digitalization of sports have created numerous opportunities for entrepreneurs while simultaneously establishing an attractive market for investors. The recognition of the sports industry as a top-tier economic sector has encouraged the development of innovative Business models in both traditional sports and emerging sports fields. This has great potential for both entrepreneurs and investors. However, sports entrepreneurship and investment opportunities extend beyond innovative products and services, representing a field that requires making significant strategic decisions in business and accurately analyzing industry trends (Funk & Pizzo, 2019).

The growing importance of sports entrepreneurship and investment opportunities is directly related to the role of technology in sports. The digitalization of the sports industry has provided entrepreneurs with numerous new Business models based on technological innovations. Technologies such as wearable devices, data analytics, artificial intelligence, virtual reality, and augmented reality have created opportunities to enhance athlete performance, improve fan experiences, and optimize the operational processes of sports organizations. The development of such innovative technologies has created new markets in sports with high growth potential for investors and has led to significant changes in investment strategies. For example, companies developing wearable devices to monitor athlete performance are being closely watched by investors, as these technologies can be utilized to improve efficiency across all areas of sports (Albrecht, 2020). These innovations enable entrepreneurs to be part of the rapidly growing sports technology market. However, sports entrepreneurship and investment opportunities are not limited to technological innovations. The emergence of new sports fields has created vast opportunities for investors. For instance, the e-sports sector has gained attention as a rapidly growing field in recent years. Beyond traditional sports, digital games and virtual competitions have attracted a new audience and created opportunities such as sponsorship deals, media rights, and digital content. These new digital sports have established a massive global market, particularly by appealing to younger demographics. E-sports organizations and digital platforms have attracted the attention of investors because the growth potential in this sector is considerable (Hamari, Koivisto, & Sarsa, 2017). Additionally, the digitalization of traditional sports organizations and strategies related to media rights has provided sports entrepreneurs with new Business models and revenue streams.

Sports entrepreneurship and investment opportunities are also closely linked to the necessity of developing financial sustainability and interactive Business models. For entrepreneurs to succeed, it is not only essential to develop innovative products or services, but also to make strategic decisions that effectively manage marketing, sponsorships, and distribution channels. Access to financial resources can be a significant barrier for sports entrepreneurs; however, in recent years, special funding sources for entrepreneurs have increased. Angel investors, venture capital firms, and private equity funds have provided financial support to sports entrepreneurs, enabling these new Business models to reach a broader audience. For example, in 2020, investment in the sports technology sector exceeded $5 billion, marking a significant financial step that supports growth and innovation in the sector (Nielsen, 2020). However, the challenges faced in sports entrepreneurship should not be overlooked. Entrepreneurs need to make the right strategic decisions to stand out in a highly competitive market. Additionally, regulatory barriers arising from the digitalization of sports organizations and new Business models may pose a risk factor for investors. Issues such as data security, player health, and intellectual property rights create important legal responsibilities for sports entrepreneurs and investors. Therefore, sports entrepreneurs must not only be innovative but also navigate legal frameworks correctly and minimize risks (O'Brien & Lyman, 2021).

Lastly, the relationship between sports entrepreneurship and social responsibility and sustainability also plays a crucial role in influencing investment opportunities. Social responsibility determines not only the environmental and societal impacts of sports but also sponsorship agreements and brand values. Sustainability is a topic that investors carefully evaluate, as environmentally friendly and socially beneficial sports projects have long-term value creation potential. In this context, sports entrepreneurs are responsible for developing solutions that reduce environmental impact and create projects that strengthen social engagement (Mason, 2018). Sports entrepreneurship and investment opportunities, in a world where technology and digitalization are rapidly advancing, offer great potential for entrepreneurs. Innovative products, digitalized sports organizations, and new sports markets create attractive opportunities for investors, while sustainable Business models and strategic financial requirements are also significant. Innovation in this field not only promotes commercial success but also encourages social responsibility and environmental sensitivity.

12.2.6 Fan Engagement and Experience

The sports industry is rapidly transforming through technology, and this transformation has deeply impacted fan engagement and experience. Traditional fan experiences were largely confined to static events centered around game days. However, with the influence of digitalization, social media platforms, and new technologies, the way sports are consumed has undergone a radical shift. With the integration of technology into sports, fans' loyalty to their teams, their game-watching experiences, and interactive engagement have significantly evolved (Smith, 2018). In this transformation, artificial intelligence (AI) and other emerging technologies play a particularly important role. These technologies have made the fan experience more interactive, personalized, and data-driven, both physically in the stadium and in the digital environment (Parker, 2021).

Artificial intelligence (AI) has become one of the most effective technologies for enhancing fan engagement in the sports world. AI uses data analysis and machine learning algorithms to predict fan behaviors and utilizes this data to create personalized experiences. For example, AI recommends content based on fans' viewing habits, encouraging interaction with game highlights or team news that will capture their interest (Huang & Liu, 2020). Additionally, AI-powered chatbots and virtual assistants enable teams to directly engage with fans, accelerating customer service and offering more personalized experiences. Such interactions transform fans from mere consumers into active participants engaging with sports organizations (Funk & Pizzo, 2019). Moreover, augmented reality (AR) and virtual reality (VR) technologies are revolutionizing how sports organizations reshape fan experiences. AR and VR allow fans to experience a different level of engagement, whether in the stadium or from home. For example, VR technology provides fans with the opportunity to watch games in a virtual environment, enabling them to experience the atmosphere of the stadium remotely. Particularly during the pandemic, VR helped fans maintain their connection to the sport despite being physically distant from the stadium (Chung & Lee, 2021). Additionally, AR applications allow fans to access real-time statistics, player information, and interactive content while watching games in the stadium. These technological innovations merge physical and digital experiences, making sports more immersive and interactive (Evans, 2021a).

New technologies are not limited to game days alone; social media and digital platforms have also become a significant part of fan engagement. Through social media, fans can stay instantly updated on the developments of their teams and players. These platforms allow fans to go beyond being passive spectators, strengthening their emotional and social connections with their teams. For example, platforms like Twitter, Instagram, and YouTube have become mediums where teams can engage with fans, receive immediate feedback, and share content (Miller & Boland, 2019). Teams and athletes can directly interact with their fans via social media platforms, further involving them and strengthening their brands. In this context, the rise of digital content and social media interactions creates new revenue streams for sports organizations and makes fans an integral part of their brands. Another important factor shaping the fan experience through technology is the emphasis on personalized experiences. With the help of artificial intelligence (AI) and big data analytics, teams can offer customized content based on fans' preferences and interests. These personalized offerings can range from news about a fan's team to ticket offers, providing tailored services across a wide spectrum (Baker & Coviello, 2019). For instance, based on a fan's past preferences, the current status of the team, and ticket prices, special discounts or content can be offered. Such personalized experiences help foster deeper fan loyalty and increase revenue for teams.

Technological advancements not only enhance the fan experience but also improve the operational efficiency of sports organizations. Digital platforms and artificial intelligence (AI) enable organizations to respond more quickly to fan demands, enhance in-stadium experiences, and generally provide more efficient services. Fan feedback and interactions can be effectively analyzed and used to develop team strategies (Funk & Pizzo, 2019). Additionally, the collection and analysis of fan data provide valuable insights for sponsors and advertisers, making advertising and sponsorship strategies more targeted and effective. As a result, technological developments in the sports industry are creating a significant transformation in fan engagement and experience. Innovative technologies such as AI, augmented reality (AR), virtual reality (VR), and digital platforms are making fan experiences more interactive, personalized, and entertaining. These advancements are generating new opportunities and revenue models, not only for fans but also for sports organizations. The future of the sports industry seems poised to be shaped by the increasing digitalization of fan engagement and experience.

12.2.7 Challenges and Opportunities for Entrepreneurs in the Sports Technology Sector

The sports technology sector has witnessed significant growth in recent years, creating substantial opportunities for investors and entrepreneurs. However, this growth has also brought a number of challenges for entrepreneurs within the industry. The rapidly changing dynamics of technology-driven innovations are disrupting traditional Business models in the sports industry, creating new business opportunities while simultaneously transforming existing structures. In this context, the most prominent opportunities for sports technology entrepreneurs are shaped by developments in innovative areas such as digitalization, data analytics, wearable technologies, and artificial intelligence (Smith & Johnson, 2022). However, the rapid changes within the sector and the competitive market conditions present significant barriers that make it challenging for entrepreneurs to achieve success.

The integration of technology into the sports industry creates significant opportunities for entrepreneurs while also presenting various challenges. First, many sports technology ventures face greater uncertainty and risk compared to traditional sports organizations. In the process of developing innovative products and services, entrepreneurs encounter substantial challenges in investing in technology and finding suitable markets to offset these investments (Foster & Lyman, 2019). Particularly in the areas of wearable devices and data analytics, factors such as the required technology, design, and functionality to gain user acceptance often serve as determining elements. Investing in these aspects appropriately also means significant costs for entrepreneurs. The risks encountered in the development of technological products present barriers for new entrepreneurs in the sector.

Another major challenge for entrepreneurs is the need to keep up with the rapidly evolving nature of sports technologies. To innovate in the sports industry, it is important to continuously monitor current technologies and develop sector-appropriate solutions. For example, while the integration of artificial intelligence (AI) and machine learning helps sports organizations improve data analytics and performance assessments, properly implementing these technologies requires a substantial amount of knowledge and expertise (Huang & Liu, 2020). Entrepreneurs must understand and apply these complex technologies correctly to survive in the market, making it a critical success factor. Furthermore, keeping pace with rapid technological changes requires entrepreneurs to continuously innovate and update their products, creating a significant challenge regarding the sustainability of financial resources. Despite these challenges, there are significant opportunities for sports technology entrepreneurs. Digitalization has initiated a massive transformation across all areas of the sports industry. For instance, wearable technologies and sensors allow for more precise tracking of athletes' performance, while data analytics and artificial intelligence enable more accurate and timely decision-making (Miller & Boland, 2020). This, especially in the areas of health and performance tracking, helps athletes train more effectively and reduce the risk of injuries. Additionally, developing technology-based solutions for sports organizations to enhance fan engagement and generate more revenue presents a major opportunity. A successful sports technology venture not only offers performance-enhancing technologies but also establishes strong partnerships with other sectors in the sports industry (Parker, 2021). Technologies such as mobile applications, social media platforms, and virtual reality provide interactive and personalized experiences for fans, helping sports organizations expand their markets.

Another significant factor contributing to the growth of sports technology entrepreneurship is the rapid development of the entrepreneurial ecosystem. In recent years, there has been a notable increase in private investors, accelerator programs, and incubators targeting sports technology startups. Organizations such as *SportTechie* and *Techstars Sports Accelerator* provide mentorship, investment, and networking opportunities, supporting the growth of new ventures (Evans, 2021b). These programs help entrepreneurs acquire the technical and commercial skills necessary for business development, equipping them with a competitive advantage in the marketplace. This, in turn, has become a key factor in increasing opportunities for sports technology entrepreneurs. Investor interest in sports technologies is not limited solely to revenue potential; the growing global popularity of sports also increases the likelihood of success for new ventures in this field (Chung & Lee, 2020). On a global scale, the digital transformation of sports organizations and the increased production of digital content have raised the demand for sports technologies. In particular, technologies such as virtual reality, augmented reality, and e-sports, which target growing markets within the sports industry, are attracting investor attention. Additionally, the increasing demand in areas such as digital media and mobile applications is creating new business opportunities, presenting attractive prospects for sports technology entrepreneurs.

12.3 Conclusion

Today, the sports industry is undergoing a profound transformation driven by digitalization and technological innovation. This transformation not only aims to enhance athletic performance but also redefines fan engagement, optimizes the operational processes of sports organizations, and expands the entrepreneurship ecosystem within the sector. In line with the themes examined throughout this chapter, the multidimensional impacts of the intersection between sports and technology entrepreneurship have been demonstrated.

The role of technology in sports extends beyond making training processes more efficient; it also reshapes strategic decision-making mechanisms. In particular, wearable technologies enable the real-time monitoring of athletes' physiological data, creating added value in areas ranging from injury prevention to performance optimization. These devices provide coaches with scientifically grounded insights into individual athletes' development and facilitate more precise performance analyses.

Data analytics and artificial intelligence (AI) applications have triggered strategic transformations both on and off the field. From sabermetric analysis and player tracking algorithms to AI-supported game planning and injury risk prediction, these technologies offer sports organizations the ability to make more informed and data-driven decisions. Moreover, analyzing fan behavior to deliver personalized digital content enhances fan loyalty and leads to the emergence of new revenue models.

Sports entrepreneurship stands at the heart of this technological transformation, reshaping Business models within the industry. Innovative solutions developed in areas such as wearable devices, mobile applications, e-sports platforms, and digital broadcasting provide entrepreneurs with opportunities to create both economic and social value. However, this dynamic landscape also presents challenges, including intense competition, high investment requirements, and the pressure of long-term sustainability. To succeed, entrepreneurs must possess not only technical expertise but also a deep understanding of sports culture, a strategic mindset, and sensitivity to ethical responsibilities.

From an investment perspective, sports technology ventures have attracted increasing attention from investors. Innovations in AI, augmented reality, e-sports, and health technologies are accelerating the digital transformation of sports and presenting high growth potential. Nonetheless, to attract investment, ventures must demonstrate transparency and sustainability, particularly in areas such as regulatory compliance, data security, and athlete well-being.

Fan experience and engagement represent some of the most visible reflections of technological transformation in the sports domain. Through virtual and augmented reality applications, social media interactions, and AI-powered content recommendations, fans have evolved from passive spectators to active participants and content creators. This shift deepens the relationship between sports organizations and their fan bases, significantly contributing to brand development processes.

Finally, the challenges faced in sports technology entrepreneurship necessitate a strategic approach to seizing opportunities in the field. Keeping pace with rapidly evolving technological trends, ensuring financial sustainability, forging partnerships with the right investors, and adhering to ethical principles are among the critical success factors for entrepreneurs in this domain. Overall, the emerging paradigm at the intersection of sports and technology entrepreneurship not only enhances existing sports practices but also contributes to reshaping the future sports ecosystem. In this context, researchers, practitioners, and entrepreneurs alike are faced with both significant opportunities and important responsibilities. The conscious and ethical integration of emerging technologies into the sports domain is essential for building a sustainable, inclusive, and innovative future for the world of sports.

12.4 Recommendations for Future Research

This study offers a comprehensive interdisciplinary analysis of the key themes at the intersection of sports and technology entrepreneurship. Nevertheless, each thematic area addressed in this chapter presents numerous unexplored research questions and methodological opportunities for future investigation. Below are several research directions organized according to the major thematic areas of the study:

The Role and Transformative Impact of Sports Technologies: While the performance-enhancing effects of sports technologies are well-documented, their psychological impacts—such as on athletes' mental resilience, motivation levels, and stress management abilities—remain underexplored. Future research could focus on the subjective experiences of athletes using technology-assisted training through qualitative methods. Furthermore, critical topics such as technological dependency, the balance between human agency and automation, and the digitalization of coaching processes warrant deeper investigation to better understand the human dimension of technology in sport.

Performance Monitoring and Wearable Technologies: The accuracy of physiological data generated by wearable technologies should be evaluated comparatively across different sports disciplines. Special populations—such as female athletes, youth athletes, and para-athletes—should be the focus of research assessing the validity and reliability of these devices. In addition, issues of data privacy, ethical use, and informed consent in the context of wearable technologies must be examined in order to guide the development of athlete-centered data governance policies. There is a growing need to establish technology usage models that align with ethical and legal standards.

Data Analytics and Artificial Intelligence: The effectiveness of AI-driven decision support systems in coaching, player transfers, and game strategy development should be examined through a larger number of empirical studies and case analyses. The predictive accuracy of machine learning algorithms in opponent analysis and match outcome forecasting should be tested across multiple sports and competitive levels to assess their universal applicability. Another crucial direction is understanding how these systems influence human decision-making. Future research should address human–machine collaboration in sports from ethical, psychological, and organizational perspectives.

Sports Entrepreneurship and Innovation: Most current studies on sports entrepreneurship are based on Western-centric examples. Future research should investigate the dynamics of sports entrepreneurship ecosystems in developing countries, with attention to cultural factors and localized innovation practices. Studies focusing on the contributions of women entrepreneurs, youth-led ventures, and university-based initiatives could enhance the inclusivity of the field. Furthermore, the role of social entrepreneurship models in creating societal value through sports constitutes an important research agenda.

Investment Opportunities and Financial Sustainability: The investment dynamics, risk factors, and scalability potential of sports technology ventures should be analyzed in greater detail from the perspective of investors. Specifically, identifying the success factors of early-stage ventures and comparing them with venture capital preferences across the sector would yield valuable insights. Additionally, the influence of sustainability and social responsibility criteria on investment decisions should be further investigated within the framework of environmental and social impact investing.

Fan Experience and Engagement: The effects of digital solutions (e.g., VR, AR, AI-powered content) designed to enhance fan experience should be assessed across different demographic groups using cross-cultural, socioeconomic, and generational comparisons. Qualitative studies examining the sports consumption behaviors of younger fan cohorts could inform the development of future marketing strategies. Moreover, the potential negative consequences of digital inequality and exclusion on the fan experience deserve further investigation.

Challenges in Sports Technology Entrepreneurship: The regulatory, data security, intellectual property, and ethical challenges faced by technology-oriented sports ventures must be addressed through interdisciplinary approaches. In particular, the scalability barriers of early-stage startups could be explored in relation to academic collaborations, public incentives, and university incubator models. Finally, future studies should evaluate the integration of sports technology education into academic curricula and the development of skilled human capital to support the growth of the entrepreneurial ecosystem in this domain.

References

Achenbach, T. (2020). Digital transformation in sports: The future of fan engagement. *Journal of Sports Technology, 12*(2), 44–57.

Albrecht, K. (2020). Wearable technology in sports: Implications for athletes and performance analysis. *Sports Technology Review, 13*(4), 112–125.

Anderson, C., & Cross, R. (2017). Globalization and its impact on sports entrepreneurship. *International Journal of Sports Management and Marketing, 28*(1), 45–58.

Baker, J., & Coviello, N. (2019). Digital transformation in sports: A framework for the future. *Journal of Sport Management, 34*(5), 431–445.

Brynjolfsson E, McAfee A (2017). *The second machine age: Work, progress, and prosperity in a time of brilliant technologies.* W. W. Norton & Company

Chung, Y., & Lee, K. (2020). Investment opportunities in sports technology: Emerging trends and market analysis. *Sport Business Review, 18*(4), 32–45.

Chung, Y., & Lee, K. (2021). Virtual reality in sports: How VR is transforming fan engagement. *Journal of Sports Media, 16*(3), 212–229.

Eichhorn, M. (2022). Augmented and virtual reality in sports fan experience. *International Journal of Sports Management, 31*(1), 89–102.

Evans, L. (2021a). Augmented reality and fan engagement in sports: New directions for sports marketing. *International Journal of Sports Marketing, 25*(1), 99–114.

Evans, L. (2021b). The role of accelerators in sports technology entrepreneurship. *Journal of Sports Innovation, 13*(1), 99–115.

Foster, R. (2021). Artificial intelligence in sports: Opportunities and challenges. *Sports Innovation Review, 15*(3), 123–136.

Foster, A., & Lyman, P. (2019). Challenges and opportunities for sports tech startups: The need for innovation and investment. *Sports Entrepreneurship Journal, 24*(2), 130–142.

Funk, D. C., & Pizzo, A. D. (2019). Sports entrepreneurship: Opportunities, challenges, and strategies for success. *Journal of Sports Management, 34*(2), 234–246.

Gustafsson, A. (2021). Fan experience and engagement through AI and big data. *Journal of Sports Management, 34*(3), 238–250.

Hamari, J., Koivisto, J., Sarsa, H. (2017). Does gamification work?—A literature review of empirical studies on gamification. In *Proceedings of the 47th Annual Hawaii International Conference on System Sciences* (pp. 3025–3034). IEEE.

Hassan, D., & McKeown, P. (2019). Entrepreneurial dynamics in the sport industry. *Journal of Business Research, 67*(12), 2383–2391.

Held, J., Cioppa, A., Giancola, S., Hamdi, A., Devue, C., Ghanem, B., Van Droogenbroeck, M. (2024). Towards AI-powered video assistant referee system (VARS) for association football. arXiv preprint arXiv:2407.12483. https://doi.org/10.48550/arXiv.2407.12483

Huang, H., & Liu, X. (2020). Artificial intelligence in sports: Transforming fan interactions and experiences. *Sport & Technology Review, 22*(3), 107–119.

Karafil, A. Y. (2023). Examination of football referees' attitudes towards video assistant referee system (VAR) by Q method. *Journal of Sport Sciences Research, 8*(1), 99–112. https://doi.org/10.25307/jssr.1178303

Klein, D. (2020). Data-driven decisions in sports: An overview of sports analytics. *International Journal of Sports Analytics, 14*(2), 120–135.

Lewis, D. (2004). Sabermetrics in sports: A revolution in game strategy. *Journal of Sport Analytics, 8*(1), 1–13.

Lewis, D. (2018). The role of analytics in sports performance management. *Journal of Performance Analysis, 10*(1), 45–56.

Mason, D. S. (2018). Sustainability in sport: Issues and opportunities for entrepreneurs. *Journal of Sports Business, 16*(3), 88–103.

Miller, T., & Boland, M. (2019). The role of social media in fan engagement in sports. *Sport Business Journal, 45*(2), 38–51.

Miller, T., & Boland, M. (2020). The growth of wearable technology and data analytics in sports. *International Journal of Sports Technology, 15*(2), 185–202.

Mohammed, A., Othman, Z., & Abdullah, A. (2024). The Role of artificial ıntelligence in enhancing sports analytics and training. *Cihan University-Erbil Scientific Journal, 8*(1), 58–62. https://doi.org/10.24086/cuesj.v8n1y2024

Müller, M. (2019). AI in injury prevention and recovery in professional sports. *Sports Medicine, 22*(4), 234–245.

Nielsen. (2020). Global sports tech sector attracts over $5 billion in investment. *Nielsen Sports*

O'Brien, R., & Lyman, M. (2021). Navigating regulation in sports technology: A modern challenge. *International Journal of Sports Law, 19*(2), 101–115.

Parker, J. (2021). Sport technology and fan engagement: Creating new opportunities for entrepreneurs. *Sport Marketing Quarterly, 30*(1), 56–69.

Pisaniello, A. (2024). The Game changer: How artificial intelligence is transforming sports performance and strategy. *Geopolitical, Social Security and Freedom Journal, 7*(1), 75–84. https://doi.org/10.2478/gssfj-2024-0006v

Rahmani, M., Majedi, N., Hemmatinejad, M., & Jamshidi, A. (2024). Application of artificial ıntelligence in the sports industry: A review article. *AI and Tech in Behavioral and Social Sciences, 2*(2), 20–27. https://doi.org/10.61838/kman.aitech.2.2.4

Smith, A. (2018). The impact of digital media on fan experience and engagement in sports. *Journal of Sports Media and Technology, 11*(4), 204–221.

Smith, J., & Johnson, R. (2022). Wearable technology in sports: Enhancing athlete performance. *Journal of Sports Science and Technology, 23*(4), 211–223.

Sokolov, R. (2020). Sports tactics and game strategy optimization using machine learning. *Journal of Sports Analytics, 13*(1), 67–79.

Tang, C., Chen, X., Gong, J., Occhipinti, L. G., & Gao, S. (2023). WMNN: Wearables-based multi-column neural network for human activity recognition. *IEEE Journal of Biomedical and Health Informatics, 27*(1), 339–350. https://doi.org/10.1109/JBHI.2022.3219364

Tang, C., Yi, W., Zhang, Z., Occhipinti, E., Occhipinti, L. G. (2025). *AI-driven smart sportswear for real-time fitness monitoring using textile strain sensors*. arXiv preprint arXiv:2504.08500.

Vanderbilt, M., & Gibson, H. (2020). AI in sports health management: Applications in injury prevention. *Journal of Sports Science and Technology, 26*(2), 98–113.

Williams, J. (2019). Data analytics in modern sports: Transforming the game with technology. *Sportech Review, 11*(3), 178–190.

Wilson, K. (2020). Technological advancements in sports: Wearables and beyond. *Sports Science Quarterly, 23*(4), 215–230.

CHAPTER 13

Building a Framework of Startup Growth in Evolving Economies: Empirical Scale Development and Validation

Pinky Bahuguna

13.1 Introduction

Start-ups represent an organizational structure designed to develop scalable Business models, whether through novel solutions to unaddressed societal challenges or by reimagining existing ideas (Blank, 2010). In the modern economy, entrepreneurs are increasingly viewed as crucial drivers of growth, competitiveness, and innovation (Singh & Hanafi, 2020; Zhao et al., 2023). In India, initiatives like Startup India, Atal Innovation Mission, TIDE 2.0 further energized the start-up ecosystem. These programs offer streamlined access to resources, investor networks, funding, mentoring, and regulatory support, aiming to foster hundreds of new ventures and thousands of jobs in the state.

P. Bahuguna (✉)
University School of Business, Chandigarh University, Mohali, Punjab 140413, India
e-mail: pinky.e17261@cumail.in

D. Kumar et al. (eds.), *Evolving Trends in Technology Entrepreneurship*, Palgrave Studies in Global Entrepreneurship,
https://doi.org/10.1007/978-981-95-7441-4_13

Start-up growth is notoriously difficult to quantify during early stages, as founders explore unproven models. Research continues to probe success factors, many of which align with both internal dynamics—such as entrepreneurial orientation, founding team composition, firm age and size—and external forces such as market demand, competitive intensity, and government support (Wiklund et al., 2007; Lau & Busenitz, 2001; Grewal & Sharma, 2024; Reddy et al., 2023). A strong entrepreneurial orientation—marked by innovativeness, proactive behavior, and calculated risk-taking—has a well-established positive correlation with small firm growth (Beugelsdijk & Noorderhaven, 2004; Azoulay et al., 2020; Kumar & Mehta, 2021). Equally, the capabilities of the founding team—experience, diversity, and cohesion—are key predictors of scale-up success (Klotz et al., 2013; Wang & Li, 2022). Product innovation, especially when leveraging lean-startup principles and emerging technologies such as artificial intelligence, enables rapid prototyping and iteration, significantly boosting developmental velocity and market fit (Wang & Wu, 2025).

Externally, favorable market conditions—including robust demand and moderate competition—aid scaling (Kemp et al., 2006; Podoynitsyna et al., 2007; Saini, 2020). In the Uttarakhand context, academic-industry linkages via institutions like IIT Roorkee and IIM Kashipur, supported by rural incubators and mentorship networks, amplify local start-up growth. Government-backed venture funds—such as a ₹200 crore state fund launched in April 2025—coupled with incubation centers in every district, monthly stipends, seed funding, SGST and patent support, and reverse-migration trends underscore the tangible impact of state-led interventions. Nevertheless, persistent challenges remain: inconsistent funding access, infrastructural and connectivity gaps, and limited national and global engagement continue to frustrate growth (Garhwal Post, 2024). A recent empirical study involving 240 small-scale entrepreneurs in Uttarakhand confirmed that while schemes are well-intentioned, finance, taxation, marketing, HR, and regulatory issues still impede success, emphasizing the need for policy refinement (Singh & Chauhan, 2021). Understanding the growth trajectory of start-up companies necessitates examining various internal and external dimensions that shape their performance and sustainability. This review categorizes literature into five major themes: entrepreneurial and managerial factors, innovation and technology, market and environmental dynamics, financial and policy support, and empirical gaps and regional context.

13.1.1 Entrepreneurial and Managerial Factors

Founders' personal attributes, experience, and management style play a pivotal role in start-up growth. Early studies such as Watson et al. (1998) and Goswami (2006) analyzed how entrepreneurial traits, family involvement, and need for achievement influence firm survival and success. These themes continue to be central in recent studies. For instance, Joseph et al. (2023) affirm that cognitive patterns and personality traits of entrepreneurs significantly impact long-term performance.

Furthermore, Konno (2021) employed a binary logit model to study over 2,500 Japanese start-ups and concluded that start-up preparation efforts were more critical to firm sustainability than managers' demographic characteristics. Similarly, Engidaw (2021) identified managerial and workplace factors as strong predictors of performance MSEs in Ethiopia. These findings align with Bakar et al. (2012), who emphasized the influence of customer orientation, management quality, and human capital in organizational growth.

13.1.2 Innovation and Technology Capabilities

Innovation remains a cornerstone of entrepreneurial growth. Bjornali and Ellingsen (2014) highlighted how innovation performance is shaped by team composition and governance mechanisms. Ghaffar and Hamidreza (2020) expanded this by incorporating constructs like business intelligence, R&D investment, and network capabilities, revealing their positive correlation with sustainability.

A notable study by Gupta et al. (2020) investigated how social media technology usage and innovation capability indirectly influence innovation performance through entrepreneurial orientation, using SEM on 164 Indian start-ups. Wang & Wu (2025) further emphasize that AI-driven rapid prototyping in product development significantly boosts time-to-market efficiency, thereby accelerating growth. Moreover, Nalintippayawong et al. (2018) found that Thai start-ups' success was directly influenced by the alignment between their innovative capabilities, customer needs, and Business models. These findings were echoed in Novanda et al. (2021), who underlined the synergistic impact of digital capabilities and adaptive Business models on start-up growth in Southeast Asia.

13.1.3 Market and Environmental Dynamics

The role of market conditions and external environments has been well documented. Lau and Busenitz (2001) and Kemp et al. (2006) confirmed that market dynamism affects scalability by shaping consumer behavior and competitive positioning. More recently, Reddy et al. (2023) observed that start-ups with proactive market-scanning abilities exhibited better market fit and revenue growth, especially in post-pandemic recovery phases.

The environmental uncertainty variable was also addressed by Kroeger (2007), who demonstrated that entrepreneurial orientation correlates with performance only when moderated by high uncertainty. The integration of such variables continues in the current work by Lee and Kim (2021), who introduced a dynamic capability framework showing how market turbulence moderates resource alignment for start-up success.

13.1.4 Financial and Policy Support

Financial access and policy backing are critical for early-stage ventures. Okrah, Nepp, and Agbozo (2018) used panel data from 13 countries and found that government policies, post-education systems, and internal market openness significantly foster innovation. This supports earlier findings by Mazzarol et al., (1999), who discussed demographic barriers to small business formation. Recent Indian studies, such as Singh and Chauhan (2021), revealed mixed perceptions toward policy interventions, despite the presence of supportive ecosystems like Startup India and the Uttarakhand Start-up Policy. New initiatives, such as Uttarakhand's ₹200 crore venture fund and incubation hubs in each district (Business Standard, 2025), have further strengthened the ecosystem, though issues like taxation and finance access remain persistent (Grewal & Sharma, 2024). Empirical studies now also consider non-monetary support. For example, Wang & Li (2022) stressed the role of informal mentorship and personal connections in improving a firm's access to capital and expertise.

13.1.5 Empirical Gaps and Regional Context

Although extensive global research exists on start-up growth, there remains a lack of empirical evidence focused on specific regional contexts such as Uttarakhand. While earlier studies have observed that newer and smaller firms often grow more rapidly than their older and larger counterparts (Davidsson et al., 2002; Kutzhanova et al., 2009), this dynamic has been largely understudied in India's hilly and semi-urban areas.

The available literature reveals the complex interplay between innovation, leadership, market dynamics, and ecosystem support. However, little empirical evidence is available on how these factors operate in geographically diverse, resource-constrained states like Uttarakhand. Most prior work focuses on national-level data or developed economies, underscoring the need for localized, perception-based research.

The present study addresses this void by empirically examining start-up growth factors from the perspective of founders operating within Uttarakhand. This regional focus adds nuance to the broader start-up literature and serves as a valuable reference for both practitioners and future researchers aiming to design targeted interventions.

13.2 Research Goals and Methodology

1. To explore and identify the key growth drivers influencing start-ups operating in Uttarakhand.
2. To empirically validate the identified growth constructs through confirmatory factor analysis.

Given the scarcity of region-specific scholarly literature on start-up ecosystems in predominantly hilly states like Uttarakhand, there is a pressing need for focused research in this domain. While the broader Indian start-up landscape has been widely examined (NASSCOM, 2021; Singh & Ghosh, 2020), studies at the sub-national level—particularly in geographically diverse regions—remain limited. To bridge this research gap, the current study seeks to empirically confirm the core factors that stimulate the growth of start ups operating in the study area.

The study focuses on four key districts—Dehradun, Haridwar, Nainital, and Udham Singh Nagar—which collectively account for approximately 90% of the state's recognized start-ups as of March 2022 (Startup India, 2022). These districts were strategically selected due to their relatively higher entrepreneurial activity and better infrastructural support compared to other regions in the state. This research adopts an exploratory design with a quantitative methodological approach. Data were gathered through a structured survey instrument administered to founders/co-founders of recognized start-ups operating in the selected districts. The questionnaire used for primary data collection was self-designed and validated through a pilot test to ensure reliability and content adequacy.

Consistent with the study's objectives, two advanced statistical techniques were employed. EFA was first conducted to uncover underlying growth constructs, followed by CFA to validate these dimensions and evaluate the model's goodness of fit (Hair et al., 2020; Malhotra & Dash, 2016). This methodological framework facilitated a thorough empirical examination of the factors influencing start-up growth within a distinct regional and developmental context.

13.2.1 Survey Process and Demographic Overview

To ensure the reliability and clarity of the survey instrument, a pilot study was initially conducted involving 48 respondents drawn from the target population. Based on the feedback received, several questionnaire items were revised and refined for clarity and contextual appropriateness. Given the relatively small population size of recognized start-ups in the target region, a census approach was adopted for the final data collection, encompassing all eligible start-ups within the four selected districts of Uttarakhand.

The final questionnaire was disseminated to 378 start-up entrepreneurs through both online and offline modes. Out of these, 212 valid responses were received, yielding a response rate of approximately 56%, which is considered acceptable in entrepreneurial and management research (Baruch & Holtom, 2008). The demographic profile of the sample revealed that 78% of respondents were male and 22% were female. In terms of age distribution, 41% of respondents were aged below 30 years, while 36% fell within the 31–40 years bracket. Additionally, 18% were between 41 and 50 years, and only 5% were aged 51–60 years. Thus, a significant 77% of the respondents were under the age of 40, indicating a youthful entrepreneurial base in the state. Regarding educational qualifications, respondents were classified into four categories: below graduation, graduation, post-graduation, and professional degree holders. The largest segment (36%) held graduate-level qualifications, followed by 31% postgraduates, 22% with professional degrees, and 11% with education below graduation level. Geographically, the highest number of respondents (116, or 55%) were located in Dehradun district, the state's

Table 13.1 Demographics of respondents

		N	%
Gender	Male	166	78
	Female	46	22
Founder's age	Up to 30 years	87	41
	31–40 years	76	36
	41–50 years	38	18
	51–60 years	11	5
Education level	Below graduation	23	11
	Graduation	76	36
	Post-graduation	66	31
	Professional degree	47	22
District	Dehradun	116	55
	Haridwar	36	17
	Nainital	31	15
	Udham Singh Nagar	29	13
	Total	212	100

Source The authors

prominent entrepreneurial hub. Haridwar accounted for 17%, followed by Nainital (15%) and Udham Singh Nagar (13%) of the total sample. The detailed demographic profile of the respondents is presented in Table 13.1.

13.2.2 *Identification of Latent Growth Determinants Using EFA*

To identify the hidden growth-related factors influencing start-up performance—a set of statistical procedures were implemented. Specifically, EFA was utilized. The study instrument included 26 items measured on a 5-point Likert scale, which were developed based on an in-depth literature review and refined with input from academic experts and field professionals. This process ensured the scale demonstrated strong face and construct validity, as recommended by Hair et al., (2019a, 2019b, 2019c, 2019d). The item development process followed established scale construction protocols emphasizing content accuracy, clarity, and item relevance (Churchill, 1979; DeVellis, 2017). Feedback from pre-testing and expert review enhanced the clarity and consistency of the questionnaire. The overall process reflects standard best practices in psychometric development, which advocate for iterative testing and refinement to

Table 13.2 The result of KMO and Bartlett's test

KMO measure of sampling adequacy		*.780*
Bartlett's Test of Sphericity	Approximate Chi-Square	3086.630
	df	190
	Sig	.000

ensure internal consistency and reliability (Hinkin, 1998; Netemeyer et al., 2003).

Prior to EFA, the dataset's adequacy for factor analysis was assessed using the Kaiser–Meyer–Olkin (KMO) measure and Bartlett's Test of Sphericity. As outlined by Chawla and Sondhi (2016), KMO values above 0.5 are considered adequate, with scores above 0.8 viewed as ideal. The KMO value obtained in this study was 0.780, indicating sufficient sample adequacy. Furthermore, Bartlett's Test of Sphericity was statistically significant ($p < 0.001$), confirming that relationships among variables were strong to proceed with factor extraction. These preliminary diagnostic results are shown in Table 13.2.

Additionally, the study evaluated communality scores to determine how well each item was explained by the extracted components. Hair et al., (2020) suggest that a communality value of at least 0.50 is acceptable, as it demonstrates sufficient shared variance. All items retained in the final analysis met or exceeded this benchmark, confirming the appropriateness of applying Principal Component Analysis (PCA). Detailed results of communalities are presented in Table 13.3. The systematic development and validation of the measurement tool ensured that the final factor structure was both statistically robust and conceptually sound, contributing to the credibility of the resulting model.

To examine the internal structure of the measurement scale, Principal Axis Factoring was performed using Varimax rotation on the initial 26-item tool. In the preliminary round of analysis, six items were excluded because their communality scores were below 0.50, suggesting they did not share adequate variance with other items in the dataset. After refining the scale, the factor analysis was re-conducted using the remaining 20 items. This procedure led to the identification of six clear and meaningful factors. These were categorized based on the thematic relevance of the items as: entrepreneurial skills, product innovation, founding team, location, government support, and market. Each of these components had

Table 13.3 Communalities

	Initial	*Extraction*
My business idea is innovative that can improve the quality of goods and services	1.000	.905
My company can adapt according to different client demands	1.000	.816
To sustain, the start-up idea needs to be innovative	1.000	.888
The commitment of the team members is high	1.000	.688
The coordination among the team members leads to proper management in the company	1.000	.828
Team members make sure that all the internal processes are in sync	1.000	.725
There are no trust issues among the team members	1.000	.729
My start-up is located near the right market	1.000	.837
My company is working well as its location is suitable	1.000	.843
I located the company near the right customers to build trust with them	1.000	.826
Various growth opportunities are provided by the government to support my company	1.000	.905
Government is directly or indirectly supporting the start-up ecosystem in India	1.000	.892
Sound policies have made it easier to access supporting infrastructure	1.000	.856
I use my creativity to work efficiently in my start-up	1.000	.808
I can communicate well to persuade investors for investing funds in my company	1.000	.771
I possess the organizational skills required to organize the work	1.000	.725
I know how to manage the company's affairs actively to perform well	1.000	.818
My business is aware of the target market to attract the right customers for its product/services	1.000	.893
My company has done market research prior to launching the product/service	1.000	.826
The timely advertisement of product/service is made online to attract new customers	1.000	.746

Extraction method: principal component analysis (PCA)
Source The authors

an eigenvalue > 1, aligning with the criteria recommended by Hair et al. (2014) for factor retention.

Collectively, these six factors accounted for 81.620% of the total variance, which is higher than the recommended threshold of 50–60% typically considered acceptable for factor solutions in the social sciences (Williams, Onsman, & Brown, 2010). The individual variance explained by each factor was relatively balanced, ranging from 12.113% to 15.519%, suggesting that each construct makes a meaningful contribution to explaining overall variance (Table 13.4). The Rotated Component Matrix revealed strong and clean loadings, with all retained variables demonstrating factor loadings exceeding 0.70—a threshold considered robust for established scales (Hair et al., 2013a, 2013b). This result confirmed the discriminant structure of the identified constructs and supported the factor solution's reliability and validity (Table 13.5).

Table 13.4 Total variance explained

Component	*Initial Eigenvalues*			*Extraction Sums of Squared Loadings*			*Rotation Sums of Squared Loadings*		
	Total	*% of Variance*	*Cumulative per cent*	*Total*	*% of Variance*	*Cumulative per cent*	*Total*	*% of Variance*	*Cumulative per cent*
1	5.077	25.387	25.387	5.077	25.387	25.387	3.104	15.519	15.519
2	3.337	16.685	42.072	3.337	16.685	42.072	2.955	14.777	30.295
3	2.610	13.048	55.120	2.610	13.048	55.120	2.696	13.479	43.775
4	2.277	11.383	66.502	2.277	11.383	66.502	2.688	13.440	57.215
5	1.945	9.726	76.229	1.945	9.726	76.229	2.459	12.293	69.508
6	1.078	5.392	81.620	1.078	5.392	81.620	2.423	12.113	81.620
7	.506	2.531	84.151						
8	.447	2.233	86.384						
9	.419	2.094	88.478						
10	.352	1.761	90.240						
11	.321	1.605	91.844						
12	.288	1.438	93.282						
13	.265	1.323	94.605						
14	.215	1.074	95.680						
15	.209	1.044	96.723						
16	.186	.929	97.652						
17	.144	.722	98.375						
18	.125	.624	98.998						
19	.104	.521	99.519						
20	.096	.481	100.000						

Extraction Method: Principal Component Analysis.
Source The authors.

Table 13.5 Rotated component matrix

	Component					
	1	*2*	*3*	*4*	*5*	*6*
My business idea is innovative that can improve the quality of goods and services			.935			
My company can adapt according to different client demands			.893			
To sustain, the start-up idea needs to be innovative			.928			
The commitment of the team members is high		.819				
The coordination among the team members leads to proper management in the company		.902				
Team members make sure that all the internal processes are in sync		.846				
There are no trust issues among the team members		.851				
My start-up is located near the right market						.913
My company is working well as its location is suitable						.908
I located the company near the right customers to build trust with them						.844
Various growth opportunities are provided by the government to support my company				.941		
Government is directly or indirectly supporting the start-up ecosystem in India				.913		
Sound policies have made it easier to access supporting infrastructure				.909		
I use my creativity to work efficiently in my start-up	.854					
I can communicate well to persuade investors for investing funds in my company	.842					
I possess the organizational skills required to organize the work	.782					
I know how to manage the company's affairs actively to perform well	.818					
My business is aware of the target market to attract the right customers for its product/ services					.868	
My company has done market research prior to launching the product/service					.875	
The timely advertisement of product/service is made online to attract new customers					.815	

Extraction Method: Principal Component Analysis.
Rotation Method: Varimax with Kaiser Normalization.[a]
[a]Rotation converged in five iterations.
Source The authors.

Table 13.6 Factor loadings of items in the measurement model

Growth factor	*Item*	*Factor loading*
Entrepreneurial skills (ES)	Entrepreneurial_skills1	0.84
	Entrepreneurial_skills2	0.80
	Entrepreneurial_skills3	0.77
	Entrepreneurial_skills4	0.91
Product innovation (PI)	Product_innovation1	0.91
	Product_innovation2	0.83
	Product_innovation3	0.95
Founding team (FT)	Founding_team1	0.79
	Founding_team2	0.78
	Founding_team3	0.91
	Founding_team4	0.73
Government support (GS)	Govt_support1	0.87
	Govt_support2	0.92
	Govt_support3	0.93
Location (L)	Location1	0.83
	Location2	0.88
	Location3	0.83
Market (M)	Market1	0.73
	Market2	0.83
	Market3	0.99

Source Authors own

13.2.3 Confirmatory Factor Analysis (CFA)

To validate the factor structure, CFA was conducted using AMOS software. The results supported the proposed six-factor model, with all items showing standardized factor loadings exceeding 0.70 and reaching statistical significance at the 1% level ($p < 0.01$). These findings indicate strong convergent validity, consistent with the guidelines provided by Hair et al., (2019a, 2019b, 2019c, 2019d) and Fornell and Larcker (1981) (Table 13.6).

13.2.4 Reliability of the Research Instrument

Reliability indicates the degree to which items within a scale are correlated and measure the same underlying construct. As per Nunnally's (1978a, 1978b) guideline, a Cronbach's alpha value above 0.70 is generally considered acceptable for exploratory research. In this study, the calculated Cronbach's alpha was 0.803 (Table 13.7), indicating strong internal consistency and confirming that the scale is both reliable and well-constructed.

To establish the construct validity of the measurement model, both convergent and discriminant validity were examined through the correlation matrix and Average Variance Extracted (AVE) values. As outlined by Hair et al. (2010), convergent validity is supported when AVE values are > 0.50, composite reliability exceeds 0.70, and CR is higher than the corresponding AVE. In this study, all constructs fulfilled these requirements, with AVE values ranging from 0.649 to 0.822 (Table 13.8), thus providing strong evidence of convergent validity (Fraering & Minor, 2006; Hair et al., 2010; Khan, 2019a, 2019b).

For discriminant validity, the Fornell-Larcker criterion was used, which asserts that the square root of the AVE for a given construct should be higher than its correlations with other constructs (Fornell & Larcker, 1981). Furthermore, Hair et al. (2010) recommend that both the maximum shared variance and average shared variance should remain lower than the AVE to affirm discriminant validity. The analysis confirmed that these conditions were met across all constructs, with discriminant validity indicators exceeding the recommended threshold of 0.70. These

Table 13.7 Reliability statistics

Cronbach's Alpha	*Number of Items*
.803	20

Source The authors

Table 13.8 Indicators of convergent and discriminant validity

Factor	*CR*	*AVE*	*MSV*	*MaxR(H)*	*ES*	*FT*	*PI*	*L*	*M*	*GS*
ES	0.898	0.689	0.426	0.911	**0.830**					
FT	0.881	0.650	0.016	0.900	0.030	**0.806**				
PI	0.925	0.805	0.055	0.940	0.218**	−0.128†	**0.897**			
L	0.882	0.714	0.055	0.885	0.149†	−0.074	0.235**	**0.845**		
M	0.892	0.736	0.426	0.974	0.653***	0.007	0.040	0.001	**0.858**	
GS	0.933	0.822	0.130	0.938	0.361***	−0.013	0.052	0.119	0.173*	**0.907**

Source Gakingston MS-Excel Validity Master Output

findings verify the distinctiveness and non-redundancy of the measured constructs.

13.2.5 Validation of the Measurement Model for Start-Up Growth Factors

The CFA analysis aimed to validate the measurement model by evaluating the extent to which the observed indicators reflected their respective latent constructs. The finalized model comprised six core constructs: Entrepreneurial Skills (ES), Founding Team (FT), Product Innovation (PI), Location (L), Market Orientation (M), and Government Support (GS). Each of the constructs ES and FT consisted of four observed items, while PI, L, M, and GS included three items each, all of which demonstrated strong standardized factor loadings (≥ 0.70), indicating satisfactory convergent validity (Fig. 13.1).

Model fit was further assessed using multiple indices: the Chi-square to degrees of freedom ratio (CMIN/DF), Tucker-Lewis Index (TLI), Comparative Fit Index (CFI), Normed Fit Index (NFI), Goodness-of-Fit Index (GFI), and the Root Mean Square Error of Approximation (RMSEA). The CMIN/DF value was 2.009, which is within the acceptable threshold (i.e., below 3.0), suggesting a good model fit. Additionally, all other indices met or exceeded the recommended cutoff values, aligning with the guidelines established by Hair et al. (2010) and Bentler and Bonett (1980). These findings, detailed in Table 13.9, confirm the structural validity and overall adequacy of the measurement model. As a result, the six-factor model is considered both statistically robust and conceptually appropriate for capturing the primary factors contributing to start-up growth in a regional entrepreneurial ecosystem.

13.3 Discussion and Implications of Findings

India's start-up landscape has grown significantly in recent years, driven by a blend of supportive government programs, innovation-oriented regulations, and an increasingly vibrant entrepreneurial mindset (Chatterjee & Das, 2021; NASSCOM, 2022). Although several studies have examined start-up success from a broader, macroeconomic lens, there remains a scarcity of empirical research that investigates firm-level growth determinants—especially within regional and emerging market contexts (Kumar & Mohapatra, 2020; Sharma et al., 2021). This study addresses

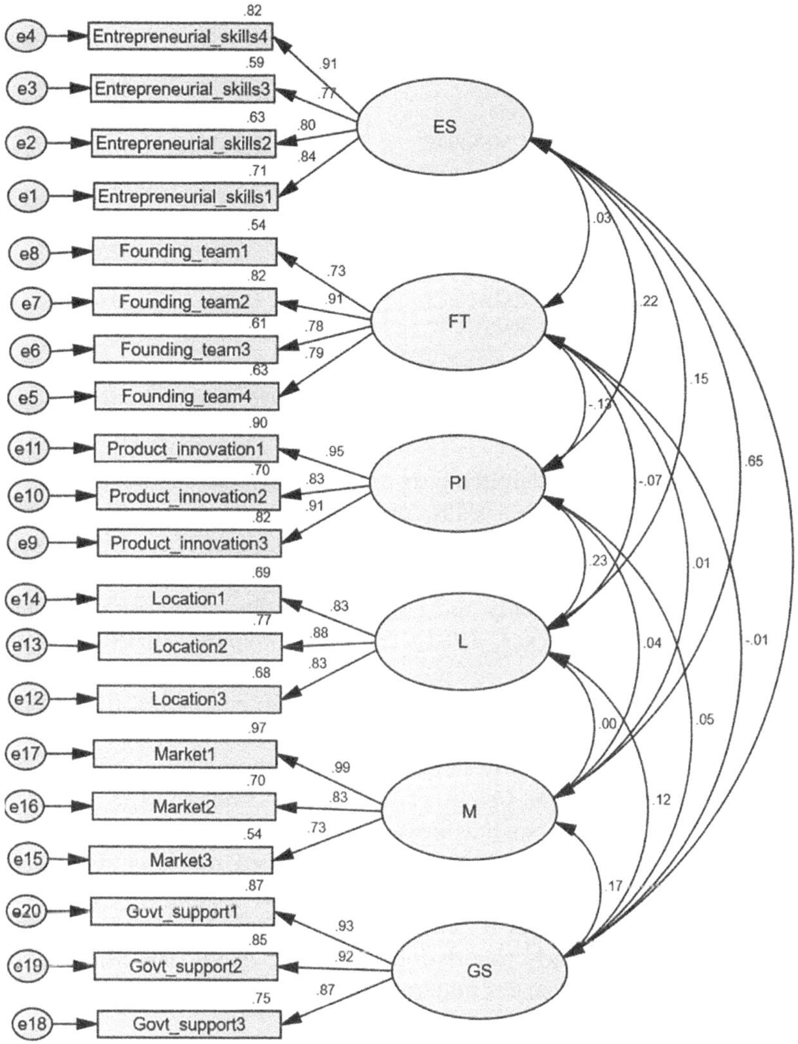

Fig. 13.1 Measurement model of start-up growth factors

Table 13.9 Model fit indices

Fitness criteria	*Measurement model*	*Acceptable range*
CMIN	311.367	–
DF	155	–
CMIN/DF	2.009	Less than 3
GFI	.876	> 0.80
AGFI	.831	> 0.80
CFI	.948	> 0.90
TLI	.936	> 0.90
NFI	.903	> 0.90
RMR	.071	< 0.09
RMSEA	.069	< 0.08

Note The study followed an acceptable range for model fit indices given by Forza and Filippini (1998) andHair et al. (2010)

that gap by empirically identifying six critical dimensions influencing start-up growth: entrepreneurial skills, product innovation, founding team, location, market orientation, and government support. These factors were validated using a rigorous two-step process involving both EFA and CFA, which ensured the reliability and construct validity of the measurement model (Fornell & Larcker, 1981; Hair et al., 2019a, 2019b, 2019c, 2019d).

The results resonate with prior studies that emphasize the importance of internal resources, including entrepreneurial capabilities and team dynamics, as essential to early-stage growth and long-term viability (Bjornali & Ellingsen, 2014; Okrah et al., 2018). Similarly, the influence of external conditions—such as government facilitation, market connectivity, and geographic positioning—was confirmed to play a significant role in performance outcomes (Ghaffar & Hamidreza, 2020; Gupta et al., 2020; Nalintippayawong et al., 2018). Among these, entrepreneurial skills emerged as a particularly foundational element, reinforcing earlier findings that this domain remains underexplored in empirical start-up research (Bjornali & Ellingsen, 2014).

From a managerial standpoint, the findings provide practical guidance: start-up founders are encouraged to build diverse and skilled teams, emphasize innovation in product development, and maintain active engagement with their target markets. Additionally, leveraging locational benefits and addressing infrastructural challenges should form part of strategic planning—especially in less urbanized or underserved regions where such factors can be either constraints or growth enablers (Autio et al., 2014; Coad et al., 2016).

The study also carries valuable policy implications. Given the significant role of government support identified in the analysis, agencies such as DPIIT and various state-level start-up missions are advised to move beyond policy design and focus more on practical implementation, region-specific support mechanisms, and inclusive outreach programs (Mehta et al., 2021; Singh & Goyal, 2022). Strengthening local ecosystems through these efforts can meaningfully enhance start-up scalability and long-term success across India's diverse geographic and economic landscape. Future research could extend this model across sectors and geographies to further generalize and deepen our understanding of regional start-up dynamics.

13.4 Research Limitations and Directions

This study offers valuable insights into start-up growth drivers but has certain limitations. First, the findings are based on a geographically limited sample, affecting generalizability. Future research should include diverse regions to enhance external validity. Second, the focus on DPIIT-recognized start-ups may overlook relevant factors affecting unregistered or informal ventures. Broader inclusion could provide better understanding of the ecosystem.

Additionally, while the study validated key growth constructs, it did not assess their direct impact on performance metrics such as revenue or scalability. Future studies could employ structural modelling to explore these causal relationships. Longitudinal research designs and examination of moderating or mediating variables—such as digital adoption or founder experience—are also recommended to deepen insights.

References

Autio, E., Kenney, M., Mustar, P., Siegel, D., & Wright, M. (2014). Entrepreneurial innovation: The importance of context. *Research Policy, 43*(7), 1097–1108.

Azoulay, P., Jones, B. F., Kim, J. D., & Miranda, J. (2020). Age and high-growth entrepreneurship. *American Economic Review: Insights, 2*(1), 65–82. https://doi.org/10.1257/aeri.20180582

Bakar, A. H. A., Tabassi, A.A, Razak, A. A. & Yusof, M.N. (2012). Key factors contributing to growth of construction companies: A Malaysian experience. *World Applied Sciences Journal, 19*(9).

Baruch, Y., & Holtom, B. C. (2008). Survey response rate levels and trends in organizational research. *Human Relations, 61*(8), 1139–1160. https://doi.org/10.1177/0018726708094863

Bentler, P. M., & Bonett, D. G. (1980). Significance tests and goodness of fit in the analysis of covariance structures. *Psychological Bulletin, 88*(3), 588–606. https://doi.org/10.1037/0033-2909.88.3.588

Beugelsdijk, S., & Noorderhaven, N. (2004). Entrepreneurial attitude and economic growth: A cross-section of 54 regions. *The Annals of Regional Science, 38*(2), 199–218. https://doi.org/10.1007/s00168-004-0192-y

Bjornali, E. S., & Ellingsen, A. (2014). Factors affecting the development of clean-tech start-ups: A literature review. *Energy Procedia, 58*, 43–50. https://doi.org/10.1016/j.egypro.2014.10.407

Blank, S. (2010). *What's a startup? First principles*. Retrieved from https://steveblank.com/2010/01/25/whats-a-startup-first-principles/

Business Standard. (2025, April 27). Uttarakhand to strengthen startups, sets up venture fund of Rs 200 crore. Business Standard. https://www.business-standard.com/finance/news/uttarakhand-to-strengthen-startups-sets-up-venture-fund-of-rs-200-crore-125042700744_1.html

Chatterjee, S., & Das, N. (2021). Indian Start-ups: Innovation, ecosystem and policy. *IIM Kozhikode Society & Management Review, 10*(2), 180–192.

Chawla, D., & Sondhi, N. (2011). *Research methodology: concepts and cases*. Vikas Publishing House.

Chawla, D., & Sondhi, N. (2016). *Research methodology: Concepts and cases* (2nd ed.). Vikas Publishing House.

Churchill, G. A., Jr. (1979). A paradigm for developing better measures of marketing constructs. *Journal of Marketing Research, 16*(1), 64–73. https://doi.org/10.1177/002224377901600110

Coad, A., Frankish, J., Roberts, R. G., & Storey, D. J. (2016). Predicting new venture survival and growth: Does the fog lift? *Small Business Economics, 47*(1), 1–18.

Davidsson, P., Kirchhoff, B., Hatemi-J, A., & Gustavsson, H. (2002). Empirical analysis of business growth factors using swedish data. *Journal of Small Business Management, 40*(4), 332–349. https://doi.org/10.1111/1540-627x.00061

DeVellis, R. F. (2017). *Scale development: Theory and applications* (4th ed.). Sage Publications.

Engidaw, A. E. (2021). Exploring internal business factors and their impact on firm performance: Small business perspective in Ethiopia. *Journal of Innovation and Entrepreneurship*. https://doi.org/10.1186/s13731-021-00167-3

Fornell, C., & Larcker, D. F. (1981a). Evaluating structural equation models with unobservable variables and measurement error. *Journal of Marketing Research, 18*(1), 39–50. https://doi.org/10.2307/3151312

Forza, C., & Filippini, R. (1998). TQM impact on quality conformance and customer satisfaction: A causal model. *International Journal of Production Economics, 55*(1), 1–20. https://doi.org/10.1016/s0925-5273(98)00007-3

Fraering, M., & Minor, M. S. (2006). Sense of community: An exploratory study of US consumers of financial services. *International Journal of Bank Marketing, 24*(5), 284–306. https://doi.org/10.1108/02652320610681738

Garhwal Post. (2024). Challenges faced by startups in Uttarakhand. https://garhwalpost.in

Ghaffar, T., & Hamidreza, P. (2020). Structural model of factors affecting survival and growth of start-ups in Iran. *Journal of Executive Management.* https://doi.org/10.22080/jem.2020.17998.3096

Goswami, N. (2006). *Entrepreneurship development in Assam a study of the influencing factors* [Thesis]. https://shodhganga.inflibnet.ac.in/handle/10603/69544

Gupta, S., Saha, R., Kaur, J., Kathuria, S., & Paul, J. (2020). Factors impacting innovation performance for entrepreneurs in India. *International Journal of Entrepreneurial Behavior & Research, 27*(2), 356–377. https://doi.org/10.1108/ijebr-09-2020-0612

Grewal, R., & Sharma, S. (2024). Determinants of startup scalability in emerging economies. *Journal of Entrepreneurship in Emerging Economies, 16*(1), 45–67. https://doi.org/10.1108/JEEE-07-2023-0154

Hair, J. F., Black, W. C., Babin, B. J., Anderson, R. E., & Tatham, R. L. (2010). *Multivariate Data Analysis.* Pearson- Prentice Hall.

Hair, J. F., Celsi, M., Ortinau, D. J., & Bush, R. P. (2013). *Essentials of marketing research* (3rd ed.). McGraw-Hill Education.

Hair, J. F., Ringle, C. M., & Sarstedt, M. (2013b). Partial Least Squares Structural Equation Modeling: Rigorous Applications, Better Results and Higher Acceptance. *Long Range Planning, 46*(1–2), 1–12. https://doi.org/10.1016/j.lrp.2013.01.001

Hair, J. F., Black, W. C., Babin, B. J., & Anderson, R. E. (2014). *Multivariate data analysis* (7th ed.). Pearson Education.

Hair, J. F., Anderson, R. E., Babin, B. J., & Black, W. C. (2019a). *Multivariate data analysis.* Cengage Learning.

Hair, J. F., Hult, G. T. M., Ringle, C. M., & Sarstedt, M. (2019). *A primer on PLS-SEM* (2nd ed.). Sage.

Hair, J. F., Hult, G. T. M., Ringle, C. M., & Sarstedt, M. (2019). *A primer on partial least squares structural equation modeling (PLS-SEM)* (2nd ed.). Sage Publications.

Hair, J. F., Hult, G. T. M., Ringle, C., & Sarstedt, M. (2019). *A primer on partial least squares structural equation modeling (PLS-SEM)* (2nd ed.). Sage Publications.

Hair, J. F., Black, W. C., Babin, B. J., & Anderson, R. E. (2020). *Multivariate data analysis* (8th ed.). Cengage Learning.

Hinkin, T. R. (1998). A brief tutorial on the development of measures for use in survey questionnaires. *Organizational Research Methods, 1*(1), 104–121. https://doi.org/10.1177/109442819800100106

Joseph, G., Aboobaker, N., & KA, Z. (2023). Entrepreneurial cognition and premature scaling of startups: a qualitative analysis of determinants of start-up failures. *Journal of Entrepreneurship in Emerging Economies, 15*(1), 96–112. https://doi.org/10.1108/JEEE-11-2020-0412

Kemp, R., & Gibcus, P., & Hart, P. M.. (2006). Determinants of growth of Start-ups in the Netherlands. *EIM Business and Policy Research, Scales Research Reports*.

Khan, M. T. (2019a). The impact of strategic planning on organizational performance: A case study of manufacturing firms in Pakistan. *Asian Journal of Multidisciplinary Studies, 7*(3), 89–96.

Khan, S. (2019b). A comparative analysis of emotional intelligence and intelligence quotient among Saudi business students' toward academic performance. *International Journal of Engineering Business Management, 11*, 184797901988066. https://doi.org/10.1177/1847979019880665

Klotz, A. C., Hmieleski, K. M., Bradley, B. H., & Busenitz, L. W. (2013). New venture teams. *Journal of Management, 40*(1), 226–255. https://doi.org/10.1177/0149206313493325

Konno, Y. (2021). Factors Influencing the continuation of start-up companies. *Cogent Economics & Finance, 9*(1), 1899368. https://doi.org/10.1080/23322039.2021.1899368

Kroeger, J. W. (2007). *Firm performance as a function of entrepreneurial orientation and strategic planning practices* (pp. 1–166). https://engagedscholarship.csuohio.edu/cgi/viewcontent.cgi?article=1169&context=etdarchive

Kumar, V., & Mehta, S. (2021). Entrepreneurial orientation and firm growth: Evidence from Indian SMEs. *International Journal of Entrepreneurial Behavior & Research, 27*(6), 1502–1520. https://doi.org/10.1108/IJEBR-01-2020-0045

Kumar, R., & Mohapatra, S. (2020). Entrepreneurial ecosystem in India: A comparative analysis. *Journal of Business and Economic Policy, 7*(1), 12–22.

Kutzhanova, N., Lyons, T. S., & Lichtenstein, G. A. (2009). Skill-based development of entrepreneurs and the role of personal and peer group coaching in enterprise development. *Economic Development Quarterly, 23*(3), 193–210. https://doi.org/10.1177/0891242409336547

Lau, C. M., & Busenitz, L. W. (2001). Growth intensions of entrepreneurs in a transitional economy: The People's Republic of China. *Entrepreneurship Theory and Practice, 26*(1), 5–20.

Lee, J., & Kim, S. (2021). A dynamic capability framework for startup success under market turbulence. *Journal of Business Venturing Insights, 15*(2), 101234. https://doi.org/10.1016/j.jbvi.2021.101234

Malhotra, N. K., & Dash, S. (2016). *Marketing research: An applied orientation* (7th ed.). Pearson Education India.

Mazzarol, T., Volery, T., Doss, N., & Thein, V. (1999). Factors influencing small business start-ups. *International Journal of Entrepreneurial Behavior & Research, 5*(2), 48–63. https://doi.org/10.1108/13552559910274499

Mehta, K., Garg, R., & Ahlawat, S. (2021). Government support and innovation in Indian start-ups: An empirical investigation. *Journal of Public Affairs, 21*(3), Article e2314.

Nalintippayawong, S., Waiyawatpattarakul, N., & Chotipant, S. (2018). *Examining the critical success factors of startup in Thailand using structural equation model.* (pp. 388–393).

NASSCOM. (2021). *India Tech Start-up Report 2021.* National Association of Software and Service Companies. Retrieved from https://nasscom.in

NASSCOM. (2022). *Indian tech start-up ecosystem: Year of the Titans.* https://nasscom.in

Netemeyer, R. G., Bearden, W. O., & Sharma, S. (2003). *Scaling procedures: Issues and applications.* Sage Publications.

Novanda, R. R., Khaliqi, M., Bakhtiar, A., & Amiruddin, A. (2021). The impact of entrepreneurial characteristics and innovation characteristics on entrepreneurial skills in Madura cattle farmers. *IOP Conference Series: Earth and Environmental Science, 782*(2), Article 022026. https://doi.org/10.1088/1755-1315/782/2/022026

Nunnally, J. C. (1978). *Psychometric theory* (2nd ed.). McGraw-Hill.

Nunnally, J. C. (1978b). *Pshychometric theory.* McGraw Hill Book Company.

Okrah, J., Nepp, A., & Agbozo, E. (2018). Exploring the factors of startup success and growth. *The Business and Management Review, 9*(3).

Podoynitsyna, K., Van der Bij, H., & Song, M. (2007). The role of mixed emotions in the risk perception of entrepreneurs. *Journal of Business Venturing, 22*(6), 798–822. https://doi.org/10.1016/j.jbusvent.2006.08.004

Reddy, K. S., Xie, E., & Huang, Y. (2023). Institutional support and startup performance in emerging markets. *Management and Organization Review, 19*(2), 361–389. https://doi.org/10.1017/mor.2022.35

Saini, T. (2020). *The sustainability of developing startup companies in Finland.* https://www.theseus.fi/handle/10024/341677

Sharma, P., Singh, A., & Gupta, S. (2021). Start-up success in India: Ecosystem challenges and policy solutions. *International Journal of Innovation Science, 13*(1), 87–104.

Singh, D. S. M., & Hanafi, N. B. (2020). Innovation capacity and performance of Malaysian SMES. *International Journal of Academic Research in Business and Social Sciences*. https://doi.org/10.6007/ijarbss/v10-i2/6956

Singh, H., & Goyal, D. P. (2022). Start-up policy implementation in India: Gaps and the way forward. *Vision: the Journal of Business Perspective, 26*(1), 57–65.

Singh, R., & Ghosh, S. (2020). Regional disparities in the Indian start-up ecosystem: A state-level analysis. *Journal of Innovation and Entrepreneurship, 9*(1), 1–15. https://doi.org/10.1186/s13731-020-00128-2

Singh, A., & Chauhan, S. (2021). Constraints faced by small-scale entrepreneurs: An empirical scale development study. *Journal of Small Business and Enterprise Development, 28*(5), 789–807. https://doi.org/10.1108/JSBED-08-2020-0296

Startup India. (2022). *State-wise distribution of recognised start-ups*. Retrieved from https://www.startupindia.gov.in

Wang, Y., & Li, H. (2022). Founding team diversity and startup performance: Evidence from technology ventures. *Technovation, 114*, 102443. https://doi.org/10.1016/j.technovation.2021.102443

Wang, Y., & Wu, X. (2025). Artificial intelligence and lean startup development: Accelerating innovation cycles. *Journal of Business Research, 172*, 114991. https://doi.org/10.1016/j.jbusres.2024.114991

Watson, K., Hogarth-Scott, S., & Wilson, N. (1998). Small business start-ups: Success factors and support implications. *International Journal of Entrepreneurial Behavior & Research, 4*(3), 217–238. https://doi.org/10.1108/13552559810235510

Wiklund, J., Patzelt, H., & Shepherd, D. A. (2007). Building an integrative model of small business growth. *Small Business Economics, 32*(4), 351–374. https://doi.org/10.1007/s11187-007-9084-8

Williams, B., Onsman, A., & Brown, T. (2010a). Exploratory factor analysis: A five-step guide for novices. *Australasian Journal of Paramedicine, 8*(3), 1–13. https://doi.org/10.33151/ajp.8.3.93

Zhao, F., Li, Y., & Wang, J. (2023). Entrepreneurial innovation and competitiveness in emerging economies. *Journal of Entrepreneurship, 32*(2), 221–240. https://doi.org/10.1177/09713557231102458

CHAPTER 14

The Future of Technology Entrepreneurship in Fitness Business

Yeşer Eroğlu-Eskicioğlu and *Kadir Yıldız*

14.1 Introduction

In recent years, cities have considered a variety of products, themes, and resources to capture a share of tourism and other external capital. Some have emphasized their qualities as cultural centers (Griffiths, 1995) or their location advantages. Others emphasized historical events or even mythical and fictional associations to compete in an increasingly symbolic

Yeşer Eroğlu-Eskicioğlu and Kadir Yıldız contributed equally to this work.

Y. Eroğlu-Eskicioğlu
Department of Physical Education and Sport, Faculty of Sport Sciences, Duzce University, Duzce, Türkiye
e-mail: yesereskicioglu@duzce.edu.tr

K. Yıldız (✉)
Department of Sport Management, Faculty of Sports Sciences, Manisa Celal Bayar University, Manisa, Türkiye
e-mail: kadir.yildiz@cbu.edu.tr

D. Kumar et al. (eds.), *Evolving Trends in Technology Entrepreneurship*, Palgrave Studies in Global Entrepreneurship,
https://doi.org/10.1007/978-981-95-7441-4_14

space economy. However, by evoking parallels with their Athenian and Roman predecessors, many cities have begun to use sport to advance their reputations (Smith, 2005). In the rapidly evolving global sports industry, the sector is considered an entrepreneurial process, as innovation and change are central to sports. In an increasingly competitive global environment, sports organizations gain a strategic advantage through innovation. In this context, one way for sports marketers to remain competitive is by embracing entrepreneurship. Therefore, entrepreneurship provides direction for sports businesses aiming to enhance their overall performance (Özkul, 2020). Entrepreneurship is defined as a process aimed at social transformation, economic growth, and the delivery of new services and products by stimulating creativity and generating innovative ideas. It is an appealing career path, as it contributes to overcoming economic crises and fostering the development of robust economies and new business opportunities. A sports entrepreneur, therefore, is someone who organizes, operates, and assumes risk in a sports-related business venture (Erkan, 2022). In the context of globalizing industries and economies, entrepreneurship has recently gained importance in business structures and national economies. It is seen as a fundamental element in economic development and social progress and is frequently highlighted in research for its role in utilizing untapped production potential. Entrepreneurs are not only individuals who establish new businesses for profit and growth by assembling necessary resources and taking risks but also innovative and determined figures capable of successfully managing small businesses (Okay & Karahan, 2010).

Tech entrepreneurship and sports are rapidly changing the way we interact with athletic performance, fan experiences, and the business side of sports. In an era defined by rapid technological advancement, the future of sport has been and continues to be heavily influenced by innovations in areas such as artificial intelligence (AI), virtual reality (VR), wearables, data analytics, and blockchain. Technology entrepreneurship plays an important role in shaping this future by focusing on creating new solutions through cutting-edge innovations.

Entrepreneurs in the sports technology sector have a symbiotic relationship with emerging technologies to develop new tools that enhance player performance, optimize team management, increase fan engagement, and revolutionize sports media. These innovations are not only transforming traditional sports but also creating new Business models, digital platforms, and ways of consuming sports content. In the coming years, the relationship between technology and sports stakeholders will continue to deepen. Startups and established companies will push the boundaries of what is possible, from personalized health data to immersive fan experiences. This will make it harder for sports businesses to remain independent from tech entrepreneurship. Looking to the future of the sports business, the synergy between tech entrepreneurship and sports promises to redefine the essence of what it means to be a fan, an athlete, and a stakeholder in the sports industry.

14.2 Conceptual Framework

14.2.1 Technology Entrepreneurship

The term "digital" encompasses not only technology but also people (Soltanifar & Smailhodžić, 2021), as digital advancements depend on population growth and the rise of new inventions. As inventions multiply, technological progress follows. Today, countries compete globally through technological superiority. The gap between countries that produce technology and those that rely on its import underscores differences in development. Technology not only enhances economic development but also fosters social and cultural transformation. In countries that cannot produce technology, cultural and social change often occurs as a result of technology transfer—a phenomenon referred to as "technological change." There is a clear relationship between technology and knowledge. Knowledge is a key component of technological development and a fundamental step in product creation, as it shapes and organizes social life (Akkaya & Arıca, 2023). The knowledge process is one of the important elements of technological development and social change.

Digital technologies have emerged as a crucial catalyst for entrepreneurial opportunities and have led to technological start-ups with significant market and societal impacts (Audretsch et al., 2020). It is the effective cooperation between research institutions, research and development centers, capital market institutions, business communities, and enterprises to disseminate knowledge and scientific potential related to technological innovations into commercial solutions (Badzińska, 2016). Governments and the public need science, industry, and entrepreneurs to find technological solutions to issues such as global warming, mobility, energy supply, population growth, demographic changes, and globalization. New inventions to overcome challenges have become the hope of many, so it is important not only to develop new technologies but also to use and commercialize them (Spiegel & Marxt, 2011).

Technology lowers the barriers to entrepreneurship and accelerates access to resources and markets. The Internet, in particular, facilitates entrepreneurship by offering access to information, finance, and global markets. Platforms such as Kickstarter and Indiegogo enable aspiring entrepreneurs to crowdfund their ventures, while e-commerce platforms like Shopify and Amazon have made it easier than ever to reach customers worldwide. Technology-driven innovations improve efficiency and productivity, helping entrepreneurs deliver more value to their customers. For instance, artificial intelligence (AI) and machine learning can automate repetitive tasks, optimize decision-making, and personalize customer experiences. By leveraging these technologies, entrepreneurs can enhance operational efficiency, reduce costs, and gain a competitive edge (Mert, 2023). Technology entrepreneurship involves identifying and capitalizing on intense business opportunities. It requires a unique mix of skills, strategic planning, and resilience. Entrepreneurs in this field often focus on turning innovative ideas from research and development into viable Business models.

The future of technology entrepreneurship is poised to be significantly shaped by the integration of digital technologies, the evolution of entrepreneurial ecosystems, and the increasing emphasis on innovation readiness. As highlighted by Bakri et al. (2024), startups that strategically leverage artificial intelligence (AI) and digital entrepreneurship practices are likely to gain a competitive advantage, particularly in dynamic environments such as Jakarta, where government support and professional infrastructure play crucial roles in fostering digitalization. This trend underscores the necessity for entrepreneurs to not only adopt advanced technologies but also to cultivate an ecosystem that supports innovation and collaboration. Mignenan (2023) emphasizes that technological entrepreneurship is emerging as a vital trend within the entrepreneurial landscape, characterized by the need for advanced technological mastery and the development of innovative solutions. This shift reflects a broader transformation in how entrepreneurs approach business challenges, moving towards less linear and more adaptive strategies that can respond to rapid technological changes. The emphasis on resilience and adaptability is critical, as entrepreneurs navigate the complexities of modern markets influenced by digital transformation (Du et al., 2018; Elia et al., 2020).

Technology Entrepreneurship is concerned with all questions related to the successful creation, exploitation and innovation of products, services, and processes in technology-driven firms. To achieve this, Technology Entrepreneurship researchers apply different perspectives and nuances to explore the question of whether technology-driven companies can create, sustain or expand their competitive position in an ever-changing environment (Spiegel & Marxt, 2011). Technology entrepreneurship can be understood as the endeavor to introduce new technologies into various industries, professions, or occupations. This approach contrasts with traditional business entrepreneurship, as it places greater emphasis on social and institutional factors rather than solely on a company's products and profitability. It encompasses broader considerations beyond the mere establishment of new businesses. It entails a form of what is termed institutional entrepreneurship, a concept first introduced by DiMaggio (1988). It encourages a shift in professions or occupations to embrace new technology (Venkataraman & Sarasvathy, 2005).

The role of digital platforms in fostering entrepreneurship is also significant, as they provide essential infrastructure for startups to innovate and scale their operations (Judijanto et al., 2024; Kumar, 2024). This interconnectedness among digital platforms, entrepreneurial activities, and technological advancements creates a fertile ground for new Business models and opportunities. However, the transition to digital entrepreneurship is not without challenges. As noted by Judijanto et al. (2024), there are substantial gaps in the literature regarding the integrated impact of digital transformation on entrepreneurship, indicating a need for more comprehensive studies that address these complexities. Moreover, the rapid pace of digitalization necessitates that entrepreneurs not only adopt new technologies but also innovate their Business models to remain competitive (Parida et al., 2019).

A review of the literature on technology entrepreneurship leads to generalizations such as operating small businesses owned by engineers or scientists; finding problems or applications for a particular technology; starting new enterprises, introducing new applications, or working with others to exploit opportunities based on scientific and technical knowledge and to produce technology change (Bailetti, 2012). Based on this generalization, it should not be ignored that technology initiatives can have a significant impact on fitness businesses, which have an important place in the sports industry.

14.2.2 *Technology Entrepreneurship and Fitness Business*

The notions of entrepreneurship and technology have developed a strong connection in recent years. The growth of digital technology and external factors has brought new opportunities and challenges to entrepreneurs. With the rise of digital technologies, digital entrepreneurs have started to emerge (Yáñez-Valdés & Guerrero, 2024). New digital technologies and knowledge have recombined in ways not previously thought possible, leading to the emergence of new Business models, especially during transformative global events. These innovative initiatives have had a significant impact on society. The process, which has an international impact, has also changed the technological change processes of fitness businesses.

Technology entrepreneurship researchers have shown that technology entrepreneurs derive competitive advantage either by a combination or singularly utilizing three basic approaches. The three distinct competitive advantage pathways are the recognition of technological possibilities, the ability to use technology to decrease transaction costs, and the ability to use new technology product paradigms to provide a solution to a market gap (Ratinho et al., 2015). Sports and fitness businesses are also part of this market.

The focus of innovation in the sport context is on sport organizations that are open to innovation to increase their membership numbers and add more services. This is a product of consumers, who play an important role in sport organizations by generating new ideas because they have a greater emotional connection. Innovation in sport is developed by consumers or participants from their high level of connection with sport. This means that sport innovation is different from other types of innovation that are usually developed within an organization through research and development activities. Most organizations develop innovation by investing time and money in internal processes that lead to commercialization that they control. Sports innovation is different in that it innovates the equipment itself, rather than waiting for users to do so. This makes innovation in sport dynamic as it is developed by members of the sporting community. The resulting innovation then diffuses within the sporting context and is used in a variety of different contexts depending on demand. Sports innovation has gained popularity because of the performance reward that results from the change made by users rather than producers. This user-driven innovation occurs in organizations that want to keep the innovation secret for revenue-sharing reasons and want to benefit from it (Ratten & Ferreira, 2017).

The internationally competitive sports industry depends on the use of digital technology to grow and sustain entrepreneurship in the sector (Ratten & Thompson, 2020). The internationalization of the sports industry means that fitness-related lifestyle habits are constantly evolving. In particular, there have been increased efforts to make participatory sport central to one's lifestyle choices and fitness goals, rather than just a casual leisure-time activity. With individuals now fully immersed in sport and fitness participation, innovations that provide opportunities to engage in new types of fitness abound. There is now a huge market for participatory sports such as CrossFit, Ironman, Tough Mudder, Spartan Race, yoga, marathons, and triathlons. These markets offer businesses a significant entrepreneurial opportunity. This interest both drives and overlaps with advanced media technologies that disseminate information about competitions and competitions (Jones et al., 2020).

Despite the great efforts made in the fitness industry and its impact on a healthy and active lifestyle, the great pace of change makes it imperative to provide up-to-date data for managerial decisions. Identifying best practices in fitness centers is important to improve the academic knowledge of the industry and to make the right managerial decisions. Therefore, the development of adequate protocols and reliable procedures in fitness centers will help increase customer participation in fitness services and lead to more stable and sustainable businesses. The most difficult tasks in the long-term management of sports organizations are taking care of people and having sufficient financial resources. In this context, building a stable and sustainable core of the organization through proper collaboration with stakeholders has a significant impact on its success. In the business world, best practices seek to provide clear guidance to professionals. Research suggests that sports programs, staff and the physical environment are the most important qualities for fitness center management, while more recent studies point to core and complementary services, facilities, and employee competencies as key elements (León-Quismondo et al., 2020). Underpinning all these institutional improvements, a strong entrepreneurial capacity is considered a necessity.

While sports businesses aim to make a profit to survive in a competitive environment, they also serve a social purpose. Social enterprises are oriented towards solving societal problems. One such enterprise type in the sports sector is fitness businesses. The recent rise in physical activity participation has led to a significant increase in the number of fitness centers—now exceeding 210,000 worldwide, serving over 183 million members, including 63,644 facilities with 64.8 million members in Europe. These businesses have become societal reference points that encourage exercise and foster a commitment to physical activity, making the fitness industry increasingly complex (Eraslan, 2024).

Today, issues such as obesity—often a consequence of rapid technological advancements—have led to growing interest in fitness programs. The unhealthy lifestyle brought on by sedentary habits negatively affects both physical and social well-being, resulting in reduced work efficiency and increased healthcare costs. Consequently, the general public's interest in fitness centers has increased, driven by a desire for healthier lifestyles, opportunities for non-professional physical activity, and socialization by overcoming personal barriers (Doğaner et al., 2018).

With the development of technology and media, sports have also become a profitable platform for advertising and promotion. Sports activities organized for show and entertainment purposes, which attract mass audiences, are rapidly transforming into a consumption sector. At the same time, they have become an attractive economic activity area for entrepreneurs, involving substantial financial dynamics (Şahin et al., 2021). A fitness business focuses on providing health and wellness services, products, or experiences to help individuals improve their physical fitness, mental health, and overall well-being.

In the sports sector, innovation is not limited to the improvement of existing services or the implementation of new technologies; it also serves as a powerful catalyst for entrepreneurial activities. Innovative ideas enable sports organizations to gain a competitive advantage, while the process of commercializing these ideas fuels the entrepreneurship ecosystem. Therefore, innovation processes in sports management are directly related to entrepreneurial activities in terms of developing new Business models, diversifying methods of reaching target audiences, and creating sustainable revenue streams. In this context, innovative approaches not only form the foundation of the entrepreneurial vision but also expand its fields of application, thereby supporting the creation of economic and social value in sports businesses.

Although general interest in entrepreneurship research is growing, the sports industry—especially due to its unique characteristics—has only recently begun to receive focused attention. The role of entrepreneurship in sports-related organizations differs from that in other industries.

Sport-specific entrepreneurial factors include mass communication power, social interaction, and broad public demand for sports. To improve their overall performance, sports organizations should approach entrepreneurship collaboratively, strategically, and with a community orientation. Key stakeholders benefiting from entrepreneurship include athletes, fans, customers, governments, sponsors, communities, and employees. Sport-based entrepreneurship offers a promising strategy for broader economic development (Dağlı-Ekmekçi & İrmiş, 2013).

Franchise Business models are among the latest schemes available in postmodern societies and are not separate from this global trend that touches concrete areas such as the fitness industry, physical movements, or sectoral professionalism (Andreasson & Johansson, 2018). This representation is widely and increasingly used by entrepreneurs seeking growth through geographical expansions, local management businesses, outlet/retail organizational dimensions, creating flexible and mobile customers, valuable franchisor inputs, and royalty rate definition. The fitness business landscape has evolved significantly, particularly in the context of Business models and consumer engagement strategies.

Recent studies highlight the transition from traditional fitness franchises to boutique fitness models, emphasizing the importance of qualitative characteristics that appeal to modern consumers. Addolorato et al. (2022) discuss the shift in fitness industry Business models, identifying key qualitative traits that define boutique fitness studios, such as personalized service and community engagement, which are increasingly valued by consumers seeking unique fitness experiences. This shift is supported by Jia's analysis of online ratings and reviews from fitness clubs, which reveals that exercisers prioritize aspects like service quality and community atmosphere, thereby influencing their overall satisfaction and loyalty (Jia, 2018). Moreover, the role of entrepreneurial marketing in the fitness sector cannot be overlooked. Anwar and Daniel (2016) emphasize how online businesses, including fitness services, leverage entrepreneurial marketing strategies to enhance customer engagement and build networks, which are crucial for sustaining competitive advantage in a crowded market. The integration of technology in fitness businesses, particularly through online platforms, has also been highlighted as a means to enhance customer experience and operational efficiency. For instance, Ardley and Hardwick explore how online member-owned communities can generate revenue through innovative Business models that cater to the evolving needs of fitness enthusiasts (Ardley & Hardwick, 2024). The impact of the global pandemic experienced in the first quarter of the twenty-first century further accelerated changes in the fitness industry, prompting businesses to adapt their models to maintain engagement and service delivery. Wiltshire et al. (2022) note that fitness professionals and organizations had to pivot quickly, utilizing digital platforms to connect with clients and provide services remotely, which has reshaped consumer expectations and business operations. This adaptability is crucial for fitness businesses aiming to thrive in a post-pandemic environment, as they must continue to innovate and respond to changing consumer behaviors. In terms of franchising within the fitness industry, research indicates that the relationship dynamics between franchisors and franchisees play a significant role in performance outcomes. Studies by Tsai et al. (2020) and Grünhagen et al. (2013) highlight the importance of operational autonomy and trust in franchise relationships, which can enhance performance and satisfaction among franchisees.

An activity tracker, commonly known as a fitness tracker, is a gadget or app that monitors and tracks fitness-related metrics such as distance walked or run, calorie consumption, and, in some cases, heart rate. It is a form of computer that a person wears on a part of their body. Smartwatches are often used because they connect wirelessly to a computer or smartphone for long-term data tracking. Standalone smartphone and software applications are also available. In recent years, wearable devices such as Fitness Trackers, Smartwatches, Heart Rate Monitors, and Global Positioning System (GPS) tracking devices have boomed, with usage ranging from children to the elderly. These devices are designed and marketed to encourage sedentary individuals to think critically about their health by creating mental anxiety about heart rate, step count/rhythm, duration and projection of current and future exercise, calorie loss, running distance, activity log, sleep patterns, and blood pressure, thus enabling them to be physically active (Kapoor et al., 2022).

The intersection of technology entrepreneurship and the fitness business sector is increasingly significant, particularly as advancements in technology reshape consumer expectations and operational strategies. The integration of digital tools and platforms has become essential for fitness businesses aiming to enhance customer engagement and streamline operations. The rise of wearable technologies and artificial intelligence has been identified as a transformative trend within the fitness industry, enabling personalized training and real-time feedback for users (Štajer et al., 2022).

This technological evolution not only improves user experience but also creates new business opportunities for entrepreneurs in the fitness sector. Moreover, the lean startup methodology, which emphasizes rapid iteration and customer feedback, is particularly relevant for technology-driven fitness startups. Silva et al. highlight that startups often begin with an idea that evolves through continuous validation and adaptation of their Business models (Silva et al., 2021). This approach is crucial in the fitness industry, where consumer preferences can shift rapidly, necessitating a flexible business strategy that can pivot based on market feedback. Entrepreneurs in this space must remain agile, leveraging technology to refine their offerings and ensure they meet the evolving needs of fitness consumers. Social media also plays a pivotal role in the success of fitness businesses, particularly for startups. Annisa and Er (2019) propose a conceptual model that underscores the importance of aligning social media strategies with business processes to enhance performance. Fitness entrepreneurs can utilize social media not only for marketing but also for building community engagement and fostering brand loyalty. This alignment can significantly impact customer acquisition and retention, which are critical for the sustainability of fitness startups. Furthermore, the concept of product-market fit is vital for the success of technology-driven fitness startups. Benkraiem et al. (2023) indicate that startups backed by corporate venture capitalists often achieve higher valuations due to the strategic alignment and resources provided by these investors. In the fitness industry, partnerships with established corporations can facilitate access to funding, technology, and market insights, which are essential for scaling operations and enhancing competitive advantage. In conclusion, the convergence of technology entrepreneurship and the fitness business sector presents numerous opportunities for innovation and growth. By leveraging advancements in technology, adopting lean startup methodologies, aligning social media strategies, and seeking strategic partnerships, fitness entrepreneurs can navigate the challenges of a rapidly evolving market. The ability to adapt and innovate will be paramount for success in this dynamic landscape. A notable example of technology-driven entrepreneurship can be found in wearable technologies. In the era of digital transformation, wearable devices—now deeply integrated into daily life—serve as both fashion trends and personal health assistants. These devices monitor physical activity, health metrics, and environmental data, analyze the collected information, and provide feedback. By acting as extensions of the human body, they simplify daily routines. The convergence of technology and fashion enhances the prominence of wearables in various industries. Covering domains such as healthcare, entertainment, sports, business, fashion, and industrial applications, wearable technologies are reshaping consumer experiences. Reflecting this growing impact, the global market size for wearable technologies reached $154.8 billion last year, marking a 20% increase from the previous year (Şener, 2025).

The convergence of technology entrepreneurship and the fitness industry has redefined business models, consumer engagement, and innovation strategies. As digital technologies, wearable devices, and AI-driven platforms become integral to fitness services, entrepreneurs are challenged to adapt quickly, personalize offerings, and build resilient, customer-centered ecosystems. This dynamic intersection offers significant opportunities for growth but also demands strategic agility and continuous innovation in a rapidly evolving market landscape.

14.2.3 The Tech-Adoption Lifecycle for Innovation Entrepreneurship in Fitness, Health, and Wellness

The convergence of technological advancement and wellness-oriented consumer behavior has given rise to a transformative era in the fitness, health, and wellness industries. Entrepreneurs operating in these domains are no longer confined to traditional service delivery models; instead, they are increasingly leveraging digital platforms, wearable technologies, AI-enabled coaching systems, and data-driven personalization to reshape how value is created and delivered (Ali, 2024). This wave of digital transformation, accelerated by shifting lifestyle trends and global health concerns, demands that entrepreneurial actors not only recognize technological opportunities but also adopt structured approaches to implementing innovation across highly dynamic markets.

This study introduces a novel conceptual framework titled the Technology Adoption Life Cycle for Fitness Entrepreneurs (TALFE), developed in response to emerging innovations and Business models at the intersection of sports and technology. Rooted in Rogers' Diffusion of Innovations Theory—originally proposed in 1962 by communication scholar E.M. Rogers at the University of New Mexico—this model draws from a theory widely acknowledged in the fields of information systems and technological innovation. According to Rogers, the diffusion of innovations typically unfolds through both mass media and interpersonal communication channels. In the modern digital age, technologies such as the internet and mobile devices, which combine features of both communication types, have become powerful tools in accelerating the diffusion process (Rogers, 2014).

Within this context, the TALFE model is designed to guide fitness entrepreneurs—particularly those operating health-oriented fitness centers—in aligning their business strategies with evolving technological trends and entrepreneurial opportunities. The framework offers a structured approach for identifying, evaluating, and integrating emerging technologies into fitness ventures. Each phase reflects critical decision points in the entrepreneurial journey: from recognizing technological trends and assessing their relevance, to engaging users, analyzing interaction data, and ultimately implementing scalable tech-based solutions that respond to dynamic market needs. By bridging theory and practice, the TALFE model provides both a theoretical foundation and a practical roadmap for navigating digital transformation in fitness-oriented enterprises.

14.3 Conclusion

Entrepreneurship is a revolutionary process that aims to develop new services, products, and ideas with a creative impulse, and thereby achieve economic growth and social transformation. This process plays an important role in making human life more qualified and for the welfare of societies. In this role, technology and human factors are effective. The technological approaches used by fitness businesses during the pandemic process have helped accelerate this process. Fitness classes connected from homes and business centers have created a new path for entrepreneurs, using the advantage of convenient time applications along with the possibility of group and individual work. Because resource management has taken its place among the main goals of businesses.

Proper management of resources, which is a fundamental business activity in entrepreneurship, depends on focusing on and implementing technological innovations. It is unthinkable for fitness businesses to be independent of cloud services, augmented and virtual reality, and artificial intelligence applications, which are 21st-century products of digital entrepreneurship that reshape business sectors and communication. For this reason, changing customer and technological tools make it a necessity for many fitness businesses to renew themselves with a focus on technology entrepreneurship. Although technological developments are developing rapidly, the important factor depends on how businesses prioritize and use these opportunities. Naturally, with the rapid change in technological developments, businesses that take advantage of this opportunity will be one step ahead. As a result, the symbiotic relationship between technology and the human factor will never weaken.

In addition, it is thought that adopting the Digital Maturity Model (DMM) developed by Deloitte and MIT Sloan Management Review in 2019, which reveals five business dimensions—customers, strategy, technology, operations, organization, and culture—used to assess the digital capacity of a business, will be an effective step in technological entrepreneurship. To ensure corporate sustainability, fitness businesses should focus on technology-oriented innovations such as artificial intelligence (AI), virtual reality (VR), and the Internet of Things (IoT) instead of traditional technological tools. This process can only be realized through adaptation to technological initiatives.

While the integration of digital technologies in the fitness sector brings considerable advantages, it also poses risks that must be carefully considered. In particular, excessive digitalization may erode the core human-centered experience that boutique fitness models are valued for, potentially replacing authentic interpersonal connections with impersonal interactions. Automation, if overextended, can unintentionally undermine the sense of personalization by making customer engagement feel mechanical rather than meaningful. Furthermore, the successful implementation of digital tools often depends on substantial infrastructure investment, comprehensive staff training, and adequate levels of digital literacy among clients—factors that may hinder the adoption process in certain markets. For this reason, technological integration should not only be strategic but also sensitive to the experiential and relational dimensions that define the fitness industry's appeal.

In conclusion, the future of technology entrepreneurship will be defined by the interplay of digital technologies, innovative ecosystems, and the ability of entrepreneurs to adapt to changing market conditions. The emphasis on collaboration, resilience, and continuous learning will be essential for navigating the complexities of the digital age. As the landscape evolves, it is imperative for entrepreneurs to embrace these changes and leverage the opportunities presented by emerging technologies and digital platforms. The answer to why technological entrepreneurship is important for fitness centers depends on the sustainability principles of businesses. Because changing technologies reshape the way people live, learn, and generate ideas. This process of social change naturally obliges businesses to reshape as well. Another dimension is related to the attractiveness of these changes. To support this adaptive transformation process in a structured manner, this chapter has proposed the Tech-Adoption Lifecycle for Fitness Entrepreneurs (TALFE), a conceptual framework that outlines how fitness entrepreneurs identify, evaluate, and integrate emerging technologies through four critical phases—Awareness, Strategic Integration, Customer-Centric Innovation, and Scalable Transformation. By embedding entrepreneurial behavior within a structured technology adoption pathway, TALFE provides a theoretical and practical roadmap for navigating digital disruption in health and wellness-oriented ventures.

In addition to these insights, while the integration of digital technologies in fitness entrepreneurship enhances accessibility and innovation, critical perspectives regarding over-dependence on digital systems, privacy concerns in fitness tracking apps, and the inclusivity of tech-driven models must not be overlooked. The sustainability of fitness ventures depends not only on embracing innovation but also on safeguarding ethical, secure, and equitable technology usage.

This chapter contributes to the literature on digital entrepreneurship and the resource-based view of entrepreneurial firms by outlining different pathways to the success of fitness businesses, with a particular focus on technological entrepreneurship.

References

Addolorato, S., García Unanue, J., Gallardo, L., & García Fernández, J. (2022). Fitness industry Business models: From the traditional franchising chain to the fitness boutique. *PODIUM Sport, Leisure and Tourism Review, 11*(1), 1–25. https://doi.org/10.5585/podium.v11i1.18287

Akkaya, E., & Arıca, F. (2023). Technology-based entrepreneurship and its applications in Turkey. *Journal of Entrepreneourship and Development, 18*(2), 33–45.

Ali, W. (2024). The role of artificial intelligence technology and innovation in disrupting traditional Business models and startup ecosystem. *International Journal of Scientific Research in Engineering and Management, 08*(008), 1–4. https://doi.org/10.55041/ijsrem37268

Andreasson, J., & Johansson, T. (2018). Glocalised fitness: The franchising of a physicalmovement, fitness professionalism and gender. *Leisure/loisir, 42*(3), 301–321.

Annisa, L., & Er, M. (2019). Impact of alignment between social media and business processes on smes' business process performance: A Conceptual model. *Procedia Computer Science, 161*, 1106–1113. https://doi.org/10.1016/j.procs.2019.11.222

Anwar, M., & Daniel, E. (2016). Entrepreneurial marketing in online businesses. *Qualitative Market Research an International Journal, 19*(3), 310–338. https://doi.org/10.1108/qmr-04-2015-0029

Ardley, B., & Hardwick, J. (2024). Business models and revenue generation: Conceptualising the development of economic value for online member owned communities. *Open Journal of Business and Management, 12*(03), 1429–1446. https://doi.org/10.4236/ojbm.2024.123077

Audretsch, D., Colombelli, A., Grilli, L., Minola, T., & Rasmussen, E. (2020). Innovative start-ups and policy initiatives. *Research Policy, 49*(10), Article 104027. https://doi.org/10.1016/j.respol.2020.104027

Bakri, B., ZM, A.A., Defitri, S.Y., & Mu'min, H. (2024). The Effect of AI technology, innovation readiness, and digital entrepreneurship on competitive advantage in start up in Jakarta. *West Science Interdisciplinary Studies, 2*(04): 841–850. https://doi.org/10.58812/wsis.v2i04.807

Badzińska, E. (2016). The Concept of technological entrepreneurship: The Example of business implementation. *Entrepreneurial Business and Economics Review, 4*(3): 57–72. https://doi.org/10.15678/EBER.2016.040305

Bailetti, T. (2012). Technology entrepreneurship: Overview, definition, and distinctive aspects. *Technology Innovation Management Review, 2*(2), 5–12.

Benkraiem, R., Gonçālves, D., & Shuwaikh, F. (2023). The Role of corporate venture capitalists in supporting the growth of their backed start-ups. *European Business Review, 35*(5), 672–693. https://doi.org/10.1108/ebr-09-2022-0183

Dağlı-Ekmekçi, Y. A., & İrmiş, A. (2013, 17–18 September). *Entrepreneurship and sport*. In *International Conference on Eurasian Economies 2013* (pp. 635–640). St.Petersburg: Beykent University. Retrieved from https://www.avekon.org/papers/754.pdf

DiMaggio, P. (1988). Interest and agency in institutional theory. *LG Ballinger*, 1–21. https://ci.nii.ac.jp/naid/10030010621/

Doğaner, S., Kaplan, M., & Özbek, O. (2018). Management problems and future plans for fitness centers: A qualitative research in Ankara. *SPORMETRE The Journal of Physical Education and Sport Sciences, 16*(4): 246–255. https://doi.org/10.33689/spormetre.498487

Du, W., Pan, S., Zhou, N., & Ouyang, T. (2018). From a marketplace of electronics to a Digital Entrepreneurial Ecosystem (Dee): The Emergence of a meta-organization in Zhongguancun, China. *Information Systems Journal, 28*(6), 1158–1175. https://doi.org/10.1111/isj.12176

Elia, G., Margherita, A., & Passiante, G. (2020). Digital entrepreneurship ecosystem: How digital technologies and collective intelligence are reshaping the entrepreneurial process. *Technological Forecasting and Social Change, 150*, Article 119791. https://doi.org/10.1016/j.techfore.2019.119791

Eraslan, A. (2024). Factors affecting success in fitness businesses. *Gazi Journal of Physical Education and Sport Sciences, 29*(2): 95–102. https://doi.org/10.53434/gbesbd.1434296

Erkan, M. (2022). Innovation and the entrepreneurship ecosystem in sport management. In Z. F. Dinç (Ed.), *Sport Sciences IV* (pp. 487–506). Ankara: Akademisyen. https://doi.org/10.37609/akya.2109 [Turkish]

Griffiths, R. (1995). Cultural strategies and new modes of urban intervention. *Cities, 12*(4), 253–265. https://doi.org/10.1016/0264-2751(95)00042-K

Grünhagen, M., Wollan, M., Dada, O., & Watson, A. (2013). The moderating influence of Hr operational autonomy on the entrepreneurial orientation-performance link in franchise systems. *International Entrepreneurship and Management Journal, 10*(4), 827–844. https://doi.org/10.1007/s11365-013-0270-7

Jia, S. (2018). Toward a better fitness club: Evidence from exerciser online rating and review using latent Dirichlet allocation and support vector machine. *International Journal of Market Research, 61*(1), 64–76. https://doi.org/10.1177/1470785318770571

Jones, P., Ratten, V., & Hayduk, T. (2020). Sport, fitness, and lifestyle entrepreneurship. *International Entrepreneurship and Management Journal, 16*, 783–793. https://doi.org/10.1007/s11365-020-00666-x

Judijanto, L., Putra, J., Ode, H., Timotius, E., & Supriandi, S. (2024). The role of digital platforms in developing entrepreneurship: A bibliometric analysis. *West Science Interdisciplinary Studies, 2*(07): 1411–1422. https://doi.org/10.58812/wsis.v2i07.1098

Kapoor, G., Chauhan, P., Singh, G., Malhotra, N., & Chahal, A.J. (2022). Physical activity for health and fitness: Past, present and future. *Journal of Lifestyle Medicine, 12*(1): 9–14. https://doi.org/10.15280/jlm.2022.12.1.9

Kumar, P. (2024). Challenges and opportunities for young entrepreneurs in digital age. *International Journal of Scientific Research in Engineering and Management, 8*(5): 1–5. https://doi.org/10.55041/ijsrem35116

León-Quismondo, J., García-Unanue, J., & Burillo, P. (2020). Best practices for fitness center business sustainability: A qualitative vision. *Sustainability, 12*(12): Article 5067. https://doi.org/10.3390/su12125067

Mert, M. (2023). The power of technology and innovation. In G. Mert & R. Kök (Eds.), *Technology and innovation-oriented ventures* (pp. 19–36). Ankara: Artikel Academy. (**Turkish**)

Mignenan, V. (2023). Contemporary perspectives for technological entrepreneurship in the age of change: Between success and resilience. *International Business Research, 16*(6), 1. https://doi.org/10.5539/ibr.v16n6p1

Okay, Ş., & Karahan, M. (2010). An Example field survey for determining of entrepreneurship characteristics of small scaled enterprises In Denizli. *Turkish Journal of Social Sciences, 1*: 291–304. [Turkish]

Özkul, G. (2020). The interaction between sport and entrepreneurship: Sports entrepreneurship and its economic reflections. In İ. Y. Gök & D. Dayı (Eds.), *Financial, economic and social research in sports* (pp. 340–356). Ankara: Nobel Akademik [Turkish]

Parida, V., Sjödin, D., & Reim, W. (2019). Reviewing literature on digitalization, business model innovation, and sustainable industry: Past achievements and future promises. *Sustainability, 11*(2), 391. https://doi.org/10.3390/su11020391

Ratinho, T., Harms, R., & Walsh, S. (2015). Structuring the technology entrepreneurship publication landscape: Making sense out of chaos. *Technological Forecasting and Social Change, 100*, 168–175. https://doi.org/10.1016/j.techfore.2015.05.004

Ratten, V., & Ferreira, J. J. (Eds.). (2017). *Sport entrepreneurship and innovation.* Routledge.

Ratten, V., & Thompson, A. J. (2020). Digital sport entrepreneurial ecosystems. *Thunderbird International Business Review, 62*(5), 565–578. https://doi.org/10.1002/tie.22160

Rogers, E. M., Singhal, A., & Quinlan, M. M. (2014). Diffusion of innovations. *An integrated approach to communication theory and research* (pp. 432–448). Routledge.

Şener, O. (2025). Geleceğin modası giyilebilir teknolojiden geçiyor. https://www.platinonline.com/teknoloji/gelecegin-modasi-giyilebilir-teknolojiden-geciyor-1092040 [Turkish]

Silva, D., Ghezzi, A., Aguiar, R., Cortimiglia, M., & Caten, C. (2021). Lean startup for opportunity exploitation: Adoption constraints and strategies in technology new ventures. *International Journal of Entrepreneurial Behaviour & Research, 27*(4), 944–969. https://doi.org/10.1108/ijebr-01-2020-0030

Smith, A. (2005). Reimaging the city: The value of sport initiatives. *Annals of Tourism Research, 32*(1), 217–236. https://doi.org/10.1016/j.annals.2004.07.007

Soltanifar, M., & Smailhodžić, E. (2021). Developing a digital entrepreneurial mindset for data-driven, cloud-enabled, and platform-centric business activities: Practical implications and the impact on society. In M. Soltanifar, M. Hughes, & L. Göcke (Eds.), *Digital entrepreneurship, impact on business and society* (pp. 3–21). Springer.

Spiegel, M., & Marxt, C. (2011). Defining technology entrepreneurship. In *2011 IEEE International Conference on Industrial Engineering and Engineering Management* (pp. 1623–1627). IEEE. https://doi.org/10.1109/IEEM.2011.6118191

Štajer, V., Milovanović, I., Todorović, N., Ranisavljev, M., Pišot, S., & Drid, P. (2022). Let's (tik) talk about fitness trends. *Frontiers in Public Health, 10*, 899949. https://doi.org/10.3389/fpubh.2022.899949

Şahin, C., Demirci, S., & Güllü, S. (2021). Examination of entrepreneurship examples in the field of sports. *Journal of Social Sciences and Humanities Researches, 22*(49), 135–156.

Tsai, F., Kuo, C., & Lin, J. (2020). Knowledge heterogenization of the franchising literature applying transaction cost economics. *Economies, 8*(4), 106. https://doi.org/10.3390/economies8040106

Venkataraman, S., & Sarasvathy, S. D. (2005). Strategy and entrepreneurship: Outlines of an untold story. In Michael A. Hitt, R. Edward Freeman, Jeffrey S. Harrison (Edt.), *The Blackwell handbook of strategic management* (655–673). Oxford: Blackwell Publishers Ltd. https://doi.org/10.1111/b.9780631218616.2006.00025.x

Wiltshire, H., Supriya, R., & Baker, J. (2022). Covid-19 impact on the sport sector economy and athletic performance. *Journal of Risk and Financial Management, 15*(4), 173. https://doi.org/10.3390/jrfm15040173

Yáñez-Valdés, C., & Guerrero, M. (2024). Determinants and impacts of digital entrepreneurship: A pre-and post-COVID-19 perspective. *Technovation, 132*, 102983. https://doi.org/10.1016/j.technovation.2024.102983

CHAPTER 15

The Evolving Dynamics of Technology Entrepreneurship: A Descriptive Approach

Rajendra Sharma, Preeti Singh, and Kishan Jee

15.1 Introduction

The modern world is undergoing rapid and significant changes, particularly in the field of information and communication technology (ICT). According to Omerovic Smajlovic (2024), the swift proliferation of digital technologies with novel features is changing competitive landscapes and altering standard company strategies, structures, and practices. In the connected economy, driven by technologies, many businesses are shrinking to one person. Due to innovative digital technologies such as AI, IoT, machine learning, social media platforms, and mobile and cloud-based technological solutions, the partnerships are also evolving. New approaches to collaboration, resource leveraging, product/service design,

R. Sharma · P. Singh (✉)
Rajarshi School of Management and Technology, Varanasi, India
e-mail: singhpreeti19vns@gmail.com

K. Jee
Dr. Shantilal K. Somaiya School of Commerce and Business Studies, Somaiya Vidyavihar University, Mumbai, India

D. Kumar et al. (eds.), *Evolving Trends in Technology Entrepreneurship*, Palgrave Studies in Global Entrepreneurship,
https://doi.org/10.1007/978-981-95-7441-4_15

creation, and launch across open standards and shared technologies are further emerging. By creating job possibilities, they are also impacting corporate operations globally. Digital technologies are bringing many job opportunities, but they are also posing several problems and challenges. They are changing the demand pattern of the labor market. To compete economically, labor-intensive nations like India and other South Asian countries must develop proactive strategies. Nations should adopt digital entrepreneurship and establish a suitable framework to address these issues.

Through the use of ICTs such as the internet, mobile devices, social computing, and digital platforms, digital entrepreneurship has boosted employment rates globally (Kraus et al., 2019; Shukla et al., 2021; Modgil et al., 2022). The simplest definition of digital entrepreneurship is an entrepreneurial enterprise that operates via a digital platform worldwide. Lately, many companies have started doing business digitally. They are selling their products and services online to capture the market globally. This is not only a requirement in changing market dynamics but also a necessity to face competition in the global market. Therefore, there is a rising need to understand how to start a digital business venture. People entering digital business must be able to understand the difference between digital and traditional entrepreneurship, the underlying risks, and the potential opportunities. For this, people need a digital entrepreneurship format or structure that includes all the information, such as its features and goals, about a new digital venture.

This paper aims to offer an in-depth primer on digital entrepreneurship, examining its key characteristics, drivers, and challenges within the context of evolving technological trends. It tends to explore the transformative impact of emerging technologies, analyze the factors propelling the rise of digital businesses, and address the critical issues faced by digital entrepreneurs. Furthermore, this research will try to explore the future trends shaping the landscape of digital entrepreneurship, including the burgeoning metaverse, the imperative of sustainability, and the expanding creator economy. By synthesizing existing literature and providing a critical analysis, this paper seeks to contribute to a deeper understanding of digital entrepreneurship and its significance in the broader setting of the technological entrepreneurship environment. Ultimately, the research aims to illuminate the pathways for future innovation and sustainable growth in the digital age.

15.2 Review of Literature

See Table 15.1.

15.3 Digital Transformation Journey of a Traditional Enterprise into a Digital Enterprise

Figure 15.1 The digital transformation journey of a traditional enterprise is a structured, multi-phase journey aimed at reimagining operations, enhancing value-added delivery, and integrating with broader digital ecosystems. According to the conceptual framework given by Paul et al. (2023). This journey progresses through six key steps, beginning with three foundational elements such as:

Foundation Stages:

1. Digital knowledge base creation
2. Digital technology adoption
3. Digital platform readiness

Core of Foundational Stages

1. Digitization Process

The digitization process act as a bridge between traditional and digital enterprise models. Once organizations move beyond this phase, they can achieve comprehensive digital transformation such as

- Business processes into digital business process.
- Organizational resources controlled through technology.
- Business models.

This transformation enables enterprises to enter into the digital ecosystem, which enhances overall operational efficiency and enables the system to enter new markets globally, which leads to leveraging the data for better decision-making and communicating with a wider customer base globally. By adopting digitalization, a traditional enterprise successfully enters into a modern digital enterprise, which can meet global

Table 15.1 Review of literature

	Section	*Year*	*Study Title*	*Key Focus Area/ Findings*	*Author(s)*	*DOI*
1	Digital Entrepreneurship	2019	Digital entrepreneurship: An interdisciplinary structured literature review and research agenda	Offers a structured framework of digital entrepreneurship literature and a future research agenda	Zaheer, H., Breyer, Y., & Dumay, J.	https://doi.org/10.1016/j.techfore.2019.119735
		2010	Digital entrepreneurship and its sociomaterial enactment	Examines digital entrepreneurship as an interaction between technology and entrepreneurial action	Davidson, E., & Vaast, E.	https://doi.org/10.1109/HICSS.2010.150
		2020	Agile business model innovation in digital entrepreneurship	Discusses how lean startup methods aid business model development	Ghezzi, A., & Cavallo, A.	https://doi.org/10.1016/j.jbusres.2018.06.013
		2024	Digital entrepreneurship: theoretical foundations, methods, and trends	Explores how digital entrepreneurship transforms SMEs' models	Fernandes, A. J., Ferreira, J. J., Fernandes, C. I., & Kraus, S.	https://doi.org/10.1561/0300000122
		2007	Taking advantage of digital opportunities: a typology of digital entrepreneurship	Framework for structuring and launching digital ventures	Hull, C. E., Hung, Y. T. C., Hair, N., & DeMartino, R.	https://doi.org/10.1504/IJNVO.2007.015166
		2021	Influencing mechanism of strategic flexibility on corporate performance: the mediating role of business model innovation	Analyzes how dynamic capabilities mediate firm performance	Xiao, H., Yang, Z., & Hu, Y.	https://doi.org/10.1080/13602381.2021.1896256

Section	*Year*	*Study Title*	*Key Focus Area/ Findings*	*Author(s)*	*DOI*
	2021	Toward a loose coupling view of digital globalization	Key themes in innovation in a digital age	Nambisan, S., & Luo, Y.	https://doi.org/10.1057/s41267-021-00446-x
	2021	On the costs of digital entrepreneurship: Role conflict, stress, and venture performance in digital platform-based ecosystems	Explores stress, role conflict, and venture performance	Nambisan, S., & Baron, R. A.	https://doi.org/10.1016/j.jbusres.2019.06.037
	2017	Visual tools for business model innovation: Recommendations from a cognitive perspective	Discusses lean startup and MVP approaches in digital business model design.	Täuscher, K., & Abdelkafi, N.	https://doi.org/10.1111/caim.12208
	2017	Digital entrepreneurship: Toward a digital technology perspective of entrepreneurship	Outlines ecosystem dynamics, crowd participation, and digital opportunity	Nambisan, S.	https://doi.org/10.1111/etap.12254
	2010	Digital Entrepreneurship and Its Sociomaterial Enactment	This paper asks how we can better understand entrepreneurship when digital technologies become deeply embedded	Elizabeth Davidson; Emmanuelle Vaast	https://doi.org/10.1109/HICSS.2010.150
	2017	The digital entrepreneurial ecosystem	Explores the structure and evolution of entrepreneurial ecosystems enabled by digital technologies	Fiona Sussan; Zoltan J. Acs	https://doi.org/10.1007/s11187-017-9867-5

(continued)

Table 15.1 (continued)

	Section	Year	Study Title	Key Focus Area/ Findings	Author(s)	DOI
		2012	Market Orientation in Digital Entrepreneurship: Advantages and Challenges in A Web 2.0 Networked World	Discusses the importance of market orientation in digital venture creation	Neil Hair, Lyle R. Wetsch, C. E. Hull, Victor Perotti, Y. Hung	https://doi.org/10.1142/S0219877012500459
		2018	Digital transformation by SME entrepreneurs: A capability perspective	Explores how SMEs leverage digital technologies for innovation and growth	Liang-liang Li, Fangjie Su, Wei Zhang, Jiye Mao	https://doi.org/10.1111/isj.12153
		2020	Agile Business Model Innovation in Digital Entrepreneurship: Lean Startup Approaches	Discusses agile methods in developing digital entrepreneurial ventures	Antonio Ghezzi, Angelo Cavallo	https://doi.org/10.1016/j.jbusres.2018.06.013
2	Digital Transformation	2021	Digital Transformation: An Overview of the Current State of the Art of Research	Shows how SMEs align digital strategies with competitive goals	Kraus, S., Jones, P., Kailer, N. et al.	https://doi.org/10.1177/21582440211047576
		2022	Business model innovation and digital transformation in global management consulting firms	Discusses dynamic capabilities for business model innovation	Tavoletti, E., Kazemargi, N., Cerruti, C., Grieco, C., & Appolloni, A.	https://doi.org/10.1108/EJIM-11-2020-0443
		2023	Sustainable digital transformation in small and medium enterprises (SMEs): A review on performance	Identifies how SMEs utilize digital capabilities for growth	Melo, I. C., Queiroz, G. A., Junior, P. N. A., de Sousa, T. B., Yushimito, W. F., & Pereira, J.	https://doi.org/10.1016/j.heliyon.2023.e13908

Section	*Year*	*Study Title*	*Key Focus Area/ Findings*	*Author(s)*	*DOI*
	2025	A conceptual framework for asymmetric collaborations between startups and big corporations in digital innovation ecosystems	Examines dynamic capabilities required to respond to crises	Felicetti, A. M., Ammirato, S., Linzalone, R., & Quinto, I.	https://doi.org/10.1108/EJIM-01-2025-0022
	2025	Analysis of key factors affecting the digital transformation of small and medium-sized manufacturing enterprises in China	Empirical evidence from China on business model innovation	Shao, Q., Lin, J., Liou, J. J., Zhu, D., & Tzeng, G. H.	https://doi.org/10.1177/2158244025133607
	2021	Does age matter? The impact of SMEs age on the relationship between knowledge sourcing strategy and internationalization	A systematic review shows digital enablers of export	Santoro, G., Mazzoleni, A., Quaglia, R., & Solima, L.	https://doi.org/10.1016/j.jbusres.2019.05.021
	2013	Digital business strategy: toward a next generation of insights	Presents digital value framework aligning strategy and tech	Bharadwaj, A., El Sawy, O. A., Pavlou, P. A., & Venkatraman, N.	https://doi.org/10.25300/MISQ/2013/37:2.3
	2023	The impact of digitalization on enterprise value creation: An empirical analysis of Chinese manufacturing enterprises	Case evidence from European firms on performance enhancement	Meng, F., & Wang, W.	https://doi.org/10.1016/j.jik.2023.100385

(continued)

Table 15.1 (continued)

Section	*Year*	*Study Title*	*Key Focus Area/ Findings*	*Author(s)*	*DOI*
	2013	Digital business strategy: toward a next generation of insights	Over the last three decades, the prevailing view of IT strategy has been to align IT with business strategy	Anandhi Bharadwaj; Omar A. El Sawy; Paul A. Pavlou; N. Venkatraman	https://doi.org/10.25300/MISQ/2013/37:2.3
	2020	Digital entrepreneurship ecosystem: How digital technologies and collective intelligence are reshaping the entrepreneurial process	Digitalization plays a major role in contributing to innovation, entrepreneurship and sustainable digital business models	Gianluca Elia, Alessandro Margherita, Giuseppina Passiante	https://doi.org/10.1016/j.jbusres.2019.12.040
	2017	Values-based network and business model innovation	Innovation management falls short in solving urgent sustainability challenges and therefore requires new approaches	Henning Breuer; Florian Lüdeke-Freund	https://doi.org/10.1142/S1363919617500281
	2010	Research Commentary—The New Organizing Logic of Digital Innovation: An Agenda for Information Systems Research	Discusses how digital technologies change innovation processes and organizational structures	Youngjin Yoo; Ola Henfridsson; Kalle Lyytinen	https://doi.org/10.1287/isre.1100.0322

	Section	Year	Study Title	Key Focus Area/ Findings	Author(s)	DOI
		2020	Digital innovation: towards a transdisciplinary perspective. In Handbook of digital innovation	Explores digital innovation processes and their role in transforming industries and organizations	Nambisan, S., Lyytinen, K., & Yoo, Y.	https://doi.org/10.1016/j.respol.2019.03.018
		2017	Firm growth, adaptive capability, and entrepreneurial orientation	Explores how firms adapt and grow through digital transformation strategies	Yoshihiro Eshima, B. Anderson	https://doi.org/10.1002/smj.2512
		2019	The digital transformation of innovation and entrepreneurship: Progress, challenges and key themes	Explores the impact of digitalization on innovation ecosystems	Satish Nambisan, Mike Wright, Maryann P. Feldman	https://doi.org/10.1016/j.respol.2019.03.018
		2023	Unlocking the full potential of digital transformation in banking: a bibliometric review and emerging trend	Identifies key drivers and strategies for successful digital transformation	Lambert Kofi Osei, Yuliya Cherkasova, Kofi Mintah Oware	https://doi.org/10.1186/s43093-023-00207-2
3	Metaverse & Emerging Tech	2016	Digital product innovation within four classes of innovation networks	Describes digital innovation in VR/AR ecosystems	Lyytinen, K., Yoo, Y., & Boland, R. J.	https://doi.org/10.1111/isj.12093

(continued)

Table 15.1 (continued)

	Section	Year	Study Title	Key Focus Area/ Findings	Author(s)	DOI
		2022	A framework for collaborative artificial intelligence in marketing	Discusses the rise of virtual marketplaces and creator tools	Huang, M. H., & Rust, R. T.	https://doi.org/10.1016/j.jretai.2021.03.001
		2012	Organizing for innovation in the digitized world	Investigate VR/AR potential for new industries	Yoo, Y., Boland Jr, R. J., Lyytinen, K., & Majchrzak, A.	https://doi.org/10.1287/orsc.1120.0771
		2011	The business model in practice and its implications for entrepreneurship research	Emphasizes virtual identity, tokenization, and decentralization	George, G., & Bock, A. J.	https://doi.org/10.1111/j.1540-6520.2010.0042
4	Technology Drivers (AI, IoT, Blockchain)	2021	Artificial Intelligence and entrepreneurship: Implications for venture creation	Explores how AI transforms new venture creation and entrepreneurial support	Chalmers, D., MacKenzie, N. G., & Carter, S.	https://doi.org/10.1177/1042258720934581
		2016	IoT applications and challenges in smart cities	Reviews IoT use cases and challenges in urban management	Scuotto, V., Ferraris, A., Bresciani, S. et al.	https://doi.org/10.1108/BPMJ-05-2015-0074
		2021	Artificial intelligence and entrepreneurship: Implications for venture creation in the fourth industrial revolution	Discusses how AI assists and challenges venture support systems	Chalmers, D., MacKenzie, N. G., & Carter, S.	https://doi.org/10.1177/1042258720934581

Section	*Year*	*Study Title*	*Key Focus Area/ Findings*	*Author(s)*	*DOI*
	2025	Blockchain-enabled value creation for circular supply chain in the tyre industry	Shows how blockchain enhances supply chain transparency	Modgil, S., & Singh, R. K.	https://doi.org/10.1108/IJLM-08-2023-0350
	2021	Digital or not—The future of entrepreneurship and innovation: Introduction to the special issue	Highlights the importance of tech platforms in new venture success	Berger, E. S., Von Briel, F., Davidsson, P., & Kuckertz, A.	https://doi.org/10.1016/j.jbusres.2019.12.020
	2019	Linking information systems and entrepreneurship: A review and agenda for IT-associated and digital entrepreneurship research	Reviews IT-associated research and proposes digital paths	Steininger, D. M.	https://doi.org/10.1111/isj.12206
	2019	The feeling economy: Managing in the next generation of artificial intelligence (AI)	Explains how AI changes the nature of economic value and labor	Huang, M. H., Rust, R. T., & Maksimovic, V.	https://doi.org/10.1177/0008125619863436
	2017	The role of enterprise systems in innovation in the contemporary organization	Digital platforms as enablers of innovation	Sedera, D., Lokuge, S.	https://doi.org/10.4324/9781315619361

(continued)

Table 15.1 (continued)

Section	*Year*	*Study Title*	*Key Focus Area/ Findings*	*Author(s)*	*DOI*
	2023	AI-driven predictive analytics for customer retention in e-commerce platforms using real-time behavioral tracking	Discusses smart agents in digital startups and their impact on customer service	Ononiwu, M., Azonuche, T. I., Okoh, O. F., & Enyejo, J. O.	https://doi.org/10.38124/ijsrmt.v2i8.561
	2016	Where is current research on blockchain technology?—a systematic review	Case study-based insights on trust, efficiency, and data control	Yli-Huumo, J., Ko, D., Choi, S., Park, S., & Smolander, K.	https://doi.org/10.1371/journal.pone.0163477
	2019	Big data analytics and firm performance: Effects of dynamic capabilities	Investigates how big data analytics capabilities influence firm performance and innovation	Wamba, S. F., Gunasekaran, A., Akter, S., Ren, S. J. F., Dubey, R., & Childe, S. J.	https://doi.org/10.1080/09537287.2017.1320576
	2018	Big data and business analytics ecosystems: paving the way towards digital transformation and sustainable societies	Discusses big data technologies and analytics ecosystems that support digital innovation	Pappas, I. O., Mikalef, P., Giannakos, M. N., Krogstie, J., & Lekakos, G.	https://doi.org/10.1007/s10257-017-0352-7
	2018	Business Models and Dynamic Capabilities	Discusses how technological capabilities enable innovative digital business models	David J. Teece	https://doi.org/10.1016/j.lrp.2017.06.007

Section	*Year*	*Study Title*	*Key Focus Area/ Findings*	*Author(s)*	*DOI*
	2017	Knowledge-driven preferences in informal inbound open innovation modes. An explorative view on small to medium enterprises	Explores knowledge systems supporting technological innovation and entrepreneurship	V. Scuotto, M. Giudice, Stefano Bresciani, D. Meissner	https://doi.org/10.1108/JKM-10-2016-0452
	2015	Business models for open innovation: Matching heterogeneous open innovation strategies with business model dimensions	Discusses how technological innovation enables new forms of business models	Tina Saebi, Nicolai J. Foss	https://doi.org/10.1016/j.emj.2014.11.002
	2011	International entrepreneurship in internet-enabled markets	Highlights the global expansion of entrepreneurs via digital platforms	Reuber, A. R., & Fischer, E.	https://doi.org/10.1016/j.jbusvent.2011.05.002
	2019	Digital entrepreneurship and field conditions for institutional change–Investigating the enabling role of cities	Case study of Uber's platform disruption and policy tension	Geissinger, A., Laurell, C., Sandström, C., Eriksson, K., & Nykvist, R.	https://doi.org/10.1016/j.techfore.2018.06.019
	2021	Knowledge-and innovation-based business models for future growth: Digitalized business models and portfolio considerations	Systematic review on how education platforms foster skills	Bouncken, R. B., Kraus, S., & Roig-Tierno, N.	https://doi.org/10.1007/s11846-019-00366-z

(continued)

Table 15.1 (continued)

Section	*Year*	*Study Title*	*Key Focus Area/ Findings*	*Author(s)*	*DOI*
	2022	Exploring influences on social entrepreneurial intentions among Indian students: the function of gender role orientation	Cross-country study using digital tools to assess intention	Dato-on, M. C., Banerjee, S., & Banerjee, P.	https://doi.org/10.1504/IJICBM.2022.127727
	2014	Industry platforms and ecosystem innovation	Describes platform business models and control mechanisms	Gawer, A., & Cusumano, M. A.	https://doi.org/10.1111/jpim.12105
	2021	The commercialization of social media stars: a literature review and conceptual framework on the strategic use of social media influencers	Examines the entrepreneurial behavior of digital influencers	Hudders, L., De Jans, S., & De Veirman, M.	https://doi.org/10.4324/9781003181286
	2019	Global platforms and ecosystems: Implications for international business theories	Explains the role of digital platforms in enabling value creation and ecosystem-based entrepreneurship	Satish Nambisan, Shaker A. Zahra & Yadong Luo	https://doi.org/10.1057/s41267-019-00262-4
	2019	The Relational Organization of Entrepreneurial Ecosystems	Explores how digital platforms support entrepreneurial growth and innovation networks	Ben Spigel	https://doi.org/10.1111/etap.12167

	Section	Year	Study Title	Key Focus Area/ Findings	Author(s)	DOI
		2019	Digital academic entrepreneurship: The potential of digital technologies on academic entrepreneurship	Examines commercialization of research and innovation through digital platforms	Pierluigi Rippa, Giustina Secundo	https://doi.org/10.1016/j.techfore.2018.07.013
		2017	Digital Entrepreneurship: Innovative Business Models for the Sharing Economy	Investigates the development of platform-based digital business models	Chris Richter, S. Kraus, A. Brem, S. Durst, Clemens Giselbrecht	https://doi.org/10.1111/caim.12227
6	Sustainability & Ethics	2019	Sustainability, FinTech, and financial inclusion	Connects fintech adoption with sustainable development and inclusion	Arner, D. W., Buckley, R. P., & Zetzsche, D. A.	https://doi.org/10.2139/ssrn.3387359
		2021	Fintech and SMEs sustainable business models: Reflections and considerations for a circular economy	Focuses on sustainable strategies integrated with digital business models	Pizzi, S., Corbo, L., & Caputo, A.	https://doi.org/10.1016/j.jclepro.2020.125217
		2021	The age of digital entrepreneurship	Analyzes challenges and sustainable opportunities in the digital era	Sahut, J. M., Iandoli, L., & Teulon, F.	https://doi.org/10.1007/s11187-019-00260-8

(continued)

Table 15.1 (continued)

Section	*Year*	*Study Title*	*Key Focus Area/ Findings*	*Author(s)*	*DOI*
	2018	Business models and business model innovation: Between wicked and paradigmatic problems	Discusses how digital business models shape ethical design	Foss, N. J., & Saebi, T.	https://doi.org/10.1016/j.lrp.2017.07.006
	2016	Understanding and tackling societal grand challenges through management research	Investigate hybrid business models promoting sustainability	George, G., Howard-Grenville, J., Joshi, A., & Tihanyi, L.	https://doi.org/10.5465/amj.2016.4007
	2019	Sustainability, FinTech and financial inclusion	We argue financial technology (FinTech) is the driver of financial inclusion and sustainability in modern financial systems	Douglas W. Arner; Ross P. Buckley; Dirk A. Zetzsche; Robin Veidt	https://doi.org/10.1007/s40804-020-00183-y
	2020	Startups in Times of Crisis—A Rapid Response to the COVID-19 Pandemic	Analyzes how startups adapt to crises through innovation and digital business models.	Andreas Kuckertz; Leif Brändle; Alicia Gaudig; Sebastian Hinderer	https://doi.org/10.1016/j.jbvi.2020.e00169
	2020	Business models shifts: Impact of Covid-19	Explores how firms transform business models in response to pandemic disruptions	P. Seetharaman	https://doi.org/10.1016/j.ijinfomgt.2020.102173
	2020	The economics of COVID-19: initial empirical evidence on how family firms in five European countries cope with the corona crisis	Discusses economic disruptions and the role of digital technologies during the pandemic	S. Kraus, T. Clauss, M. Breier, J. Gast, A. Zardini, V. Tiberius	https://doi.org/10.1016/j.jbusres.2020.10.016

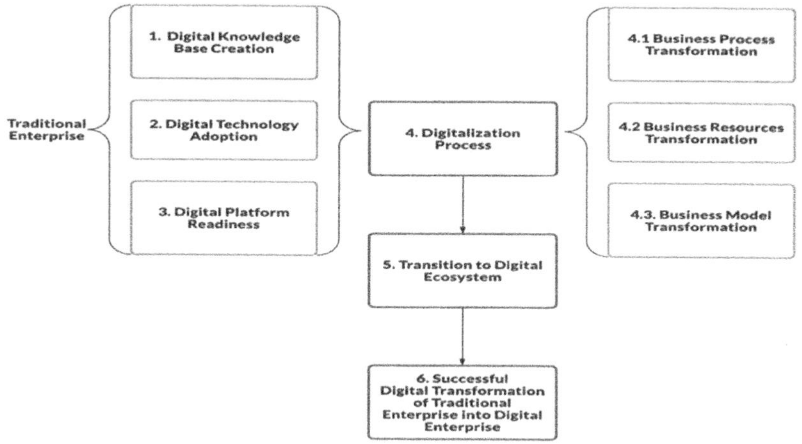

Fig. 15.1 Conceptual framework of digital entrepreneurship. (*Source* Paul et al., 2023)

demands. However, this linear representation of the process may underestimate the number of real-world practical challenges. Success in digital transformation demands parallel and simultaneous execution with regularly upgrading technology, regular training programs for employees, and evolving business processes. Truly, it also requires strong leadership and a commitment to continuous, adaptive technological changes.

Ultimately, this transformation is not merely about adopting digital tools but about innovative thinking, enterprise logic, fostering digital entrepreneurship, and creating sustainable competitive advantage in an increasingly digital economy.

Figure 15.2 The Digital Entrepreneurship Orientation Cycle represents an energetic and iterative process that captures the transformation from traditional model to digital entrepreneurial models. Digital entrepreneurship thrives on alertness, scalability, and platform-based ecosystems, in contrast to traditional entrepreneurship's roots in physical infrastructure, fixed locations, and linear traditional business practices.

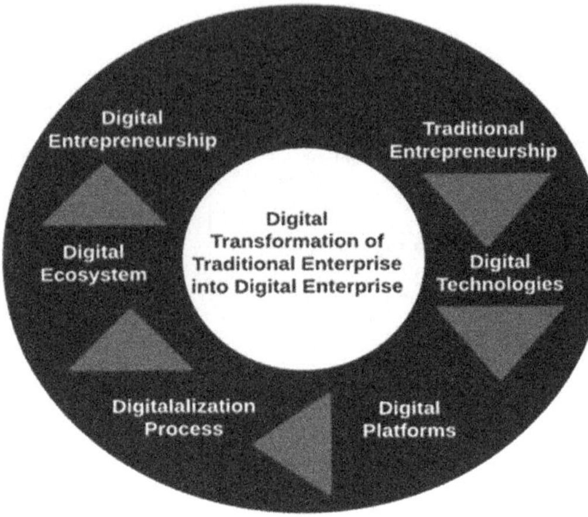

Fig. 15.2 Digital entrepreneurship orientation cycle. (*Source* Paul et al., 2023)

15.3.1 Key Characteristics of the Digital Entrepreneurship Orientation Cycle

1. Transformation from Physical to Digital Infrastructure:

Traditional entrepreneurs depend on assets tied to specific locations and face-to-face interactions with business stakeholders while digital entrepreneurs utilize AI, cloud computing, automation, and remote platforms such as Shopify and AWS to scale quickly and connect with global customers and vendors.

2. Business Model Reinvention:

Digital entrepreneurship encompasses more than just the adoption of tools, such as CRM software and ERP software. This requires reimagining business logic, including a shift from one-time product sales to subscription-based or service-based models.

3. Ecosystem Integration:

The digital orientation is highly ecosystem-dependent, requiring interoperability, proper API integration, and seamless digital platform connectivity. This interconnectedness accelerates growth, minimizes the physical effort, increases the efficiency, and sustainability in a competitive digital economy.

4. Transformation Enablers:
   - The process of digitalization acts as a catalyst for organizational change, embedding technology into core operations and enabling a smoother transition into digital models.
   - The cycle promotes the strategic adoption of innovation and disruptive technologies, reinforcing adaptability and future-readiness.

The Digital Entrepreneurship Orientation Cycle is not linear but cyclical and adaptive, emphasizing regular and consistent transformation. It demands a continuous commitment to innovation, platform integration, and strategic reorientation. Enterprises that successfully embrace this cycle can unlock scalable growth, improve market responsiveness, and sustain competitive advantage in the evolving digital landscape.

In comparison to a typical entrepreneurial business, starting a digital venture is simple, but high technical knowledge is required. It takes less time to create a website and digital platforms that sell already-existing products and services globally. Existing large corporations, such as Flipkart, eBay, and Amazon, and a number of other corporations, allow people to take advantage of the chances to establish small company operations quickly. This is due to the fact that many suppliers fall short in providing high-quality products and services, which hinders the success of digital entrepreneurship. This procedure creates challenges for ventures that are only partially digital, as some tasks require more labor. When a significant amount of work is required, businesses with lower entry capabilities may fail. Additionally, it may serve as inspiration for business owners whose ventures utilize digital technologies. Digital entrepreneurship leverages technological innovations to create, operate, and grow businesses in the digital realm. This approach is characterized by internet-based operations, agile methodologies, and a firm reliance on emerging technologies that are capable of minimizing the manufacturing cost along with the storage cost and handling cost.

15.4 Main Features of Digital Entrepreneurship

15.4.1 High reliance on technology and digital platforms/tools

Digital entrepreneurship is inherently based on the application of modern technology, both as a driver and facilitator of innovations in new tools of functioning. Cloud-based applications, artificial intelligence, blockchain, and IoT are not tools but pillars that enable technical entrepreneurs to build scalable, efficient, and innovative products and services. The dependence on technology has reduced the barrier to entry, and even small and new ventures/start-ups can play catch-up with big players by using leading-edge tools and platforms.

15.4.2 Internet-Based Business and International Accessibility

The internet has facilitated smooth access to global markets with low-cost interaction with a big customer base across different geographical boundaries. Operations over the internet allowed companies to tap into a vast market base, optimize supply chains, and distribute products or services online in the global market. This has brought higher growth of e-commerce, SaaS (Software as a Service), ERP and other online Business models that are transforming traditional sectors into tech-driven sectors. The internet also enables real-time communication with customer, collaboration, and customer interaction, which are essential for digital success.

15.4.3 Innovative and Agile Business Models for Functioning in the Global Market

A characteristic that distinguishes digital entrepreneurship is alertness. Digital entrepreneurs thrive on flexibility and adaptation to new technology on regular basis, in contrast to traditional enterprises that could rely on inflexible structures and long-term planning. They readily adapt their strategies, experiment with new ideas, and respond to consumer feedback or a change in the market. Such an adaptable strategy is particularly important in a high-tech, rapid-paced environment where customer preferences and fashions constantly changing with time.

15.4.4 *Transforming the Local and Global Economy*

Digital entrepreneurship is revolutionizing the local and international economy both, and it does not remain limited to specific industries. Now new markets have been opened, outsourcing business began, traditional Business models were turned upside down/renewed, and innovative ways of working, such as remote employment and the gig economy, have emerged. Cross-border commerce, access to healthcare and education, and financial inclusion have all been enabled by digital platforms. Moreover, the rise of digital entrepreneurship has driven economic growth, the establishment of new industries and competencies, and job creation worldwide.

15.5 Technological Drivers of Digital Entrepreneurship

15.5.1 *Artificial Intelligence (AI)*

Efficiency and Automation: Artificial Intelligence makes it possible for organizations to slash several expenditures substantially, maximize procedural efficiencies, and automate tedious operations within a very short time frame. In addition, using chatbots, online entrepreneurs can advance customer support infrastructures, and machine learning programs can help make supply chains more efficient.

Personalization: Modern AI-based data analytics enable businesses to provide personalized experiences that vary from product suggestions to individual customers according to their individual tastes and preferences, thus enabling targeted marketing campaigns on a regular basis.

Innovation: Currently, AI is helping to drive the creation of previously unforeseen products and services worldwide, such as autonomous systems, virtual assistants, and predictive analytics applications, thereby forming completely new markets globally.

Difficulties: To ensure that AI is implemented ethically, it is important to solve moral issues like biases in AI algorithms and job displacement.

15.5.2 *Internet of Things (IoT)*

Connected Ecosystems: The Internet of Things allows devices to be interconnected, which makes it possible for organizations to gather and analyze data in real time. This technology revolution is changing different industries such as manufacturing (smart factories), healthcare (wearable technology), and agriculture (precision farming).

Improved Customer Experiences: Currently, IoT devices, such as smart home appliances, provide businesses with valuable insights into consumer habits, thus enabling them to make improvements in products and services based on customer tests and preferences.

Operational Efficiency: The Internet of Things helps businesses with resource management, reducing downtime, and monitoring and optimizing entire processes in order to enhance efficiency levels.

Challenges: The implementation of Internet of Things has several major practical challenges, such as security vulnerabilities and data privacy issues.

15.5.3 Blockchain

Decentralization and Transparency: The blockchain decentralized framework ensures transparency and protection to customers, making it viable for uses like supply chain tracking, digital identity verification, and monetary transactions.

Smart Contracts: They are the self-executing contracts that mechanize and enforce obligations under contract, thus eliminating the need for intermediaries and minimizing transactional costs.

Cryptocurrencies and Fintech: Blockchain has revolutionized the financial sector fundamentally by allowing direct-to-direct payments and encouraging the growth of decentralized finance (DeFi).

Challenges: Operations scalability, uniform regulatory uncertainty, and energy usage are major barriers to the mass implementation of blockchain technology.

15.6 External Drivers of Digital Entrepreneurship

15.6.1 Globalization

15.6.1.1 Access to International Markets

E-commerce and digital platforms enable business people to access global customers, eradicating geographical barriers.

15.6.1.2 Talent and Cooperation
Globalization enables businesses to tap into a global talent pool and cooperate across borders, thus driving innovation and growth.

15.6.1.3 Competition and Innovation
The global nature of digital marketplaces naturally creates competitive forces that push entrepreneurs to innovate and differentiate their products and services.

15.6.2 Changing Consumer Behavior

15.6.2.1 Digital-First Mindset
Now young consumers of age group 20–35 desire to use digital modes of shopping, banking, entertainment, and communication, thus creating a demand for new digital offerings.

15.6.2.2 Convenience Demand
After COVID-19, the rise of on-demand services, including food delivery and streaming services, is an indicator of consumers' demand for instant access and convenience.

15.6.2.3 Sustainability and Ethics
Nowadays, consumers have become interested in sustainability and ethical practices while choosing products and services, which have given an impetus to create business models that keep sustainable and ethical practices at the center.

15.6.3 Government Support

15.6.3.1 Incentives and Policies
The government supports innovation through grants, rebates in taxation, and various funding schemes.

15.6.3.2 Digital Infrastructure
Ultra-speed internet connectivity, next-generation 5G networks, and smart city development initiatives help to create a favorable ecosystem for the growth of digital businesses.

15.6.3.3 Regulatory Frameworks

Governments led regulatory policies encourage the usage of disruptive technologies. They also help to address issues of privacy of data, cybersecurity, and intellectual property rights.

15.7 Challenges and Strategies

Digital entrepreneurship brings both immense opportunities and practical challenges since it has several technical and legal issues. Digital entrepreneurs face a unique set of challenges, such as intense competition, cybersecurity attacks, and ethical issues. These challenges require anticipatory approaches that involve differentiation, holistic security practices, and ethical behavior to achieve sustainable growth and a positive social contribution. By addressing these problems head-on, entrepreneurs can create robust businesses that thrive in the dynamic digital economy while maintaining trust and credibility with their customers and stakeholders. The key challenges, however, include technical competitiveness from the global business players, cybersecurity threats, and ethical issues that are unique to different nations. Careful and considerate managerial interventions and practices are required to ensure long-term success and a fair, positive societal impact. The difficulties are:

15.7.1 Intense Global Competition

The online environment has an extremely competitive character due to near-zero entry barriers, due to WTO agreements, worldwide availability, and rapid technological development in developed and developing countries. This results in an oversaturated market where companies have difficulty distinguishing themselves and remaining faithful to their customers.

15.7.1.1 Low Barriers to Entry

With little starting investment and the potential to utilize digital platforms, essentially anyone is capable of launching an online business, leading to waves of entrants into desired domains like e-commerce, Software as a Service (SaaS), and content creation.

15.7.1.2 Global Market Access

Whereas globalization stimulates growth globally, it also demands that entrepreneurs compete against businesses from around the world, oftentimes featuring strong institutions with extensive resources.

15.7.1.3 Regular and consistent Innovation

The high accelerated rate of technological progress forces every company to constantly innovate in order to remain appropriate and competitive in the global market. Businessmen are threatened by the possibility of being overtaken by competitors who have new technologies, growing technologies or business models more quickly to sustain in the market.

15.7.1.4 Strategies to Overcome Penetrating Competition

Entrepreneurs can differentiate themselves based on innovative value propositions, superior customer experiences, niche-focused marketing, and leveraging data-driven insights to stay ahead of the competition.

15.7.2 Cyber Security Threats

The digital entrepreneurs are heavily dependent on technology and data; they are increasingly susceptible to cyber-attacks, data breaches, and various security threats.

15.7.2.1 Data Breaches

Unauthorized access to confidential customer or organizational information can result in significant financial penalties, legal expenses, and reputational damage. For example, data breaches on e-commerce sites may expose customers' payment information, which potentially leading to cyber frauds.

15.7.2.2 Ransomware and Malware

Globally, cyber attackers are consistently targeting digital businesses with ransomware attacks. They now encrypt critical data and may ask for an extortion payment for its decryption. These can interfere with operations and pose a threat to sensitive information.

15.7.2.3 *Phishing and Social Engineering*

Through phishing methods, customers, employees, and clients can be targeted and exploited, tricked into revealing passwords or other sensitive information.

15.7.2.4 *Strategies to Counter Cybersecurity Threats*

Employees and customers need to be educated about these threats, and businesses need to develop effective cybersecurity solutions, such as data encryption, multi-factor authentication, firewalls, and regular security assessments as Airtel is practicing by informing the customer regarding fraud calls or spam calls.

15.7.3 *Ethical Considerations*

Digital entrepreneurs must navigate intricate ethical complexities when using technology, maintain data privacy, and create a positive societal impact. Failure to deal with these issues may lead to public disapproval, legal impacts, and damage to their credibility.

15.7.3.1 *Data Privacy and Customer Consent*

Collecting customers' data and using it may raise certain ethical questions of privacy and customer consent. Therefore, these organizations, while collecting personal information, are required to follow the General Data Protection Regulation (GDPR) and be transparent in their operations related to the type of information collected, stored, and used by them.

15.7.3.2 *Algorithmic Bias consideration*

Artificial Intelligence and Machine Learning algorithms have the potential to increase biases; therefore, it is necessary to design and regulate them carefully.

15.7.3.3 *Misinformation and Content Moderation*

Businesses that run on user-generated data need to strike a balance between free speech and false information.

15.7.3.4 *Environmental Impact*

The high energy consumption use of digital technologies, like data centers and blockchain networks, raises serious sustainability concerns.

Entrepreneurs must therefore ensure to incorporate environmentally friendly practices and technology in their systems.

15.7.3.5 Strategies to Meet Ethical Issues

Nowadays, credibility and trust in the business world are greatly improved when entrepreneurs are following ethical guidelines, regularly inspect their automated systems, are transparent with their consumers, and use sustainable methods. So, digital entrepreneurs need to develop frameworks on this ground.

15.8 Additional Challenges Faced by Digital Entrepreneurs

15.8.1 Global Governing Complexity

Keeping pace with the global shifts in rules about how data is kept private, how ideas are protected, and how commerce is done online presents a difficult challenge to entrepreneurs, especially those with new companies that have limited resources.

15.8.2 Talent Retention and Acquisition

The ever-rising demand for skilled human resources in areas like generative AI, machine learning, software development, and data science often creates shortages in supply. This poses a serious challenge to retaining a skilled team for a longer duration.

15.8.3 Funding and Cash Flow Management

The seeking of financial funding and cash flow management remains the most critical challenge, particularly for first-stage start-ups, which have unproven Business models.

15.8.4 Technological Obsolescence

Rapid technological development rapidly makes products or services obsolete, and therefore, continuous innovation and a flexible approach are highly required.

Table 15.2 SWOT analysis of digital entrepreneurs

Category	*Strengths*	*Weaknesses*	*Opportunities*	*Threats*
Technology	Agile adoption of AI/no-code tools	High dependency on third-party APIs	Rising open-source ecosystems	Cybersecurity breaches (e.g., API hacks)
Market Access	Global reach via digital platforms	Algorithmic volatility (e.g., SEO/SEO)	Emerging markets (e.g., Africa's fintech boom)	Platform policy changes (e.g., Apple's ATT)
Funding	Lower start-up costs (cloud, remote work)	Limited access to traditional VC	Revenue-based financing models	Economic downturns reduce ad spend
Talent	Remote global talent pools	High competition for skilled development	AI-augmented productivity tools	Burnout from "always-on" culture

15.9 SWOT Analysis of Digital Entrepreneurs

See Table 15.2.

15.10 Trends in Digital/ Technical Entrepreneurship

The path of the digital or technical entrepreneurs is shaped by the evolving and disruptive shifts in paradigms that incorporate innovative technologies, understanding and adapting to changing consumer trends, and also changes in social dynamics. The key trends are the rise of the metaverse, the intense focus on sustainability, and the spread of the creator economy.

15.10.1 The Ascendance of the Metaverse

The metaverse, as a virtual, networked digital environment, is quickly evolving into a new frontier for digital entrepreneurship. It quickly incorporates augmented reality (AR), virtual reality (VR), blockchain technology, machine learning, deep learning, and artificial intelligence (AI) to enable immersive, interactive experiences.

Recent Examples

- *Meta (formerly Facebook):* Meta has invested heavily in the metaverse, building VR platforms such as Horizon Worlds and acquiring VR hardware companies like Oculus. Mark Zuckerberg views the metaverse as the internet's next evolutionary step, creating changes in the industry where users can conduct innovative work, socialize, and play in virtual spaces with an enhanced entertainment experience.
- *Decentral and The Sandbox*: These virtual worlds, based on blockchain, allow users to buy, sell, and trade virtual property and assets using cryptocurrencies. Companies like Adidas, Samsung, and Atari have created virtual presence on such platforms to create differentiation in the market.
- *Gucci and Nike*: Leading fashion brands are entering the metaverse by selling designed virtual clothes and accessories for avatars. For example, Gucci sold a virtual handbag on Roblox for $4,115, which was higher than its real-life counterpart. Gucci generated new opportunities for fashion brands to think out of the box and establish a presence in the virtual world, with the opportunity to get a higher return.

Building virtual real estate, digital fashion, interactive gaming experiences, and hosting virtual events can be seen as opportunities for Entrepreneurs, along with offering tools and platforms for developing and maintaining metaverse experiences, such as VR/AR hardware and software. However, challenges may include high development costs and complex technical requirements, as well as uncertainty in regulatory environments for virtual assets globally, and similarly for financial transactions.

15.10.2 The Critical Emphasis on Sustainability

Consistent sustainability has moved from the periphery to the core of the agenda for digital entrepreneurs. Now, consumers have become more vigilant and knowledgeable, so consumers, investors, and governments are increasingly focusing on environmentally sustainable and socially responsible business practices.

Recent Examples

- *Too Good To Go*: This app brings consumers together with restaurants and grocery stores to buy excess food at reduced prices, thus by doing this they reduced the food waste. It has helped save millions of meals globally and has spread its wings to various nations.

- *Allbirds:* A green footwear company using sustainable resources like merino wool and foam from sugarcane to attract green consumers towards their products and services. Allbirds has utilized online marketing and digital commerce efforts to increase the attention of green consumers.
- *Microsoft's AI for Earth:* The program uses artificial intelligence to understand environmental challenges like climate change and biodiversity loss by giving funding and access to resources to entrepreneurs and scientists.

The development of green technologies, such as renewable energy platforms, carbon footprint measuring applications, and circular economy projects, may bring Entrepreneurial opportunities in the development of sustainable goods and services responding to eco-minded consumers.

15.10.3 The creator economy

It includes the ecosystem of independent creators, influencers, and online entrepreneurs who monetize their talent and creativity using platforms like YouTube, TikTok, Patreon, and Substack.

Recent Examples

· *MrBeast (Jimmy Donaldson)*: Perhaps the most famous YouTuber, Mr Beast has built a large following by creating fantastic, philanthropic content. His brand has expanded to encompass gaming, merchandising, and even a chain of virtual restaurants known as Mr Beast Burger.

· *Patreon*: Using this platform, artists can give paying supporters access to exclusive material and experiences. Artists, musicians, and podcasters use Patreon to build a loyal base of supporters and receive a steady income.

· *NFT Artists*: Using blockchain technology, digital artists like Beeple (Mike Winkelmann) have transformed how creators sell their work by selling NFTs (non-fungible tokens) for millions of dollars.

Building platforms and tools, such as content management systems, payment channels, and analytics software, to support creators can bring entrepreneurial opportunities; however, dependence on platforms, as artists often rely on external platforms that can modify their rules or algorithms, can pose challenges.

15.11 Recent International and National Case Studies & Interviews of Successful Digital Entrepreneurs

Recent case studies of International and national digital entrepreneurs who set milestones in the global business world.

15.11.1 International case studies

Amazon started as an enormous online retailer for businesses, selling a massive selection of products from office supplies to industrial machinery. Just as with standard Amazon, businesses enjoy sweet benefits such as free 2-day shipping on larger orders and exclusive discounts. This was a master stroke on the part of Amazon. It enabled them to venture into the humongous wholesale market, worth trillions of dollars in the U.S. alone. They earn their revenues by charging a small percentage (6–15%) from other businesses that sell their goods under Amazon Business. It's all about making business shopping as easy and convenient as your individual shopping.

Unilever, a global leader in consumer products, implemented Workday HCM to streamline and unify its HR operations. With over 3 billion transactions handled weekly by this company's vast digital infrastructure, ongoing digital transformation is an essential yet challenging task. Unilever partnered with Berkeley to adopt a new HR IT strategy that modernized its core HR platform, enhanced the functionality of its L&D software, and streamlined people management for more than 174,000 employees in 90 countries. This was done in order to align its HR operations with growth objectives.

15.11.2 National case studies

Bhavish Aggarwal (Promoter of Ola & Krutrim): In 2025, Bhavish Aggarwal created history by promoting a "Made in India" AI ecosystem through Krutrim, which focuses on creating Large Language Models (LLMs) that are specific to India. He overcame linguistic hurdles by acknowledging the necessity of vernacular AI, promoting AI sovereignty to aid in national digital self-reliance. By providing highly customized user experiences at scale, he further integrated Krutrim's AI capabilities throughout Ola's vast mobility and energy platforms.

Siya Kapoor (Promter MedGenie): With MedGenie, an AI-driven diagnostics system and digital platform driven by clever algorithms, Siya Kapoor is transforming diagnostic healthcare. Her invention upended conventional lab models and reduced the gap in healthcare between urban and rural areas by making testing quicker, cheaper, and more accessible, particularly in underprivileged rural communities. By combining telemedicine and diagnostics and using data to generate insights into public health, she is now broadening MedGenie's reach.

Rohan Iyer (Promoter SkillUp): With SkillUp, an online learning platform that focuses on providing in-demand, employable skills, Rohan is taking graduate unemployment head-on. SkillUp seeks to democratize access to high-quality education beyond traditional degrees by fusing virtual collaborative tools with digital course delivery. Looking ahead, the platform is forming key alliances to promote widespread worker up-skilling and incorporating cutting-edge technology like virtual reality (VR) to offer immersive, adaptive learning experiences.

NishaVerma (Promoter CodeMate): With CodeMate, an AI-powered B2B platform that automates code reviews, debugging, and security checks, NishaVerma is revolutionizing the software development industry. She is revolutionizing the way that modern software is developed and putting India at the forefront of AI-driven development tools by increasing developer efficiency and guaranteeing quality and security at scale. She is currently extending CodeMate's AI capabilities throughout the whole software development lifecycle and providing customized solutions to meet a range of industry demands.

Aadit Palicha & Kaivalya Vohra (Promoters Zepto): By incorporating hyper-local digital marketing, superior logistics optimization, and predictive AI into Zepto's operations, both Zepto promoters are revolutionizing fast e-commerce. They have shown that rapid commerce can be profitable even when it comes to more than just groceries by using AI-driven inventory control and route optimization. Their quick expansion into Tier 2 and Tier 3 cities has been made possible by their data-driven strategy. They are now concentrating on expanding Zepto's product line to include more items beyond just everyday essentials.

Dr. Rhea Sharma (Promoter Neuro Connect): With Neuro Connect, an AI-powered platform that uses Natural Language Processing (NLP) to provide individualized, digital mental health care, Dr. Rhea Sharma is trying to close the gap in mental health. Her approach provides scalable, discreet, and easily accessible therapy, having a significant societal impact, particularly in marginalized populations. She is contributing to the development of preventative mental health initiatives, more focused therapies, and more comprehensive public health insights by analyzing aggregated data.

Arjun Desai (Promoter Agri Vision AI): With the use of satellite photos and AI-powered drones, Arjun is revolutionizing Indian agriculture by providing farmers with hyper-local insights through a mobile app. His invention optimizes resource utilization, boosts yields, and encourages sustainable, intelligent farming methods by giving smallholder farmers the ability to make data-driven decisions. In order to increase resilience and production, Agri Vision AI is now branching out into predictive analytics for weather forecasting and market trends, as well as integrating with automated farm equipment.

MeeraSanyal (Promoter Crafts Bazaar): Through Crafts Bazaar, an online marketplace that links craftspeople with international markets through Web3 technologies like blockchain for safe payments and NFTs for provenance, she is fusing tradition and technology. She's using digital innovation to preserve cultural heritage and increase artisan incomes by guaranteeing transparency, authenticity, and global reach. In order to increase customer involvement and appreciation, the platform is currently growing its network of crafts and producers and creating immersive digital experiences.

Vikram Singh & Priya Rao (Promoter EcoSwap): With EcoSwap, a digital marketplace that uses AI for intelligent item classification, dynamic pricing, and effective matching of secondhand products and materials, both are advancing the circular economy. They are cutting waste, carbon footprints, and opening up new micro-business opportunities by making reuse more commonplace. To further speed up sustainable commerce, EcoSwap is now branching out into intricate industrial waste streams and enabling direct business-to-business transactions.

Recent Interviews

1. Lucy Guo—Co-Founder of Passes *(Age: 30, now the youngest self-made female billionaire). In her interview for the New York Post, dated 20 July 2025, she said,* "I feel like the title changes every year." Guosaidin her interview about the Forbes magazine ranking. "It means almost nothing to me personally," She shared. She climbed from early roles at Facebook, Snapchat, and Quora, to co-founding **Scale AI**, and later launching **Passes.** A creator monetization platform now serving thousands and enabling millions in creator earnings. She is known for her mantra, **"Act broke, stay rich."** Guo emphasizes disciplined growth and product-first thinking despite entering billionaire status.

2. Divyesh Patel—Founder & CEO, Radixweb (*celebrating 25 years in business in 2025*)

In an interview with the India Times dated 15 July 2025, he said how Radixweb transformed into an AI-first innovation company, balancing ethical AI frameworks (RxWeb, TezJS) with long-term sustainability. He stressed clarity over trend-chasing, responsible tech, and inclusive innovation through open developer tools and community engagement.

3. Aravind Srinivas—CEO & Co-Founder, Perplexity (*Leading a $14B AI-powered search startup*) In a talk at Combinator's AI Startup School on 19 July 2025 Srinivas said "Sleeping with fear that your competitor will steal your idea is key to the success." He credits this mindset for Perplexity's rapid ascent, positioning it as a compelling challenger to giants like Google and OpenAI. Published at TOI Tech Desk/ The Times of India/Updated on 20 July, 2025.

4. Kim Perell—Serial Entrepreneur and Mentor (*Sold her digital ad agency for $20 M by age 30*). In an interview on 18 July 2025, Perell recounted building her agency from a $10 K loan. Her story emphasizes risk-taking, normalization of failure, and the power of perseverance. She now mentors founders while balancing family life and career aspirations.

5. Dolly Chaiwala—Viral Tea Vendor Turned Franchise (Founder *of "Dolly Ki Tapri"*)

A profile published in The Economic Times dated 21 July 2025 describes Dolly's rapid shift from local street-side tea fame to a national franchise. Within 48 hours of launching, the brand received over 1,600 franchise applications. Financial educator AkshatShrivastava cautioned against viewing such viral successes as standard startup templates, emphasizing structured planning and sustainability.

6. Anupam Mittal—Founder of Shaadi.com & Shark Tank India Judge (Viral *LinkedIn reflections on unconventional startup paths*) A post by AnupamMittal exposed how he launched Shaadi.com *with no money, no plan, and no safety net*. Mittal highlights resilience and boldness, advocating for embracing unorthodox risk-taking as a route to exponential growth. Published at The Economic Times dated 07 June 2025.

15.12 Discussion

Innovation is intrinsic to digital entrepreneurship, often acting as a driver of new technological and related developments. Here, entrepreneurs are at the forefront of adopting and developing newer technologies such as 5G, blockchain, AI, and the Internet of Things. These technologies create new markets, disrupt existing industries, and enable novel Business models around the world. As an example, companies like SpaceX (space exploration) and Tesla (electric vehicles) have their origins in technology entrepreneurship but primarily depend on digital platforms for innovation, data analysis, and operational effectiveness. Through innovation that drives the boundaries of what is possible and sets the stage for broader adoption, digital entrepreneurs are often the first to pilot and ramp up new technologies for expansion and greater returns within a short time frame. To translate technology innovations into functional solutions, the digital entrepreneurs are needed who can address critical problems in the real world. They use digital platforms to identify market opportunities to create products and services that can meet with evolving customer demands. For instance, the Ola, Uber, and Airbnb took advantage of digital technologies to remove inefficiencies of existing Business models of transportation and hospitality industries, respectively, and created new value propositions. Digital entrepreneurs through their sincere efforts ensure that these technological developments utilized to promote growth and progress in the economy. The transformation has helped to transcend national boundaries and has helped these organizations extend their business operations globally. Firms such as Shopify had made small business to access global markets by allowing them to set up their online stores and sell their products in international markets. More and more, people are reaching to online platforms and buying things and using services online. They like to be things tailored for them. This shift in consumer behavior provides online business owners with a chance to make stuff that people want. Digital entrepreneurship offers numerous benefits, but at the same time, numerous risks, such as ethical dilemmas, concerns related to the privacy of data, and risks associated with cybersecurity. These challenges need to be addressed considerably to enjoy success in the long run. The advent of AI has fueled the debate regarding algorithmic bias and the shortening of jobs, prompting entrepreneurs to develop moral codes and transparent procedures. Addressing these issues is crucial for maintaining public trust and ensuring that digital entrepreneurship is good for society.

Technological entrepreneurship and digital entrepreneurship go hand in hand. Digital entrepreneurship uses them to develop new, scalable Business models, while technological entrepreneurship is about creating and bringing to market new technologies. As an example, the metaverse is a product of technology entrepreneurship (advances in blockchain, VR, and AR), but is also created by digital entrepreneurs creating virtual communities, marketplaces, and experiences. This partnership ensures that technological advances are effectively integrated into the economy and stimulates innovation.

15.13 Conclusion and Recommendation

Digital entrepreneurship is the foundation of today's economy, powering innovation, solving global problems, and redefining business for the future. Its power is its capacity to respond to changing technology trends, consumer preferences, and international markets. Through the use of digital technologies and tools, entrepreneurs are not just generating wealth for themselves but also contributing to general economic and social development. But to unleash its full capability, digital entrepreneurship has to prioritize ethical issues and challenges so its influence is encompassing, lasting, and constructive for everyone. In the bigger picture of techno entrepreneurship, digital entrepreneurship serves to connect innovation to market use and plays a pivotal role in what industries are indeed incorporated into the economy. Online entrepreneurship presents unlimited opportunities for expansion; entrepreneurs need to operate in a highly competitive market, face risks to security, and address ethical issues. A successful business hinges on harnessing the advancement of technology, market trends, and adjusting to regulatory conditions while upholding ethical business practices. Digital entrepreneurship is constantly changing, driven by emerging trends that transform business models and consumer experiences. Some of the most important trends are the growth of the metaverse, the focus on sustainability, and the growth of the creator economy.

To foster robust digital entrepreneurship in today's fast-evolving tech ecosystem, a multi-stakeholder approach is essential. The following recommendations outline strategic actions for various actors supporting digital ventures:

15.13.1 Tech Entrepreneurs (SaaS, AI, Dev Tools)

- **Adopt Product-Led Growth**: Offer freemium models (e.g., Slack, Notion) and in-app upselling to drive organic user acquisition.
- **Optimize Tech Stack**: Leverage server less architecture (e.g., AWS Lambda, Vercel) and open-source analytics tools (e.g., PostHog).
- **Use Data to Reduce Churn**: Track feature engagement and implement personalized onboarding.
- **Build Developer Communities**: Engage on platforms like GitHub and Hacker News, and contribute content/tools to build trust and visibility.

15.13.2 Investors in Tech Start-ups

- **Support Vertical SaaS**: Back niche solutions targeting specific industries (e.g., Toast for restaurants).
- **Fund Critical Infrastructure**: Invest in "unsexy" but vital areas like compliance, security, and B2B SaaS.
- **Embrace Global Talent**: Prioritize remote-first teams, especially in emerging tech hubs like Ukraine and Nigeria.

15.13.3 Governments and Policymakers

- **Provide Cloud Credit Subsidies**: Support programs like Start-up India to lower entry barriers for founders.
- **Accelerate Tech Visas**: Adopt models like Canada's Global Talent Stream to attract global experts.
- **Enact Ethical AI Regulation**: Clarify data and IP rights early to ensure innovation with accountability.

15.13.4 Universities & Tech Educators

- **Promote Practical Learning**: Focus on startup launching skills; require capstone projects to deploy real MVPs.
- **Bridge AILiteracy Gaps**: Teach not only the usage of AI tools, but also fine-tuning and development of LLMs.

15.13.5 Corporates (Tech Partnerships)

- **Adopt API-First Strategies**: Build open ecosystems, similar to Stripe's API model, to foster third-party innovation.
- **Pursue Strategic Acqui-Hiring**: Acquire startups for their talent and IP, as seen in deals like Google–DeepMind.

15.13.6 Incubators & Accelerators

- **Focus on "Zero to IPO" Metrics**: Train founders on fundraising readiness, cap tables, and unit economics.
- **Run Mock Technical Diligence**: Stress-test codebase scalability and readiness before demo day.

References

Arner, D. W., Buckley, R. P., Zetzsche, D. A., & Veidt, R. (2019). Sustainability, FinTech and financial inclusion. https://doi.org/10.2139/ssrn.3387359, https://doi.org/10.1007/s40804-020-00183-y

Berger, E. S., Von Briel, F., Davidsson, P., & Kuckertz, A. (2021). Digital or not–The future of entrepreneurship and innovation: Introduction to the special issue. *Journal of Business Research, 125*, 436–442. https://doi.org/10.1016/j.jbusres.2019.12.020

Bharadwaj, A., El Sawy, O. A., Pavlou, P. A., & Venkatraman, N. V. (2013). Digital business strategy: Toward a next generation of insights. *MIS Quarterly, 37*(2), 471–482. https://doi.org/10.25300/MISQ/2013/37:2.3

Bouncken, R. B., Kraus, S., & Roig-Tierno, N. (2021). Knowledge-and innovation-based business models for future growth: Digitalized business models and portfolio considerations. *Review of Managerial Science, 15*(1), 1–14. https://doi.org/10.1007/s11846-019-00366-z

Breuer, H., & Lüdeke-Freund, F. (2017). Values-based network and business model innovation. *International Journal of Innovation Management, 21*(03), 1750028. https://doi.org/10.1142/S1363919617500281

Chalmers, D., MacKenzie, N. G., & Carter, S. (2021). Artificial intelligence and entrepreneurship: Implications for venture creation in the fourth industrial revolution. *Entrepreneurship Theory and Practice, 45*(5), 1028–1053. https://doi.org/10.1177/1042258720934581

Dato-on, M. C., Banerjee, S., & Banerjee, P. (2022). Exploring influences on social entrepreneurial intentions among Indian students: The function of gender role orientation. *International Journal of Indian Culture and Business Management, 27*(4), 488–509. https://doi.org/10.1504/IJICBM.2022.127727

Davidson, E., & Vaast, E. (2010, January). Digital entrepreneurship and its sociomaterial enactment. In *2010 43rd Hawaii international conference on system sciences* (pp. 1–10). IEEE. https://doi.org/10.1109/HICSS.2010.150

Elia, G., Margherita, A., & Passiante, G. (2020). Digital entrepreneurship ecosystem: How digital technologies and collective intelligence are reshaping the entrepreneurial process. *Technological Forecasting and Social Change, 150*, 119791. https://doi.org/10.1016/j.jbusres.2019.05.021

Eshima, Y., & Anderson, B. S. (2017). Firm growth, adaptive capability, and entrepreneurial orientation. *Strategic Management Journal, 38*(3), 770–779. https://doi.org/10.1002/smj.2532

Felicetti, A. M., Ammirato, S., Linzalone, R., & Quinto, I. (2025). A conceptual framework for asymmetric collaborations between startups and big corporations in digital innovation ecosystems. *European Journal of Innovation Management*, 1–33. https://doi.org/10.1108/EJIM-01-2025-0022

Fernandes, A. J., Ferreira, J. J., Fernandes, C. I., & Kraus, S. (2024). Digital entrepreneurship: Theoretical foundations, methods, and trends. *Foundations and Trends in Entrepreneurship, 20*(6), 574–678. https://doi.org/10.1561/0300000122

Foss, N. J., & Saebi, T. (2018). Business models and business model innovation: Between wicked and paradigmatic problems. *Long Range Planning, 51*(1), 9–21. https://doi.org/10.1016/j.lrp.2017.07.006

Gawer, A., & Cusumano, M. A. (2014). Industry platforms and ecosystem innovation. *Journal of Product Innovation Management, 31*(3), 417–433. https://doi.org/10.1111/jpim.12105

Geissinger, A., Laurell, C., Sandström, C., Eriksson, K., & Nykvist, R. (2019). Digital entrepreneurship and field conditions for institutional change–Investigating the enabling role of cities. *Technological Forecasting and Social Change, 146*, 877–886. https://doi.org/10.1016/j.techfore.2018.06.019

George, G., & Bock, A. J. (2011). The business model in practice and its implications for entrepreneurship research. *Entrepreneurship Theory and Practice, 35*(1), 83–111. https://doi.org/10.1111/j.1540-6520.2010.0042

George, G., Howard-Grenville, J., Joshi, A., & Tihanyi, L. (2016). Understanding and tackling societal grand challenges through management research. *Academy of Management Journal, 59*(6), 1880–1895. https://doi.org/10.5465/amj.2016.4007

Ghezzi, A., & Cavallo, A. (2020). Agile business model innovation in digital entrepreneurship: Lean startup approaches. *Journal of Business Research, 110*, 519–537. https://doi.org/10.1016/j.jbusres.2018.06.013

Hair, N., Wetsch, L. R., Hull, C. E., Perotti, V., & Hung, Y. T. C. (2012). Market orientation in digital entrepreneurship: Advantages and challenges in a web 2.0 networked world. *International Journal of Innovation and Technology Management, 9*(06), 1250045. https://doi.org/10.1142/S0219877012500459

Huang, M. H., & Rust, R. T. (2022). A framework for collaborative artificial intelligence in marketing. *Journal of Retailing, 98*(2), 209–223. https://doi.org/10.1016/j.jretai.2021.03.001

Huang, M. H., Rust, R., & Maksimovic, V. (2019). The feeling economy: Managing in the next generation of artificial intelligence (AI). *California Management Review, 61*(4), 43–65. https://doi.org/10.1177/0008125619863436

Hudders, L., De Jans, S., & De Veirman, M. (2021). The commercialization of social media stars: A literature review and conceptual framework on the strategic use of social media influencers. *Social Media Influencers in Strategic Communication*, 24–67. https://doi.org/10.4324/9781003181286

Hull, C. E. K., Hung, Y. T. C., Hair, N., Perotti, V., & DeMartino, R. (2007). Taking advantage of digital opportunities: A typology of digital entrepreneurship. *International Journal of Networking and Virtual Organisations, 4*(3), 290–303. https://doi.org/10.1504/IJNVO.2007.015166

Kraus, S., Clauss, T., Breier, M., Gast, J., Zardini, A., & Tiberius, V. (2020). The economics of COVID-19: Initial empirical evidence on how family firms in five European countries cope with the corona crisis. *International Journal of Entrepreneurial Behavior & Research, 26*(5), 1067–1092. https://doi.org/10.1108/IJEBR-04-2020-0214

Kraus, S., Jones, P., Kailer, N., Weinmann, A., Chaparro-Banegas, N., & Roig-Tierno, N. (2021). Digital transformation: An overview of the current state of the art of research. *Sage Open, 11*(3), 21582440211047576. https://doi.org/10.1177/21582440211047576

Kuckertz, A., Brändle, L., Gaudig, A., Hinderer, S., Reyes, C. A. M., Prochotta, A.,... & Berger, E. S. (2020). Startups in times of crisis–A rapid response to the COVID-19 pandemic. *Journal of Business Venturing Insights,* 13, e00169. https://doi.org/10.1016/j.jbvi.2020.e00169

Li, L., Su, F., Zhang, W., & Mao, J. Y. (2018). Digital transformation by SME entrepreneurs: A capability perspective. *Information Systems Journal, 28*(6), 1129–1157. https://doi.org/10.1111/isj.12153

Lyytinen, K., Yoo, Y., & Boland Jr, R. J. (2016). Digital product innovation within four classes of innovation networks. *Information Systems Journal, 26*(1), 47–75. https://doi.org/10.1111/isj.12093

Melo, I. C., Queiroz, G. A., Junior, P. N. A., de Sousa, T. B., Yushimito, W. F., & Pereira, J. (2023). Sustainable digital transformation in small and medium enterprises (SMEs): A review on performance. *Heliyon, 9*(3). https://doi.org/10.1016/j.heliyon.2023.e13908

Meng, F., & Wang, W. (2023). The impact of digitalization on enterprise value creation: An empirical analysis of Chinese manufacturing enterprises. *Journal of Innovation & Knowledge, 8*(3), 100385. https://doi.org/10.1016/j.jik.2023.100385

Modgil, S., Dwivedi, Y. K., Rana, N. P., Gupta, S., & Kamble, S. (2022). Has Covid-19 accelerated opportunities for digital entrepreneurship? An Indian perspective. *Technological Forecasting and Social Change, 175*, 121415. https://doi.org/10.1016/j.techfore.2021.121415

Modgil, S., & Singh, R. K. (2025). Blockchain-enabled value creation for circular supply chain in the tyre industry. *The International Journal of Logistics Management, 36*(3), 1014–1033. https://doi.org/10.1108/IJLM-08-2023-0350

Nambisan, S. (2017). Digital entrepreneurship: Toward a digital technology perspective of entrepreneurship. *Entrepreneurship Theory and Practice, 41*(6), 1029–1055. https://doi.org/10.1111/etap.12254

Nambisan, S., & Baron, R. A. (2021). On the costs of digital entrepreneurship: Role conflict, stress, and venture performance in digital platform-based ecosystems. *Journal of Business Research, 125*, 520–532. https://doi.org/10.1016/j.jbusres.2019.06.037

Nambisan, S., & Luo, Y. (2021). Toward a loose coupling view of digital globalization. *Journal of International Business Studies, 52*(8), 1646–1663. https://doi.org/10.1057/s41267-021-00446-x

Nambisan, S., Lyytinen, K., & Yoo, Y. (2020). Digital innovation: Towards a transdisciplinary perspective. In *Handbook of digital innovation* (pp. 2–12). Edward Elgar Publishing. https://doi.org/10.1016/j.respol.2019.03.018

Nambisan, S., Wright, M., & Feldman, M. (2019). The digital transformation of innovation and entrepreneurship: Progress, challenges and key themes. *Research Policy, 48*(8), 103773. https://doi.org/10.1016/j.respol.2019.03.018

Nambisan, S., Zahra, S. A., & Luo, Y. (2019). Global platforms and ecosystems: Implications for international business theories. *Journal of International Business Studies, 50*(9), 1464–1486. https://doi.org/10.1057/s41267-019-00262-4

Omerovic Smajlovic, M. (2024). Strategic implications of digital transformation: Navigating the evolution of traditional organisations through sustainable and agile practices (Doctoral dissertation)

Ononiwu, M., Azonuche, T. I., Okoh, O. F., & Enyejo, J. O. (2023). AI-driven predictive analytics for customer retention in e-commerce platforms using real-time behavioral tracking. *International Journal of Scientific Research and Modern Technology, 2*(8), 17–31. https://doi.org/10.38124/ijsrmt.v2i8.561

Osei, L. K., Cherkasova, Y., & Oware, K. M. (2023). Unlocking the full potential of digital transformation in banking: A bibliometric review and emerging trend. *Future Business Journal, 9*(1), 30. https://doi.org/10.1186/s43093-023-00207-2

Pappas, I. O., Mikalef, P., Giannakos, M. N., Krogstie, J., & Lekakos, G. (2018). Big data and business analytics ecosystems: Paving the way towards digital transformation and sustainable societies. *Information Systems and E-business Management, 16*(3), 479–491. https://doi.org/10.1007/s10257-018-0377-z

Paul, J., Alhassan, I., Binsaif, N., & Singh, P. (2023). Digital entrepreneurship research: A systematic review. *Journal of Business Research, 156*, 113507. https://doi.org/10.1016/j.jbusres.2022.113507

Pizzi, S., Corbo, L., & Caputo, A. (2021). Fintech and SMEs sustainable business models: Reflections and considerations for a circular economy. *Journal of Cleaner Production, 281*, 125217. https://doi.org/10.1016/j.jclepro.2020.125217

Reuber, A. R., & Fischer, E. (2011). International entrepreneurship in internet-enabled markets. *Journal of Business Venturing, 26*(6), 660–679. https://doi.org/10.1016/j.jbusvent.2011.05.002

Richter, C., Kraus, S., Brem, A., Durst, S., & Giselbrecht, C. (2017). Digital entrepreneurship: Innovative business models for the sharing economy. *Creativity and Innovation Management, 26*(3), 300–310. https://doi.org/10.1111/caim.12227

Rippa, P., & Secundo, G. (2019). Digital academic entrepreneurship: The potential of digital technologies on academic entrepreneurship. *Technological Forecasting and Social Change, 146*, 900–911. https://doi.org/10.1016/j.techfore.2018.07.013

Saebi, T., & Foss, N. J. (2015). Business models for open innovation: Matching heterogeneous open innovation strategies with business model dimensions. *European Management Journal, 33*(3), 201–213. https://doi.org/10.1016/j.emj.2014.11.002

Sahut, J. M., Iandoli, L., & Teulon, F. (2021). The age of digital entrepreneurship. *Small Business Economics, 56*(3), 1159–1169. https://doi.org/10.1007/s11187-019-00260-8

Santoro, G., Mazzoleni, A., Quaglia, R., & Solima, L. (2021). Does age matter? The impact of SMEs age on the relationship between knowledge sourcing strategy and internationalization. *Journal of Business Research, 128*, 779–787. https://doi.org/10.1016/j.jbusres.2019.05.021

Scuotto, V., Del Giudice, M., Bresciani, S., & Meissner, D. (2017). Knowledge-driven preferences in informal inbound open innovation modes. An explorative view on small to medium enterprises. *Journal of Knowledge Management, 21*(3), 640–655. https://doi.org/10.1108/JKM-10-2016-0465

Scuotto, V., Ferraris, A., & Bresciani, S. (2016). Internet of Things: Applications and challenges in smart cities: A case study of IBM smart city projects. *Business Process Management Journal, 22*(2), 357–367. https://doi.org/10.1108/BPMJ-05-2015-0074

Sedera, D., & Lokuge, S. (2017). The role of enterprise systems in innovation in the contemporary organization. In *The Routledge companion to management information systems* (pp. 276–289). Routledge. https://doi.org/10.4324/9781315619361

Seetharaman, P. (2020). Business models shifts: Impact of Covid-19. *International Journal of Information Management, 54*, 102173. https://doi.org/10.1016/j.ijinfomgt.2020.102173

Shao, Q., Lin, J., Liou, J. J., Zhu, D., & Tzeng, G. H. (2025). Analysis of key factors affecting the digital transformation of small and medium-sized manufacturing enterprises in China. *Sage Open, 15*(2), 21582440251336077. https://doi.org/10.1177/21582440251336077

Shukla, A., Kushwah, P., Jain, E., & Sharma, S. K. (2021). Role of ICT in emancipation of digital entrepreneurship among new generation women. *Journal of Enterprising Communities: People and Places in the Global Economy, 15*(1), 137–154. https://doi.org/10.1108/JEC-04-2020-0071

Steininger, D. M. (2019). Linking information systems and entrepreneurship: A review and agenda for IT-associated and digital entrepreneurship research. *Information Systems Journal, 29*(2), 363–407. https://doi.org/10.1111/isj.12206

Sussan, F., & Acs, Z. J. (2017). The digital entrepreneurial ecosystem. *Small Business Economics, 49*(1), 55–73. https://doi.org/10.1007/s11187-017-9867-5

Täuscher, K., & Abdelkafi, N. (2017). Visual tools for business model innovation: Recommendations from a cognitive perspective. *Creativity and Innovation Management, 26*(2), 160–174. https://doi.org/10.1111/caim.12208

Tavoletti, E., Kazemargi, N., Cerruti, C., Grieco, C., & Appolloni, A. (2022). Business model innovation and digital transformation in global management consulting firms. *European Journal of Innovation Management, 25*(6), 612–636. https://doi.org/10.1108/EJIM-11-2020-0443

Teece, D. J. (2018). Business models and dynamic capabilities. *Long Range Planning, 51*(1), 40–49. https://doi.org/10.1016/j.lrp.2017.06.007

Wamba, S. F., Gunasekaran, A., Akter, S., Ren, S. J. F., Dubey, R., & Childe, S. J. (2019). Big data analytics and firm performance: Effects of dynamic capabilities. *Journal of Business Research, 70*, 356–365. https://doi.org/10.1016/j.jbusres.2016.08.009

Xiao, H., Yang, Z., & Hu, Y. (2021). Influencing mechanism of strategic flexibility on corporate performance: The mediating role of business model innovation. *Asia Pacific Business Review, 27*(3), 470–492. https://doi.org/10.1080/13602381.2021.1896256

Yli-Huumo, J., Ko, D., Choi, S., Park, S., & Smolander, K. (2016). Where is current research on blockchain technology?—A systematic review. *PloS One, 11*(10), e0163477. https://doi.org/10.1371/journal.pone.0163477

Yoo, Y., Boland Jr, R. J., Lyytinen, K., & Majchrzak, A. (2012). Organizing for innovation in the digitized world. *Organization Science, 23*(5), 1398–1408. https://doi.org/10.1287/orsc.1120.0771

Yoo, Y., Henfridsson, O., & Lyytinen, K. (2010). Research commentary—the new organizing logic of digital innovation: An agenda for information systems research. *Information Systems Research, 21*(4), 724–735. https://doi.org/10.1287/isre.1100.0322

Zaheer, H., Breyer, Y., & Dumay, J. (2019). Digital entrepreneurship: An interdisciplinary structured literature review and research agenda. *Technological Forecasting and Social Change, 148*, 119735. https://doi.org/10.1016/j.techfore.2019.119735

Index

A
Access to capital, 54, 81, 108, 109, 300
Access to technology, 55, 72, 174
Adjustment, 14
Adjustment speed, 98, 99, 101
Adoption behavior, 13, 71
AI-driven analytics, 39
AI-driven applications, 20, 123
AI governance, 16
AI Regulation, 375
Algorithmic decision-making, 7
Artificial Intelligence (AI), v, 1–7, 9–11, 13–16, 18, 20, 22, 23, 29–45, 51–56, 58–73, 82, 90–92, 113, 122–138, 149, 153–155, 161, 167, 173, 174, 198, 210, 211, 216–219, 221–223, 225–230, 232, 234, 237–239, 248, 271–276, 278–281, 283, 285–292, 298, 299, 320, 322, 328, 330–332, 339, 356, 358, 359, 364, 365, 366, 368–373, 375
Artificial Intelligence Startups, 137
Augmented Reality (AR), 136, 149, 151, 152, 155, 167, 227, 228, 273, 276, 283, 285–287, 289, 290, 292, 366, 367, 374
Automation, 7, 13, 39, 63, 65–67, 69, 70, 99, 105, 107, 110, 115, 155, 291, 332, 356, 359

B
Barriers to adoption, 182
Blockchain ecosystems, 111–113
Blockchain technology, 37, 68, 90, 99, 101–104, 106, 107, 109, 111–116, 174, 210, 224, 226, 230, 235, 360, 366, 368
Bootstrapping, 15, 181
Business ethics, 34, 36
Business models, v, 1–3, 6, 9, 13, 19, 20, 24, 29–45, 52, 79–81, 88,

D. Kumar et al. (eds.), *Evolving Trends in Technology Entrepreneurship*, Palgrave Studies in Global Entrepreneurship,
https://doi.org/10.1007/978-981-95-7441-4

90, 92, 93, 156, 174, 187, 211, 217, 219, 222, 225, 229, 232, 237, 239, 271, 273, 275, 276, 280, 281, 283, 284, 287, 289, 297, 299, 320, 322–324, 326, 327, 329, 330, 341, 358, 359, 361, 363, 365, 373, 374

C

Capital structure, 14, 98–101, 104–108, 113–116
Capital structure adjustment, 14, 100, 104, 105, 107, 114, 116
Characteristics, 40, 60, 61, 179, 195, 203, 299, 326, 327, 340, 356
Circular economy, 14, 80, 82–84, 86, 92, 221, 237, 239, 254, 368, 371
Cloud computing, 6, 130, 356
Collaboration, 4, 11, 13, 15, 20, 81, 90, 129, 155, 160, 167, 175, 217, 233, 240, 258, 291, 322, 325, 332, 339, 358
Commercialization, 18, 155, 174, 181, 184, 185, 232, 324
Conceptual foundations, 13
Conscious entrepreneurship, 211, 212, 214, 215, 217, 220, 227–229, 231, 235
Consumer behavior, 197, 300, 330, 373
Contextual adaptation, 13, 53, 54
Crowdfunding, 15, 98, 178, 181–184, 186, 202

D

Data analytics, 4, 9, 15, 137, 271–276, 279–281, 283, 286–289, 320, 359
Data-driven innovation, 273
Data governance, 4, 72, 291
Data protection, 63, 226
Decentralized Autonomous Organizations (DAOs), 114
Decentralized Finance (DeFi), 11, 15, 18, 20, 99, 101, 104–107, 114, 115, 174, 178, 188, 360
Decision support, 291
Digital business, 340, 341, 361, 363
Digital Business models, 2, 30, 40, 44
Digital entrepreneurship, 6, 16, 22, 253, 322, 323, 331, 333, 340, 355, 357–359, 366, 373, 374
Digital platforms, 3, 6, 7, 18, 41, 125, 166, 271, 273, 276, 282, 284, 286, 287, 320, 323, 328, 330, 332, 340, 357–360, 362, 366, 373
Digital transformation, v, 3, 4, 6, 7, 13, 16, 19, 23, 24, 37, 38, 55, 149, 174, 289, 290, 322, 323, 329–331, 341, 355, 369
Distributed ledgers, 41
Dynamic Capabilities Theory, 8, 9, 11

E

Effort expectancy, 53, 56, 60, 61, 65, 66, 70, 73
Emerging economies, v, 7
Empirical Scale Development, 298
Entertainment and recreation, 14, 146–153, 155, 160, 165–168
Entertainment industry, 157, 159–163
Entrepreneurial agility, 9, 10, 19
Entrepreneurial ambition, 24, 71
Entrepreneurial ecosystems, 3, 5, 7, 10, 11, 13, 20, 22, 23, 322
Entrepreneurial Ecosystem Theory, 8, 10, 12
Entrepreneurial education, 23, 198, 217, 235, 237, 250
Entrepreneurial environment, 52

Entrepreneurial processes, 4, 6, 16, 197
Entrepreneurship education, 198, 211, 212, 225, 236, 240, 248, 250, 252–260
Entrepreneurship research, 5, 20, 326
Environmental, Social, and Governance (ESG), 10, 11, 86, 88, 112, 113, 181, 249, 255, 257
Ethical awareness, 15, 220
Ethical challenges, 16, 282, 292
Ethical concerns, 3, 30, 45, 229
Ethical dimensions, 34, 203
Ethical governance, 11, 17, 113
Ethical implications, 152, 220, 228
Ethical issues, 2, 3, 30, 31, 40–43, 45, 282, 362, 374
Ethical leadership, 215, 231
Ethical outcomes, 44
Ethics, 2–6, 10, 11, 13, 16, 17, 20–24, 30–43, 45, 72, 82, 88, 167, 196, 203, 204, 209, 214, 223, 227, 228, 231–233, 235–237, 361
Expected value, 68, 69
Experiential learning, 22, 220, 221, 231, 236

F

Fan engagement, 14, 122, 125, 129, 137, 138, 271, 273, 274, 276, 277, 285–289, 320
Financial constraints, 79, 91, 92, 184
Financial flexibility, 99, 107, 108, 115
Financial inclusion, 20, 115, 359
Fitness industry, 325–330, 332
Frugal innovation, 81, 194
Future trends, 15, 99, 113, 235, 281, 340

G

Global competition, 145, 362
Globalization, 16, 238, 282, 321, 363
Governance, 4, 7, 10, 12, 13, 20, 23, 24, 40, 43, 70, 72, 86, 88, 114, 174, 194, 226, 232, 247, 248, 250, 299
Governance mechanisms, 4, 10, 20, 23, 299
Green innovation, 4, 6, 221, 236, 237, 240

I

Immersive experiences, 152, 157
Inclusion, 4, 13, 23, 32, 59, 167, 178, 199, 232, 313
Inclusive innovation, 7, 204, 372
Innovation, v, vi, 3–16, 18, 20–24, 51, 52, 55–57, 65, 70–73, 80, 81, 83–86, 101, 102, 105, 110–116, 129, 136, 138, 144, 145, 151–153, 155, 156, 158, 163, 165, 167, 173–175, 180–183, 185–187, 197, 199, 200, 202, 209–212, 214–216, 221, 222, 227–229, 232, 233, 235, 237, 239, 240, 248, 256, 257, 280–284, 291, 297–301, 304, 308, 310, 312, 320, 322–326, 329, 330, 333, 340, 357, 361, 365, 371 376
Innovation ecosystems, 24, 71, 183
Institutional Theory, 8, 10, 11, 13, 15, 22
Interdisciplinary curricula, 219, 233, 236
International case studies, 369
Internet of Things (IoT), 3, 15, 16, 90, 92, 113, 126, 130, 132, 216, 219, 222, 225, 226, 228, 248, 332, 339, 358–360, 373

Interoperability, 72, 90, 111–113, 356
Investment trends, 137
IoT integration, 126

K
Kosovo, v, 7, 10, 13, 52–58, 60, 61, 63–66, 68, 70–73

L
Latent Dirichlet Allocation (LDA), 194, 196–198, 200, 202–204
Leadership, 88, 163, 196, 227, 230, 231, 301, 355
Legitimacy, 4, 7, 10, 11, 13, 15, 16, 18, 72, 109, 175, 179, 182, 183
Life Cycle Assessment (LCA), 86, 89

M
Machine learning, 33, 62, 131, 133–137, 149, 153–155, 167, 223, 275, 285, 288, 291, 322, 339, 359, 364–366
Market dynamics, 15, 301, 340
Match prediction systems, 131, 133

N
National case studies, 16, 369
Network effects, 7

O
Online gaming, 158, 159

P
Performance expectancy, 13, 56, 60, 61, 63–65, 70, 73
Platform economies, 20, 174
Policy frameworks, 7, 72, 114, 175, 187
Policy support, 232, 298, 300
Predictive analytics, 7, 14, 52, 126, 136, 359, 371
Privacy, 2, 4, 11, 13, 18, 30, 39, 41, 63, 82, 90, 112, 113, 138, 155, 226, 229, 230, 291, 333, 360, 362, 364, 373
Project-based learning, 217, 227, 228, 233

R
Regulation, 2, 3, 30–32, 36, 44, 45, 90, 92, 112, 115, 166, 174, 178, 185, 187, 232, 251, 252, 310
Regulatory support, 81, 251, 297
Resource-Based View, 4, 8–10, 12, 14, 15, 22
Responsible Innovation (RI), v, 3, 4, 6, 8, 10–15, 17, 18, 21–23, 39, 80–85, 88–93, 229, 236, 240
Risk management, 102–104

S
Scalability, 19, 72, 89, 90, 99, 111–113, 136, 185–187, 200, 292, 300, 313, 355, 360, 376
Sectoral applications, 5
Seizing opportunities, 238, 290
Smart contracts, 10, 99, 102–107, 109–111, 114, 115, 360
SMEs, 54–56, 181, 183, 184, 239
Social factors, 67, 147
Social value, 194, 290, 326
Societal impact, 6, 8, 13, 82, 147, 152, 197, 230, 274, 281, 284, 321, 362, 364, 371
Sports analytics, 135, 136, 138

Sports industry, 14, 15, 122, 123, 125–127, 134, 138, 271–275, 278, 280–283, 285–288
Sports performance analysis, 131
Sports technology entrepreneurship, 273, 288, 290
Startup performance, 92
Startups, v, 4, 5, 9, 10, 14, 19, 20, 23, 52–54, 56–59, 61, 70, 73, 79–86, 88, 90–93, 98–102, 107–110, 115, 134, 138, 174–176, 178–180, 182–187, 217, 228, 232, 234, 236, 237, 239, 292, 322, 323, 329, 376
Sustainability goals, 82, 85, 88, 91, 211, 217, 220
Sustainable business models, 43, 92, 93, 234, 282, 285
Sustainable Development Goals (SDGs), 4, 19, 193, 198, 211–213, 216, 235–237, 248, 251, 260
Sustainable education, 5, 7, 10, 11, 16, 226
Sustainable entrepreneurship, 6, 38, 92, 211, 215, 218, 234, 238, 239, 248–250, 253, 259
Sustainable growth, 5, 80, 81, 84, 92, 166, 340, 362
Sustainable innovation, v, 3, 72, 80, 81, 92, 220, 222–225, 227, 235, 238, 255
Sustainable technology entrepreneurship, 11, 15, 209, 211–213, 219, 229, 233, 236–238, 240, 248, 250–261

T
Technological change, 4, 5, 11, 18, 143, 145, 159, 321, 324
Technological innovation, v, 5, 8, 10, 14, 23, 81, 82, 137, 194, 204, 213, 214, 216–218, 220, 233, 239, 289, 330
Technology, v–vii, 1, 3–17, 19–24, 29, 33, 34, 40, 41, 51–58, 60, 62, 65–73, 80, 84, 86, 88–90, 98, 99, 102–104, 107, 111–115, 122, 124, 128, 129, 132, 134, 137, 143–148, 150, 151, 154–156, 161, 162, 164–166, 174, 176, 179–185, 187, 188, 193, 194, 199, 202, 209–214, 216–222, 224, 227–231, 233–238, 240, 248, 250–260, 272–276, 281, 283–292, 298, 299, 320–333, 339, 341, 355, 357–359, 363–365, 370, 371, 373, 374
Technology acceptance, 13, 53, 54, 57, 58, 60, 73
Technology adoption, 14, 17, 52–54, 56, 57, 70–72, 333, 341
Technology entrepreneurship, v–vii, 4–9, 11–17, 19–24, 194, 196, 210, 216, 218, 237, 248, 251–254, 256, 259, 260, 272, 273, 289, 290, 292, 321–324, 328–330, 332, 373, 374
Technology startups, 6, 14, 80, 81, 84–86, 88, 98, 99, 107, 114, 173, 174, 176, 182, 288
Technology transfer, 181, 184, 321
Technology ventures, 10, 98, 287, 290, 292
Topic modeling, 15, 194, 196, 197, 203
Traditional enterprises, 16, 358

U
Unified Theory of Acceptance and Use of Technology (UTAUT), 10, 13, 53, 54, 58–60, 65, 70, 71, 73

UTAUT-3, 10, 13, 53, 54, 58–60, 65, 70, 71, 73

V

Value creation, vi, 3, 5, 6, 9, 14, 15, 20, 22, 52, 92, 215, 284
Value creation logic, 4
Venture capital, 7, 15, 89, 91, 101, 102, 109, 137, 174, 175, 178, 179, 181–186, 284, 292
Virtual Reality (VR), 14, 136, 149, 151, 152, 155, 161, 166, 167, 216, 227, 228, 273, 276, 281, 283, 285–289, 292, 320, 331, 332, 366, 367, 370, 374

W

Wearable technologies, 126–129, 138, 272–274, 276–278, 280, 281, 287–289, 291, 328–330, 360

The manufacturer's authorised representative in the EU is Springer Nature Customer Service Centre GmbH, Europaplatz 3, 69115 Heidelberg, Germany. If you have any concerns regarding our products, please contact ProductSafety@springernature.com

Printed and bound by CPI Group (UK) Ltd, Croydon, CR0 4YY

10/10/2026

02231311-0004